THE HORN ENGAGING THE GULF

THE HORN ENGAGING THE GULF

Economic Diplomacy and Statecraft in Regional Relations

Aleksi Ylönen

BLOOMSBURY ACADEMIC
LONDON • NEW YORK • OXFORD • NEW DELHI • SYDNEY

BLOOMSBURY ACADEMIC
Bloomsbury Publishing Plc, 50 Bedford Square, London, WC1B 3DP, UK
Bloomsbury Publishing Inc, 1359 Broadway, New York, NY 10018, USA
Bloomsbury Publishing Ireland, 29 Earlsfort Terrace, Dublin 2, D02 AY28, Ireland

BLOOMSBURY, BLOOMSBURY ACADEMIC and the Diana logo are trademarks of
Bloomsbury Publishing Plc

First published in Great Britain 2024
Paperback edition published 2025

Copyright © Aleksi Ylönen, 2024, 2025

Cover design: Adriana Brioso
Cover image © Bandar Algaloud/Saudi Kingdom Council/Handout/Anadolu Agency/
Getty Images

A catalogue record for this book is available from the British Library.

A catalog record for this book is available from the Library of Congress

ISBN: HB: 978-0-7556-3515-3
PB: 978-0-7556-3516-0
ePDF: 978-0-7556-3519-1
eBook: 978-0-7556-3518-4

Typeset by Deanta Global Publishing Services, Chennai, India

For product safety related questions contact productsafety@bloomsbury.com.

To find out more about our authors and books visit www.bloomsbury.com and
sign up for our newsletters.

CONTENTS

ILLUSTRATIONS

Figure

Tables

ACKNOWLEDGMENTS

This work was made possible by interactions with various institutions and people in the Horn of Africa and the Middle East. Without the support of the "Fundação para a Ciência e Tecnologia" (FCT) under UIDB/03122/2020, the study would not have been possible. I also benefited from the generosity of the Finnish Institute in the Middle East (FIME) and the "Centre français des études éthiopiennes" (CFEE) which supported a research visit and fieldwork that importantly contributed to this study's success.

People I would like to thank are many. First and foremost, I would like to extend my gratitude to Dr. Nasir Ali for his friendship and assistance and to Dr. Muzaffer Şenel for his support. Also, I would like to mention Dr. Anu Leinonen and Ambassador Ari Mäki who introduced me to new contacts and acquaintances. Joint projects with various colleagues, especially with Dr. Jean-Nicolas Bach, Dr. Alexander Meckelburg, and Dr. Jan Záhořík, also contributed to the maturing of the ideas presented in the findings of the research.

In addition, I would like to thank colleagues who I worked together with to organize the "New Gulf Streams – Middle East and Eastern Africa Intersected" conference and the subsequent publication of a thematic issue in the "Cadernos de Estudos Africanos." I am also thankful for various collaborations with the HORN International Institute for Strategic Studies, Institute for International Political Studies (ISPI), and the Barcelona Centre for International Affairs (CIDOB).

Moreover, I have been a beneficiary of knowing Dr. Fatuma Ali and Prof. Manuel João Ramos for many years. Our numerous discussions have helped to further refine my work. Many colleagues and friends in and from Ethiopia, Eritrea, Somalia, Somaliland, and various places in Europe not only facilitated my research but also gave insightful feedback on some of the central ideas presented in this book.

All these invaluable relationships have helped to refine my thoughts and generate new ideas on theoretical dimensions and how to interpret empirical evidence. I am grateful to you all.

Finally, above all else, I would like to thank Grace for her incredible patience with me and my obsession with research which often requires sacrifices from her. I am truly blessed to be yours!

In Addis Ababa, November 5, 2022,

Aleksi Ylönen

PREFACE

This book discusses theoretical and in-depth research-based aspects of the Horn of Africa–Middle East/Persian Gulf relations founded on several years of observation. The discussion in this work should not be considered as a comprehensive account but, rather, an attempt to tease how the connections between state and non-state actors in the overall Horn of Africa–Middle East/Persian Gulf relations can be seen from the perspective of African agency. The motive behind the research presented here is to steer away from the currently prevalent, and perceivably skewed, International Relations theory framework used to interpret international affairs in the Middle East and, by extension, the Horn of Africa. In particular, the dominant conceptualization of state and power in the realist strand of the International Relations discipline, shaped by the Western experience, is questioned from the perspective of the Horn of African state and non-state actors. The study shows that re-conceptualizing the state and power by including the "sub-national" and "local" actors and forces in the analysis of external connections enriches our understanding of African agency and the overall Horn of Africa–Middle East/ Persian Gulf relations.

The theoretical dimensions discussed in this work are based on observations of the political and economic aspects of the relations. Empirical analysis shows that due to the nature of the states and political regimes involved, Horn of Africa–Middle East/Persian Gulf relations are largely personalized, pragmatic, and transactional, which makes them in most cases volatile due to frequently changing emphases, orientations, and alignments. Based on empirical observation and numerous discussions with experts and stakeholders further supported by the existing, and ever-growing, literature and other documented sources, the main propositions of the study rely on several elaborated examples which, however, should be seen as representative of a wider phenomenon. The book is therefore an attempt to provide a glimpse into the Horn of Africa–Middle East/Persian Gulf relations, but without shutting out other regional and international actors and influences.

Zooming in on bilateral ties, and recognizing the importance of complex networks of relations involving state and non-state actors, the discussion seeks to highlight the dynamics of the relationship between the parties. While doing this, it underlines some of the caveats of the dominant concepts in the realist mainstream International Relations literature, including that of the monolithic state, power between the so-called powerful (strong) and small (weak) states, and the narrow conceptualization of inter-relations that largely excludes the significant agency of non-state actors. Therefore, power, a central concept in the realist view of the International Relations discipline, is looked at more comprehensively based on several years of proximate observation, which helps to elucidate the actual power dynamics between actors beyond the simple understanding based on relations between unitary actors. In the Horn of Africa, for example, governments often lack the capacity to monopolize the state's foreign connections, and sub-state and non-state actors maintain their own external linkages which affect the country's overall foreign relations. These external connections contribute to state and non-state actors' domestic strength, as they use their local power (influence and control over strategic assets and resources) to bargain favorable deals with foreign actors and engage in domestic political and economic power competition. Their local strength results in power asymmetry and relative autonomy toward external actors. This, in turn, enables careful balancing between various external partners, which is aimed at maximizing space and minimizing constraints in maintaining foreign relationships. Therefore, local power and domestic rivalries are an important consideration in the Horn of Africa's engagement with foreign partners from the Persian Gulf, the wider Middle East, and elsewhere. It is expected that this perspective founded on prolonged observation contributes to refining the view on power in the Horn of Africa–Persian Gulf/Middle East interactions and helps to enrich the wider debate on the subject in the International Relations discipline.

The selected country case studies do not pretend to holistically cover all Horn of Africa or provide comprehensive histories of the particular countries. But they seek to provide examples of the interaction between the local actors (governments, sub-state, and non-state) and their Middle East/Persian Gulf counterparts in the wider regional and international context. This necessarily includes some discussion on their relations with other powers beyond the Middle East. As indicated earlier, the case studies, based on long-term observation, point out the importance of understanding power and foreign relations in the so-called weak, or fragile, states in the Horn of Africa, going beyond the limitations of inadequate realist interpretations. This seeks to improve our comprehension of the domestic political dynamics behind foreign policy and external connections and how foreign relations and linkages of various actors contribute to the overall domestic and regional dynamics. Various domestic power centers revolving around the state, sub-state, and non-state actors, individuals and groups alike, sustain such foreign connections by engaging in personalized, pragmatic, and transactional relations focusing on material, and to an extent reputational, elements related to maintaining or gaining local power. In these highly personalized and often obscure relations, actors in the Horn of Africa exchange local resources, both material and intangible, for financial and economic benefits to enhance their local power. This puts them in a strong position in their relationship with external partners seeking local influence.

These empirical observations of the Horn of Africa–Middle East/Persian Gulf relations, in turn, motivated the study's emphasis on economic diplomacy and statecraft as a relevant theoretical frame. Rather than pursuing a holistic explanation, the work seeks to highlight the importance of pertinent aspects of these economic approaches to foreign relations. It considers them particularly useful in relationships in which one party possesses significant financial resources and the other politically, strategically, and economically desirable material and reputational resources.

The in-depth chapters which focus on three influential states in the Horn of Africa, Ethiopia, Somalia, and Eritrea highlight the connections between state, sub-state, and non-state actors with their Middle east/Persian Gulf partners. They seek to elucidate the local power and influence of the Horn actors and demonstrate the mainstream International Relations interpretations' lack of ability to account for the local agency. The book, therefore, aspires to make an important contribution to discrediting the dominant, but distorted, realist International Relations discourse applied to the Horn of Africa–Middle East/Persian Gulf relations.

INTRODUCTION

The view from Ras Siyan is impressive. Surrounded by the deep blue waters of the Red Sea, the peninsula's northernmost point, one of the Sawabi or Seven Brothers together with the nearby islands, marks Djibouti's closest point to the Arabian Peninsula. An observer can easily appreciate the traffic of large tankers and container vessels through one of the world's busiest shipping lanes, the Strait of Bab al-Mandab. This area, literally translated as "the Gate of Tears,"[1] forms a strategic and treacherous choke point dividing the Red Sea from the Gulf of Aden opening to the Arabian Sea and the Indian Ocean. Extending over less than 30 kilometers, Bab al-Mandab is divided into two channels, by the Yemeni island of Perim (also known as Jazirat Mayyun). The larger of the two, Dact al-Mayyun, or the large pass, serves as the main international shipping lane through the strait, while the smaller Bab Iskender, or Alexander's Strait, lies entirely in the Yemeni coastal waters.

The strategic significance of Bab al-Mandab is crucial since it connects Asia with Europe together with the Suez Canal through which up to 10 percent of world trade passes. Historically, Bab al-Mandab and the surrounding areas have epitomized great and regional power rivalries, such as those between the Ottomans and the Portuguese, the British and other European powers, the United States (US) and the Soviet Union, and the Arab states, Iran, and Israel. It has been estimated that a 7 percent share of world trade, including a significant and increasing amount of food and fertilizers,[2] and about 30 percent of global oil shipments pass through the strait.[3] Trade, including petroleum from the Persian Gulf, shipped through Bab al-Mandab has been on the rise in recent years. For example in 2009 the oil passing through accounted for an estimated 3.2 million barrels per day,[4] while five years later the amount had grown to 4.7 million barrels per day.[5] The trade growth has marked a parallel increase in Bab al-Mandab's strategic significance as a chokepoint, particularly for the petroleum and natural gas exporting Persian Gulf countries.[6]

In recent years, securing the Red Sea shipping lanes and containing the regional influence of rival states, namely, Iran and Türkiye, has turned the attention of the Arabian Peninsula's most powerful states, Saudi Arabia and the United Arab Emirates (UAE), toward the shores and interior Horn of Africa. Although Arab, Israeli, and Iranian engagement in the sub-region has existed for a long time, the recent attention is significant in the context of the rising influence of middle and regional powers. Particularly after the Arab Spring, their attempt to ensure political influence, desirable foreign policy alignment, security, and economic benefits has entailed diplomatic and political efforts. The Saudi-led intervention against the Houthi in Yemen led to further efforts to woo especially the Red Sea and Gulf of Aden coastal states to collaborate in security affairs, as well as politically and economically. The Gulf Cooperation Council (GCC) crisis in which Saudi Arabia and the UAE sought to isolate Qatar led Ankara to support Doha and intensified competition among the Gulf and Middle East powers also in the Horn of Africa. Apart from the coastal states, their efforts have entailed seeking increasing influence and economic access in Ethiopia perceived as a key state in the Horn of Africa due to its centrality, population size, and rapidly growing markets.

In contrast, governments in the Horn of Africa have taken the opportunity to capitalize on the intensification of the Persian Gulf and Middle East states' interest in the sub-region. While pursuing their interests through foreign relations, largely to ensure domestic regime survival and consolidation, they have readily engaged the Gulf and Middle East states. In this, the 2011 Arab Spring, the Saudi-led intervention in the war in Yemen, and the GCC crisis provided opportunities for the Horn states, and local sub-state and non-state actors alike, to take advantage of the Middle Eastern interest to obtain crucial material and nonmaterial resources for domestic consolidation and competition against internal political and economic rivals. While the Horn governments are generally unable to fully monopolize their foreign relations, the local sub-state and non-state actors' external connections often contribute to the countries' overall foreign relations, particularly with their proximate Red Sea, Persian Gulf, and Middle Eastern counterparts.

The Dilemma and Argument

The terms "Horn of Africa," "Persian Gulf," and "Middle East" are used in this work to describe constructed and geographically delimited "regions" consisting of ethnically and culturally similar polities neighboring each other. It is recognized here that such regions have been constructed over time mainly according to the interests of external empire makers. Indeed, the delimitations of these regions are clearly understood, and their ancient, historical, and current connections over the narrow bodies of water, the Red Sea, the Gulf of Aden, and the Nile River, blur any such differentiation. However, when exploring the relations between a selection of states in what constitutes the "Horn of Africa," strictly speaking, and the leading Persian Gulf countries and Türkiye (and to an extent Egypt) from the so-called "Middle East," referring to these terms facilitates author's expression and reader's understanding due to the established understanding of approximate limits of these "regions." What is referred to as "regional relations" then becomes understood as relations between significant actors from the conceived "regions," the so-called "Horn of Africa" and the "Persian Gulf/Middle East."

In the study of International Relations, and particularly its realist strand, geographical determinism and realist geopolitical interpretations are often seen to guide a one-way foreign policy from the perspective of what are considered great or middle powers. They are seen as projectors of power toward smaller, often fragile,[7] states to advance their interests, while such target states tend to be regarded as rather passive recipients of great and middle power influence. This view is based on the realist view of states as monolithic units and fails to account for the significant role of a wider spectrum of players, including small states, and sub-state and non-state actors, in international affairs. The role of the so-called societal actors is even more pronounced in the weak or fragile states, as in the Horn of Africa, in which the leaders of the governing regime are just one player competing to survive in the domestic political landscape[8] and, as a government, do not have the capability to monopolize significant foreign connections. Foreign relations are therefore influenced by multiple administrative and societal actors that maintain autonomous external linkages and form part of regional or international networks. Overall, they are a complex collection of foreign relationships between state and non-state actors in which the government constitutes one, albeit central, player.

In the prevalent realist interpretations of international relations, which mainly emerge in the United States after the First World War and continue to provide the dominant frame for the analysis of international politics in the Middle East, there is a tendency of looking at interstate affairs from the perspective of powerful states or through the lens of hegemony. This is in part because of the realist fascination with power as a relational concept between states which are deemed as unitary actors. Considering international relations as a power projection from the perceivably more powerful states to the weaker ones has especially been the case of how realist interpretations consider Africa where states are mostly viewed as targets and objects of external actors and interveners.[9] This prevailing view continues to be perpetrated in the International Relations discipline[10] and is still present in the dominant Western discourses about Africa.[11] As such, this perspective recreates the bias of perceiving outside powers with the capacity and interest to intervene in Africa as "strong" or "powerful," while looking at African states through a negative, pessimistic, lens, generally considering them as weak, fragile, or outright failed objects of intervention.[12] As such, Africa has often been depicted as a poor, hopeless, needy, and dependent continent living in a state of permanent crisis,[13] an interpretation to which structural critical approaches, including many of those drawing on Marxist foundations,[14] have arguably contributed. Structural narratives of the wholesale domination of Africa by the powerful states continue to linger and are still endorsed by sections of African intellectuals and leaders.

Lately, however, the more actor and agency-based narratives of "rising Africa" have gained momentum, albeit not without criticism.[15] The logic of dominant views continues to draw on the assumption that the foreign actors involved in Africa are powerful and can take advantage of the continent and its resources. Yet, this perception fails to consider the African agency, namely, the ability of African governments and non-state actors engaged in external relations to pursue their interests.[16] It also ignores local power, the influence, and control over strategic assets and resources, wielded by African actors, which leads to asymmetric interactions[17] and relative autonomy, enabling careful balancing in their foreign relations. As Brown notes, the agency in African external relations is multiple,[18] in part due to the fragility of formal state structures and the high level of informality in governance and political affairs. This goes against the persisting view in realist International Relations that considers the state as the sole agent in external relations and the accompanying conceptualization of power between such monolithic states as relative according to differences in their overall capabilities.

Although little nuanced in-depth analysis exists, the narrow conception of power and agency dictated by the dominant views in the International Relations discipline is often assumed to apply to the foreign relations of the states in the Horn of Africa. Indeed, when considering the past ten years of developments in the Horn of Africa and the Red Sea neighborhood, and the affairs of the countries in the African sub-region with those in the Middle East, from a shallow realist perspective it can be assumed that these relations fall into the above pattern. As a result, recent analyses of the current relations between the states in the Persian Gulf/Middle East and the Horn of Africa often discard more comprehensive accounts.[19] They fail to engage with the complexity of domestic, regional, and international affairs from the perspective of the Horn actors, while depicting these relations as a one-sided projection of relative power and influence through the powerful Persian Gulf/Middle East (center) actors' pursuit of political, security, and strategic economic interests in the weak, fragile, turbulent, and insecure Horn of Africa (hinterland).[20]

While most such analyses have adopted the classic "eagle eye" perspective of international relations, and are inherently realist in their focus on rational-materialist interests and the Western conception of the state, their weakness lies precisely in that they portray such relations as monolithic and one-sided. This owes to their bias and narrow understanding of power according to the dominant, mainly Western, classical realist epistemological groundings,[21] failing to recognize a distinct structure of power and agency. The realist state-centered view is limiting and constrains the understanding of international relations from the perspective of non-Western states, particularly in the case of the so-called weak or fragile, mostly postcolonial, states in Africa.[22] Especially realist interpretations, which dominate the analysis of international relations in the Middle East, have been applied to the Horn of Africa and perpetuate the perspective of external powers on the sub-region they engage in.

However, these perspectives are yet to reconcile their failure to consider the condition of the heterogeneous and largely informal African state as distinct from a typical nation-state. They do not fully recognize its endemic fragility, which allows sub-state and non-state actors, and political, economic, and social dynamics, space and enable societal actors to engage in activities and external linkages that affect the state's overall foreign relations. The failure also to understand the importance of state and societal actors' local power and leverage in their interactions with foreign players results in a limited perception of the Horn of Africa's overall external relations. Therefore, by concentrating strictly on monolithic state-level relative power relations, the realist mainstream views result in a limited and inaccurate general understanding of the complexity of African state and societal actors' external affairs. This is where comparative political analysis has sought to step in, with scholars establishing frameworks for analyzing various types of sub-national units.[23]

In the case of African states, it is important to remind us that they are a product of relatively brief but intense and deeply incisive colonial brutality. The imposition of the colonial state, an alien and violently extractive territorial governing structure, led to arbitrary borders splitting heterogeneous and socially and culturally distinct population groups between polities and resulting in new exploitative political, economic, and social realities. Colonial governance, lifting some individuals and groups over others, and imposing order by violence, without an attempt to create legitimacy that is crucial for any strong state, led to the institutionalization of political structures and dynamics, governance, and behavior, in the postcolonial era that did not significantly differ from practices during colonialism. It led to power hierarchies and competition without a strong formal European-like institutional setup capable of mitigating violence, and in most cases led to exclusionary politics along ethnic, clan, kin, religious, or other cultural identity markers. In the postcolonial era, minority rule by privileged political elites remained prevalent, as did governance by repression and violent extraction. This has led to generally inherent state weakness and instability, even more so than in other postcolonial world regions. The power of most African states concentrates on the capital and central areas of the state, the central government having limited means to project national identity as a salient unifying element and maintain control of their outlying territories. Citizens inhabiting such peripheral areas have little contact and affinity with the central government and at times identify stronger with ethnically or culturally connected identity groups living across the border. This, along with the exclusive configuration of political power, lack of legitimacy among parts of the population, and intense competition of state leadership and resources that due to widespread societal informality largely takes place outside the formal state institutions, tends to generate a perpetual sense of political insecurity among the governing elites.

The aforementioned characteristics of African states have important implications for their foreign relations. African elites often draw on collectivism among themselves, and incumbents seek to secure their rule against political rivals by maintaining the status quo. This hegemonic logic and preoccupation with political power, mainly due to the accompanying financial and material benefits increasing individuals' economic power, translates into states' foreign policies in several ways. Although the leaders' understanding of their interests is influenced by political, economic, and cultural ideas, and at times by particular ideologies, which result from socialization, education, and training, there is necessarily a heavy materialist aspect to them associated with the idea of maintaining political power in a fragile state. Some of the salient features of foreign policy in such contexts are the incumbent's monopolization of foreign relations, particularly in highly authoritarian states, or them being driven by a narrow section of the governing elite. This is largely aimed at obtaining material and other resources from abroad to buttress political power at home. As an approach, this extraversion, through a mix of transactional relations and short-term alignments, and longer-term alliances, is aimed at confronting domestic opponents who are considered the biggest threat to maintaining power. Through foreign relations, leaders seek to create domestic reality and conditions in which their power will not be contested at a level that becomes destabilizing to their rule. These dynamics are particularly important in the largely authoritarian states in the Horn of Africa.

Yet, due to state fragility and the government's lack of capacity, the governing elite's control of foreign relations is limited. Here, other state-related, sub-state, and non-state actors engaging in local politics and maintaining external connections may play a significant role. Similarly to the governments, they may obtain significant resources from abroad and use them for advancing their domestic position and power as well as affecting the state's overall relations with outside actors. In the Horn of Africa, for example, this has been the case with armed and non-violent opposition movements, some of which have toppled governments, as well as with sub-state actors, such as federal states, and powerful groups and individuals related or not related to the state.[24] These examples show how in their international affairs states are not unitary actors and that various sub-state and non-state actors wield power, but also that the engagement of the latter in foreign relations may allow them to challenge the state and the incumbent government's domestic position. The non- and sub-state actors' engagement therefore not only poses a theoretical challenge to the dominant realist perceptions in International Relations discipline but also has practical empirical implications for states in terms of local power and overall interstate relations.

As a result, by considering states largely as unitary actors, the mainstream International Relations theory largely fails to account for this reality. Although in the Middle East–Africa relations realism has been used as the dominant framework, foreign relations of African states, particularly in the Horn of Africa, do not, at least in full, adhere to the monolithic assumption maintained by the realist International Relations theory. Consequently, the mainstream approaches focusing on a narrow conception of power and exclusive agency tend to overlook various manifestations and expressions of power, and multiple state, sub-state, and non-state actors.

This view, which often misses the significance of mutual vulnerabilities and interdependence of the actors involved, has been prevalent in the international relations interpretations of the Middle East powers' relations with Horn states. Although the realist international relations analysis has deemed Arab, Iranian, and Turkish involvement in the Horn of Africa as destabilizing, the effects of Horn actors' foreign interactions with the state and non-state players in the Persian Gulf, Türkiye, and Egypt have been largely produced by the domestic political context and dynamics. The importance of the Horn actors' financially and materially beneficial foreign linkages is highlighted by the countries' domestic political and economic situation. When states are fragile and the ruling actors are insecure, facing significant threats to their power such as a powerful opposition or insurgency, it is increasingly important for the state leadership to be able to control beneficial foreign relations and seek to minimize the opposing party's external assistance. While in the so-called proxy conflicts during the Cold War these dynamics were particularly prevalent in the Horn of Africa, it is possible to observe them later as well, for example in the context of the ongoing state-building process in Somalia since the early 1990s and the Ethiopian political transition since 2018.

This reality is at the helm of power relations and defies the view of the Middle East–Horn of Africa relations as centered on monolithic state entities as depicted by the realist conception in the International Relations discipline. It neglects power asymmetries generated by local power of domestic actors in the Horn, including governments, sub-state, and societal actors who can bargain autonomously with external players due to their local influence and control of strategic and economic assets, such as political influence and alignments on the ground, strategic locations (e.g., land and infrastructure), and natural resources. Therefore, the realist state-centered unitary perspectives provide a distorted view of the actual power relationships between actors. Instead, the Middle East actors which seek to advance their influence in the Horn of Africa face the power of domestic actors and dependence on local partners which leverages the latter in the relationship and provides them an advantageous position when engaging in pragmatic and transactional partnerships. Local actors wielding considerable control and influence over local strategic assets and resources result in power asymmetries that enable them to exercise relative autonomy in their foreign connections. This local power allows them to engage in careful balancing between foreign partnerships and alignments to minimize constraints and maximize the space to maneuver between current and potential allies.

Moreover, in the Horn of Africa–Middle East relations, the mainstream realist perspectives mainly focus on security and strategic political and economic concerns of what are perceived as the more powerful actors. In this, they often not only miss the internal insecurities and vulnerabilities of what they see as the more powerful states but also fail to understand the extent and configuration of power the Horn actors wield in their local context and their immediate neighborhood. This caveat is particularly salient in the recent literature discussing the Middle East states' engagements with the countries in the Horn of Africa.[25] While in such analyses it often appears that it is the middle-level, regional, or smaller powers that approach what are seen as fragile states, the vulnerabilities of the more powerful actors are often forgotten.

But even more importantly, it is the agency of the so-called recipient actors that is little understood. This is a crucial shortcoming because using monolithic theoretical underpinnings limits one's thinking to Western-type realist interstate relations in which strong governments are assumed to have monopolized the state's foreign affairs. However, perceiving power relations in a classical manner based on states as unitary actors results in a one-sided view. This orientation sways thinking away from a more nuanced understanding of such relations which is a particularly important consideration in the Horn of Africa–Middle East relations. As discussed earlier, due to the fragmentation of the political power within states in the Horn of Africa, the picture is more complex as several actors within states engage in foreign relations in which they wield important bargaining power over local strategic assets.

This study deals with Horn of Africa–Persian Gulf/Middle East relations. It is motivated by the perception of significant historical and current connections across the Red Sea, through the Nile River, and beyond, and the Persian Gulf countries and Türkiye's resurgent interests in the sub-region. The study seeks to shed light on the politics in the Horn of Africa and how the local actors have dealt with the Middle East powers. This is done by engaging in the daunting task to discuss the little-understood agency and power of the governments and sub-state and non-state actors from a selection of countries in the Horn of Africa in their interaction with Middle East partners. The country case studies seek to highlight multiple actors and agency in the Horn of Africa–Middle East relations to demonstrate that the currently dominant realist international relations analysis is inadequate for appreciating their complexity. The study suggests that a more nuanced analytical framework that includes local actors is necessary for an improved understanding of interactions that together constitute the overall relations between the Horn actors and their Middle East counterparts.

What is deemed as the Horn of Africa in this work departs somewhat from the conventional narrow and wide understanding of what constitutes the sub-region.[26] Because of various constraints, the largest three of its four constituent states, Ethiopia, Somalia, and Eritrea, have been chosen as the main sources of analysis. These countries in the Horn were selected also due to their intimate historical connections and particularly intense current engagements with the Middle East. In recent times, the coastal Horn states have gained currency in part due to their strategically significant position at the Red Sea, while the government of the dominant state in the sub-region, Ethiopia, has increasingly sought to capitalize on its position through improved Middle East relations. The Horn of Africa countries' Persian Gulf and Middle East counterparts most closely considered in this study include Saudi Arabia, the UAE, Qatar, and Türkiye which are among the top of those states that have increased their involvement in the sub-region over the past decade. But the study also necessarily discusses other great and regional powers, including China, the United States, Iran, Israel, and Russia when related to advancing the study's main arguments. This focus on the Horn countries' foreign engagements primarily with their Middle East counterparts helps one to understand power differently from the mainstream realist international relations discourse and to highlight the agency, interests, and objectives in the Horn countries' generally pragmatic and transactional foreign relations toward their seemingly more powerful external counterparts. Here the foreign relations approach includes an array of techniques and instruments mainly aimed at survival, consolidation, and extending power in the local context. Foreign relations and partnerships can be seen as an extension of local political rivalries in the process of state-making, state-building, and regime consolidation against local opponents. In such a political environment protracted state fragility is the norm, and the local political "game" extends to external alignments and alliances. The local players seek to use outside partners and patrons to strengthen themselves when negotiating local status and power relations, at times engaging in coercion and violence. The study, therefore, does not view states and regimes as monolithic actors that monopolize foreign relations, as the realist international relations interpretations do, but recognizes the importance of prominent individuals, groups, and organizations engaging in relations with external players. When seeking to understand these dimensions of external relations, considering how relational power is structured, understood, and practiced is essential. This draws on the understanding of the domestic political landscape, including players, dynamics, and realities and their interaction with external actors and forces.

In sum, the analysis here seeks to challenge the common misconceptions related to the current, rather superficial, international relations accounts of the Middle East–Horn of Africa encounters. The focus on rigid state-to-state relative power relations between the countries in the Persian Gulf/Middle East and the Horn of Africa lacks a nuanced understanding of these interactions. As a result, the attempt here is to shed light on these relations and their dynamics from the perspective of the Horn of Africa to demonstrate that the interactions are not merely a one-way street of agency, power, and influence dictated by state-level relative differences in capabilities. From the rather simplistic unitary state-to-state perspective, African countries continue to be perceived as "small" and fragile target states, and positioned low within the overall power hierarchy of states, while seen to be structurally dependent and without significant agency. While this misconception appears to arise mostly in the analysis of those security and strategic studies scholars who are more used to looking at international relations from the viewpoint of the great or middle powers, and the Middle East–Africa affairs from the perspective of what they perceive as internationally more powerful Middle East states, others more familiar with African states and regional politics from African perspective would argue that African actors command a significant degree of agency in their relations with foreign partners, including those from the Middle East.

In this study, it is shown that ordering states according to such hierarchy based on relative power is in itself flawed because it relies on a narrow conception of power and a strict view of interstate relations. It is argued that any nuanced analysis needs to re-conceptualize power and influence, central concepts in the study of International Relations, to better understand the structure and practice in external relations among state and non-state actors in the Horn of Africa. The re-conceptualization should take into account aspects such as the regime types, local political dynamics, and formal and informal power structures, as well as the actors engaging in external relations, and most importantly the ability to control and exchange local strategic, material, and nonmaterial assets which are essential elements contributing to the Horn states' largely pragmatic and transactional overall foreign relations.

On Power and Its Local Dimensions

Power is inherent to any social relationship. It is also a defining concept of the realist theoretical strand in the discipline of International Relations. Realist interpretations consider power to be based mainly on material resources and capabilities, and it has been given a central position in the understanding of how states conduct themselves in their affairs with other states. In the early days of the International Relations discipline, authors of its realist school of thought built the epistemological understanding of power on their interpretations of classical works that describe politics, governance, and war. From early on, the realist theoretical lens focused on the leadership's ability to ensure the survival of the state and its independence and freedom from external domination.[27] This understanding is heavily grounded on power as a narrow relational concept of the coercive capacity of the stronger party to dictate the rules of the political game and exert influence on the weaker party which is forced to comply[28] unless it outwits the stronger party.[29] Similarly, realists adopt a conception of sovereignty and independence of foreign policy as conditional to the coercive and noncoercive influencing capacity of bigger powers without deeper inquiry into local dimensions of power, including its social and institutional foundations and manifestations. From a systemic perspective, such interpretations view international politics as a struggle for power that is exercised in conditions of anarchy,[30] again overlooking inter-relational social factors and institutional arrangements.

Enriching views on power in international relations emerged in response to the lack of ability of the narrow military view to explain noncoercive influence.[31] In 1990, Joseph Nye introduced the concept of soft power and elaborated on the characteristics of power over time in his subsequent works.[32] While hard power is coercive, soft power is the noncoercive ability to use diplomacy and foreign policy to appeal and to attract others and shape their preferences for favorable outcomes.

Explaining what the foundation for power consists of, and how it plays out in a given relationship, French and Raven's five-element framework (legitimate, referent, expert, reward, and coercive) has been particularly influential in understanding power in social sciences.[33] Even more importantly for the study of International Relations, power can be seen as essentially relational between states and/or non-state actors, or based on relative standing and gain as classical and neorealists often perceive it,[34] or based on absolute position and gain as perceived by liberal realists and neoliberal institutionalists.[35] As Powell has noted in his excellent review of the two points of view,[36] they constitute fundamentally different perspectives and understandings of how the interstate system works, based on conflict or cooperation, or essentially as either a zero-sum or non-zero-sum game. While these understandings of power in international politics and political economy rely heavily on material considerations and are strongly resource-based, liberal realists and constructivists claim that ideas give rise to identities and interests and form a defining factor behind states and their behavior driving international politics.[37]

In addition, the perceived position or considered status matters for power in International Relations. Together, the real material and resource endowment and how power is perceived by others define state power. This goes beyond the understanding of power as hard, or raw, based on coercion through threats of military or economic action, made possible by advantages in material resources and operational capabilities. It includes soft power, consisting of more subtle ways to persuade and influence others by employing culture, history, and political and economic values through noncoercive appeal, attraction, and co-optation.[38] However, in practice, diplomatic efforts and states' foreign policies can often draw on both ways of applying power to a varying degree, depending on the other actor(s) and the context. It is also not clear what exactly qualifies as hard and soft power because each diplomatic and foreign policy measure may include both. Exportation of the sender state's political and economic values may be considered noncoercive by the state itself but can have deep transformational effects in the recipient state and be deemed coercive. For example, Western states' promotion of liberal democracy, neoliberal capitalist economic order, and other liberal political, economic, and social values has not always been received well elsewhere in the world. However, wielding power (e.g., in terms of resources) enables the powerful one to dictate a relationship, and it renders the other party subordinate, at times creating dependence when options for alternative relationships are limited.[39] This, however, depends on how power is conceptualized, observed, and practiced.

As discussed earlier, various types and combinations of power have been identified and explained in the scholarly literature. The literature has also engaged in explaining how states use foreign policy, including diplomatic efforts and military engagements, as an important vehicle to exercise power and influence. Broadly, power is often perceived as relational, as one actor's capacity to influence another actor, and get the other actor to do what that recipient actor would otherwise not do. This involves being able to shape other actors' beliefs or affect their actions or overall behavior.

Concerning the subject of this study, it is important to consider that since in realist international relations analysis states are likened to individuals and considered as "persons" in terms of international law, mechanisms that explain inter-personal psychology and communication can help understand relational power between states as well.[40] In the International Relations discipline, the notion of relative power is intended to illustrate the hierarchy in terms of political and economic influence and control between two or more states. Here, power is often seen as either symmetric or asymmetric, reflecting the differences in the state's ability to exert influence and control over another state. In the case of an asymmetric power relationship, the actual influence and control of the stronger state appear less overpowering than the perceived difference in the level of states' capability would indicate.[41]

However, this view of power based on the state as a unitary actor fails to account for its local dimension which is crucial for understanding power relations between weak, or fragile, states and their perceivably stronger counterparts. In this type of state, the government has less control over the country's overall external relations because of its lack of influence on non-state actors. As a result, actors who have gained domestic power through control of strategic material and reputational assets and resources engage in their independent foreign connections with state and societal actors abroad. They use these linkages to gain mainly financial and material resources to strengthen themselves against domestic political and economic rivals. The external interactions of such prominent societal actors contribute significantly to the country's overall foreign relations and their local power propels relative autonomy toward perceivably more powerful external actors. This enables the state and societal actors to engage in a careful balancing of relationships between various external actors in an attempt to maximize benefits from foreign partnerships.

As a result, when looked at from the perspective of the less powerful, or so-called fragile, states, as can be observed in the Horn of Africa, it can be observed how external relations with foreign state or non-state actors are not a privilege of one unitary and coordinated state actor but rather exercised by several actors, state and non-state actors alike. This contrasts with powerful states which have monopolized their highly coordinated and concentrated foreign policy. The difference arises largely from state weakness, the strength of non-state actors, and local competition for power which give various domestic actors significant agency both locally and in their external relationships.

Political and Economic Power

In the International Relations discipline, two major forms of power are particularly relevant to our analysis. Both represent states' international reach in terms of influence, including the ability to shape the beliefs and behavior of other states and convince them to act according to their interests. The first is political power which draws largely on status, authority, legitimacy, and material and nonmaterial resources. It can be used in both a coercive and noncoercive manner depending on various considerations such as interests, context, relationship with the other party, and available resources and capabilities. Instruments of exercising political power in interstate relations are also varied, but the main formal channels are diplomacy, foreign policy, and coercive means such as military and sanctions mechanisms.

Second, economic power plays an important role in International Relations. However, extricating it from political power is difficult because in combination they are largely viewed as an expression of countries' ability to influence others. In Marxist analysis, for example, intertwined and inseparable political and economic power has informed structural approaches to understanding the international system of states, but the resulting theories have often not engaged in an in-depth analysis of how individual states or non-state actors use economic power in their international relationships.[42]

While a state's economic power is largely perceived through its wealth, economic strength, and material resources, it can be measured according to the extent to which it is capable of using economic means to influence other states. Again, diplomacy and foreign policy, along with negotiation and commercial arrangements in which private actors play an important role, denote the main channels of exercising such power in international relations. Instruments such as foreign direct investment, agreements and terms of trade, and various financial mechanisms and arrangements form part of using economic power through which other states can be influenced. Creating or strengthening transactional interstate relations can be a powerful tool in exerting economic power although any mutually agreed financial or economic arrangements also require mutual compliance. However, the application of economic power to influence other states also has its limits because this kind of power is constrained and limited by the agency and sovereign political autonomy of the target states where governments are often able to drive and exert control over the relationships, especially with investors.[43] It should be noted though again that the influence exerted by a state whose investors intervene in another state largely depends on its political reach in which economic aspects are again important. Such economic determinants may also not be motivated by foreign policy objectives targeting another state, but by domestic interests for economic benefits and consolidation. While Strange argues that rich states exercise economic power in international relations by using successful bargaining with poorer states to promote the market economy which spreads their influence over such states,[44] it is important to understand that for example, fragile states may have important ideological or material domestic objectives which drive their foreign policy approach as is the case of the Horn of Africa. Depending on their strength, they also exert more or less influence on the local political and economic landscape which empowers them in their relations with external partners.

While bargaining power is important in helping to determine who gets their way in a negotiation, it is more significant to seek to contextualize it, understand where it comes from, and how it plays out in international relationships. Economists often equate bargaining power with the means to buy something or as an exercise of power coming from a dominant position in the market (e.g., market share). Although this provides bargaining leverage in economic terms, in the International Relations discipline bargaining has traditionally been viewed through a political lens relating it to peace and war. There are, however, political roots to economic bargaining power as well involving the power position and status of the state or the state's ability to capitalize on a strategic position or a resource. Here, it is often the case that in its relations with a powerful state, a weaker state can wield a level of bargaining power and leverage that can yield an opportune negotiation result. Arguably, this is often the case in the Horn of Africa where local actors control assets that outside powers seek to acquire. It is therefore not the mere power position and status that determines a relationship between states and/or non-state actors, internationally, but in it, factors such as local power, interests, strategic assets, political influence, and natural endowments play an important role.

Power and Elites

Who exactly exercises power in international relations? This question is crucial to the understanding of state and other actors' international interactions. Generally, in states such as those in the Horn of Africa and the Persian Gulf, foreign policy decision-making is concentrated on the leadership of one or a small closed circle of individuals. In the case of the Horn of Africa, foreign policy decisions are strongly associated with the extraversion of principally financial and economic resources from abroad which are often channeled through personal relationships. This adds to such individual leaders' personal resource base and ability to direct resources to clients to buy legitimacy and support. Here the role of individual leaders and narrow circles of elites is particularly significant in foreign relations that are mainly used to maintain power and status. This produces a particularly personal type of foreign relations which in the case of the Horn of African relations with the Middle East countries correspond with the exercise of power by narrow governing (and at times local) elites at both ends and has been keenly endorsed and maintained by them. The preference by the elites in Saudi Arabia, the UAE, and Qatar to engage in personalized dealings with individual national or sub-national level leaders in the Horn of Africa, and the latter using such relationships to ensure exclusive benefits, has helped to further consolidate this long-established practice.

In hierarchical states in the Horn, such as Eritrea and Ethiopia, the leader and the governing elite seek to control the main foreign sources of resources exclusively for maintaining the status quo. For example, in Ethiopia, the individuals of the ruling party routinely use resources from external sources to control possible rivals and restrict the federal system, while in Eritrea the president and a tight circle of few advisors have dominated resource flows from abroad in name of the state. However, more horizontal states, such as Somalia, where political authority and legitimacy are yet to concentrate in the federal government hierarchically, are less able to monopolize external relations and sub-state and non-state actors, such as individual political, religious, and economic leaders, including presidents of the key federal states, heads of religious groups, and businessmen, have been able to establish significant foreign connections and tap into significant external sources of resources. In Somalia, the central government has therefore been reduced to one player among several rivals competing for domestic political and economic power.

Elites exercise power formally and informally. While the Western theoretical propositions about elites, arising from Italian or American schools of thought in political sociology, are useful for an improved understanding of elite power, they are largely tied to formal institutions and therefore do not fully capture the informality related to elites, states, and governance in the Horn of Africa or the Middle East. The established practices, traditions, and conduct within or behind the façade of formal institutions and offices are key to understanding the internal politics and external relations of such states. Such relations, depending on the vision and pragmatic considerations of individual or closed circles of leaders, are also volatile. They are pragmatic and oriented toward material gain. Because of their largely material nature, they may allow buying temporary alignment or generating one-off deals but they hardly guarantee longer-term alliances unless they are in the interest of the leaders involved.

This also departs from the realist blanket approach to power. It elucidates how the locus of power does not necessarily lie in what is considered as the militarily or economically more powerful state but may be seen as more related to the individual leaders who control local political, religious, or economic assets. For example, the exchange of financial benefits in return for promises for certain political orientation or conduct, or resources such as land or strategic assets, places the power in the relationship on those who control the latter. This is particularly the case in volatile settings such as the Horn of Africa where financial or economic goods may buy influence, strategic presence, or resources but this is only ensured by the willingness of the local actors who control such assets. It is often the case that the recipients of material advances from external actors do not hold their end of the bargain or that circumstances will arise that prevent the fulfillment of the set goals. This has been the case in the highly volatile political scene in Somalia and in what have been considered somewhat more stable political systems such as Eritrea and Djibouti. It is the local actors who receive the material overtures that are often the more powerful party in the bargain. These aspects of power and external relations are further elucidated in the chapters that deal with individual states.

Guide to Chapters

This book is organized in a case study form in an attempt to focus on the agency of the state and non-state actors in the Horn of Africa in their relations with their Persian Gulf/Middle East counterparts. These interactions must be discussed in the wider context of regional and international relations. As a result, the chapters will necessarily have to include discussion on the relevant great and middle powers, but due to the focus on the Horn of Africa's engagement with the Persian Gulf/Middle East, it will not be possible to deal with these and other relevant actors and the surrounding dynamics exhaustively. Chapter 2 will discuss the theoretical aspects of this study. It introduces the study's framework for strategic foreign relations analysis, incorporating the theoretical concepts of "economic statecraft" and "economic diplomacy" along with other foreign policy elements. The chapter also briefly discusses the general empirical applicability of the framework in the Horn–Gulf foreign relations. Before the study engages in the particular case studies, Chapter 3 provides a general overview of the relations between the Horn of Africa and the Persian Gulf/Middle East. It seeks to address the need to gain a deeper understanding of the agency of the actors from the Horn of Africa in their relations with their Persian Gulf/Middle East counterparts and serves as an introduction to the subsequent chapters which deal with particular states in the Horn of Africa and their relations with the Persian Gulf and Middle East countries more profoundly. The chapter provides a brief general background to these interconnections while looking at the contemporary relationship from a general perspective.

Chapter 4 presents Ethiopia as the first nuanced and historically contextualized country study. As the most populous and centrally located, Ethiopia is a dominant state in the Horn of Africa and a desired partner for foreign powers interested in the sub-region. Within the context of the Horn, Ethiopia is also the dominant state and influential actor which further underlines its central role in regional affairs. The chapter discusses Ethiopia's relations, particularly with those Gulf States and Türkiye which have recently intensified their relations with the country but also includes a brief discussion of other relevant actors in Ethiopian external relations. It highlights the significance of Ethiopia's dominant position in the Horn and the importance of its domestic politics in shaping the country's external relations with the Persian Gulf and the Middle East. The chapter provides a theory-based analysis of empirical evidence of Ethiopia's agency in its foreign relations.

The following Chapter 5 deals with Somalia's relations with the leading Persian Gulf and Middle East states. Drawing on historical experience, it argues that despite its endemic weakness, and being seen as a battleground of external interests, local actors in Somalia have maintained agency and certain power leverage in their relations with the Persian Gulf/Middle East powers. The chapter shows how the main actors in Somalia, the central government, federal states, and non-state actors have sought to advance their particular interests through these relations which has resulted in political rivalries being affected by diverging external alliances.

Chapter 6 focuses on Eritrea and provides a historically conscious analysis of its relations with the Persian Gulf and the Middle East. Eritrea emerged from a colonial entity with deeply entrenched connections with several Middle East countries. More recently, faced with international isolation, Eritrea opted to work with Persian Gulf powers and has since maintained strong alignment with a selection of Gulf countries. Questioning whether Eritrea can be seen as a staunch ally and not only a strategic partner of the leading countries of the Persian Gulf, the chapter examines the Eritrean regime's perceived strategies and interests as it exercises agency in its international relations. It seeks to provide a deeper understanding of aspects of Eritrea's foreign policy and external relations, especially in the context of its connections across the Red Sea.

Finally, by examining the Horn of Africa–Middle East relations, the concluding chapter advances the argument for the need of a more nuanced understanding of agency and power relations in the external affairs of states. As the agency of the Horn of Africa actors in relations with their Persian Gulf and Middle East counterparts demonstrates, governments, administrations, and non-state actors of the so-called small and weak states may have important levels of control, leverage, and bargaining power in their affairs with larger and seemingly more powerful states and non-state actors. Although their agency should not be exaggerated due to various constraints, these actors can advance their interests through external relations and exert a variable degree of influence on their partners and their engagement. Due to the Horn countries' domestic political contexts, the utility of their external relations is mainly local since the material and nonmaterial resources obtained through foreign partnerships are mainly used for relative strengthening against domestic rivals.

Chapter 1

THEORETICAL CONSIDERATIONS

ECONOMIC ASPECTS OF FOREIGN POLICY

Theoretical aspects discussed in this study center on a selection of current approaches in International Relations and International Political Economy that are relevant to the discussion of small (weak, fragile) states' relations with middle and great powers. However, here the analysis is done contrary to the current trend from more powerful states toward the weaker by examining these relations from the perspective of small states' external relations. Moreover, unlike the dominant views in the International Relations literature on the Middle East, it attempts to highlight agency and complexity in the Horn of Africa–Persian Gulf/Middle East relations by discussing states, and sub-state and non-state actors in the Horn of Africa and their relationships with their Persian Gulf/Middle East counterparts and other regional and great power actors. It seeks to highlight the perspective of domestically relevant political actors in the Horn as they reach out to the Middle East. Informed by geostrategic and geo-economic considerations of major and middle powers, the study discusses various government and non-state actor strategies, approaches, and objectives as part of their agency in their external relations toward the Persian Gulf/Middle East players. The study's deliberate focus is bilateral relations, so it purposefully leaves other relations, including multilateral fora, to lesser attention. This allows more intense focus on the particular foreign policy and external relations strategies and approaches that various actors in the Horn states use in their relations with the Persian Gulf/Middle East countries. The study also proposes a framework for a clearer understanding of economic statecraft as a strategy and economic diplomacy, containing various noncoercive and coercive policy instruments, as a practical approach in foreign relations.

This chapter discusses relevant theoretical considerations of the Horn of Africa–Persian Gulf/Middle East relations and provides a framework for analyzing them from the political-economic perspective. It highlights the inability of the realist theoretical frame in International Relations, which is currently dominant in the analysis of Middle East politics to provide a nuanced interpretation of these relations because of its narrow understanding of actorness and power. The study, therefore, calls for more in-depth multiple-actor-based interpretations for an improved understanding of the Horn of Africa's relations with the Middle East.

Types of International Powers and Interstate Relationships

Generally, international relations analysis recognizes that in terms of international power and influence states stand hierarchically at different positions. In International Relations, it is possible to distinguish various types of states in terms of their power and influence. Roughly, however, three categories of states based on the level of their international power and influence can be identified: the great (major, international, global) powers, middle (regional) powers,[1] and small states.[2]

Great powers have been in the eye of the realist international relations analysis largely due to its long-standing focus on power and hegemony in international politics. The essentially anarchic international realm in which there is no ultimate authority is seen to be shaped by the complex system of states, and more recently non-state actors, which the most powerful states considered as unitary actors dictate. Indeed, in the mainstream, mainly Western-centric, versions of international political history the most powerful states and their empires are given a major role, while some lesser powers are mentioned, but the agency of small states is rarely recognized except through exceptional events.[3]

What are such major powers? They are states with an extraordinary ability to influence international political dynamics and economic and social discourses and trends. Great powers have the capacity and the willingness to exert influence at a global scale. They have leverage over other states due to their capabilities that emerge from their large base of material and nonmaterial resources. These major powers are economically big and strong and have an unusual capacity to exert coercive influence militarily and diplomatically while also being able to draw on their social (e.g., education) and cultural (e.g., liberalism) resources to shape international affairs and discourses according to their agendas and interests. They play leading roles in international institutions and maintain effective influence globally among peoples and regions beyond their own. If state leaders perceive a certain power to have consolidated international presence and influence, and generated interest in shaping world politics, these peers tend to recognize and treat it as a major power.

Middle, or regional, powers are powerful states which do not have the same reach as the globally strong great powers. However, they are influential and can challenge or be more powerful than major powers in their surrounding neighborhood. Since the consolidation of US unipolarity after the Cold War, the number and importance of middle powers have increased. Regional powers have gained assertiveness due to factors such as political and economic consolidation, as well as rising military capacity and population growth, resulting in a range of powers with various levels of regional and international influence.[4] Several middle powers have become significant in their own right, and to an extent local challengers to the US hegemony or other regionally dominant states, but some also serve as the hegemon's allies in confrontation against rival powers.[5]

It is important to understand the role of regional powers in international politics. This is because they are crucial in shaping their neighborhood in the increasingly regionalized world and because the most powerful of them may challenge major powers in areas where they are strongest. As processes of political, economic, and security regionalism have become increasingly popular and accelerated since the end of the Cold War, regional powers have been able to carve themselves consolidated zones of influence in which some of them have been able to assert themselves as the leading states. Others have faced great powers or regional rivals in their primary zones of influence and sought to establish their leading status. The rising regionalism has therefore not only offered opportunities to the regional powers but also generated rivalries in the leadership of given regions.[6]

Regions themselves are composed of several states and therefore often include rivalries and aspirants to become the dominant state. However, what also seems to be the case is that the rivals within the region appear to have more influence among certain peoples and certain territories while their opponents seem to have more in others. This influence tends to be strongest in the most proximate neighboring or particularly strategic territories of interest for each such state. For example, in the Middle East, Iran's zones of major influence are across the border in Iraq and Syria, as well as in strategic areas such as southern Lebanon and to a lesser extent in northern Yemen. Meanwhile, its regional rival Saudi Arabia employs strategies of cooperation and confrontation in its attempts to exert a level of control in the Arabian Peninsula and proximate territories, such as the Horn of Africa, while challenging Iran in some of its territorial strongholds. In Northeast Africa, Egypt and Ethiopia are lesser regional powers connected by the Nile River, but the two rivals are both influential in their neighborhood.

However, when considering middle, or regional, power status what again matters is perception. Similarly to great powers, regionally influential states gain and lose in status based on the way they are considered by other states. If such a state is seen to wield important power and influence among states in that region and perceived to legitimately lead it, the state is more readily accepted as a true regional power. In contrast, a state that cannot assert regional power status due to its fewer capabilities, or is simply viewed as a lesser power, falls short.

The implication of the perception of power is that reputational considerations matter. The state may be viewed and treated as lesser or greater than its actual material power because of perception. Here, soft power and leverage among other states are important, but *who* determines and believes the state's status is crucial for the wider assessment of its position. For example, Turkish leadership might consider the country a great power, but because of the limits of its material and nonmaterial power and influence, both hard and soft, beyond its neighborhood, and perception among other states about its status, it is often perceived as a middle, or regional, power.

The generally cited third category is small states. These are considered "small" not necessarily because of their lesser geographical extension or low population number, but rather due to their limited power and influence in international politics. In the International Relations literature, from the Cold War period onwards, small states have been considered to be peripheral to the understanding of the salient dynamics of the international system.[7] They have been often considered weak and in need of great power assistance to fend for their survival against more powerful states. This has had the far-reaching policy implication that great powers should use their resources to support such small state allies with the reward of maintaining or extending their sphere of influence and dictating the "rules of the game" of international politics.

However, it can be observed that many small states, especially when referred primarily to their geographical size, are more influential than their relative size might suggest. Such influential small states, for example, the UAE and Qatar (albeit some might consider them as middle powers),[8] are likely to be financially or economically strong and have resources, capabilities, governance systems, interests, and aspirations that enhance their international power. As Ennis suggests, such states may be able to capitalize on the opportunities emerging in the context of the decline of the unipolar world order for their benefit and "influence a multiplicity of outcomes in the international order."[9]

Yet, there are also small states which are considered politically and economically weak. These states, often described as fragile,[10] have much less international influence and are constrained in their foreign policy[11] to maneuver in a limited policy space in which they often need to align themselves with bigger powers. In such states, due to the limited state capacity,[12] the governing elite is less able to monopolize external relations and sub-state and non-state actors. The latter often pursue their foreign connections which affect the state's overall external relations and challenge the governing forces leading to further state weakness, fragility, or outright failure (collapse).[13] While great powers have been traditionally viewed to be the main beneficiaries of relations with small states, more recently middle, or regional, powers have increasingly taken advantage of their influence relative to small states, especially in their neighborhood in the growingly multipolar international system.

Still, governments of weak states have their interests which in most cases relate to securing their domestic position and predominance. They are often able to use their juridical statehood and foreign policy to maintain external legitimacy and strengthen themselves against internal rivals[14] by gaining recognition and extracting resources from their allies.[15] And, as can be observed to have been the case with Somalia (from the 1960s to mid-1970s) and Ethiopia (especially since the 1998-2000 Eritrean–Ethiopian War) in the Horn of Africa, state weakness is not static since states can become powerful enough to convert into important players in regional politics in their neighborhood.[16]

The transformation of the international system in terms of power hierarchy is seen to have implications for the small states' foreign policy options. This is because the rise of new powers is considered to provide them with new opportunities for bandwagoning.[17] Some neorealist approaches also consider the great and middle powers' attempt to gain security through expansion, and by asserting their position and norms in international politics and economy, while pointing out that small states with fewer resources and capabilities are "more exposed to the vagaries of international security and economic competition."[18] As a result, small state leaders' main preoccupation becomes preventing external intervention and devastating effects of international market forces which limits their policy choices to the space provided by the structure of the international system and the great power maneuvering in international politics and economy.[19] Even today, especially from a security analysis perspective, some realist International Relations scholars continue to associate state smallness with the difficulty of successfully pursuing one's aspirations through foreign policy.[20] This, however, may be considered as a somewhat erroneous and analytically antiquated view because small states, even some considered as fragile as in the Horn of Africa, can often overcome significant constraints in their foreign relations and are capable of pursuing their interests internationally, for example through bilateral and multilateral diplomacy and political and economic alignments.[21]

As a result, state smallness should be seen neither as a determining factor of state strength and weakness, nor a definitive indicator of its power and influence.[22] For example, the state behavior in the Horn of Africa may often not comfortably fit the definition of bandwagoning because the governments may gain relatively significantly more from cooperation and alliances than their powerful allies. This is evident in the case of the foreign policy approach of most governments in the Horn where their efforts and alliances with great and regional powers have brought significant benefits in terms of material and nonmaterial resources (e.g., diplomatic and political support, domestic popularity, and legitimacy) for regime survival while they may have yielded lesser returns to their more powerful allies. The Horn regimes tend to have an important level of local power over their affairs and through it, they have important leverage and bargaining power in the affairs with states that seek to collaborate with them in their political and territorial space. While this kind of power does often not translate into far-reaching international influence, it is particularly present in bilateral relationships with even much more powerful states especially when such states seek to advance their interests in or through the territorial space of such small states. For example, especially since 2015 a number of the governments in the greater Horn of Africa, among them Djibouti, Eritrea, Ethiopia, Somalia, and Sudan, have taken advantage of the opportunities opened up in the changing regional context provided by the Saudi-led intervention in Yemen and the GCC crisis resulting isolation of Qatar and drawing in Türkiye. The interest of the powerful Gulf States, particularly Saudi Arabia and the UAE, to increasingly exert influence over the Red Sea in the changing regional dynamics has placed governments in the Horn of Africa in a favorable bargaining position. A number of the Horn governments engaging in new or changing external alignments have capitalized on the emerging opportunities to strengthen themselves.

Geopolitics and Geo-economics

When dealing with external relations of states another important aspect to consider is the role of geopolitics and its economic aspects, geo-economics. This is significant not only because of relations among states in a given region, but also because it provides a frame for understanding how they also relate to extra-regional states, such as major powers, and how those relationships affect regional and interregional state relations. Geopolitics studies human and physical geography's impact on politics and international relations between states. Through the lens of geographic variables, it explores how geographic space relates to political power and how geopolitical spaces are constituted and organized. The geopolitical inquiry has been largely concerned with great powers[23] and links to foreign policy analysis in that it analyses international political behavior and the global structure of international political relations.[24]

Similarly, geo-economics considers geography as an important factor in its study of economic aspects of politics. Generally, geo-economics can be conceived as the extension of geopolitical competition associated mainly with strategic and security perspectives into the realm of economics.[25] It centers on the use of economic instruments and power to reach geopolitical objectives, emphasizing spatial, political, and strategic aspects of economies and resources. However, the term has not been universally defined and its independence from geopolitics has not been established. The lack of definition has led to several understandings of the concept. While some scholars consider geo-economics to form part of a broader notion of geopolitics, others have sought to differentiate between the two to gain analytical clarity.[26]

Indeed, geo-economics can be seen as an outgrowth of the geopolitical paradigm which has dominated International Relations analysis, especially in the fields of strategic and security studies. Its development as an analytical framework is propelled by the understanding that the "strategic competition of today is largely driven by economic means."[27] Yet, until today the concept's independence from geopolitics has not been well-established largely because it has not been shown that despite highlighting economic aspects the term appears not to bring substantial new analytical light that differs from the more established concept of geopolitics. For example, in a recent attempt to distinguish between geopolitical and geo-economic strategies, it was claimed that as geopolitical actors leaders pursue strategic objectives "by employing diplomatic and military means, as well as intelligence capabilities" while geo-economically they would engage in the same "through the control over markets, resources, and rules that shape international economic interaction."[28] Again, however, the means and overall strategies to reach the strategic objectives are largely the same and draw from the geopolitical analytical toolbox.[29] Simply highlighting economic and geographical aspects as sources of and ends of strategic considerations is not convincingly different from the geopolitical paradigm unless a substantial difference can be established in terms of analytical perspective.

However, rather than analytically rewarding, geo-economics as a concept may be somewhat more empirically convincing. For example, it has been suggested that geo-economics can be seen as a form of application of economic power in foreign policy to reach strategic objectives in which there should be a clear geographical dimension.[30] Moreover, others consider geo-economics, at times in combination with military means, as a form of statecraft for political ends,[31] including using the state and businesses together to increase economic power by obtaining gains, resources, and economic security.[32] Yet, this can be considered as reducing the concept to a foreign policy instrument in the geopolitical game[33] and may result in confusing the term with concepts such as economic statecraft and economic diplomacy which have been employed extensively in the field of foreign policy analysis.[34]

Foreign Policy and Power

In their international relations, states seek to advance their interests through foreign policy. Bridging domestic politics and international relations, foreign policy inquiry elucidates how states' interests come about and how they engage each other to reach their strategic objectives.[35] It shows how domestic and foreign actors and forces have to pass through the states' political structures to influence their foreign policy decision-making units[36] and only then affect their relations with other governments and non-state actors. Here, one encounters two major perspectives for the starting point of the analysis. First, from a realist or neorealist perspective, but somewhat uneasily, one can see foreign policy reflect the states' nature as a unitary and rational actor and their attempt to survive in the anarchical international system which may impose certain structural conditions on them that guide their behavior.[37] This, however, does not account for domestic determinants of foreign policy which are often even more important than the dynamics of the international system. Indeed, the "innerpolitik" tradition subscribing to the idea that foreign policy emerges within the social and economic structures of the state has been strong in the tradition of foreign policy analysis.[38]

Second, from a constructivist viewpoint, one can argue that foreign policy preferences grow out of domestic political, economic, social, and/or cultural realities, reflecting various societal actors' identities, ideas, and values.[39] While, social constructivism, as a broader approach in social sciences, appears to open the way for a more nuanced foreign policy analysis than unitary actor or systemic approaches in International Relations, as an approach rooted in domestic realities alone it falls short of gaining an understanding of varying state behavior in international politics. Therefore, an intertwined domestic and international level analysis combining the two spheres is necessary for an improved understanding of how states relate to and behave toward their counterparts.[40] This enables an analysis to shed light on the decision-making and policy space taking into account domestic and international systemic constraints.

While foreign policy has been analytically explored through various frameworks, its domestic dimension has gained important scholarly focus. The most widely used among them is the rational actor approach[41] which is also the most suited for our study exploring the foreign relations and approaches adopted by the states in the Horn of Africa toward their Middle Eastern neighbors. This model based on rational choice theory considers the actors in charge of the state, or its authoritative foreign policy institutions (e.g., presidency), as the main actors determining foreign policy. These actors are relied on to make rational and informed decisions based on preference ranking of possible policy options and seeking to maximize value. However, the purest form of the rational actor approach is undermined by several factors relating to real-life situations. It assumes state leaderships to base their decisions on complete information and consistent, coherent, and optimized decision-making which can be seen as not fully reflecting the empirical reality.

A more nuanced reading suggests that state leaders work in a constrained empirical environment and often do not exert total control of the country's external relations. Their decisions on foreign policy are often influenced by numerous factors such as outlook, mentality, ideas and ideology, and national psyche. However, due to constraints often dictated by power differences, they may be forced to abandon their most preferred policy options and may be obliged to decide among their least preferred choices. At times such foreign policy decision-makers do not have access to complete information or they may make decisions that may rationally favor their own interests while these might go against any conceivable "national" interest or be seen as less than ideal choices for the interests of other groups within the state.[42] For example, rationality may be defined along the interests of an individual leader, group, or coalition while other societal groups (e.g., middle or working class) would rationally choose other policy options. These decision-makers would also not necessarily consider all possible foreign policy options if this is not rationally feasible, but decide among the most available choices.

Another focus, which can be grouped together as a set of similar approaches, centers on broader decision-making in foreign policy. It is headed by bureaucratic, or governmental and administrative, politics.[43] Initially emerging from Allison's interpretation of the Cuban Missile Crisis,[44] this approach seeks to take into account various actors deemed to affect the making of foreign policy within a state. The main model sees foreign policy decisions as a collective outcome of bargaining by the individual leaders who occupy government posts. It seeks to highlight the role of policy actors in the government.[45] Inter-branch model, which draws on the same bureaucratic logic but views foreign policy more clearly as a combined product of interactions among various government and international agencies than individual leaders and civil servants,[46] and the political process model, which emphasizes individuals' objectives, mindset, and ideology among various power centers in government to determine foreign policy decisions,[47] can be seen as extreme variations of this approach. However, although often seen to explain why a state might embark on irrational action these approaches often fail to account for the relative power and its concentration on certain individuals in foreign policy decision-making. They may not account for the most significant determinants guiding behavior and inaccurately diminish the role of the main individual or organ steering the state's foreign policy, particularly in the case of authoritarian political systems in which power is heavily concentrated on a few individuals in the executive. This is particularly the case with states this study focuses on.

As can be observed in the above discussion, foreign policy analysis has a heavy emphasis on agency and includes various levels of analysis.[48] Having originated largely as a North American disciplinary orientation during the Cold War, in the most basic form the analysis can be seen to consist of three elements; actor (independent variable), process (intervening variable), and outcome (dependent variable).[49] It can focus on any of such elements, such as choices, processes, outcomes, or implementation, and most often emphasizes the comparison of single case studies in an attempt to generalize and build theory.[50] According to such analyses, again in the simplest form there are three major instruments for a state to conduct foreign policy which include diplomacy, aid, and military force. These instruments pertain mostly to capable states because they entail the application of power, although the state or sub-state and non-state actors in weak states may use the same tools in their competition for prominence which takes place mainly in their domestic political setting.

In this study, drawing on the rational actor logic, the attempt is to primarily discuss the relations between the states in the Horn of Africa and the Persian Gulf/Middle East countries. Given that the states in the sub-region are largely authoritarian, as are most of their Middle East counterparts, it sees the leading individuals of the regimes in the Horn of Africa being mainly in charge of foreign policy orientation and pursuing their own and the narrow governing elite's interests through their external relations. Since they lack the capacity to monopolize external relations, sub-state and societal actors often maintain their own external connections which help them in their competition with the state and contribute to the country's overall foreign relations as illustrated in Figure 1.

Countries' overall external relations are a complex web of individual foreign connections of various state, sub-state, and non-state actors. As Figure 1 seeks to elucidate, in fragile states the state actors are unable to monopolize the most important foreign connections due to the strength of sub-state and societal (non-

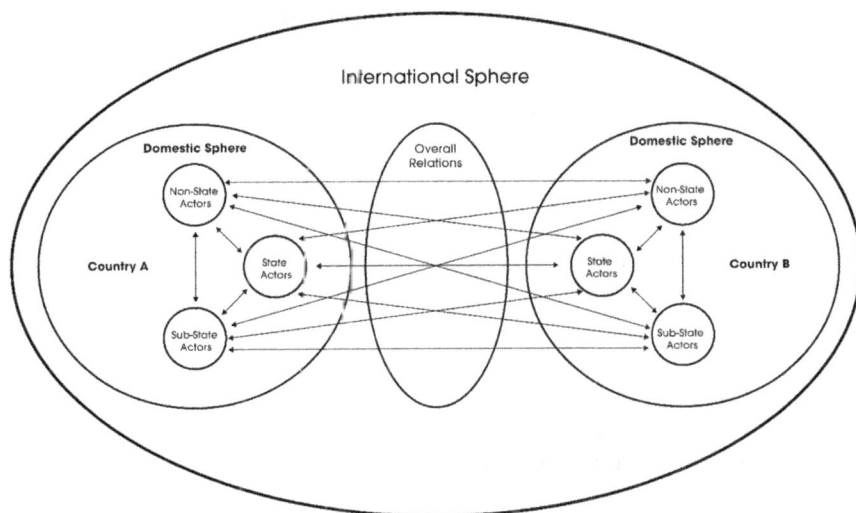

Figure 1 Countries' overall foreign relations.

state) actors which compete with them in the domestic sphere and engage in their own external linkages. As a result, several domestic actors' simultaneous engagement in significant external connections and partnerships produces a complex network of relationships of variable intensity and significance which together constitute the country's overall foreign relations. Although the governmental actors may use the state's international legal recognition as leverage, the advantage they may gain is limited by their own weakness and the relative strength and external connections of their domestic rivals.

We, therefore, discuss above all motivations, strategies, and approaches of state, sub-state, and societal actors in the Horn of Africa in their relations with their counterparts in the Persian Gulf and the Middle East. In these external partnerships, we emphasize their local power which gives them leverage in the domestic setting and sets limits to the influence of external actors. Therefore, the big question we seek to explore concerns the power dimensions of these relations. Based on empirical observation, the configuration and exercise of power are more complex than the impression given by the realist International Relations paradigm. While most Horn states can be considered small and weak in comparison to their counterparts in the Persian Gulf, their governments do maintain a degree of leverage and bargaining power in their affairs with their perceivably more powerful counterparts. In particular, political and politico-economic features of the overall affairs between the Horn states with their powerful Persian Gulf neighbors, to which both governmental and societal actors contribute, are highlighted in an attempt to understand their agency and its significance in these interactions. Leaders of authoritarian states in the Horn of Africa have clear objectives of what to gain from their foreign relations, especially in terms of financial and material resources for regime survival, as often do the competing societal actors who maintain their particular external linkages. This enables local actors to approach external partnerships from a position of strength, as in the case of the securitization agenda in Africa,[51] which their control of locally strategic, material, and reputational assets buttresses. Due to the observed importance of geostrategic, including geo-economic, aspects in these relations, economic aspects, such as the strategy of economic statecraft and the practice of economic diplomacy, are deemed highly relevant in this endeavor.

Economic Aspects in Foreign Relations

In their international relations, powerful states seek to use economic power to influence others. As the growing scholarly interest in geo-economics and economic statecraft demonstrates,[52] focus on economic power and its use has become recognized as a crucial dimension of foreign policy and diplomacy. It not only involves the most powerful states but is also a salient feature in foreign policy strategies of middle (regional) powers.

However, in the scholarly analysis, various economic characteristics relating to foreign policy are still not highlighted, as shown by the lack of clarity and understanding of the used terminology. For example, the terms "economic statecraft" and "economic diplomacy," often referred to in the context of economic aspects of foreign policy, tend to be confused and sometimes used interchangeably[53] while other more specific terms, such as the dollar and checkbook diplomacy, have at times also been used erroneously. Yet, the use of agreed and correct terminology to delineate analytical distinctions is significant when engaging in scholarly exercise. Clarifying the terms and giving them precise meaning helps our understanding and analysis. This is particularly important in the case of not well-defined aspects of scientific inquiry, such as analyzing the economic characteristics that form part of foreign policy. Here we seek to shed light on several terms that are relevant to understanding the economic aspects of states' foreign policy in the Horn of Africa.

Economic Statecraft and Economic Diplomacy

The terms "economic statecraft" and "economic diplomacy" are at times used interchangeably. However, they carry some important distinctions and should be considered in a nuanced manner pinpointing what are their salient characteristics. As explained earlier, this should go beyond simplistic notions of the "state" and understand the individuals, motives, and objectives involved.

In the International Relations discipline, the term "economic statecraft" derives from the concept of "statecraft." In his seminal research note, Morton Kaplan defines statecraft as "the construction of strategies for securing the national interest in the international arena."[54] Economic statecraft can therefore be considered to entail the economic aspects of a strategy to promote national interest and achieve foreign policy objectives. What is often assumed is that the national interest is dictated by the state and formed to benefit it. This narrow understanding, however, may miss the crucial viewpoint that in authoritarian states, for example, the "national interest" only exists the way it is dictated by the leading individuals of a narrow governing elite and is often oriented mainly for individual, specific group, or regime benefit. When discussing largely authoritarian states, as in the case of this study, it is important therefore to highlight that such formulation of interests as "national" does not correspond with the concept of "national interest" as generally understood in International Relations, and, in reality, benefits certain individuals and societal groups but may undermine others and the state and the nation as a whole.

Moreover, economic statecraft has a strong emphasis on the exercise of economic power for political ends from the perspective of the relatively more powerful actor.[55] Indeed, it is strongly associated with strategies of great powers, and increasingly with middle powers, in their attempts to exert power and influence over smaller and weaker states. Therefore, economic statecraft as a strategy features coercion as an important element to achieve one's interests to a much greater degree than economic diplomacy which is a term used to describe the practice of interactions mainly between state representatives aimed at an economic benefit.[56] As a result, economic statecraft is often associated with security issues[57] and channeled through instruments that offer "carrots and sticks,"[58] but it has inherently political objectives which it seeks to achieve by generating political opportunities and costs to the target state.[59] When putting economic statecraft into practice, the states' foreign policy actors employ instruments such as diplomacy and sanctions in an attempt to apply economic pressure to achieve political ends.

However, it is suggested here that economic statecraft should not be understood as a use of economic power only in the classical realist sense. Economic statecraft should not be seen as a strategy reserved for monolithic states alone but rather for all relevant actors in International Relations. The economic power of a state, and sub-state or non-state, actors can be considered in various ways and should not be constrained to the financial capability of a given regime as is overwhelmingly the case. Instead, economic power and the foreign policy strategy of economic statecraft pursued by a given regime should be understood more broadly. This is because financially less powerful states, and non-state actors engaging in external relations, can use their other economic assets, such as geopolitically strategic location, natural endowments, land, or labor, as part of their foreign policy or external affairs strategy. As part of this strategy, they practice economic diplomacy and use their economic assets to gain financial or other material resources for domestic political objectives, namely, for strengthening against domestic rivals and competitors from neighboring states as in the case of the fragile states in the Horn of Africa. This domestic dimension of statecraft is often forgotten in general, state-centric, International Relations interpretations of the concept.

Furthermore, economic statecraft can be confused with economic diplomacy because it shares features with the latter, such as trade, investment, borrowing and lending, and aid, grants, and other financial flows and economic assistance as instruments to achieve foreign policy objectives. However, a crucial difference between the two concepts is that while economic statecraft can be seen as an overarching foreign policy strategy, economic diplomacy is a practical technique of interactions through which designated representatives of a state or non-state entity seek to achieve the set objectives.[60] Composed of substantial strategic foreign policy or external relations objectives, economic statecraft, therefore, includes economic diplomacy as a technique of interactions which, in turn, includes various noncoercive and coercive instruments depending on the state's capabilities.

As a whole, economic diplomacy, as a related concept in International Relations, refers to the salient economic features of a state's diplomatic interactions mainly with another state, sub-state, and non-state actors. It is therefore a technique of economic statecraft, for example, practiced by state officials who engage representatives of the target state and use a spectrum of economic tools at their disposal to persuade their counterparts and achieve their set interests.[61] These instruments are principally economic policy mechanisms or concrete economic assets dictated by the strategic considerations of the state's foreign policy. In practice, economic diplomacy in realist international relations interpretations employs diplomatic contacts, communication, and interactions as a tool to advance interests such as regime survival and economic security.

However, as with economic statecraft, the narrow conceptualization of economic diplomacy suffers from state-centrism that does not reflect the plurality of actors engaged in external relations. It fails to include sub-state and non-state actors which hold particularly important external agency in weak states, such as in the Horn of Africa. Many such actors, for example, the *de facto* state of Somaliland and various rebel or opposition movements in Ethiopia and Somalia, maintain "diplomatic-like" representative linkages with foreign state and non-state actors and engage in economic diplomacy to advance their interests and achieve their strategic goals and objectives.

While economic statecraft and economic diplomacy should be conceived as relatively broad strategic and practical concepts, narrower terms are also used to describe the economic aspects of states' foreign policy. Most such terms derive from economic statecraft or diplomacy but include more specific aspects which largely fall within the umbrella of the two broader concepts. For example, the term "financial statecraft" has been employed by scholars to understand the monetary aspects of economic statecraft.[62] Similarly, financial aspects have been highlighted by employing similar concepts such as "Dollar,"[63] "Yen,"[64] "Yuan,"[65] or "Riyal"[66] diplomacy related to great and middle powers' efforts to extend their economic power and influence through financial means. While in the past this policy was largely reserved for the hegemon, the rise and economic strengthening of middle powers have enabled them to engage in the same strategy as part of their foreign policy. Although erroneously denoted as a type of diplomacy, this strategy forms part of economic statecraft, the broader foreign policy planning, and practice.

The term "checkbook diplomacy," however, refers to the use of investment and economic aid for gaining influence and recognition.[67] These tools are used as bargaining chips in diplomatic interactions to reach foreign policy objectives as part of the strategy of economic statecraft. Such financial injections are meant to generate goodwill in the recipient economy and function as a mechanism to extend soft power. In particular US-based analysis, the instrument for economic statecraft has been most closely associated with Chinese foreign policy,[68] but the Chinese media has sought to downplay the claimed existence of any such policy mechanism.[69] Another term Western policymakers and analysts have recently associated with China's foreign policy strategy of economic statecraft is "debt trap diplomacy."[70] This concept emerged based on observations of how China was issuing extensive loans mainly for infrastructure development to partners in key locations of its geostrategic master plan, the Belt and Road Initiative.[71] The proponents of this idea believe that the Chinese government uses high levels of debt to trap partner countries and gain power and influence to affect decision-making.

Finally, an important concept to mention in the context of this study is "petrodollar recycling." The term "petrodollar" emerged from the early 1970s deal between the United States and Saudi Arabia to standardize oil prices using the US dollar which sought to maintain its central role in the international financial system.[72] This mutually beneficial deal increased US political influence and involvement in the Middle East and convinced other states belonging to the

Organization of the Petroleum Exporting Countries as well. Consequently, the predominance of the US dollar in energy markets boosted its desirability as the world's preferred reserve currency. It began dictating the global oil economy and related politics and gave growing incentives for countries to invest in US dollar-denominated assets. States enriched by their oil wealth could not absorb all financial returns from petroleum sales and began investing and spending proceeds outside of the country. While much of this money found its way back to the US as foreign investment, an important quantity was also spent by states to advance their political interests abroad in the context of the Cold War. This dimension of petrodollar recycling has been especially important for the oil-rich states in the Persian Gulf which have used their petrodollars in an attempt to extend influence and reach foreign policy objectives, especially in their neighborhood.[73] For the Horn of Africa, this has meant that especially from the 1970s onward there has been a variable degree of efforts from the leading countries of the Persian Gulf to primarily use financial power to influence political and economic realities and developments in the sub-region. These states have especially targeted the geostrategically significant, resource-rich, and culturally somewhat similar, littoral countries on the African side of the Red Sea and the Gulf of Aden.

Theoretical Considerations for the Horn of Africa–Middle East Relations

The literature on the Horn of Africa–Middle East relations, and especially that focusing the Gulf States' interactions with countries in the Horn of Africa, has depicted these interactions as largely state-centric and based on unitary actor power projection. The Horn states have been portrayed as rather passive reactionaries in state-centered relative power relations heavily tilted toward the financially strong countries of the Persian Gulf. This perspective is founded on a view of the Persian Gulf countries' superior power as they seek to extend their political influence and secure the Red Sea and Gulf of Aden neighborhood. However, it fails to account for the plurality of actorness and various state and non-state players in the Horn of Africa wielding local power that enables them to advance their interests by engaging their Persian Gulf/Middle East counterparts in favorable terms.

The realist interpretation particularly dominates the International Relations analysis of the Middle East. It demonstrates strategic and security analysts' persisting use of realism as an analytical frame and its extension to the Middle East-Africa relations especially from the Cold War onward. However, there is a strand of literature, which first emerged in the 1970s, that defies the realist view.[74] This literature indicates that considering international and domestic politics as inherently separate does not reflect the prevailing reality. In the case of the fragile state entities in the Horn of Africa, the state-centric realist approach fails to recognize multiple domestic state and non-state actors that maintain significant international connections. Equally important is its inability to capture how power emerges locally and how it is exercised in the domestic formal and informal institutional context, and how it manifests itself in the connection between the local and international spheres. Understanding social dynamics, attitudes, beliefs, and convictions and their relationship with material and reputational dimensions of power in the particular local institutional settings is overlooked, resulting in diminished explanatory power in the case of the Horn of Africa where various actors, state and non-state alike, exercise agency both domestically and externally. This reality defies the realist interpretation based on unitary states and the more powerful states' projection of relative power on their weaker counterparts.

While may not have always been so, the hydrocarbon bonanza in the Middle East came to emphasize transactional dimensions of the Persian Gulf polities' interactions with the Horn of Africa. This trend gained traction from the recycling of petrodollars in the 1970s and early 1980s but strengthened further due to the heightened political, security, and economic competition among the Gulf States and Türkiye since the Arab Spring, and in the context of the Saudi–Iran rivalry, Yemen civil war, and the Qatar diplomatic crisis.[75] In the simplest sense, the approach has been to use their financial muscle to provide rewards for political influence and invest in strategic sectors of the economy, infrastructure, land, and natural resource concessions. However, these transactional interactions, from which the Horn actors seek to benefit, are inherently volatile and often result in endemic weakness and instability in the established partnerships. Although these transactions are sometimes supplemented by more formal and observable pacts, such as defense or technical cooperation treaties, such agreements have not added significant stability to the volatile relationships. This is largely because the Horn actors, state and non-state actors alike, exercise local power in such relationships and often prefer to shift external political alignments and economic partners according to their interests, as required by the domestic political and economic rivalries. As a result, the Horn actors' ambiguity to honor partnerships in the long term creates uncertainty and insecurity among their Middle East partners.

The unpredictability of relations and the inability to dictate alliances and alignments in the long term weaken the relative position of the Persian Gulf countries toward their partners in the Horn of Africa. In this context, state and non-state actors in the Horn gain leverage in bilateral relationships. The emphasis on financial and economic aspects of strategic partnerships by engaging partners mainly in transactional terms also diminishes the importance of other layers of interaction, including identity, religious, and cultural dimensions which often provide social substance on which to base more profound connections. Here, Turkish "humanitarian' development and culturally emphasized engagement among Muslim populations in the Horn of Africa, and especially in Somalia, have provided somewhat of an exception and has resulted in important local influence, significant economic investment and trade benefits, and long-term cultural, religious, and military partnerships. Meanwhile, the largely volatile and material nature of transactional relations encourages mainly a dynamic based on short-term convergence of interests and favors temporary alignments over the formation of deeper and more lasting alliances.

Moreover, depictions of the relations between the Horn and the Persian Gulf/ Middle East are composed of a combination of their perceived hierarchical position in international politics. From the perspective of the state and non-state actors in the Horn, however, the relative power between monolithic states that International Relations scholars emphasize is less relevant because their focus is pragmatic and oriented toward gaining crucial resources from abroad for domestic consolidation and competition against local political and economic rivals. Accordingly, governments and non-state actors in the Horn of Africa take part in the regional and international political "game" based on the perceptions they have principally on their domestic political and economic position. These considerations help frame their interests and approaches toward external actors in the geostrategic (geopolitical and geo-economic) context and guide behavior on a spectrum of possible actions such as confrontation, alignment, and alliance. Collectively the Horn states have various types of mainly authoritarian governance systems, and they tend to be heterogeneous and diverse in terms of geography, population, and natural, financial, and material resources. In the Horn, the states are generally ruled by narrow governing elites but are at the same time enormously diverse and endowed with a wide variety of different exchangeable assets such as natural resources, geostrategic location, markets, fertile land, and labor. These assets generate leverage and bargaining power in external relations, but the states' weakness and fragility often allow sub-state and non-state actors to pursue their particular foreign relations, sometimes in competition with the government, undermining the central authority's ability to establish a monopoly of the most significant external connections. Yet, each particular state has unique political, economic, social, and cultural features, and the way they tend to engage other states depends on factors such as the leadership and the governing elite's strategic and practical approaches, the nature of the overall relations, and bargainable assets.[76]

It is therefore important to underline that in their relations with the Persian Gulf and other external partners, the Horn actors, both state and non-state, have not been mere passive targets of influence and intervention. The agency of state and non-state leaders has been important in shaping relations with external parties irrespective of relative power differences. Many actors in the Horn actively look for foreign connections for their own benefit and negotiate transactions and partnerships from a position of power due to their local status, significance, and control of strategic assets and resources.

Similarly to middle powers, which in their neighborhood are in some ways more powerful than great powers, the Horn state and non-state actors exert power and influence principally in their local context and immediate surroundings. Here, due to their local status and ability to control significant assets and resources, they maintain an advantage against their regionally powerful Persian Gulf and Middle East partners. While the influence of the Persian Gulf and Middle East states extends to the sovereign space of the Horn states, local actors in the latter are often much stronger in their own political, economic, and social context and able to take advantage of this influence. As a result, by offering the possibility for external actors to involve themselves in their space, these local state and non-state actors have leverage in their relations with these external players. For example, this is the case with attracting investment and tying the investing individual or entity into a relationship in which the local actor controlling the targeted asset has significant power. The external investor is unlikely to give up on his financial commitment easily and the local recipient is likely to exercise relative power in the relationship. This also applies to financial injections, including loans and grants, which are often paid with an expectation of certain political favors or economic action from the recipient who is made responsible for the delivery of particular political or economic good.

Consequently, the more powerful the actors in the Horn of Africa are in their domestic context, the more leverage they appear to have in their external relations. However, internally weak states tend to have less bargaining power and face more constraints in their foreign policy options. They may fall under the influence of a particular external partner and become easier targets of more invasive external action. Although the leaders and the governing elites in such weak states often obtain benefits from foreign relations, they are often interested in using the resources for maintaining the domestic status quo and less focused on advancing any broader national interest. This is because they are preoccupied with domestic political and economic competition and contestation of power mainly by rival non-state actors which seek to use their particular external connections for strengthening themselves in the domestic competition. What therefore is evident in the Horn of Africa is that regimes' internal strength reduces their necessity to rely on external sources of survival and consolidation. Such governments have the privilege to pursue more assertive foreign policy, maneuver in a more ample strategic and policy space, and have more leverage in terms of bargaining power to negotiate better terms for cooperation with foreign powers.

Foreign Relations of the Horn Countries

Generally, the regimes in the Horn of Africa are led by individuals hailing from narrow political-economic elites and are considered authoritarian.[77] These elites tend to have various broader ethnic constituencies, but the concentration and dynamics of political and economic power often result in the leading individuals being the main beneficiaries of governing the state and associated resources. They seek to use various aspects of the state, such as its international legal status, as a vehicle for establishing beneficial foreign connections that provide resources for their and the government's domestic strength to fend off rivals and maintain the favorable political-economic status quo. While there is a degree of difference in this between states, sovereign political power, foreign policy decision-making, and the conduct of most crucial external relationships often concentrate on the head of the executive and at best on a few other individuals surrounding them.

Therefore, external relations of the regimes in the Horn of Africa are overwhelmingly the responsibility of their executives. This applies both to the presidential and parliamentary systems. Due to the narrow concentration of power in these regimes, the foreign policy strategy and decisions are largely made by the regimes' leading individuals with a close circle of advisors. This, however, should not blind one from recognizing that there are differences in the degree to which leaders are able to impose their personal preferences in the foreign policy strategies and approaches as they may be swayed by interests or dynamics of groups and coalitions in or close to the government[78] depending on the configuration and practice of power and influence in foreign policy making.[79] These considerations highlight and help understand the decision-making processes and their outcomes, and they may also contribute to unearthing the wider foreign policy approaches, strategies, and diplomatic techniques and practices.

As shown in Table 1, generally state actors in the Horn pursue pragmatic foreign relations motivated by the maintaining of political and associated economic power and the domestic status quo. They tend to resist change and transition to a robust democratic form of governance which could undermine their position. They maintain transactional relationships with foreign partners to obtain financial, material, and nonmaterial resources from abroad for strengthening against and establishing dominance over domestic challengers. They employ formal and covert diplomacy for making exchanges of domestic assets for foreign resources but also engage in private and unofficial dealings.

However, the executives in the Horn of Africa have limited power over their respective countries as a whole. Their formal institutions are weak, and the governing individuals and groups are often challenged by strong sub-state or societal actors, leading to state weakness and fragility. In the Horn of Africa, the sub-state actors are in many cases regional or provincial administrations which exercise wide autonomy due to their local power that enables them to also pursue their own foreign relations. Similarly to the state actors, they generally pursue a pragmatic approach and transactional exchanges in foreign relationships to gain resources aimed at buttressing their local political and economic position and consolidating themselves against domestic state and non-state rivals.

In the Horn, influential non-state actors, such as prominent individuals or leaders of kinship, clan, cultural, or religious groups, often exert significant local power and also engage in external connections and partnerships independently. While competing with state and other non-state players, these societal actors also build and use their foreign linkages to strengthen themselves. At times, they are powerful enough to control a variety of local assets and resources that they can

Table 1 Foreign Relations in the Horn of Africa

	Overall Approach—Pragmatic		
	Motivation/Interest	**Strategy**	**Techniques**
State Actors, Sub-State Actors, and Non-State Actors	- Domestic/local status quo - Political and economic power - Establish dominance over domestic rivals	- Transactional to exchange local assets for financial, material, and nonmaterial resources from abroad	- Formal and covert Diplomacy - Nonofficial/ private partnerships

transact for financial, material, or nonmaterial support. Although these exchanges may be formal business dealings, for example, they are mainly private and as such unofficial. But they can be highly effective in empowering societal actors in their domestic rivalries for political and economic power.

Yet, highlighting the agency of the Horn states and non-state actors in their relations with the Persian Gulf and Middle East countries requires comprehension of their external relations strategies, approaches, orientations, and objectives. This can improve our knowledge of the relative power dynamics involved in these relations. Concentrating on these bilateral relations and elucidating agency, leverage, and bargaining power in them enables filtering out other variables and influences in an attempt to locate the power of these actors in their interactions with their Persian Gulf and Middle East counterparts.

Moreover, the leadership of governments and non-state actors in the Horn dictating states' foreign policy should be considered rational actors. It is assumed that policymakers, for example, make decisions weighing on their perceptions of the nature and dynamics of international politics, their country's regional and international position in the international and regional system, possible partners and rivals, and how to best benefit from foreign connections. Rational decisions based on these considerations result in foreign policy strategies, approaches, and objectives. In this, individual and collective worldviews of those making foreign policy are significant. Consequently, the rational actor model, in which it is important to understand the appropriate decision-making units and their dynamics, can be seen as the most appropriate framework for observing the Horn state and non-state relations with their Persian Gulf and Middle East counterparts. For example, in each case, it is important to recognize the role of governing individuals, groups, and coalitions, in the making of a government's foreign policy, but more importantly in this study, it is essential to understand how such foreign policy contributes to the regime's agency in its bilateral foreign affairs with its foreign partners. This is done to answer the bigger question what indeed is power in such a relationship? And how is such power constituted and used? By aiming above all at gaining a better understanding of agency and power, the country case chapters engage in a nuanced, historically conscious, discussion on the strategies, approaches, and objectives that the regimes and non-state actors alike in the Horn of Africa pursue in their foreign relations.

In our analysis, it is important to remind us that most states in the Horn are commonly deemed weak or fragile.[80] A number of them struggle with legitimacy and authority, the use of coercive force, and economic and social issues. Therefore, among the main concerns of the regimes in power is their survival, and, due to the state's fragility, their biggest threats tend to be domestic.[81] Meanwhile, these governments only exceptionally experience foreign invasions or interventions that would remove them from power. These realities have several implications for their foreign policy strategy, approaches, and objectives. For example, such regimes, in light of their Cold War background, consider their foreign policy a critical strategic instrument for obtaining resources from abroad to ensure survival. During the post–Second World War period, governments in Africa and the Horn developed foreign policy strategies in which they tapped into the superpower competition by forming and exploiting strategic alliances. Arguably, this practice barely changed in the post–Cold War environment, and the active international presence of middle, or regional, powers has enabled these regimes again to choose among various influential strategic partners. Moreover, the emerging multi-polarity in the international system is likely to further widen the foreign policy space for these states.

As a result, the Horn governments' foreign relations are normally used to ensure the domestic status quo. Primarily concerned about maintaining power and consolidation as the state's leading force, the Horn leaders engage heavily in efforts to obtain resources from abroad. Such resources are often more financial than material, but they help to provide funding for the regimes in which patron–client networks feature heavily within and outside the official structures and institutions and boost economies which helps to maintain the status quo and appease popular discontent against the variably authoritarian regimes. Maintaining a good economic standing and high level of economic growth, therefore, helps regimes to justify their rule. Making sure that important sectors of the population benefit from it at least to a degree keeps these groups content and boosts the government's legitimacy. It helps prevent widespread protests and demands for the government to step down. Ensuring sufficient economic rewards for key groups of the population while maintaining a credible level of coercive force to secure the government's position elevates their opportunity cost for causing political disruption and increases the likelihood of regime survival in the longer term.

It is therefore important for our discussion to understand the domestic political context of each state to assess the strength of a particular regime, as well as its rivals, and its ability to manage domestic affairs. Internal political vulnerabilities arising for example from the apparent mismatch between the highly centralized, hierarchical, and narrowly based regimes and the high level of diversity among the population and heterogeneous territorial divisions may expose vulnerabilities that may lead to regimes losing to domestic rivals or falling under the influence of other states or external non-state actors. To prevent this, regimes in the Horn seek to consolidate themselves by utilizing externally obtained resources extensively for strengthening their authority. Consequently, it is important to draw on two intertwined dimensions of analysis, domestic and regional (international), to gain an improved understanding of the agency and power of the Horn states in their relations with the regionally important Persian Gulf and Middle East countries.

Economic Engagement as a Foreign Relations Framework

When considering the Horn regimes' foreign policy strategies and approaches toward other states it is important to highlight that three elements, in particular, have been relatively consistent over time. As indicated in the earlier discussion, the way foreign policy is planned, designed, and practiced has a clear continuity over time. The endemic weakness and fragility of the state, and the largely authoritarian, in some cases highly hierarchical, and relatively narrowly based political systems, shape foreign policy orientation toward ensuring the domestic survival of the regimes in power. The success of foreign policy strategy largely depends on its ability to generate sufficient material returns for maintaining the internal status quo by securing resources to feed the given regime's formal and informal structures and networks involving key institutions, offices, groups, and individuals. It is for this reason that foreign policy becomes highlighted as a strategic vehicle delivering resources for regime survival and strengthening.

In their foreign relations, the Horn states often target bilateral, and largely transactional, interactions with great and middle powers. This is mainly because they ensure necessary economic returns and diplomatic and political support for regime survival through alignments and partnerships with such states. This orientation owes in part to domestic vulnerability and endemic mistrust toward other states, arising from history and continued interference in their internal affairs.[82] This has been a salient feature of regional affairs in the Horn of Africa as regimes have sought to strengthen themselves by exerting power and influence across their borders. As a result, the Horn states fear destabilization by their neighbors and prefer bilateral relations with extra-regional states, or international or regional multilateral fora, as opposed to deeper relations with their neighbors or sub-regional organizations influenced by the most powerful states in their neighborhood.[83]

While the foreign policy in the Horn states arises from the domestic need of the governments to survive, it is affected by the regimes' strategic considerations and orientation in the regional and international political structures and dynamics. Therefore, any analysis of their foreign policy strategy and approaches toward other states should take into account domestic, regional, and international level politics. In this study, while focusing on the Horn countries' relations with the Persian Gulf and Middle East states, reference to other countries is made when relevant and necessary for understanding the realities of their foreign connections.

As discussed earlier, geostrategic considerations are important for understanding foreign policy. In these, geo-economic aspects have become increasingly salient and captured in the politics of economic statecraft. For the states in the Horn of Africa, remedying their endemic internal weakness is a priority that can be alleviated through a highly economic foreign policy approach aimed at obtaining material resources for regime survival and consolidation. This is why, despite their relatively inferior state-to-state level power relative to their main external partners, the foreign policy institutions of the Horn states engage heavily in economic statecraft and employ economic diplomacy to achieve domestic objectives. They use diplomatic techniques and instrumentalize specific strategic political and economic assets by exchanging them for financial and material resources. As part of their strategic approach, they often offer physical economic assets under their control, such as strategic locations or natural resources, or political goods and guarantees,[84] in exchange for financial and other material returns. For example, as in the case of Djibouti, Eritrea, or Somalia's coastal regions, a state could offer development, management, and operating rights of strategically significant locations, such as port or airport facilities, to a foreign power for a designated time in exchange for financing, investment, economic development, or other material compensation.[85] They can also offer nonmaterial political assets, such as influence on decision-making, with an expectation of financial or material returns.

On the other hand, for the leading Persian Gulf countries, there are important geostrategic (e.g., security and economic) considerations in their relations across the Red Sea. Here the strategy of economic statecraft is operationalized to extend economic influence and address security concerns. Many of the Persian Gulf economic ventures in the Horn are not meant to be particularly successful in terms of profit generation but play an important strategical role in establishing a presence, securing the Red Sea/Gulf of Aden space, and setting the stage for expanding political influence. While in recent years the leading Persian Gulf countries' approach has been largely oriented toward competition against regional rivals, it also has an important dimension in securing the regimes at home by supporting favorable governments and the political status quo in their neighborhood. Meanwhile, the Turkish approach has somewhat differed due to its more holistic engagement, especially in federal Somalia where Turkish state and nongovernmental actors combine economic, humanitarian, military, and social spheres for significant returns in terms of wealth and political influence. Although the approach among Middle East actors differs, for example, Saudi Arabia and the UAE favoring top-down and Qatar and Türkiye a bottom-up or mixed approach, the attempt is to advance preferable political systems in the Horn of Africa to maintain favorable strategic alignments and alliances in the Red Sea/Gulf of Aden neighborhood. Through the support of nearby authoritarian governments, the Persian Gulf powers aim at minimizing pressure for regime change at home and continue to impose the prevailing conditions in their domestic political systems. As a result, despite the seeming differences between the Horn and the Persian Gulf countries in terms of international power, there are mutual concerns about regime survival which are significant in their relationship.

In terms of power considerations, the web of Horn of Africa–Persian Gulf/Middle East connections is more complex than depicted in the International Relations literature. The realist analysis deems power as a relative concept between monolithic states, and uneven due to perceived differences in capabilities. But a more nuanced look at power beyond the simple interstate consideration reveals that the agency and leverage of the seemingly less capable Horn regimes and non-state actors in their relations with the Persian Gulf countries, for example, is considerable. This owes to their control of strategic local assets and resources. It is apparent in current partnerships that it is the Horn regimes, and societally powerful actors, which control most of the local material and nonmaterial assets that their Persian Gulf/Middle East counterparts desire in their attempt to advance their regional influence. This provides the Horn actors with local power and an advantageous bargaining position when interacting with foreign players.

However, perhaps even more importantly, it is ultimately the Horn governments or non-state actors who determine the assets that they allocate to the Persian Gulf/Middle East states in exchange for financial benefits. In addition, since all such transactions involve their territories and/or populations, the Horn regimes maintain an important level of control over the realities produced (or not) in exchange for financial or economic benefits. While they engage in these kinds of transactional relations from a variety of motivational perspectives, including due to individual, group, or coalition considerations in political leadership, they continue to maintain an important level of control in them. This results in an asymmetric power relationship and relative autonomy which the Horn actors can use to balance relations between various external actors in order to minimize constraints in their foreign engagements.

Reaching into the sovereign space of their Horn partners puts the Persian Gulf and Middle East actors in a vulnerable position due to the local political power of their hosts. While this shows the significant agency of the Horn state and non-state leadership in their relations with their Persian Gulf counterparts, it also exposes the limitations of power that internationally more powerful actors can project in the local setting. Although some strategic objectives may undoubtedly be reached this way, such involvement has many uncertainties and unintended consequences due to the agency of local actors. These include other aspects of the overall foreign policy approach to accompany the strategy of economic statecraft to ensure reaching the desired objectives set on the basis of established motivations and interests. Having a more comprehensive approach that includes the economic strategy as one aspect may improve the chances of success. While great and middle powers, especially the financially affluent countries of the Persian Gulf, often use economic statecraft as a significant component in their overall foreign policy approach, small and weak states often lack the means to engage in it. They tend to prefer techniques and strategic instruments that require fewer financial resources and often settle for achieving less ambitious objectives.

Salient aspects of the economic approaches which feature prominently in foreign policy in the Horn of Africa–Persian Gulf/Middle East relations are captured in Table 2. Here, economic imperatives connected to political power, security, and survival concerns play a crucial role for the states and non-state actors in the Horn as well as their Persian Gulf counterparts. From the perspective of the governing elites in the Horn, which often face contestation for power from strong societal actors, economic statecraft presents an attractive and much-used strategy option through which material and nonmaterial resources can be obtained for competition against domestic challengers. At the same time, their local or regional non-state or sub-state rivals engage in more informal external connections for gaining resources to consolidate themselves in the domestic competition for political and economic power.

In the day-to-day, these external relationships are operationalized through various techniques. In the Horn of Africa–Persian Gulf/Middle East relations, economic diplomacy is practiced as a major technique that involves the use of specific noncoercive or forceful instruments to advance one's interests. These instruments include noncoercive strategic material and nonmaterial assets and resources, capital injections, investment, aid, and trade, as well as coercive sanctions. At any given situation, and depending on the domestic political landscape and power structure and distribution, interests behind foreign relations are formed mainly according to individual, group, or coalition motivations of the given government or societal actor's foreign relations setting body, and, because of being oriented by self-preservation and strengthening, they take into account the broader state and societal interests to a variable degree. Essentially, economic diplomacy, as part of the wider strategy of economic statecraft, is a technique of survival and therefore has the main function of securing material (and nonmaterial) resources for the leadership of the given state or societal actor.

As described above, actors in the leading countries of the Persian Gulf approach relations with the Horn of Africa from a strategic standpoint of economic statecraft in which they seek to use their financial resources, capabilities, and economic instruments for gaining political and economic influence and benefits. Equipped with financial and economic power, they have a wider toolbox of instruments, and, consequently, a greater policy space, to maneuver in their foreign relations than their Horn counterparts. By employing their strengths, the Gulf state actors also seek to ensure the domestic political status quo, in part by increasing influence in their neighborhood. When pursuing regional power in the Horn, they exercise principally economic means through official diplomatic and informal channels by employing mainly noncoercive instruments. Although the Persian Gulf countries, as in the case of Saudi Arabia, the UAE, and Iran, also use coercive measures such as sanctions and military interventions as part of their foreign policy strategy,[86] this has not been the case in the Horn of Africa. Instead, the leading Persian Gulf states, including Saudi Arabia, UAE, Qatar, and Iran, have overwhelmingly used financial means, such as occasional injections of capital to politically relevant parties, as well as investment and aid, to seek strategic alignments and alliances in the Horn. Türkiye has employed similar instruments, although its engagement has included strong humanitarian and cultural components[87] along with economic imperatives. These efforts have been made to pursue strategic objectives, in most cases increasing political and economic influence and benefits.

Table 2 Economic Aspects of Foreign Relations Approach

	Approach		
Motivation/Interest	**Strategy**	**Operationalization/ Technique**	**Instruments**
Domestic Survival/ Strengthening (Power)	Economic Statecraft	Economic Diplomacy	Noncoercive - Strategic Material, and Nonmaterial Assets/ Resources - Investment - Capital Injections and Aid - Trade Coercive - Sanctions (Interventions)

Table 2 illustrates strategic and practical aspects of foreign relations in the Horn of Africa–Persian Gulf/Middle East relations. It is meant to explain how leaders of regimes and sub-state and societal actors on both sides of the spectrum, preoccupied with their domestic survival, engage in a strategy of economic statecraft that they practice through economic diplomacy and by employing a variety of practical, or policy, instruments. While the more powerful actors may have wide interests and ambitious strategic objectives and have a larger variety of instruments at their disposal, including coercive ones such as sanctions and outright interventions, their seemingly weaker counterparts with fewer options concentrate on economic diplomacy and use mainly noncoercive instruments such as exchange of strategic material and nonmaterial assets. Whereas the governments of what appear as more powerful Persian Gulf/Middle East states may employ their capabilities for attempts of exerting influence on their weaker counterparts, the leaders of the Horn states seek to use their countries' foreign relations mainly for domestic purposes.

The degree of concern about survival is related to a particular regime's domestic strength and consolidation. It varies greatly among the Persian Gulf and Middle East powers and the Horn of Africa states depending on the level of domestic threats and rivalries. While internationally more powerful regimes, such as the leading Persian Gulf countries and Türkiye, are able to seek regional power and influence through a strategy of economic statecraft, what are considered weaker states, such as Somalia, Ethiopia, and Eritrea, are more likely to concentrate on securing domestic power and stability through economic diplomacy. Whereas the Horn states engage significantly in economic diplomacy with their Middle East counterparts, by invariably using instruments such as offering political goods and guarantees or economic and strategic assets to satisfy their chronic need for financial and material returns, their Middle East partners primarily use their financial muscle to advance their interests in the Horn of Africa.[88] The various instruments available for states, or non-state actors, vary based on their capabilities and resources, as well as their international legal recognition which ensures access to external funding. Noncoercive instruments are available for those with significant financial or economic power, such as the Persian Gulf countries, or important local power and control of strategic assets as in the case of state and non-state actors in the Horn of Africa. Stronger states are also often able to use coercive instruments, such as military/humanitarian interventions and sanctions, to advance their interests. The internationally powerful actors often have a wider range of instruments at their disposal relative to those who are unable to project significant power beyond their borders.

Conclusion

The theoretical discussion in this chapter has sought to highlight the importance of looking beyond the realist lens when seeking to understand Horn of Africa–Persian Gulf/Middle East relations. The prevailing International Relations literature has mainly analyzed these relations from the perspective of what many authors deem more powerful Persian Gulf/Middle East countries through the understanding of states as unitary actors that monopolize a country's external relations. They conceptualize power as relational between monolithic state actors and deem it relative, based on the perceived capabilities of each state.

However, as the discussion here has underlined, such a theoretical framework cannot capture the complexity of Horn of Africa's relations with the Persian Gulf/Middle East. Above all, it fails to account for the agency of the Horn state and non-state actors by erroneously depicting the Horn as a passive and weak sub-region intervened on by stronger external actors who spread their influence and control. This results in inaccuracies in both the analysis and the findings.

Instead, a more nuanced account that recognizes state fragility, which includes domestic political, economic, and social realities, and governments' associated inability to monopolize significant foreign connections, is necessary for an in-depth understanding of these relations from the perspective of the Horn countries. Such a narrative helps to appreciate the complexities of political and economic power and the strengths of the state and non-state actors in the Horn as well as the vulnerabilities of their Persian Gulf/Middle East counterparts. An in-depth understanding of the importance of local power in the Horn of Africa also permits richer inquiry and more accurate observations regarding the intricacies of power than a realist international relations analysis can produce.

The theoretical discussion provided here seeks to provide a structure for a better understanding of power and its political and economic aspects, as well as the significance of state and societal actors' foreign connections in the countries' overall external relations. It enables the reader to discover the complexity of agency, involving both state and non-state actors, in the Horn of Africa–Persian Gulf/Middle East relations. The next chapter provides a brief overview of these relations.

Chapter 2

OVERVIEW OF THE HORN OF AFRICA–PERSIAN GULF/MIDDLE EAST RELATIONS

Uncovering the perspective of the key countries in the Horn of Africa in their affairs with the most influential Persian Gulf and Middle East states is a daunting task. Indeed, the main narratives of the Horn-Persian Gulf/Middle East relations mostly observe them from the view of the latter. This is a common posture in the realist International Relations literature which tends to observe international affairs from the perspective of what are deemed as great or middle powers.

The emphasis of this chapter is on providing a general overview of Horn of Africa–Persian Gulf/Middle East relations. The chapter provides a brief background leading up to the current dynamics and because it attempts to shed light on the perspective of the Horn countries some time is spent on providing an understanding of their foreign relations strategies and interests in general.

A salient underlying determinant and a common denominator of the Horn countries' approach to the Persian Gulf/Middle East states is the concern for regime survival. This has been a driving factor behind the Horn states' effort to benefit from the external interest in general, and the Persian Gulf countries' engagements in particular. From the perspective of the Persian Gulf countries, proactive foreign policy is seen as a necessity for increasing international presence and securing the surrounding environment.[1]

Along with these considerations, and as part of its regional power competition with Iran, Saudi Arabia assumed the leading role as the most influential state in the Red Sea/Gulf of Aden region and the Horn of Africa. Since the 2010s its position as the leading Middle East power in the sub-region has become increasingly challenged by Türkiye,[2] which, as an important actor with less immediate security concerns, has offered a serious alternative for the Horn countries in terms of humanitarian, economic, and political partnership. This, along with the active role of Qatar and the United Arab Emirates (UAE), has propelled intense competition among regionally influential states.

In addition, the leaders of all main Persian Gulf actors and Türkiye realize the salience of great power dynamics as the main driving factor of international affairs in the Horn of Africa. The primarily economic but increasingly permanent physical presence of China especially since the 2000s has resulted in a dynamic in which it is surpassing the previously dominant Western actors. The Horn governments, and leading Persian Gulf countries, have embraced strategic and increasingly durable alignments with China. In the Horn, this has meant that other foreign actors have faced an increasing necessity to not only accept Beijing's presence but to engage China and take advantage of its leverage to promote their own political and economic interests. Recently, the leading Persian Gulf countries and Türkiye have collaborated with China in their affairs in the Horn of Africa to a variable degree.

After making its initial entrance into Sudan in the early 1990s, China has significantly expanded its economic presence in Africa and the Horn. Djibouti has become one of the key logistics entry points to Africa in Beijing's strategic master plan, the Belt and Road Initiative. Djibouti's importance owes to its geographic location at the mouth of the Red Sea and providing an access to the interior Horn of Africa as Ethiopia's primary import-export route. The Chinese-built Standard Gauge Railway and highway, which have replaced the obsolete colonial railway, and the port and container terminal at Doraleh that are secured by a Chinese naval support base since 2016, ensure logistics access to the landlocked Ethiopian markets where Chinese companies and financiers have invested significantly for production facilities in various industries. The logistics link to Djibouti, therefore, is an important manifestation of Beijing's strategy and economic connections that result in Chinese influence in both countries. Persian Gulf powers, particularly the UAE, and Türkiye have sought to utilize Chinese linkages in their regional aspirations.

Meanwhile, the chronic weakness of the Horn governments has made regime survival mainly against domestic challengers an existential issue. While the narrowly governed regimes of the leading Persian Gulf countries experience similar domestic vulnerabilities, theirs are a much less severe threat to the incumbent governments. The leading Gulf governments consider the Horn of Africa a concern for their security mainly due to the situation in Yemen, but, along with other Middle East powers, they are also interested in securing the Red Sea and the Gulf of Aden. As a result, from the Cold War onward, the leading Persian Gulf countries have perceived the Horn sub-region as an opportunity to extend their influence in and across the Red Sea. Due to the Horn of Africa's many conflicts, investing in land, food production, logistics, and lately hospitality and other sectors, has been considered risky but potentially productive. On the one hand, in part due to high risks and volatile relationships with various stakeholders in the Horn, the Persian Gulf actors are content with the local stakeholders' insistence on pragmatic and transactional relations. On the other hand, the governments in the Horn seek multiple simultaneous partnerships, which enables them to carefully balance to maximize benefits and minimize constraints in their foreign policy space. Aligning with various foreign partners, including states that rival each other, also enables the Horn governments to maximize payoffs from their external relations. While much of this effort is self-serving for the regimes' leading individuals, groups, and coalitions, it provides resources to strengthen and consolidate the governing forces and formal and informal governing institutions and practices.

Exercising power amid state weakness, the leaders and governments of the Horn countries seek to tap into external interest in their states and various types of assets and resources. Over time, the flurry of foreign actors interested in the Horn of Africa, as in the case of the current "scramble," has allowed pragmatic reorienting and recalibration of the transactional foreign policy of the states in the sub-region. The leaders in the Horn frequently offer interested external actors access to strategic assets such as logistics hubs, land, natural resources, or political influence, in exchange for financial or material rewards they can use against their rivals in the domestic political and economic competition. They exercise considerable local power over assets and resources under their control, and due to this control are able to exercise bargaining power in their relationships with external actors. However, due to the endemic state weakness, leaders in the Horn are limited in their ability to monopolize foreign relations and their domestic competitors often engage in parallel external connections beside the state. These non-state, and at times sub-state, actors pose the main threat to the power of incumbent leaders and therefore the Horn countries' foreign relations largely emerge from the domestic political and economic dynamics and competition.

This shows that when seeking to understand foreign relations in "fragile" states, as in the case of the Horn of Africa, monolithic views, such as the classical realist interpretation of international relations, are not particularly helpful. In the conditions of the lack of central government authority and control, sub-state and non-state actors may have sufficient legitimacy and power to challenge them. In these circumstances national and local level political rivalries may manifest in the country's overall foreign relations. While the governing elite uses the state's foreign policy as an instrument to extract resources from abroad to strengthen its hold on the state and strengthen the regime, its local rivals, such as opposition individuals and groups, may seek to advance their power by pursuing foreign relations. In this situation, the local political and economic rivalries are likely to extend to foreign relations and affect partnerships, alignments, and alliances with foreign powers and non-state actors.

Background to Contemporary Horn of Africa–Middle East Relations

The Horn of Africa and the Arabian Peninsula have been connected by long and deeply entrenched cultural, economic, and political ties.[3] The historical record of ancient times indicates that rather than a barrier, the Red Sea served as a transportation route facilitating commerce, migration, and travel, as well as the spread of cultural and political influences. Indeed, various factors, such as the genetic evidence indicating the pattern of domestication of the dromedary,[4] demonstrate the close interconnectedness between the Horn of Africa and the Arabian Peninsula.

The relations between political entities in the Horn of Africa and the Middle East have been equally multidimensional. For many centuries, the connections across the Red Sea and the Gulf of Aden have formed an important consideration in the strategies of the rulers and elites of political entities in the Horn of Africa. Some of the polities in the Horn of Africa, largely focusing on trade, extended their spheres of influence to the southern Arabian Peninsula and facilitated the exchange of goods and ideas. For example, the Aksumite Empire (*c* 80 CE–960 CE), based at the highlands of today's northern Ethiopia, extended its influence to the Arabian Peninsula and engaged in brief territorial control of its southernmost part, while its merchants maintained commercial relations with faraway empires and regions.[5] The traders of Somali city-states and sultanates also practiced commerce as a significant form of livelihood and encouraged migration over the Red Sea, the Gulf of Aden, and further afield.

Islam, which emerged in the seventh century, quickly reached the Horn of Africa. Arab-Muslim migrants crossed the Red Sea and settled in the sub-region. Their presence and intermarriage with locals led to a gradual adoption of Arab cultural traits and Islam in the local cultures.[6] Islam gradually became the majority religion in the coastal areas, lowlands, and plains in northeastern Africa but Ethiopian highlands, with consolidated biblical tradition, remained largely Christian.

With the spread of Islamization and Arab culture came not only cultural hybridity but also the Muslim-led slave trade of the perceived non-believers in which many local entrepreneurs participated. From the seventh century onward Arab and Arabized Muslim merchants' leadership in the business of slaves led to the intensification of the Trans-Saharan, Red Sea, and Indian Ocean trade involving violent capture and forced removal of millions of non-Muslim Africans from their homes in southern margins of the eastern Sahel region and their subsequent shipping to slave markets in Egypt, the Arabian Peninsula, and the wider Middle East.[7] This background, with the formal abolition of slavery in much of the Arabian Peninsula as late as the second half of the twentieth century and the enduring practices of forced and low-cost labor, has resulted in a still-persisting attitude of superiority over "the African." A manifestation of this is an Arab-Muslim-dominated social hierarchy in which Black Africans have been considered the lowest source of labor.[8]

Over the centuries the depth and intensity of interactions crossing the Red Sea and the Gulf of Aden space have been such that they defy the geographical classification of the Horn of Africa and southern Arabia as two distinct regions. People interacted, migrated, and settled on both sides of the maritime routes. With the arrival of Islam, Arab migrations, and the extension of the Ottoman Empire in Sudan and the Red Sea coastal areas, Arabic and Middle Eastern cultural influences in the Horn of Africa became increasingly manifested. Thousands of years of interaction and mixing, including through voluntary and forced migration, have resulted in important ethnic, linguistic, and cultural similarities that provide an underlying social and cultural fabric merging the peoples on both sides of the Red Sea and the Gulf of Aden.

As part of their interactions with the Arabian Peninsula and the wider Middle East, the kingdoms and sultanates of the Horn of Africa engaged in commercial activities that contributed to wealth accumulation enabling the concentration of power and building internal political order of the local polities. For example between the fourteenth and sixteenth centuries, Mogadishu city-state maintained trade networks extending to Asia, and Berbera and Bulhar[9] became key trading ports connecting the Horn of Africa with the Arabian Peninsula in the eighteenth to nineteenth centuries.[10] These coastal cities used trade to accumulate wealth and establish themselves as important logistical centers for the polities of the interior Horn of Africa.

In the sixteenth century, the rivalry between the Portuguese and Ottomans over control of the Red Sea and the western Indian Ocean culminated. It engulfed the interior Horn of Africa in a competition over influence along religious lines in which the Portuguese came in support of the Abyssinian Christian highlanders and Ottomans assisted the Muslim Adalites. Both Abyssinian and Adalite rulers engaged the external powers for gaining an advantage in the Abyssinian-Adal War (1529–43), which shows how the Horn leaders have used the strategy of engaging in foreign partnerships to strengthen themselves against local rivals for centuries.

In the nineteenth century, the Horn of Africa faced the expansion of the Turco-Egyptian Ottoman khedivate of Egypt under Muhammed Ali. This resulted in the Egyptian conquest of Sudan until the rise of the Mahdists in the 1880s as well as in brief and intermittent occupation of ports in the coastal extensions of today's Eritrea and Djibouti and the subjection of the Sultanate of Aussa. During the nineteenth century, Britain and France became increasingly fixated on Egypt, loosely part of the Ottoman Empire, and sought to secure the strategic Suez Canal (1869) which had opened a new maritime route to Asia. In 1882, Britain occupied Egypt and brought the canal under its effective control.

In the Horn of Africa, France became the first European imperial power to make territorial claims. In 1862 the local Afar Sultan Raieta Dini Ahmet sold land to the French who meant to establish a coaling station in Obock to service the ships passing through the Suez Canal. This served as a springboard for the French colonization of the Gulf of Tadjoura that was complemented by an 1885 treaty in which the Somali Issa agreed to French protection in a plan to expel competing Somali clans from the territory. These territorial claims led to the establishment of French Somaliland in 1896.

Italians followed suit. They acquired land around Assab from the Sultan of Raheita and operated a coaling station that serviced vessels traveling through the Suez Canal. Italians then expanded their territory to the highlands and officially declared the colony of Eritrea in 1890 after the Treaty of Wuchale with Abyssinia represented by King Menelik of Shewa.

Meanwhile, in the mid-1880s, following a series of agreements with local clans, the British established a protectorate of Somaliland with the main purpose of checking other colonial powers and supplying meat to their stronghold in Aden. Italy, which eyed the fertile Abyssinian highlands as the grand prize, was also eager to control ports on the Indian Ocean side of the Horn and made a deal with Sultan Yusuf Ali Kenadid of Hoboyo and Sultan Boqor Osman Mahamuud of the Majerteen which converted both sultanates into Italian protectorates. Both leaders had sought an alliance with Italians to strengthen their own rule, gain territories from their local rivals, and exploit the European competition to maintain independence,[11] but they were eventually forced to succumb to Italian overrule. Meanwhile, Abyssinia acquired the Somali territories of Haud and Ogaden with British consent but was stopped short of gaining sea access despite Menelik II's triumph against the Italians in the Battle of Adwa in 1896.

The First World War had little impact on the Horn of Africa in part because the three colonial powers were on the same side. However, it was again the ambitions of European powers which interrupted the more peaceful period. The rise of fascism in Italy fed its expansionist ambitions in the Horn of Africa, and it invaded Ethiopia; this time conquering it and declaring the Italian East Africa consisting of Eritrea, Ethiopia, and Italian Somaliland in 1936.

The European scramble for Africa resulted in the formation of new colonial political entities in the Horn of Africa. These were largely authoritarian states in most cases led by a small group of Europeans subjecting the local population to their rule. In a number of these dominions, some local subjects willing to collaborate were at times appointed to administrative positions and some eventually ascended to positions of power during the process of decolonization. In the process, and as part of the colonial administration, the local collaborators learned ruling strategies and methods associated with maintaining the colonial state and were inclined to use similar methods after they came to power. Following independence, after brief democratic attempts, mostly authoritarian regimes emerged in the Horn of Africa. While the monarchic, dictatorial, and highly centralized Ethiopia annexed the democratically governed Eritrea in 1952, Somalia and Djibouti succumbed to authoritarian rule respectively in 1969 and 1977.

Cold War Politics

While several Middle Eastern and Arabian countries gained independence in the course of the 1920s to 1940s, states in the Horn of Africa, with Ethiopia as a notable exception, became independent from the 1950s onward.[12] After the Second World War, in the context of confrontation with Israel, the most powerful Arab countries sought to extend their influence in the Red Sea region. Especially from the Suez Crisis onward, the Persian Gulf and Middle East powers in the relative proximity of the Horn of Africa became interested in influencing it. In the context of the simultaneous departure of the colonial powers, they sought to extend influence in the neighboring areas southward and across the Red Sea because autonomous political and economic developments in these areas were seen to resonate with their own or immediate surrounding territories. From the 1950s onward, this led the states in the Arabian Peninsula and Egypt to pursue pragmatic foreign policy in the Horn of Africa aimed at addressing security and political concerns and supporting the stability of their regimes. For example in Riyadh, Saud bin Abdulaziz preferred to maintain good relations with monarchical Ethiopia, which had regained sovereignty from the British, due to the US pressure, although also sympathizing with the Muslim Eritrean cause for liberation and

Somali nationalism and expansionism in the surrounding lowlands largely due to religious and cultural affinities.

Meanwhile, Gamal Nasser's Egypt played an important role in the politics of the Horn. Seeking to extend its control over the strategically crucial Nile River and influence in the territories south of it, the Egyptian regime struck a partnership with the Sudanese leadership and a favorable treaty on the Nile waters in 1959. In return, the Sudanese military regime of Ibrahim Abboud gained improved relations with Egypt and support against its southern Anyanya rebels which was countered by Israel.[13] Simultaneously Nasser's government sought to weaken US-aligned Ethiopia by providing early support for the Eritrean rebels and Somali expansionism and irredentism in eastern Ethiopia.

At the same time, Haile Selassie's Ethiopia instrumentalized the historical differences and confrontation between the Christian highlands and the surrounding Muslim lowlands by pushing Amharic cultural traits as the core of "Ethiopianness." This alienated those more culturally connected to the Arab world. Ethiopia's foreign policy discourse drew from the Amharic definition of the nation and sought to draw the necessary external resources to face both Egypt and Somalia by deepening Addis Ababa's partnership with the West and especially the US.[14] Selassie also used his reputation and international influence gained through active diplomacy and participation in the League of Nations and the United Nations to help establish the Organization of African Unity (OAU) in 1963 which came to vigorously endorse the existing state borders drawn by imperial and colonial powers, including Ethiopia. While fears of secessionism and irredentism were common to the nascent independent states in Africa, a strong commitment to the existing borders among African states certainly favored the Ethiopian regime. This deterred Egyptian support for anti-state forces and led to improved relations with Ethiopia, while several Arab states continued giving nominal support to Eritrean rebels.[15]

The Cold War politics in the Horn of Africa and the western Arabian Peninsula revolved largely around the strategic importance of the Red Sea. The superpower competition over influence in the Horn states overshadowed the regional power rivalries between the Arab states and Israel and the feuds and proxy wars among the Horn of African countries themselves. The significance of Bab al-Mandab as a chokepoint for maritime oil shipments and trade through the Suez Canal became emphasized in the US-led Western policy in which Israel's security also played an important role. The attempt was to stabilize and minimize Soviet interference on both sides of the Red Sea and the Gulf of Aden.

Until the mid-1970s, Ethiopia formed the center of the US alliances in the Horn of Africa, and Washington endorsed Haile Selassie's annexation of Eritrea which helped to safeguard its strategic Red Sea coastline. Ten years earlier, Moscow had adopted a new policy to step up its naval presence in the Red Sea and Indian Ocean. Soviet-aligned Arab states, such as Egypt, took advantage of Moscow's interest in the region and strengthened their regional standing. Similarly, Somalia and Sudan subscribed to Soviet support along with their alliances with pro-Soviet Arab states. Somali nationalism, boosted by Arab support, advocated bringing in

Somali-inhabited territories as part of the Somali state. Socialist military officer coups both in Somalia and in Sudan in 1969 were seen to bring the countries closer to the Soviet Union and enabled both to build their militaries.

In the course of the 1960s, the Arab states became divided in their ideological and pragmatic approach toward Addis Ababa. Already at this time, it was recognized that containing Ethiopia, seen as the most powerful state in the Horn, was central for any attempt to diminish Israel's influence[16] and extend pan-Arabist and pan-Islamic ideologies in the sub-region. Especially, ideologically oriented regimes such as Iraq, the People's Democratic Republic of Yemen (PDRY, or South Yemen), and Syria equated Ethiopia's warm relations with Israel, in part triggered by Emperor Haile Selassie's disappointment of the lack of Arab approval for his plans to federate Eritrea, with Zionism. However, more proximate states, mainly Egypt, Saudi Arabia, and Sudan, with direct security concerns arising from Ethiopia's geographical and strategic centrality in the Horn, pursued a more pragmatic and cooperative approach toward Addis Ababa.[17]

While the other Horn of African states kept their distance from Israel and rather positioned themselves on the Arab side, Haile Selassie considered intimate relations with Tel Aviv essential for the Ethiopian regime. Already in the late 1950s, Addis Ababa had established diplomatic relations and an alliance with Tel Aviv which helped Selassie to survive coup attempts and resulted in generous military assistance in support of Ethiopia's counterinsurgency campaign in Eritrea. In exchange, Israel gained sea access and political leverage in the Horn of Africa and support in its attempts to destabilize Sudan and its ally Egypt through the support of southern Sudanese rebels.[18] These types of transactional relations were essential for the survival of the imperial regime in Ethiopia until its downfall in 1974 but also continued informally throughout the remaining 1970s and 1980s despite the changing ideological orientation and superpower alliances in Ethiopia. The communist Mengistu regime also counted on these transactional and largely pragmatic relations which allowed obtaining Israeli intelligence, training, and military support until its collapse in 1991.[19]

Political turbulence and the involvement of regionally powerful states in the Horn of Africa and the Red Sea politics internationalized the sub-regional issues and put pressure on superpowers to compete for influence in the strategic region. The US and Soviet Union each considered that they could not afford the other to maintain overwhelming alliances and influence in the Horn of Africa and the Red Sea.[20] The emergence of the Suez Crisis and the ensuing Arab–Israeli conflict led to the intensification of the Cold War in the Red Sea region in the 1960s, and the war in Yemen in which Egypt and Saudi Arabia took opposite sides strengthened superpower involvement. Egypt's initial target in the Red Sea was Israel which it tried to deprive of oil shipments, but after Egypt's defeat in the 1967 Arab–Israeli War and Saudi Arabia's relative strengthening Riyadh assumed this role.[21] Saudi Arabia seeking US assistance to deter socialist Yemeni forces and Egypt eventually led to Washington's support that helped Riyadh's consolidation as a regional powerhouse, allowing it to influence superpower politics in the Horn of Africa and the Middle East. Meanwhile, with Egypt's defeat to Israel, Cairo's prominent position in the region deteriorated as it withdrew from Yemen. This led to Riyadh taking the leading role in Red Sea politics and marked the end of President Gamal Nasser's pan-Arabist project.

During the 1960s, the surge of socialist, Moscow-aligned states and rebel movements in the Red Sea region forced those states allied with Washington on the back foot. The 1967 Arab–Israeli War led to Egypt closing the Suez Canal. Later the same year, the Federation of South Arabia and the Protectorate of South Arabia came together and formally established a communist state of South Yemen in 1969, which then drifted to the Soviet Bloc. Partly as a response to pressure from Iraq, Libya, and Syria in favor of the Eritrean movement, South Yemen sought to establish a blockade against Israeli ships at Perim Island in Bab al-Mandab but failed.[22]

The same year military coups in Somalia and Sudan brought initially socialist regimes into power. In the Horn of Africa, Ethiopia and Somalia sought weapons and aid from their allies, and Somalia counted on Soviet assistance to build its military for confrontations to build Greater Somalia.

From the late 1960s onward, the Eritrean war of liberation became central to the Arab and Israeli pursuits in the Horn of Africa. Due to its strategic location on the Red Sea coast across Saudi Arabia and Yemen, and commanding the whole stretch of Ethiopia's sea access, Eritrea came to be seen as a significant security concern. Arab states supported Eritrean struggle for various reasons, including because of perceiving it as a Muslim cause to contain Christian Ethiopia's efforts for increasing power and dominance in the Horn and an opportunity to extend influence on the African side of the Red Sea coast near the strategically important Bab al-Mandab. Israel, on the other hand, was particularly concerned about the Eritrean rebels' Arab alignment as part of the spread of Arab influence on the African side of the Red Sea coast. It especially worked against Saudi Arabia's aspiration to turn the Red Sea neighborhood into an Arab-dominated region.

In the 1970s positions of several African and regionally powerful Arab states toward superpowers shifted. There was a preoccupation that Arab involvement could destabilize the Horn of Africa by undermining the OAU principles of state sovereignty and territorial integrity of the Horn of Africa. Sudan's 1969 military coup in which the traditional sectarian parties had been expelled and found safe havens in the Gulf and Egypt, and the following 1971 aborted coup attempt that led to national reconciliation and alignment with the US, paved the way for changing superpower alignments. Egypt ending its partnership with the Soviet Union and embracing relations with the US served as an example to other Arab states in the Red Sea region which aligned with the US as the decade progressed. The 1973 Arab–Israeli War and the associated oil embargo produced high revenue for the petroleum-producing states and allowed them to increasingly exercise economic and associated political power in their neighborhood. Driven by their financial wealth, Persian Gulf countries sought to isolate Israel, boost authoritarian regimes, strengthen Islam, and endorse local "Muslim" and "Arab" movements through their bilateral relations with Horn countries. Most African states, seeking to benefit from alignment with Arab states, turned their backs on Israel and began supporting the Arab cause.[23]

Using its petroleum receipts, Saudi Arabia emerged as a powerful regional actor projecting its influence across the Red Sea and the Gulf of Aden. It led the way in agreeing to exclusively trade oil in USD in response to Washington's petition due to economic stagnation and rising inflation in the US. This left the other Organization of the Petroleum Exporting Countries with no other feasible option than to follow suit and bind their economies increasingly to the dollarized system which helped boost the US economy and expand the US dollar massively as the world's desired exchange currency. Merging interests between Riyadh and Washington included battling Soviet influence in the Red Sea/Horn of Africa Region as well as the wider Middle East. Egypt, which had lost the leading position in the Red Sea, aligned with Saudi Arabia, although, at the same time, it reconciled with Israel. Sudan, North Yemen, and Somalia forming part of the pro-Western camp served as a counterweight to Soviet-aligned Ethiopia, South Yemen, and Libya[24] after the Somali invasion of eastern Ethiopia also known as the Ogaden War (1977–8).

The reopening of the Suez Canal in 1975 re-emphasized the strategic importance of Bab al-Mandab and propelled Arab interest in the Horn of Africa. Enriched by the 1973 Arab oil embargo, focused against those states supporting Israel in the 1973 Arab–Israeli War, Saudi Arabia recycled petrodollars and assumed the leading role in combating communism[25] and undermining Israeli interests in the Red Sea/Horn of Africa region. It supported the regimes in Somalia and Sudan by first financing arms purchases and then providing generous aid, but at the same time, it began an ambitious effort to expand its influence using religious channels. It promoted the conservative Saudi (Wahhabi) orientation within the broader Salafist movement by training religious teachers and funding schools and mosques in the Horn countries. This effort intensified after Iran began its own projects promoting the Shia doctrine and formed part of their rivalry for influence in the Red Sea region.

Strong financial connections developed between the Persian Gulf countries and their Horn of African partners in which the former sought to use their financial power as a geo-economic strategy to persuade the latter from joining the Soviet and Israeli camp. They recycled petrodollars through various foreign policy instruments such as aid, investment, and cash injections and provided political and military support. Riyadh led the way in what can be deemed as a pseudo-pan-Arabist and pan-Muslim agenda to assist Eritrean Muslim factions and Islamist political opposition in Sudan. This was largely aimed at thwarting communist expansion as in Somalia, where its assistance strengthened Mogadishu's nationalist and irredentist claims especially toward Ethiopia (but also Djibouti and Kenya) that after the 1974 Marxist officers' coup aligned with the Soviet Union. Gulf States, especially Kuwait but also others such as the UAE, ventured with Saudis to countries such as Sudan and South Yemen and used their financial muscle to persuade them of the importance of forming part of the pro-Western camp. Kuwait along with the US also used financial measures to prevent North Yemen from choosing the Soviet side. In the course of the decade, Ethiopia converted into a Marxist-Leninist bastion surrounded by American-/Arab-aligned states. Saudi Arabia promoted political Islam in the Horn to extend its influence and as a counterweight to communism emanating from Ethiopia with a silent blessing from the US.

With Kuwait as a junior partner, Saudis extended generous economic aid and investment in Sudan. They saw Sudan, with its abundance of fertile land and the Nile as a source of irrigation, as the potential "breadbasket" for the Persian Gulf, where large-scale farming was not possible due to the lack of adequate land and water resources. The Sudanese government, chronically short on foreign exchange, welcomed Arab investment but turning Sudan into a "breadbasket" for the Arabian Peninsula largely failed. Saudi Arabia also led the way in supporting President Jaafar al-Nimeiri's national reconciliation and assisted Sudanese Islamic opposition groups in the diaspora which through their networks gained influence in the country. Particularly the National Islamic Front (NIF), headed by Hassan al-Turabi, took advantage of the Saudi funding and remittances of the sizable Sudanese diaspora in the Persian Gulf countries, commanding financial flows largely through the Islamic banking system, namely, from Faisal Islamic and al Baraka banks.[26] This enabled NIF to infiltrate and gain influence in the state apparatus and expand from its elitist, intellectual, and urban groundings through charity activity. Facing the inevitable, previously publicly secular President Nimeiri took a religious turn and defined the regime and the state increasingly as Islamic. This became one of the reasons for the intensification of a nascent second rebellion in Southern Sudan in the early 1980s supported by leftist Ethiopia and Libya.

In the context of heating superpower rivalry in the sub-region, the Horn regimes aligned with Arab states on either side of the Cold War superpower divide. While Egypt and Sudan turned toward the US and its long-term ally Saudi Arabia, and Egypt also improved its relations with Sudan, the Derg regime in Ethiopia established a Marxist-Leninist state and became the centerpiece of Soviet influence in the Horn. However, at the same time, perhaps somewhat paradoxically, the communist Ethiopian junta fought rebels in Eritrea and Tigray which upheld Marxist ideology. Toward the end of the decade, particularly after the war in Ogaden (1977–8), Ethiopia converted into an island of communism surrounded by pro-Western states and got entangled in proxy wars with its most potent neighbors, especially Somalia and Sudan, which provided and channeled support for armed opposition factions in Ethiopia.

The Eritrean liberation war continued to split the regional external actors. While Libya and the PDRY initially gave covert support to the Eritrean liberation movements, as a consequence of the 1974 revolution in Ethiopia they phased out aid to the Eritrean People's Liberation Front (EPLF) and subsequently supported Ethiopia. Meanwhile, the US allies Saudi Arabia and Egypt, having their own pan-Arabic and pan-Muslim interests, worked against the Soviet influence, Cairo leaving the earlier confrontation with Israel aside. Empowered by oil receipts, Saudi Arabia became the most powerful regional actor employing economic statecraft and adopted Nasser's earlier attempt to convert the Red Sea into an "Arab lake." As an important regional partner to the US, it continued to support Eritrean Muslim elements despite the Christian highlanders having gained command of the Eritrean liberation movement and provided assistance to the Somali regime to undermine communist Ethiopia.

While in the early 1970s Egypt had emerged as a somewhat less influential US partner, its role in the Middle East elevated as a consequence of the 1978 peace treaty with Israel which left Riyadh as the main Red Sea power opposing Tel Aviv. In the Horn, Egypt continued to draw on its historical relationship with Sudan to prevent Khartoum from drifting into an alliance with the Soviet Union since this would have left it isolated. Through Sudan, Cairo was keen to safeguard its interests on the Nile. With the downfall of imperial rule in Ethiopia, it was able to maintain an influential stand toward the Horn and work against Addis Ababa interrupting the flow of the Blue Nile.[27] While Sudan became central to the US strategy in the Horn, Washington sought to sandwich Ethiopia by encouraging its allies, especially Saudi Arabia and Egypt, to provide support for Somalia and Eritrean opposition. Despite facing several coup attempts in the late 1970s and rebellion by the Sudan People's Liberation Movement/Army (SPLM/A) in the south in the early 1980s, the Sudanese regime was able to draw sufficient resources from alignment with the US and its Arab partners to fend off opposition rivals.

In 1977 the continuous confrontation between Mogadishu and Addis Ababa led to Somalia's invasion of eastern Ethiopia. On July 13, less than three weeks after the independence of Djibouti which both Ethiopia and Somalia recognized, the Somali army entered eastern Ethiopia intending to liberate the local people and edge closer to the ideal of "Greater Somalia."[28] Forced to make a choice, and sensing its geopolitical presence in the Horn being threatened, the Soviet Union and its allies threw their force behind Ethiopia, the dominant state in the sub-region. Despite Western-aligned Egypt, Saudi Arabia, and Sudan assisting Mogadishu, and seeking US support for Somalia, an overwhelming Soviet, Cuban, and South Yemeni assistance aided Ethiopia to deliver a devastating blow to Mogadishu that effectively ended its aspiration to establish "Greater Somalia."

This led the Somali regime to revert from its expansionist outlook and concentrate on survival against domestic opponents. The government sought to deal with the increasing domestic, albeit often externally backed, challenges to its rule.[29] Somali opposition organizations sprang up and sought support from other states. For example, the Somali National Movement (SNM), which became the main liberation movement among the Isaaq in Somaliland, was founded and initially funded by members of the Isaaq diaspora in Saudi Arabia but became backed by Ethiopia. Other important rebel groups, United Somali Congress (USC) and Somali Salvation Democratic Front (SSDF), based on Darod clan affiliation, were founded in Ethiopia which was their biggest supporter until the late 1980s. Arab countries which still embraced relations with the Soviet Union and improved ties with Ethiopia, such as Libya and PDRY, also played a role in supporting the Somali rebels.

Saudi Arabia's support of Somali nationalism and irredentism as part of its pan-Arabist and Pa-Muslim aspirations contributed to the radicalization that had led to the war in Ogaden. The war resulted in a reversal of superpower alignments as the Soviet Union, in a massive effort with other, particularly Cuban and South Yemeni,[30] allies, rescued Ethiopia and allowed it to beat back the Somali army. After losing Somalia, Moscow remarkably gained Ethiopia. External support not only allowed Ethiopia to defeat Somalia but also gave it momentum against the Eritrean armed opposition. Meanwhile, Arab states, namely, Saudi Arabia, Egypt, and Sudan, came to Somalia's aid, with Riyadh supporting Mogadishu's war effort with a generous financial contribution.[31] Its Arab allies assisting Somalia forced the US to switch its support to Mogadishu soon after the war. Having reluctantly lost Ethiopia, the US started backing Somalia in the late 1970s, and the Somali leadership took the opportunity to become Washington's strategic ally in the Gulf of Aden.

Following the 1979 revolution, Iran's involvement in the Horn of Africa intensified shortly. It began supporting the Eritrean cause, justifying its position by portraying it as a Muslim struggle against the reality on the ground,[32] but with the outbreak of the Iran–Iraq war in 1980 Horn governments chose to align or maintain their alliances with the US and marginalized Iran in their foreign relations.[33] Iran's relations with the Soviet Union also remained cold largely due to ideological reasons until the 1983 US arms embargo pushed Tehran closer to Moscow and to establish sporadic contacts with Ethiopia.

With the Ethiopian victory Saudi Arabia's ambitious plan for turning the Red Sea into an "Arab lake" and deter external influence failed. Addis Ababa was able to use the momentum to gain further Soviet support to pursue its campaign against the Eritrean liberation movement and a socialist form of economic development. While the Eritrean liberation war intensified and the confrontation with Somalia continued, the Ethiopian government was facing an increasing number of ingrown armed opposition groups, including the Tigray People's Liberation Front (TPLF) and much weaker Oromo Liberation Front (OLF) and Ogaden National Liberation Front (ONLF). However, with the support of the Eastern Bloc, the Derg government had enough resources to fend off these threats and also support insurgents in neighboring Somalia and Sudan. On August 20, 1981, Ethiopia signed a defense cooperation agreement with other Soviet allies South Yemen and Libya in Aden to strengthen its position in the strategically central areas of the Red Sea/Gulf of Aden.[34] In an unofficial capacity, Israel also played a role in supporting Ethiopia and its regional allies because Tel Aviv's main concern was to deter Arab influence in the Red Sea. As a result, Moscow gained an important geostrategic advantage over Washington through alliance on both sides of the Bab al-Mandab "chokepoint."[35]

Through Soviet military support Ethiopia could leverage its position toward the Arab rivals Saudi Arabia, Egypt, and Sudan, and provide rear bases and increasing assistance for anti-government groups in Somalia. South Yemeni support also ensured a measure of influence over the Bab al-Mandab, although Ethiopia itself was entangled in the struggle over Eritrea. In contrast, the US solidified its alliance with Egypt, Saudi Arabia, and Israel in the Red Sea region, and engaged Somalia and Sudan, both seen as proxy battle states that faced strengthening armed opposition due to Ethiopian and its allies' interference.

By the early 1980s, the Horn regimes had become increasingly desperate in maintaining power over domestic rivals who gained assistance from external powers. Ethiopia's struggle against a growing number of ethnically organized armed opposition movements led Addis Ababa to lean stronger on its few external partners, especially Moscow and Tel Aviv. Siad Barre's government in Somalia also faced increasing domestic dissent and reached out to the US, but the Carter administration was reluctant to engage further than through an arms deal which gave a certain level of strategic access and ensured Somalia's alignment against Soviet influence.[36] In Sudan, the ailing Nimeiri regime maintained a strategic alliance with the US through which it obtained financial and material resources, and in Djibouti Aptidon regime opted for close ties with former colonizer France and the US.

In the meantime, pro-Western Arab powers, headed by Saudi Arabia, continued to support Muslim factions in Eritrea but became discontented by the Marxist and largely Christian EPLF gaining a leading role in the Eritrean struggle. They also assisted the ailing government of Somalia which in the course of the decade faced strengthening armed opposition supported by Ethiopia and its allies. In February 1982 another border conflict between Ethiopia and Somalia ensued. This time Ethiopian forces, joined by armed opposition fighters of the Somalia Salvation Democratic Front, invaded central Somalia. After some territorial gains, the invasion was halted and the hostilities ended in August. The US weapons and military and economic aid, along with Arab support, helped the defenders, although much of the external assistance was received afterward and used in an attempt to repress the Somali government's internal rivals, who, with Ethiopia's assistance, became militarily potent enough to challenge the authority of the central government in various parts of the country by the late 1980s. Although Ethiopia returned the occupied areas to Somalia before the end of the decade, the situation in the country had deteriorated into a civil war.

A regime change in April 1985 in Sudan, however, again led to changing alignments. It opened space for Khartoum's closer collaboration with the Soviet bloc, Iran, and Libya. By reducing reliance on the West, the new regime led by Sadiq al-Mahdi sought to diversify foreign relations amid escalating civil war in southern Sudan. By the end of the Iran–Iraq War, Sudan continued with the US and its regional allies as its major arms suppliers while also benefiting from weapons shipments from Libya.

The Islamist military takeover in Sudan on June 30, 1989, formed another watershed moment for regional relations in the Horn of Africa. It served as a prelude to the final stages of the East–West ideological battle in the Horn which was replaced by the confrontation between US-led Western liberalism and conservative political Islam. A significant factor was the growing role of Libya and Sudan, and Somalia among several countries improving ties with the Gaddafi regime and receiving arms in the battle against domestic rivals. The coup in Sudan brought Islamist officers influenced by the NIF to power which resulted in the new regime pursuing top-down Islamist politics domestically and in foreign policy. Partly because of Sudanese agitation, political Islam became increasingly prevalent in parts of the Horn and provoked a confrontation with the West. The Sudanese regime used its foreign relations to draw support from the Persian Gulf countries in its attempt to become the beacon of political Islam in the region and beyond.

For most of the 1980s, the Iran–Iraq War (1979–88) dominated Middle East politics. With an important sectarian dimension, it was a warning sign to Saudi Arabia about the power of post-revolution Iran. As a result, after the war, Riyadh's attention turned increasingly to Tehran as a regional rival and the Saudi leadership became preoccupied with Iran's sectarian connection in its neighborhood. From the early 1990s onward, competition between the two regional powers extended to the Horn of Africa as Tehran built ties with various governments.

In the first half of 1986, the oil price plummeted. This led to the diminishing capacity of the petroleum-exporting Persian Gulf countries to engage in economic statecraft and pursue their strategic objectives. In June, Saudi Arabia pegged its currency to the USD to avoid a monetary crisis which strengthened the Saudi monarchy's relationship with the US further.[37] The leading Persian Gulf countries' temporarily shrinking financial capacity also meant that their engagement of the Horn of Africa lessened significantly until the oil price recovered, conservative political Islam strengthened as a potent ideological force, and regional competition between Saudi Arabia and Iran intensified.

As the Cold War drew to a close, it became apparent that the US engagement with the Horn of Africa had been successful in limiting Soviet influence. By 1988–9 both superpowers began withdrawing from the sub-region. The indications of Soviet withdrawal from the Horn diminished its importance in terms of strategic competition, and the superpower rivals phased out their support for the local regimes. What soon followed was the collapse of the Soviet Union. In connection with this and the withdrawal of the superpower and their Arab allies' support, the regimes in the Horn of Africa facing domestic rivals and armed opposition experienced significant turbulence. While the two Yemens seemed to have initially overcome their differences and united in 1990, Sudan experienced an Islamist military takeover (1989) which was followed by state collapses in Ethiopia (1990) and Somalia (1991), respectively. Eritrean and Somaliland liberators used the tempestuous political situation to establish independent Eritrea (1993) and the self-declared Republic of Somaliland (1991), respectively, as new states, while soon after interstate tensions and conflicts involving Asmara became frequent. However, political turbulence and conflict in Ethiopia, Somalia, and Sudan continued, and Djibouti experienced a civil war (1991–4).

The end of the Cold War, therefore, shocked several regimes in the Horn of Africa. On short notice, their practice of using foreign policy orientation and external alliances for essential resources, which they had relied on as a prominent strategy for survival, became much less beneficial. However, several regimes, similar to the Arab rentier states which rely on their natural resources for revenue, had become reliant almost solely on single external sources of financial and material benefits and were unable to compensate for drastically reduced superpower assistance through other sources. This was compounded by their Persian Gulf allies experiencing a decrease in oil revenues and consequently being reluctant to provide financial and military aid to their Horn partners. Although in

Sudan the June 1989 military takeover salvaged the north-central elite-dominated state which faced significant military gains by the southern rebels, Ethiopian and Somali regimes collapsed due to overwhelming opposition by several armed groups. Also, out of this unprecedented shake-up, one newly recognized (Eritrea) and one non-recognized (Somaliland) state were born.

Post–Cold War Developments

The superpowers pulling back in the Horn at the end of the Cold War opened room for the regionally powerful states to play a more significant role in the Red Sea/Horn of Africa geopolitical space. However, the petroleum-rich Persian Gulf powers had little incentive to use their financial resources in the sub-region due to the triumph of the US against communism and the low oil prices. At this juncture, the Horn generated little external interest except among actors promoting political Islam, both in its violent and non-violent form.

Various conflicts within states that devastated the Horn of Africa continued and provided a fertile ground for feuds among neighbors. Sudan's Islamic revolution of national salvation led Khartoum to assert itself in its neighborhood through the promotion of political Islam. The Arab powers also became preoccupied with Sudan's effort to export its project for revolutionary political Islam which could have a destabilizing effect in the Arabian Peninsula especially after Tehran began developing closer ties with Khartoum. At the same time, Khartoum continued in a civil war that pitted the Islamist government at the state's center against various armed and political opposition groups in its periphery. The Islamic project's potential destabilization of neighboring countries invited direct and proxy assistance and military operations on Sudanese soil.

Khartoum's unfolding alignment with Tehran, which included Iranian cultural propagation, and Iran's economic and military assistance and presence in the Red Sea, led to Saudi, Egyptian, Israeli, and American concerns and isolated Sudan further. The Horn states bordering Sudan, especially Eritrea and Ethiopia, aligned with Washington and assisted the opposition against the Islamist government with US support.

After the collapse of communism, the US soon identified radical political Islam as the main opponent to its hegemonic liberal project and as a threat to itself and its regional allies. The leading Persian Gulf monarchies also began deeming revolutionary grassroots Islamic movements dangerous for the stability of regimes in the Horn of Africa and their governments at home. However, at the same time, the Saudi–Iranian rivalry for regional influence intensified as both sought to win over those left with an ideological void after communism by promoting religious education and indoctrination. For example, after the state collapse in Somalia, the Salafist doctrine gained ground among prominent individuals who appropriated and used it to increase their authority and legitimacy. In Mogadishu, a politically powerful Salafist business elite emerged which maintained linkages with Islamists abroad, particularly in the Arabian Peninsula. Connections to Yemen were also maintained from the Somali side of the Gulf of Aden. This facilitated arms flow especially through Somalia's Puntland.

In 1994 Yemen on the other side of Bab al-Mandab went through a period of civil war in which northern forces came on top. The country subsequently solidified economically due to increasing oil export revenue, but faced various conflicts with its neighbors and harbored ties with Islamists who extended their networks to the Horn of Africa. Precisely after Yemen's provision of a haven for Islamists came to light in the course of the 1990s it began experiencing external pressure. With the emergence of al-Qaeda and the assertion of Shia Muslim tribes of their power in northern Yemen, the US-aligned regional powerhouses Saudi Arabia and Egypt grew increasingly alarmed.

Meanwhile, the independence of Eritrea in 1993 birthed another assertive state actor in the Horn of Africa. The EPLF under Isaias Afwerki converted into the governing force which effectively marginalized other political forces. This included Eritrean Muslims linked to the various Eritrean Liberation Front factions. Eritrea almost immediately confronted its neighbors Sudan and Yemen, which had both aspired to consolidate their status as key states in the region. Pursuing assertive foreign policy in which it did not hesitate to use military strength, Asmara then took on Ethiopia in the Eritrean–Ethiopian War (1998–2000), the most devastating interstate conflict in the Horn of Africa since Somalia's invasion of eastern Ethiopia. While Eritrea's independence and Somaliland's de facto departure from Somalia in 1991 further enriched the regional spectrum of state actors, state fragility and weakness in the Horn sub-region have allowed space for sub-state and non-state actors to pursue their local interests through their own external connections.

Toward the late 1990s, due to the chronic dependence on food imports, the Persian Gulf powers also became interested in reviving their earlier "breadbasket" strategy in the Horn of Africa. This strategy got wind under its wings during the 2007–8 financial and subsequent economic crisis leading to global food shortages, while higher oil prices enabled investment. The Persian Gulf actors, however, sought to engage a wider spectrum of countries in the Horn than during the 1970s and the local leaders intended to gain financially from the investment to increase their domestic political and economic influence. This led to Arab investors, at times through local proxies, purchasing large patches of land especially in Ethiopia and Sudan for agricultural use, cordoning them off from the use of local pastoralists in the Horn countries. As a result, a growing network of interactions and influences emerged which again increasingly entangled the Persian Gulf political and security concerns with the Horn of Africa.

As a result of renewed interest, the engagement of Middle East regional powers in the Horn of Africa increased. While these actors pursued their own strategic political, economic, and security objectives, their interests were to an extent shaped by the sub-regional and local political, economic, and social realities in the Horn. They were in part drawn in by the state and non-state actors in the sub-region, which in the context of the waning of superpower interest oriented their external relations more toward obtaining financial and economic resources from regional powers.

This, in turn, contributed to Middle East and Arab competition and rivalries. In the view of some authors,[38] these dynamics produced a geo-economic reality in which economic factors, particularly financial and investment flows, became increasingly important in strategies that formed part of perceived geopolitical power projections. While the renewed engagement seemingly leveraged the regional political power of the financially affluent Persian Gulf countries, their influence within political, economic, and social spaces within the Horn of Africa was constrained by the local power of domestic actors. The agency of these state and non-state actors became paramount in shaping the relations with and constraining the influence of external players in the local context.

The new regimes that took over in the Horn of Africa after the Cold War continued to pursue a similar strategy to their predecessors in terms of external relations. However, in the post–Cold War environment in which there was no significant superpower interest that one could overwhelmingly rely on for financial and material resources, the Horn governments generally felt obliged to diversify their foreign connections. Therefore, their largely pragmatic and transactional, and in most cases less ideological, external relations became increasingly driven by attempts at diversification. At home, the governments used an important part of their resources to centralize power and consolidate the political and economic status quo to avoid the faith of the previous regimes. In their domestic battle for survival, the leaders of these governments often faced potent rivals, mainly non-state actors with significant political and economic power, to challenge the governing forces. Most notably in Somalia, but also in Sudan, the armed opposition's relative strength was significant, while in Ethiopia as well armed groups remained as local challengers to the central government's power. Many of these non-state actors had foreign connections not only to neighboring states but toward the Arabian Peninsula, which hosted sizeable diaspora communities from the Horn countries. As their strategic interest in the Horn grew, some regimes and non-state actors in the Persian Gulf and the Arabian Peninsula began obscurely endorsing opposition elements there.[39]

In the Horn, pragmatic and transactional approaches favoring bilateral relations continued to carry the day in relations with the financially affluent Persian Gulf/ Middle East states. From the perspective of the Horn state and non-actors direct financial and economic returns ensuring power in competition against domestic rivals have continued to play the main role in their Persian Gulf/Middle East relations, while their Persian Gulf/Middle East counterparts have emphasized the security of maritime shipping routes through Bab al-Mandab, minimizing influences from the Horn that could undermine domestic political stability, and gaining political and economic influence in the Horn.

Over time, the recurrent economic problems and chronic shortages of foreign currency pushed the Horn governments closer to the financially affluent Persian Gulf countries. Migratory flow from the Horn of Africa where job opportunities are scarce to Gulf States has been incessant since the oil and gas discoveries and the accompanying increase in demand for formal and informal labor to fuel economic development and cater for service provision. Especially from the 1970s onward, Persian Gulf countries became an important and relatively proximate destination for migrants from the Horn of Africa, and the remittances from the diaspora communities and migrants converted into a crucial source of income in the Horn countries. This has involved the institutionalized *kafala*, or sponsorship, system, especially for domestic workers. Although at times facing ill-treatment because of misconceptions, racist views, and abuse, and often subjected to labor in difficult conditions, migrants from the African side of the Red Sea and the Gulf of Aden have contributed significantly and built successful businesses in their host countries in the Middle East. For example, state-building in the UAE owes significantly to the Sudanese contribution and Somali businesses use the financial hub Dubai extensively for their banking,[40] while migrant labor from the Horn countries has contributed to infrastructure development and service provision in all Gulf States. The financial flow through diaspora investment and remittances, and funds brought back by returnees, have had a significant impact on promoting monetary stability and economic development in the Horn. Migration and its economic and social aspects have bound Horn and Gulf countries together.

The mid-1990s also saw China's renewed interest in Africa. Driven by the need to secure new sources of natural resources to feed booming economic development, Beijing first settled in Sudan, where oil resources remained untapped mainly due to the confrontation with the West. China's return to the African continent, drawn largely by Sudan's oil, equipped Khartoum with new financial resources, as well as arms and diplomatic capital, to withstand the political and military onslaught directed by the US. Through alignment with Beijing and Tehran, Khartoum survived, but the al-Bashir regime was eventually forced to succumb to the US-led international pressure to sign the 2005 Comprehensive Peace Agreement as a prelude to its partition and the independence of South Sudan in 2011.

The first decade of the 2000s saw a renewed interest among state actors in the Arabian Peninsula and Persian Gulf toward the Horn of Africa. The recovery of oil prices fed political and economic interaction and growing interdependence between the Horn and the Persian Gulf players. Arab finances, aid, and investment again became emphasized in these relations, and in exchange, the Horn countries provided fertile land, natural resources, and labor, or granted political favors or influence. But various political and security agendas also continued to be significant in the network of relationships among state and non-state actors in the Horn and the Persian Gulf.

The Arab and Iranian interest was largely driven by strategic considerations related to the desire for securing the Red Sea/Gulf of Aden space and increase political influence and economic presence in the Horn. At the same time, there was an interest in tapping into the resource base and the growing commercial potential in the sub-region. Concrete manifestations of this interest were the Emirati government's foreign policy instrument Dubai Ports World's (DP World) thirty-year concession agreement with the Djibouti government in 2006 to develop and operate the Doraleh Container Terminal and Qatar's mediation in Sudan and peacekeeping between Djibouti and Eritrea until 2017.

For Saudi Arabia as the leading power in the Arabian Peninsula, competition with Iran became an increasing concern. This was especially due to political instability caused by tribal and sectarian conflicts in Yemen, in which Tehran seemingly supported the potent Houthi tribal militia, a Zaidi Shia formation, with its homeland around the Saudi border. Another concern was the inroads Iran had made across the Red Sea, particularly in Sudan and Eritrea. Khartoum's cooperation with Tehran had momentarily diminished the long Egyptian and more recent Saudi influence in the country and, as in the case of Eritrea, given Iran a foothold on the shores of the African side of the Red Sea. Eritrea was also deemed to channel Iranian arms and train militias for the Houthi in Yemen. In addition, there have been continuous concerns about potential Iranian attempts to undermine state-building in Somalia. Repeated allegations have been made about Iranian presence in the country and weapons being channeled through Yemen in favor of Islamist elements and opposition forces, above all al-Shabaab.[41] Saudi Arabia and the UAE have sought to capitalize on these allegations, as well as on accusations of Qatar's destabilizing role through purported Islamist connections, to advance their ambitions in the country.

In these conditions, Saudi Arabia and its allies sought to intensify the pragmatic and transactional ties with Horn governments to eject Iran from the Horn of Africa. However, Horn governments and non-state actors maintained ties with other Middle East powers that were in the region, such as Qatar, and Türkiye through nongovernmental organizations. Saudi Arabia and the UAE deemed the two to empower religious grassroots movements, Islamists, and the Muslim Brotherhood which generated concern due to fears of politically destabilizing currents emerging on the African side of the Red Sea/Gulf of Aden and extending to the Arabian Peninsula, where the Arab Spring led to the Yemeni Revolution and an uprising in Bahrain.

Consequently, strategic geopolitical, security, and (geo)economic considerations, as well as religious and socio-political identity and ideological (sectarian) alignments, have been at the forefront of the external powers' approaches toward the states in the Horn of Africa. Meanwhile, for the Horn states, the regime consolidation against internal rivals has been a major driver of their foreign policy toward external powers, including the Persian Gulf/Middle East countries.

Recent Dynamics

The political and security relations between the Persian Gulf countries and Turkey and the Horn of African states have intensified particularly since the second decade of the twenty-first century. Among the key events kicking off the recent surge of interaction were the Arab Spring uprisings which led to civil wars and governmental changes, bringing an end to the incumbent regimes in Egypt, Libya, Tunisia, and Yemen, and causing instability in for example in Bahrain and Sudan. In the Persian Gulf monarchies, this led to security concerns related to increasingly powerful non-state actors and externally induced forces potentially threatening domestic stability. In particular, instability emanating from Yemen and Somalia has been a source of concern partly due to "multibillion-dollar shadow business networks spanning the Gulf of Aden."[42] Saudi Arabia and the UAE have countered the perceived threats by seeking more political influence in their neighborhood. During the Arab Spring, they supported the incumbent regimes against popular uprisings deemed to be fueled by Qatar, Türkiye, and Iran, and, when possible, sought to reverse revolutions. In Egypt, after the toppling of the Hosni Mubarak regime in 2011, such reversal came two years later when the military, under Abdel Fattah al-Sisi, took down the Muslim Brotherhood government led by Mohamed Morsi.[43] Supporting the military's return to power, days after the coup Saudi Arabia and the UAE pledged USD 8 billion in a mix of financial and material support to revive Egypt's economy.[44] Since the 2019 Sudanese Revolution, the same countries, accompanied by Egypt, have again deliberately undermined the grassroots democratic transition by supporting the Sudanese military and security apparatus in its attempt to maintain authoritarian rule after the demise of the al-Bashir regime. These actions owe to fears that significant political changes on the other side of the Red Sea could be replicated at home, especially after the experience of the Arab Spring which led to the Yemeni Revolution (2011) and the Bahraini Uprising (2011–14).[45]

Meanwhile, the economic dimension of the Persian Gulf and Middle East powers' approach to the Horn of Africa has not only aimed at political influence but also access to strategic economic assets and logistical locations. Although at times linked to security interests, Arab investment in the Horn seeks to benefit from market access and tap into the rapidly growing service, financial, logistics, and hospitality and tourism sectors as well as in food production. With the gradually emerging middle classes in the Horn, the future market potential, as in the case of Ethiopia, is enormous. At the same time, Ethiopia, Sudan, and, to some extent, Somalia are deemed as potential overseas food production hubs. The Middle East powers recognize these realities and have focused many of their strategic and economic activities to woo the largest and most populous Horn country, Ethiopia, as a desired partner.

In their economic approach, the Persian Gulf and Middle East states work under the shadow of the overarching economic power, China, which through its strategy and size has managed to develop close ties with most governments in the Horn. Ethiopia, Eritrea, Somalia, and, above all, Djibouti[46] have welcomed Chinese investment in various sectors of the economy, and they have taken large loans that have resulted in significant Chinese political influence which the West under the US leadership has sought to counter. Some Persian Gulf actors see their role as complementary to the Chinese economic onslaught and have chosen to work in sectors that are less affected by Chinese activities or in which they can also benefit from the Chinese engagement.

After the Arab Spring, Saudi Arabia's political and security concerns regarding its regional rival Iran came to the fore in its approach to the Horn of Africa. Riyadh became determined to deal with Sudan's close long-term collaboration and

Eritrea's more recent alliance with Iran which allowed Tehran to exert influence in the strategic Red Sea region and among African Muslims. Iran's influence in Yemen through the Houthi movement was a crucial concern when it also seemed that particularly Eritrea was complacent to Iranian support through its territory. Riyadh, therefore, used its financial leverage and pressured Khartoum and Asmara to choose between continuing to work with Iran, an internationally isolated pariah, or establishing deeper ties with Saudi Arabia and its wide spectrum of allies, including the US.

In 2011 southern Somalia experienced severe famine which the Turkish leadership used to make new inroads in the Horn of Africa. In the famine caused by droughts, conflict, rising food prices, lack of humanitarian access, and the absence of international food agencies,[47] the Turkish state stepped in as a humanitarian actor, although its efforts could not save thousands of people. Following several years of groundwork by the Turkish nongovernmental organizations in the sub-region, the Turkish government initially engaged Muslim populations in the Horn of Africa through an ideological neo-Ottoman approach that celebrates Ottoman heritage. This sought to appeal to Muslims in regions that had been historically under the Ottoman rule to welcome Türkiye as a brotherly state without the colonial baggage. Although Türkiye's soft power approach emphasizing economic, humanitarian, and cultural engagement has been successful in several countries bordering the Red Sea and the Gulf of Aden during the first ten years of the intensified relations, it so far has appeared to resonate less in areas with fewer perceived historical and cultural connections with Türkiye.

Increasing Turkish connection with Somalia led to increasing cooperation and influence, which in turn put Ankara as a regional power in competition with the leading Arab states in the Horn of Africa. Türkiye developed friendly ties with Qatar during the Arab Spring because both were inclined to support religious grassroots movements, such as the Muslim Brotherhood. Ankara then expanded its influence especially during the Mohamed Abdullahi Mohamed "Farmaajo" presidency (2017-2022) to become the most significant external partner for Mogadishu, while making inroads with Ethiopia, particularly during the Tigray conflict. Ankara also came to Doha's aid during the Qatar diplomatic crisis (2017–21) which was engineered by the leading GCC states. This, however, put Türkiye in a growing rivalry with Saudi Arabia and the UAE which sought to extend their influence in Somalia, Ethiopia, and elsewhere in the Horn sub-region.

In March 2015, in response to the escalation of the civil war in Yemen and the growing threat of the Houthi movement taking over the whole country, Saudi Arabia convoked a multinational military intervention force. This was in part motivated by the Iranian support for the Houthi militia, mostly composed of Zaidi Shia Muslims, and the Saudi fears of the spread of the conflict to its territory, which form part of the wider competition between the two regional powers, Iran and Saudi Arabia, along sectarian lines. With promises of financial benefits, Sudan joined the Saudi-led coalition and also sent much-needed troops to reinforce the Arab ground forces to largely replace the UAE military which had carried the weight of the early campaign. Soon Eritrea followed suit by allowing the UAE to establish a military base in Assab for its Yemen operations, and ostensibly sending troops to Yemen in exchange for financial assistance, fuel, infrastructure, and diplomatic support.[48] Both governments, Khartoum and Asmara, hoped to improve their dire financial standing and economic problems by demonstrating closer alignment with Saudi Arabia and its junior partner, the UAE. Crucially, closer ties with the UAE paved the way for Eritrea's reconciliation with Ethiopia in 2018.

Aligning with the Saudi-led coalition provided an opportunity for a number of the Horn governments to obtain economic resources and external support against their domestic rivals. Through negotiation and economic diplomacy, they exchanged strategic assets, including ports, land for bases, and military support, for financial and material resources. Stronger ties with regionally powerful states could also help them in diplomacy with their neighbors as was the case with the 2018 rapprochement between Eritrea and Ethiopia. Saudi Arabia aspired to build on this alignment and elevate its regional role further by taking leadership in cooperation on Red Sea affairs and established the Red Sea Council in 2021 (originally an Egyptian initiative) that includes Djibouti, Egypt, Eritrea, Jordan, Somalia, Sudan, and Yemen.

In July 2017, the tension between Qatar and Saudi Arabia, and its close allies UAE, Egypt, and Bahrain, led to Doha's isolation to which countries in the Horn of Africa that desired to demonstrate their commitment to Riyadh and Abu Dhabi participated. The diplomatic crisis included accusations of Doha supporting terrorism, engaging in media propaganda and agitation through Aljazeera (especially encouraging grassroots movements against their governments), and maintaining good relations with Iran. Saudi Arabia shut Qatar's land crossing and the countries, and Riyadh and its allies closed their airspace and sea territories from Doha. They passed a list of thirteen demands,[49] including Qatar to stop supporting anti-government groups and those they have designated as terrorists, cease interference in internal affairs of states and assistance to opposition elements in Saudi Arabia and the other three states, shut down Aljazeera and news outlets it funded abroad, downgrade its relations with Iran, and end its long-term military cooperation with Türkiye. However, Ankara came to Doha's aid and helped it to withstand the isolation.

Sudanese leadership was divided about how to react to the crisis and sought to remain neutral to maintain a good relationship with both parties. While sending reinforcements to Yemen, it offered to mediate between the parties. Similarly, Ethiopia and Somalia, the latter especially interested in maintaining its external sources of income and political support, expressed their concern but remained neutral. However, Somali sub-state actors, federal states of Puntland, Hirshabelle, and Galmudug, which have close relations, particularly with the UAE, condemned and cut ties with Qatar.

In Somalia, the division among state, sub-state, and non-state actors about foreign connections and alignment with the Persian Gulf powers and Türkiye encouraged domestic competition for political and economic power. For example, both the federal and individual state administrations sought foreign support to get an edge in local power rivalries. In one incident, in April 2018, the federal authorities sized USD 9.6 million from Emirati diplomats claiming that the money was intended for rivals to destabilize the federal government rather than to pay the Somali National Army salaries as the UAE officials argued.[50] This gives a glimpse of the severity of domestic political competition over survival and consolidation.

In April 2015, after Djibouti fell out with the UAE over a dispute about the Doraleh Container Terminal and a personal spat between officials, it expelled the Emirati and Saudi forces. Consequently, the DP World lost its concession to develop and operate the Doraleh Container Terminal to Djibouti's Chinese partners, the Hong Kong–based China Merchants, including its loss of exclusivity rights and control of direct logistics access to the developing and potentially massive Ethiopian market. While this undermined the UAE's geopolitical and economic objectives, the DP World entered into an intractable legal dispute in which it has won several rulings in various courts.[51] Djibouti government, however, has defied the rulings and stuck with its Chinese partners while falling increasingly under Beijing's influence.[52] Meanwhile, the UAE government has downplayed the importance of the legal case on Abu Dhabi's strategic overall relationship with Beijing.

The UAE and Saudi Arabia had hoped to use military installations in Djibouti for their Yemen operations but were forced to look for new partners in the coastal Horn of Africa. In their strategic calculations, the Emirati were keen to establish port and logistics operations elsewhere to replace Djibouti and still gain access to the Ethiopian market, while also obtaining support bases for their campaign in southwest Yemen.

Soon after the Emirati and Saudi exit from Djibouti, the UAE stroke deals with the opportunistic leaderships of Eritrea and Somaliland and developed close relations with both. Eritrea entered into a defense deal with Saudi Arabia and allowed the Emirati to build a port and overhaul the airstrip in Assab, as well as to establish a military base and train troops to support their Yemen operations. Similarly, Somaliland entered into an agreement with the UAE for the DP World to develop and manage the port, reconstruct the airport, and build a military facility in Berbera. In March 2018, Ethiopia agreed to assume a 19 percent stake in the DP World–led Berbera port consortium which demonstrates the importance of the Berbera Corridor as an alternative import-export route to Ethiopia. Various external investors, including state and non-state actors from the UAE and the UK, have since invested in its development.

During the Qatar crisis, due to their close ties with Saudi Arabia and the UAE, Eritrea and Somaliland were inclined to side with the Saudi bloc. Djibouti, keen on improving ties with Saudi Arabia and the UAE, also joined them which led to the departure of the Qatari peacekeepers who had monitored its disputed border with Eritrea. Subsequently, Saudi Arabia stepped in to mediate in the Djibouti–Eritrea border conflict which promised to improve ties between the two countries.

More significantly for regional affairs, Emirati and Saudi support was also crucial in the groundbreaking rapprochement between Eritrea and Ethiopia in July 2018. They used financial and material incentives as well as promises that Eritrea's international sanctions would be lifted. Although the US played an important role in the diplomatic behind-the-scenes dialogue that laid the groundwork for the rapprochement, it was particularly Emirati efforts that facilitated the eventual coming together of the new Ethiopian Abiy Ahmed and Eritrean Isaias Afwerki-led governments.

Part of the reconciliation between Ethiopia and Eritrea was the sidelining and neutralization of the Tigray People's Liberation Front (TPLF) which had governed Ethiopia and dominated the Horn sub-region for almost three decades. In September 2018 Somali president Mohamed "Farmaajo" was invited to form a tripartite alliance between the heads of governments to cooperate closely in politics, economy, development, and, above all, security. On November 3, 2021, Ethiopian forces initiated what the government called a "law enforcement operation" in the Tigray region to eliminate the rebellious TPLF old guard leadership. The TPLF had been sidelined from the helm of political power, and rejecting political reforms by the new government it had decided to withdraw to Tigray, where it vehemently defied the new national political order.

The confrontation between the federal government and the TPLF led to the Tigray conflict, in which the Eritrean military participated and Somali recruits were deployed. As the war escalated and the Tigray Defense Forces (TDF) advance threatened the Ethiopian capital, Addis Ababa purchased and various external powers provided weapons and other material support which reversed the tide and led to the rebels withdrawing back to Tigray. Arab powers, Saudi Arabia and the UAE, and Türkiye, with significant investments in Ethiopia, have been among the top backers of the Abiy government, while China and Iran have also provided arms. Since then the TDF has been confined in Tigray and, following the resumption of hostilities in August 2022, Ethiopian forces and its allies advanced in the region which, together with the dire humanitarian situation, forced the TPLF and the TDF to agree to a peace deal on November 2, 2022, in South Africa approximately two years after the beginning of the conflict. External actors, particularly the United States, played an important role in pressuring the parties to an agreement under the auspices of the African Union mediation.

After significant delays, the presidential election in federal Somalia took place in mid-May 2022. The indirect election, which took place within Mogadishu Airport due to security concerns, led to the return of Hassan Sheikh Mohamud who had also served earlier (2012–17) as the country's president. The new leadership sought to improve ties with the UAE, and Prime Minister Mohamed Hussein Roble, who the month before had apologized for the seizure of money from the incoming UAE diplomats in April 2018 which had caused a diplomatic spat and exit of the UAE from Mogadishu, returned the confiscated funds.[53] Hassan Sheikh then chose the UAE as the destination for his first foreign visit while in office. This rapid policy change indicates that Hassan Sheikh, whose past administration maintained good ties with Abu Dhabi, seeks to prioritize Somalia's relationship with the UAE. Through these relations, as well as those with other external partners, the Mogadishu leadership attempts to mobilize resources for domestic use. Of particular concern is the severe drought especially in southwestern Somalia which has the potential to escalate into famine-like conditions. The UAE and other external partners have already dispatched relief. The new Somali administration's shift in policy toward the UAE, and Abu Dhabi's interest to again play a bigger role in Somalia, which it has already demonstrated by sending humanitarian aid, may have far-reaching consequences for the fickle foreign alignments and domestic rivalries in the Horn of Africa.

Recent developments affecting the Middle East, such as various Arab countries recognizing Israel, the Chinese-brokered rapprochement between Saudi Arabia and Iran, and Riyadh and Abu Dhabi strengthening their ties with Beijing and the BRICS (Brazil, Russia, India, China, and South Africa grouping), as well as Russia's invasion of Ukraine, are likely to have repercussions on the Horn states' foreign policy toward the Persian Gulf countries. However, they are unlikely to change the established dynamics dictated by pragmatic calculations and transactional engagement through which the state and societal actors seek to extract financial and economic benefits from the Persian Gulf.

Pragmatism, Transactionalism, and Power

Due to the nature of the international system, which is guided by international law focusing on the rights and responsibilities of states, it is precisely the states that continue to be considered as its main autonomous constituent units. While states have established a plethora of international and regional organizations, and despite the rise of non-state actors as an important force in international affairs, they still continue as the paramount legally recognized units that constitute the structure and influence the dynamics of the international system. States also have the advantage that they can also use sovereignty over the people and territory for extracting resources and exchanging economic and strategic assets with non-state and external state actors. In this sense, it is the bilateral relationships between states that continue to shape international politics and political economy, at least when viewed from the perspective of Horn of Africa–Persian Gulf/Middle East relations.[54]

Generally, African states have been described as neo-patrimonial due to the state leaders using public resources to secure their position and power through extensive patron–client networks that bind the state with the society. These networks require resources that the patrons, also often called the "big men,"[55] are expected to distribute to their selected clients to ensure their societal prestige and political status. This is particularly the case in authoritarian states in which the political and accompanying economic power is concentrated in the hands of the few. The state and the public resources are captured by the "big men" who use them for their private ends. Here, state or regime survival by maintaining the status quo becomes personalized by those who govern. Most often in authoritarian states, as in the Horn of Africa, which are based on the marginalization of large parts of the population and their exclusion from effective political representation and access to resources and economic opportunities, the biggest threats to the continuity of the "big man"–led status quo are domestic. Internal rivals engage in competition over resources to increase their relative power locally to be able to challenge, and at times overthrow, the patrons of the state. In the Horn of Africa, direct external threats to regime survival tend to be a less immediate concern,[56] although external powers' support of domestic actors may destabilize state leadership. Endemic weakness and fragility, based on the government's general lack of authority, legitimacy, and capacity to control population and territory, expose a state to domestic threats. Leaders of such states seek to mitigate these threats by extracting resources for consolidation against domestic rivals and using foreign relations as a significant component for obtaining additional resources. It is argued that since the Cold War African elites have concentrated on foreign aid as a significant external resource for self-enrichment and maintaining political power,[57] and deliberately presented the "African condition" as perpetually dependent on external assistance.[58] This has led states in the Horn of Africa to pursue pragmatic foreign relations with expectations of significant returns. During the Cold War, alignment with one superpower often ensured large amounts of aid. But since the end of the Cold War, the Horn governments have felt obliged to diversify their foreign partnerships, sometimes by balancing simultaneously relations with various powers that compete against each other, to maximize benefits from external engagements and secure several sources of resources from abroad for regime survival.

In their most basic form, relations between states can be characterized as pragmatic, transactional, and often reciprocal. Historically, pragmatic and transactional logic governed relations between many pre-state polities, forming basic strategy and practice that was passed on to modern states.[59] It can be argued also that an important element of pragmatic transactionalism and reciprocity is also behind ideologically driven foreign policy approaches. This can be observed in the way many of the so-called Third World governments shifted ideological positions during the Cold War in their relations with the two superpowers based on reciprocal gain. While some governments engaged in far-reaching ideologically driven political and economic transformation, many others did not. In such cases, the essence of the foreign policy approach was arguably pragmatic and transactional and not based on any particular ideological groundings. The politics of aid, for example, also reveal the importance of such transactionalism by proportioning the recipient financial and material resources in exchange for its alignment with the donor. As a result, in a realist world, where states are seen to be mostly preoccupied with their own survival, interstate relations have been viewed largely on a pragmatic and reciprocal basis. From the realist standpoint, bilateralism plays an important role in this logic as long as the state does not lose its sovereignty over its foreign relations. While liberalist approaches to interstate relations emphasize cooperation and the formation and role of supra-state organizations, the realist perspective would emphasize that individual states are the constituent units of such organizations and wield power in them.[60] Their bilateral dealings outside or within such organizations are significant. Thus, through the lens of their bilateral relations agency of individual states with other states still forms an important part of current international interactions.[61]

However, any nuanced study on countries' foreign relations and international affairs needs to include other significant actors apart from the state. In the Horn of Africa, non-state actors, including political, ethnic, and religious groups, armed movements, and powerful individuals and families often maintain their own external relations, at times in competition against state patrons and other non-state actors. This is particularly the case in countries where the state does not maintain a monopoly on major foreign connections, but in which non-state, and sub-state, actors exercise significant autonomy in their political and economic dealings and are interested in challenging the governing elite's power. As with the state actors, their external connections tend to be geared toward increasing their local power against domestic political and economic rivals. In the Horn of Africa, some non-state actors openly challenge the state leadership at the local or national level.

In the foreign policy strategy of states and non-state actors in the Horn economic aspects are salient. Obtaining financial and material resources from abroad helps to increase their local power and domestic position relative to their rivals. In their relations with financially endowed Persian Gulf and Middle East actors, the Horn actors, therefore, embark on economic diplomacy (official or informal) and mainly seek to exchange economic (e.g., land, natural resources, and labor), strategic (e.g., concessions to logistics, ports, and airfields), and nonmaterial (e.g., promises for political influence) assets for financial or material benefits. This approach is aimed at ensuring survival, consolidation, and gaining an edge against domestic competitors.

In the International Relations discipline, Horn of Africa's relations with the Persian Gulf and Middle East states have predominantly been analyzed from the perspective of the latter due to the consideration that they are dominant in the relationship. This assessment is made due to a type of understanding based on perceived state capabilities. Power relations based on different relative levels of capabilities between states are often seen as the main explanatory element of the interactions between the Horn and the Persian Gulf countries. In such a viewpoint, the deep penetration of external influence is seen to be in a major role in causing domestic changes, but such interpretations exaggerate the capacity of external actors to exert local influence. It also erroneously diminishes the importance of domestic state and non-state players as the main local actors. For example, although constrained in their foreign relations by their limited capabilities, Ethiopian, Somali, and Eritrean governments, and some cases non-state actors, are the main forces dictating political, economic, and social realities at the local level in their respective states. Despite pressure to gain financial and material resources from abroad, they often involve the Persian Gulf and Middle East actors willingly and on their terms. They tend to engage interested external partners who approach them pragmatically and exercise power locally according to their own interests, which may, or may not, align with those of external powers.

The local power of the state and societal actors in the Horn of Africa constrains the influence of their external partners, including those from the Persian Gulf and the Middle East. The pragmatic and largely transactional nature of the relations allows the actors in the Horn to wield significant power due to their control of local assets and material and reputational resources. They tend to have an advantage in bargaining processes in which the external actor seeks to advance its interests in the local setting. A classical realist international relations analysis, which focuses on relative power between unitary states is ill-equipped to deal with this reality due to its epistemological groundings.

Therefore, simply adopting the viewpoint of considering Middle East states stronger than their Horn of Africa counterparts is insufficient for gaining an in-depth understanding of multiple manifestations of power in the relationship. Instead, it is important to consider that these bilateral relations cannot be limited to states alone. In the Horn of Africa, states are not unitary and monolithic actors in external relations because of their limited capacity to dominate and monopolize major foreign connections. Sub-state and non-state actors often exercise significant external linkages which provide resources that allow some of them to locally challenge state actors.

Generally, over time, the governments in the Horn of Africa have tended to maintain transactional foreign relations with other states. They have pursued this approach pragmatically, ranging from great powers to small state partners, but transactionalism has been particularly apparent in their relations with the Persian Gulf countries. This owes in part to the leaders of such affluent Gulf countries being comfortable in pursuing foreign policy interests through their financial muscle. These transactional relations feature money in exchange for local assets and resources in the Horn of Africa controlled by state or non-state actors. They result in both types of actors becoming involved in foreign engagements and exercising local power in such transactions through their influence or control over domestic assets and resources.

Transactional exchanges are featured by reciprocal win-win, but the mutual benefit may often not be obvious. As a result, although Horn-Persian Gulf/Middle East relations might seem uneven from an interstate perspective, power in the transactional exchanges lies with both actors involved. Moreover, those exchanging strategic assets and resources under their control in the domestic space, as is often the case with the Horn actors, exercise significant bargaining power in a contractual relationship. The actor that reaches out to the other actors' space must have a reasonable amount of trust because of its lesser ability to ensure that a contract is respected in the local setting. As a result, although African Red Sea littoral states have often been depicted as mere recipients of power projection and interests of more powerful states and forced to engage the more influential Arab partners on an unequal basis,[62] this does not reflect the reality unveiled by a more nuanced understanding of the Horn of Africa–Persian Gulf/Middle East relations. In these interactions, both African state and non-state actors exercise significant local power and agency.

The Horn governments and non-state actors command different levels of leverage in relations with their Persian Gulf counterparts. This depends on several factors, including their internal cohesion and relative strength as well as their ability to negotiate from a position of power in the local context. In states where the governing regimes are more fragmented, politically powerful individuals, groups, or coalitions may find themselves in a position to exploit the interests of external actors for their benefit in local competition for political and economic power. Equipped with local knowledge and power, actors in the Horn may force their Persian Gulf partners to make choices by offering incentives and imposing constraints. They tend not to base their pragmatic and transactional relations on trust in durable long-term partnerships with extra-regional powers but prefer to diversify their foreign connections to ensure domestic survival and relative strength against local and national competitors.

Variably minority-ruled and authoritarian, most Horn states and their Persian Gulf partners have leadership and political reality based on the "big man" logic. The political leader, a president or a prime minister (or monarch in the case of the Gulf States), often counseled by a small group of advisors and confidants, is a crucial figure in determining the governments' foreign relations. This means that his personal views about international politics and his country's position in it, the values he subscribes to, his education and experiences, and contextual societal attitudes and norms he might be affected by, are all important to consider when trying to understand the leader's decisions on the country's foreign policy. In this sense, there are significant similarities between the Horn states and their Persian Gulf counterparts.

Recently, in a significant development, and after slim results in its effort to edge closer to Egypt, Türkiye has sought to improve ties with its rivals the UAE and Saudi Arabia. Experiencing a significant financial crisis, Türkiye has reached out to its rivals which could ease somewhat the Saudi–UAE and Türkiye–Qatar competition in the Horn of Africa. In November 2021, the UAE offered USD 10 billion worth of investments to alleviate Türkiye's economic troubles,[63] which should somewhat alleviate the Turkish financial crisis and gives Abu Dhabi access to the Turkish defense industry and military technology as well as other sectors of its economy. In the first half of 2022, Türkiye also initiated a rapprochement with Saudi Arabia by ending its investigation into the murder of dissident journalist Jamal Khashoggi which was followed by President Erdogan's visit to Riyadh and Crown Prince Mohammed bin Salman's reciprocal visit to Türkiye.[64] Erdogan's motivation to improve ties was to secure Saudi funding and investment to address Türkiye's severe financial crisis ahead of the 2023 presidential election while it has been speculated that bin Salman is interested in Turkish military technology.[65] This pragmatic and transactional foreign policy approach continues to guide the countries' regional relations.

However, increasing cooperation in the Horn of Africa, notably in Ethiopia and Somalia-Somaliland, where all three states have invested significantly, would require diminishing ambition for regional hegemony, economic presence, and political influence. Yet, Saudi Arabia and Türkiye unquestionably remain as the main middle power competitors in the Red Sea and Horn of Africa region, and the UAE's swiftly renewed commitment to Somalia, including the provision of humanitarian aid similar to what Türkiye did to make inroads in the country in 2011. The new Somali president Hassan Sheikh's first foreign visit to Abu Dhabi[66] signals the potential for continued rivalries in the Horn of Africa as the UAE seeks to continue punching above its weight in the Red Sea and Gulf of Aden neighborhood.

Conclusion

The states and non-state actors in the Horn of Africa are also highly pragmatic and transactional in their foreign relations. Due to the prevailing conditions of state fragility, they are in most cases preoccupied with their own survival and/ or gaining an edge against their domestic rivals who constitute the main threat to their political position and social status. This means that they use foreign relations for financial and material strengthening and political and diplomatic support. Ideological aspects are only important for pragmatic reasons because they may allow identifying the most suitable external partners and alignments, but such partnerships are highly volatile and uncertain because the Horn actors continuously seek to maximize benefits from their external connections.

A difference between most Horn of Africa and Middle East states is that in the Horn the foreign relations are less concentrated on the single state actors because of state fragility and the existence of powerful sub-state, non-state, and diaspora actors. These relations are therefore not monopolized to the same extent as among their Persian Gulf/Middle East counterparts, but the various actors pursuing such relations wield a degree of local power and influence. This defies the accuracy of analyses based on relative interstate power relations in a classical sense because local actors in the Horn, state and non-state alike, normally control strategic material, human, or political assets which they use to bargain with external actors for beneficial exchanges. As a result, their local power is often significant which puts the external actor reaching out to their space in a vulnerable position. Their strong bargaining position can largely dictate the terms and conditions of their external partners' involvement.

As a result, due to domestic realities in the Horn of Africa and the transactional nature of engagements, the Horn-Persian Gulf/Middle East relations are unpredictable and inconsistent. Alignments particularly between states, but also among politically and economically influential non-state actors, are often temporary and changeable. This owes to the primacy of pragmatic transactionalism in these relations and the Horn actors' careful balancing between various external partners to maximize benefits and minimize constraints. The lack of underlying ideological fabric or long-term interests that bind the actors together in consistent and durable alliances characterizes their uncertainty. Yet, any change in preference for bilateral, pragmatic, and transactional relations would require a fundamental change in the nature of domestic power competition and political and economic realities, which could, in turn, transform perceptions and conduct toward foreign relations and external partnerships.

Chapter 3

ETHIOPIA

THE DESIRED PARTNER

Ethiopia is a dominant state in the Horn of Africa and crucial for understanding the sub-region. With ancient linkages to the Arabian Peninsula, Ethiopia, as one observer put it, can be seen as "an outpost of Middle Easter and Semitic civilization, dislodged on the continent of Africa, as historically involved in the affairs of Yemen and Saudi Arabia as with those of its African neighbors, and with its languages of the northern highlands related to Hebrew and Arabic."[1] Historically, the heart of Ethiopia as a political entity rests in its central highlands where its core kingdoms were situated. The fertile highlands encouraged the development of mainly sedentary populations which enabled the establishment of relatively centralized political entities based on a hierarchical societal structure.

Contemporary Ethiopia's relations with the Arabian Peninsula, Persian Gulf, and the wider Middle East draw from the long ancient and historical connections that have bound Abyssinian kingdoms and empires to lands across the Red Sea. Over time, economic, political, and cultural contacts and influences have gone both ways, and locally powerful Ethiopian actors have exercised significant agency in these relations. Local power, therefore, is a key to understanding Ethiopian state and non-state actors' role in their external relations. Ethiopia's relations with Arabian Peninsula, the Persian Gulf, and the Middle East have been mainly pragmatic and transactional and intended to increase one's local power relative to domestic rivals. In these relations, regional (middle) powers have played, and continue to maintain, a prominent role. The discussion here centers on Ethiopia's relations with the Persian Gulf and Middle East states and seeks to highlight the importance of local agency and the external relations' dynamics in which actors controlling local material and nonmaterial resources exercise significant bargaining power.

Ancient and Historical Abyssinia

The ancient Kingdom of Aksum (*c.* 80 CE–960 CE) was a salient hierarchical polity that expanded into an empire. As a commercial power, Aksum dominated the narrow stretches of the Red Sea and at its height extended its control to the southern Arabian Peninsula. Aksum was one of the influential empires of its time and maintained relations with polities in other world regions. The decline of Aksum gave way to the founding of the much less-known Zagwe dynasty confined in the highlands. However, the Zagwe dynasty was defeated by Yekuno Amlak and replaced by the Solomonic dynasty which from the late thirteenth century onward became the core of the monarchical political system in the Ethiopian highlands. The hierarchical Solomonic Christian dynastic dominance in the Ethiopian highlands enabled vertical control of the sedentary population and concentration of resources for the establishment of centralized power. It contrasted the polities in the surrounding Muslim lowland areas based on nomadic and semi-nomadic lifestyles and horizontal social order.

While the interaction between these polities was often peaceful, the highland kingdoms not only struggled among themselves but experienced repeated confrontations with lowland sultanates. In the fourteenth century, European powers ostensibly sought an alliance with Abyssinia against Muslim polities in an attempt to choke Egyptian trade in the Red Sea, which presumably triggered Abyssinian-European relations and confrontation between Mamluk rulers in Egypt and the Ethiopian Empire.[2] In the course of the fourteenth and fifteenth centuries, several Solomonic Abyssinian rulers sought to expand their dominion in the surrounding eastern lowlands, the home of the Walashma dynasty-led sultanate of Ifat. The initial campaigns were waged by Emperor Amda Seyon I, who had been provoked by Egyptian Mamluk ruler Al-Nasir Muhammad's persecution of Coptic Christians and subsequent pillaging of Christian Abyssinian highlands by Haqq ad-Din I, Sultan of Ifat. The war ravaged both sides. Notably, through his envoy to Cairo in 1321–2, Amda Seyon threatened to divert the Blue Nile, which Egypt mainly depends on for its sweet water, and to reciprocally persecute Muslims under his dominion. Amda Seyon's threat set the precedent for Egypt's fear of Ethiopia's manipulation of the Nile water flow.[3] Depending on the source, during the first or second decade of the fifteenth century, Abyssinian emperor Dawit I or Gabra Masqal II delivered a terminal blow to the Ifat Sultanate by killing Sultan Sa'ad ad-Din II and burning Ifat's main port city of Zeila.[4]

However, toward the end of the century, part of the Walashma family founded the Sultanate of Adal based in Harar. While Harar's centrality as a trading hub connected to the Indian Ocean commerce through ports in the Gulf of Aden strengthened the new sultanate, weak rulers and internal conflicts, including those over succession, weakened the Abyssian Empire which lost many of its lowland tribute-paying territories. With Adalite ruler Ahmad Ibn Ibrahim Al-Ghazi seeking to conquer Abyssinia in a jihadist campaign, another era of confrontations ensued during which Abyssinia obtained support from the Portuguese and the Adalites from the Ottoman Empire who competed for the control of the Red Sea and the western Indian Ocean. Adal Sultanate's conquest of Abyssinia (1529–43) saw the Portuguese providing an expedition landing in Massawa as critical support for Abyssinians while Ottoman Turkish, Arab, and Yemeni troops from the Arabian Peninsula came to reinforce the Adalites. Both acquired firearms from their allies. While al-Ghazi's death in the Battle of Wayna Daga ended the

Adal invasion, the conflict ended in a stalemate treaty in 1548 and left both parties weakened. It opened further space for the southern Great Oromo Expansion to the Abyssinian highlands and the surrounding Adalite lowlands, which culminated in the sixteenth century,[5] and allowed Ottomans to wrest control of the key coastal areas and use them to exert influence on the interior Horn of Africa.

By the mid-sixteenth century, Ottomans had brought the key coastal ports of Sawakin and Massawa under their control and went on to establish the *Eyalet* (province) of Habesh. Their interest lay in establishing a presence in the coastal areas of the Red Sea and the Gulf of Aden from which passage through Bab al-Mandab could be controlled against maritime powers, especially the Portuguese who dominated the Indian Ocean. Their expeditions into the interior, largely motivated by securing their coastal possessions, securing Hajj and wresting maritime control from the Portuguese, and religious duty for conquest and to aid local Muslim states to face Abyssinia, led to the Ottoman control of most of what constitutes contemporary Eritrea.[6] But by the end of the century, they had withdrawn from most of the highlands. The Ottoman Habesh province was then placed under the administration based in Jeddah.

The Making of Modern Ethiopia

In the eighteenth century, divisions among monarchical elites in the Ethiopian highlands led to a dynastic decline during the Era of the Princes (*Zemene Mesafint*). This time, a collection of Afar sultanates centered on Aussa came to dominate the northern lowlands around Danakil, and partly today's Eritrea and Djibouti. Meanwhile, the Abyssinian highlands remained divided into several feuding regions which alone were weak to fend off encroachment of the surrounding lowland polities. With Kassa Hailegiorgis, a Christian nobleman from Dembiya, defeating internal rivals, and ascending to the throne as Tewodros II in 1855, the Era of the Princes came to an end. Tewodros II embarked on building a centralized state, in part relying on the Orthodox Church and seeking to restore the glory of the Solomonic dynasty. This led to the emergence of the modern state in Ethiopia.

As can be observed from the above discussion, the growing pains of the modern Ethiopian state have had to do with nation and state-building. Its multiethnic character and efforts by its rulers to centralize power and form a strong nation-state have been at odds until today. This has been an important factor shaping Ethiopian foreign policy which has aimed at ensuring the state's security, sovereignty, and territorial integrity. The largely governing elite exclusive and authoritarian nature of Ethiopian governments has resulted in narrowly based decision-making on foreign policy either by the emperor and his advisors or leaders and narrow executive bodies of military governments. Due to its central and strategic geographical location in the Horn of Africa, Ethiopian rulers have pursued a foreign policy in which external alliances and alignment with great and middle powers have been crucial. Since the time of Tewodros II, foreign policy instruments, especially diplomacy and the military, have been utilized to achieve the key objectives of what modern Ethiopian rulers or ruling bodies have perceived as their perception of the "nation's" interest.[7] In their foreign policy orientation, Ethiopian rulers have given empires and regional powers a prominent role.

Tewodros II's foreign policy was pursued as an extension of the domestic political reality. Arising from the perceived need to strengthen the central power and to build a Christian nation-state, Tewodros II's foreign policy considered Muslim lands encircling the Ethiopian highlands as a security threat. During his reign, Tewodros II pursued alliances with the main European powers, particularly Britain, seeking material and military assistance mainly against what was perceived as Turco-Egyptian and Ottoman encroachment. But the British government refused due to geopolitical considerations in which it preferred an alliance with the Ottoman Empire. In 1868, Britain sent an expedition to Ethiopia to rescue British delegates held as prisoners and punish the emperor which led to his suicide.[8]

Following Tewodros II's demise, Lij Kasa Mercha, who had gained control of Tigray and emerged as the strongest contender to the throne, was crowned Emperor Yohannes IV. Like his predecessor, Yohannes IV envisioned a united Christian Ethiopia which he sought to achieve by military force, but his foreign policy also included more pragmatic and less emotional and abrupt diplomacy. In military campaigns against external adversaries, he was able to draw on the support of Ethiopian lords although some occasionally rebelled against him. In the mid-1870s Yohannes IV and his generals were decisively victorious against the invading Turco-Egyptian Ottoman forces sent by Khedive Ismail to occupy Abyssinia, which set the starting point for Ottoman Egypt's diminishing role in the region[9] and the eventual tripartite Treaty of Adwa in 1884 with Britain and British controlled Egypt.[10] Although the emperor sought to secure a port for strategically important sea access, reaching the agreement appeared more important and he eventually settled for Ethiopia being granted free transit of goods through the port of Massawa. When retreating, however, the British allowed Italians to take over Massawa in 1885 which led to an increasing confrontation between Ethiopia and Italy that had colonial ambitions in the Horn of Africa. After defeating the Sudanese Mahdists[11] in the Battle of Kufit, the emperor's general Ras Alula, who had hosted the negotiations for the Adwa treaty, confronted the Italians in Dogali and Sahati. This ended Yohannes IV's diplomatic effort to reach an agreement with the Italians and reluctantly accept a two-front engagement as he was entering into an increasing confrontation with the Mahdists. As Ras Alula's action confirmed that Ethiopia was facing two enemies on its doorstep, the emperor unsuccessfully sought a pact with the Mahdists against the Italians. Yohannes IV died in 1889 in the Battle of Metemma when fighting the Mahdists.

A Competing Imperial Power

Following the death of Yohannes IV, King Menelik of Shewa, claiming direct male lineage to King Solomon and Queen of Sheba, announced himself as the new emperor. Important sections of Ethiopian nobility and the church supported

Menelik's claim and in November 1889 he was crowned as Emperor Menelik II. From the 1870s onward, Menelik engaged in an ambitious campaign to incorporate the surrounding lands into his Shewa-based kingdom and impose centralized Amhara rule over them. This effort, to an extent continuity of Tewodros II and Yohannes IV's ambitions, was exemplified by the founding of a new centrally located capital, Addis Ababa. However, Menelik II's extension of centralized rule and the perception of a top-down directed cultural Amharicization generated discontent, particularly in Tigray where it was seen to be the result of the region's decay.[12]

In his foreign policy, Menelik II used conquest, forceful incorporation of peoples and territories, and skillful diplomacy to extend the borders of the empire.[13] He ascended to power during the European colonial expansion and had to face the Italian colonial ambitions which constituted the biggest threat to Ethiopia. In May 1889, already before officially being crowned as the emperor, Menelik used his claim to the imperial throne to sign a treaty on behalf of Ethiopia with Italians in Wuchale.[14] The agreement was made in a moment of disputed imperial succession and from a position of weakness Menelik officially conceded Eritrea to Italians, justifying the decision by stating that the lands of contemporary Eritrea were not Abyssinian. This was a calculated move, however, to strengthen his claim to the emperorship, halt the Italian expansion, and demonstrate to Italians that Ethiopia was not leaderless.

Yet, the treaty did not stop the Italians who claimed that article 17 recognized Italian power over all of Ethiopia. The situation gradually escalated into an Italian invasion which culminated in Ethiopian victory in the Battle of Adwa in 1896, causing the Italian government in Rome to fall and grinding its expansion toward Ethiopia to a halt. Meanwhile, Menelik sought to use the Mahdist Sudan as a buffer against British encroachment and consolidate the gains of imperial expansion with a series of border treaties with the surrounding European powers.[15] The victory of Adwa led to European countries considering Ethiopia as a serious imperial power and establishing diplomatic relations with it. This allowed Menelik to ensure Ethiopia's internationally recognized sovereignty and statehood which carried its foreign relations for decades to come.

The centralization of power and territorial demarcation led to the consolidation of the imperial political system in and beyond the Ethiopian highlands.[16] Menelik established a semblance of modern government, including a foreign ministry that was answerable to the emperor. In consultation with his advisors, Menelik personally dictated foreign policy which was largely conducted by sending emissaries and delegations to foreign powers. In his foreign policy, Menelik was pragmatic and sought to engage major powers for what he saw as Ethiopia's benefit. Menelik also pursued a defensive foreign policy approach seeking to ensure the survival of its governing regime and aimed at securing Ethiopia's sovereignty and territorial integrity. This approach set the precedent for the patrons of the Ethiopian state to come. By any measure, during Menelik's reign, Ethiopia became the leading indigenous state in the African continent and central to understanding political reality in the Horn of Africa.

In the 1910–16 period, following Menelik II's incapacitating stroke, a council of regency ruled Ethiopia. *Lij* Iyasu, the emperor's grandson, governed shortly but was deposed and succeeded by Menelik's oldest daughter, Askala Maryam, as Empress Zewditu I.[17] The empress's power was limited, however, and she sought to rule through her regent, Ras Tafari Mekonnen. Ras Tafari picked up the initial modernization effort of Menelik which brought him into an increasing confrontation with more conservative Zewditu. After efforts to remove him failed, culminating in an aborted palace coup in 1928, Empress Zewditu was compelled to crown Ras Tafari, who commanded support among the state's security apparatus and the highland population, as king. In 1930, the empress's husband Ras Gugsa Welle, who had been inspired by the conservative nobility to rebel against Negus Tafari, was defeated and killed. In three days, Empress Zewditu suddenly died.[18] Seven months later, Negus Tafari was crowned as Emperor Haile Selassie I.

Post-Liberation Imperial Period

From his time as the regent, Ras Tafari sought to grow his international image and use diplomacy to strengthen Ethiopia's position relative to colonial powers. During this period, he traveled widely representing the country and managed to negotiate Ethiopia's membership in the League of Nations. This not only lifted Ethiopia's international profile but ensured a level of protection against European colonial aspirations while also boosting his domestic popularity and support for reforms. Ras Tafari used his international prestige, contacts, and partnerships to gain a reputation and strengthen himself in struggles against local rivals, mainly the conservative nobility in the highlands. After becoming emperor and having defeated his main domestic opponents, Haile Selassie embarked on further modernization and building an increasing bureaucratic empire to consolidate the central power. In 1931, he introduced a written constitution that included some features tending toward democratization, but in which the emperor maintained firm control over governance and foreign policy.[19]

In 1936 Italy invaded and subsequently occupied Ethiopia. Haile Selassie went into exile and appealed for support in a famous address to the League of Nations. In 1941, Ethiopia was finally liberated by Allied forces supported by Ethiopian patriots,[20] but even upon Haile Selassie's return from exile, Ethiopia remained a British protectorate until the beginning of the following year. Notably, after the 1942 Anglo-Ethiopian Agreement, which resumed Ethiopia's sovereignty, the British governed parts of its territory and controlled Ethiopia's ability to engage in foreign trade through the Addis Ababa–Djibouti railroad, a crucial import-export lifeline which had been completed in 1917. Access to the sea to engage in unrestricted trade became a long-term key concern in imperial Ethiopia's external relations and continues to play an important role in Ethiopia's foreign policy strategy today. In the 1940s, the internationally charismatic emperor sought to expel the remaining British administrators and reinvigorate the imperial modernization project.

Haile Selassie envisioned an internationally active and influential Ethiopia. After the Second World War Ethiopia became a founding member of the United Nations (UN) and Haile Selassie oriented his foreign policy toward the US to gain support for putting pressure on the British to abandon Ogaden and Haud they still occupied, and lay claims on the British controlled Eritrea and former Italian Somaliland. In his pragmatic, and often transactional, foreign policy approach, Haile Selassie offered the US a partnership in its fight against communism in the Horn of Africa. In exchange for the centrally located Ethiopia's alignment in a strategically important neighborhood, the US offered economic and technical assistance which culminated in a defense agreement in 1953.[21]

An essential objective of Haile Selassie's foreign policy was to secure Ethiopia's access to the sea and overseas trade. Although, as a maximalist objective in the post–Second World War political environment, he also aspired to annex British and Italian Somalilands, Selassie focused on the most realistic option, Eritrea, which provided the main opportunity to reach his goal. The emperor used his leverage as a US ally in the UN, also committing a contingent to serve in Korea to advance collective international security, and repeatedly argued for Ethiopia's claim on Eritrea. Washington, which saw both Ethiopia and Eritrea as strategically important in the Red Sea region, and had already been operating from the Kagnew Station near Asmara at least since 1943, was keen on securing its regional presence by supporting its ally's claim. In December 1950, UN General Assembly passed Resolution 390 A (V) which recommended that Eritrea would become an autonomous federal unit within Ethiopia.[22] Following the departure of British administrators from Eritrea, the UN General Assembly welcomed the annexation of Eritrea as an autonomous federal part of Ethiopia.[23]

By the late 1950s, Ethiopia appeared internationally influential. Addis Ababa was awarded the headquarters of the United Nations Economic Commission for Africa (UNECA) in 1958, while Haile Selassie sought to further diversify its foreign relations. In a 1959 visit to Moscow he secured a 400 million ruble loan from the Soviet Union,[24] but soon after, in December 1960, suffered a coup in his absence which was aborted with Israeli assistance. This, along with the increasing subversion from Gamal Nasser's Egypt[25] which Haile Selassie needed to counter, emphasized the benefit of maintaining a strong alignment with Israel, and especially its main ally, the US.

However, this did not sway the emperor from being internationally and regionally industrious. Ethiopia supported the UN Mission in the Congo, and in September 1961 Haile Selassie attended the founding conference of the Non-Aligned Movement. Meanwhile, Ethiopia sought to undermine the nascent and heavily nationalist Somalia. Addis Ababa purportedly played a hand in seeking to convince Somaliland leaders to reject union with Somalia, allegedly having a role in a secessionist mutiny in 1961, along with other plots to weaken Somalia in the 1960s.[26] Around the same time, political wrangling and Ethiopia's attempt to strengthen its hold on Eritrea had generated armed opposition, but in November 1962 Addis Ababa fully annexed it as an Ethiopian province.[27] In the following year, the Organization of African Unity (OAU) came into being as a culmination of the pan-African and anti-colonial movement with Haile Selassie as its first chairperson. In conjunction with this, the Ethiopian regime began pursuing a pan-Africanist foreign policy approach through which it supported anti-colonial and anti-apartheid movements. This added further to Ethiopia's regional and international weight and swayed Egypt to temporarily seize its confrontational stand toward Ethiopia.

However, as the 1960s progressed, international involvement in the Horn of Africa grew with the Soviet Union challenging the US in the Middle East and the Arab powers competing for influence in what they often perceived as mainly Muslim sub-region. In this context, the Ethiopian regime began facing increasing opposition and became entangled in proxy wars. Eritrean Liberation Front (ELF) emerged in Cairo, which initially served as the main protector of the Eritrean opposition, hoping to keep Addis Ababa's aspirations to build a dam on the vital Blue Nile at bay.[28] Egyptian fears were not unfounded because Ethiopia had invited the US Bureau of Reclamation to conduct a survey (1956–64) that indicated a suitable location for a future dam to the Blue Nile which generates much of Egypt's sweet water resources.

Meanwhile, intellectuals in Ethiopia were more and more inspired by Marxist ideas,[29] while attempts to impose a more efficient tax regime, for example in the state's outlying areas in Ogaden (1963), Bale (1963–70), and Gojam (1968–9)[30] faced fierce violent resistance. Multiple local groups particularly among the Oromo and Somali, but also others, often contested the perceived overrule of the Amhara-based government and their areas became sources of unrest that undermined the imperial regime. Waqo Gutu, the Oromo leader of the Bale Revolt, exemplifies how powerful local actors have exploited the central government's weakness and lack of legitimacy and control in remote areas of the Ethiopian state to engage with external actors, gain power locally, and challenge the government's authority. He initially armed followers with Somali support and became an important figure in the Somali-supported resistance[31] and later fought for Oromo self-determination against the Ethiopian government.

Adding to Ethiopia's troubles, the Eritrean war of liberation escalated. The Muslim-led Eritrean Liberation Front began receiving external support from socialist and Soviet-aligned Arab states, particularly Syria,[32] some of which viewed Eritrea on pan-Muslim and pan-Arab grounds as part of a wider Muslim struggle and sought to undermine Christian Ethiopia and its allies.[33] Along with the US, Israel, which had an effective security treaty with Ethiopia since 1954,[34] aided the Ethiopian regime against the Eritrean opposition[35] and also engaged Ethiopia in its support for southern Sudanese rebels.[36] Especially after the 1956 Suez Crisis, the Cold War superpower competition and middle power intervention in the Horn of Africa intensified, and Haile Selassie sought to capture material benefits from external interests in Ethiopia. These partnerships catered to the modernization project and the strengthening of the Ethiopian military.

However, Addis Ababa's objection to Egyptian president Gamal Abdel Nasser's nationalization of the Suez Canal greatly inflamed Ethiopia's relations with the Arab states. Among them, Ethiopia became to be seen increasingly as an outpost of the imperialist and Zionist bloc and integrally anti-Arab and anti-Muslim. Haile Selassie experienced difficulty to shake this image given Ethiopia's close relations with Israel and uneasy history with Arab and the neighboring Muslim territories.

In the early 1960s, Ethiopia also faced the intensification of Somali nationalism which strengthened irredentist sentiments in the Somali-inhabited eastern part of the country. Similarly to other outlying areas, the state sought to strengthen its grip on the Somali region by introducing a head tax. This was despised especially in the context of rising irredentism, and armed groupings emerged which received support from Somalia. The confrontation between Addis Ababa and Mogadishu led to Somalia's invasion of Somali-inhabited eastern Ethiopia in early 1964 and a brief conflict mainly around Togochale in which Ethiopian forces expelled the Somali military. Subsequently, the OAU passed a resolution calling for the member states "to respect the borders existing on their achievement of national independence."[37] The conflict also led to Somalia plunging deeper into the Soviet sphere by entering into a USD 30 million assistance program to strengthen its military, which accompanied an already existing USD 60 million economic aid agreement.[38] Despite the failure of the invasion, the pact with the Soviet Union resulted in an increasingly capable military, enabled a coup that brought Major General Siad Barre to power, and strengthened the nationalist and expansionist sentiments in Somalia.

Haile Selassie took the opportunity of the Arab defeat in the 1967 Arab–Israeli War to end the Eritrean insurgency by force. But the Eritrean liberation movement obtained increased Arab support,[39] channeled through Sudan and South Yemen (People's Democratic Republic of Yemen, PDRY).[40] In the context of the closure of the Suez Canal which highlighted the importance of access through the strait of Bab al-Mandab, Ethiopia's relations with Arab states remained hostile as Arab states worked against Israel's presence in the Red Sea neighborhood and the Horn of Africa. Haile Selassie, on the other hand, legitimized close relations with Israel on religious and cultural grounds although their strategic dimensions, including the provision of a Red Sea port and a base to destabilize Sudan in exchange for political and military support, were largely pragmatic and transactional.

In the early 1970s, Haile Selassie sought to elevate Ethiopia above regional entanglements. The regime continued to enjoy international prestige and benefit from an alliance with the United States, while maintaining good relations with pre-revolution Iran and Israel,[41] establishing diplomatic relations with China, and playing the role of peacemaker in the Sudanese civil war.[42] Following the October 1973 Arab–Israeli War Ethiopia and its OAU counterparts came under pressure from Arab states[43] to sever diplomatic ties with Israel. Around the same time, a serious famine hit Wollo and parts of Tigray, with the 1973 oil crisis and high petroleum prices compounding its effect. Despite Selassie's attempts to appease people, the protests ensued, and a coup by a military committee, the Derg, composed mainly of Marxist junior officers, brought the reign of the emperor to an abrupt end by symbolically removing him from the palace on September 12, 1974. A military junta, headed by Mengistu Haile Mariam, took power and imprisoned and then assassinated Emperor Haile Selassie.[44]

The Derg Regime

The new regime assuming power in Addis Ababa caused a shift in Ethiopia's domestic politics and foreign relations. The junta sought to transform Ethiopia's political and economic system along its Marxist-Leninist ideological principles. Rooted in the idea of effecting socialist transformation, the foreign policy was oriented to gaining support from ideologically similar states, principally seeking partnership with the Soviet bloc. The regime sought consolidation principally by boosting its military capability which could be used against dissent and armed opposition in various parts of the country and safeguard Ethiopia's sovereignty and territorial integrity against external threats. However, poor economic conditions and political instability at home made the regime dependent on external economic and military support.

Despite Moscow's initial reluctance toward the new Ethiopian regime,[45] Mengistu was able to gain Russian favor by convincing the Soviets of its communist credentials. This intensified the great power competition in the Horn of Africa and made it the primary site of the rivalry in Africa for more than a decade. Gaining Soviet support enabled Mengistu to emerge as the undisputed leader of the junta, particularly after the execution of his most potent competitors Sisal Habte, Tafari Benti, and Atnafu Abate, while two major arms deals, USD 100 million in 1976 and USD 385 million in 1977 respectively, sealed Ethiopia's Soviet alignment.[46]

Soon after coming to power, the Derg military junta launched a campaign called Red Terror (1975–7) aimed at consolidating its rule by doing away with opponents. This, however, generated increasing internal opposition, notably in Tigray, where the Tigray People's Liberation Front (TPLF) was formed, gaining initial support from the Eritrean People's Liberation Front (EPLF), an ELF splinter group, which began to dominate the Eritrean liberation struggle.[47] The TPLF, in its 1976 manifesto, claimed unique distinctiveness from the rest of Ethiopia and vowed to build a republic of greater Tigray extending to the Red Sea and interior Ethiopia. This manifesto made other Ethiopian and Eritrean stakeholders wary of the organization's ultimate objectives and caused concern for the EPLF's Christian highland leadership that sought to differentiate its version of Eritrean identity from that of the neighboring Tigray, and among those ethnic Amhara who saw themselves as the essence of what constitutes Ethiopia. The TPLF gained external assistance from Sudan and other states which were interested in weakening the Derg regime. The armed opposition counted on the TPLF which grew in strength, and on the EPLF which used its ideological credentials to draw external assistance from and through South Yemen and utilized regional and international linkages for material and political support notably from Sudan and Arab states.

The foreign policy of the Derg regime came to be motivated principally by the pursuit of national security, regime survival, and societal change.[48] Mengistu Haile Mariam, the leading figure of the regime, saw most threats to Ethiopia as external and perpetrated by its historical and contemporary enemies while seeking to position Ethiopia as the Marxist-Leninist ideological leader in the continent by supporting anti-colonial and anti-apartheid struggles. He pursued these interconnected foreign policy goals by attempting to ensure the territorial integrity of the state faced with the rising tide of armed opposition in Eritrea and northern highlands, and irredentist aspirations in the Somali region. These efforts were in vain in part due to the highland dominant EPLF leadership being strongly linked to highland Ethiopia, and the Somali-inhabited eastern Ethiopia having a strong identity connection with Djibouti and Somalia through kinship, pastoral lifestyle, and livestock-based economy. National security was also to be ensured by advancing ethnic and cultural unity through Amharicization, which ethno-nationalist opposition forces, headed by the TPLF, interpreted as forced homogenization.[49] For this, the regime needed external allies willing to help secure Ethiopia's sovereignty and territorial integrity and tolerate the Derg's coercive domestic policies, including land confiscation and nationalization, and distancing the state from the Orthodox Church, the bulwark of the previous empire. The second related and equally important element of the Derg foreign policy was to ensure the survival of the regime by using foreign policy to defend and strengthen it. For this, the regime needed to have external legitimacy in the Cold War international system and adequate external support from its partners to fend off internal challenges. The third foreign policy element was the ideologically driven social transformation through the implementation of a planned economic system of production according to Marxist-Leninist ideals. This tied Ethiopia to the Soviet Bloc, which ensured the support of its socialist transformation.

Since the formation of the Derg, Ethiopia's foreign and domestic policies were determined by the leading institution of the Ethiopian worker's party, the Politburo. Headed by Mengistu, the Politburo consisted of men selected due to their loyalty which meant that policy-making power concentrated on the leading figure of the regime. Mengistu's successful neutralization of rivals and promotion of his personality cult were in part responsible for his control of the Derg and the Politburo and for allowing him single-handedly to decide on policy matters. His conviction to eliminate domestic opposition forces and impose unity through centralization and highly hierarchical state power resembles that of imperial times. In the case of foreign policy, the concentration of power on one individual, and the lack of institutionalization of decision-making, obscured and undermined its systematic formulation and implementation. Under orders from Mengistu, various actors in the state administration engaged in foreign relations, but his personal despise of Somalia and Eritrean opposition, as well as the conviction that Ethiopia under his rule would be a leading Marxist state driving the future of the continent, came to define Ethiopian foreign policy.[50]

The Derg's Middle East relations were initially shaped by the aftermath of the 1973 Arab–Israeli War. Ethiopia took leadership to denounce the Apartheid regime in South Africa and related it to Israel's treatment of the Palestinians. However, it simultaneously maintained covert ties with Israel throughout most of the 1980s. Ethiopian regime condemned Arab states aligned with the West, or those supporting the Eritrean cause for independence irrespective of their ideological inclinations or ties with the Soviet Bloc. Despite Mengistu's efforts to make headway, the Derg had generally uneasy or outright cold relations with Arab states and its Arab-aligned neighbors, which was largely driven by the collaboration between the two but also not disconnected from the legacy of mistrust emanating from the history of confrontation between the Ethiopian highland kingdoms and the sultanates of the surrounding Muslim lowlands. Ethiopia's foreign policy toward Arab and Muslim states continued to be marred by suspicion, as the Derg supported dissident groups to undermine its most powerful neighbors Somalia and Sudan, faced Egypt for its influence in the latter and on the issue of the Nile River, and confronted Arab states supporting the Eritrean struggle. To counter the perceived threats, Mengistu sought to maintain strong alignment with the Soviet Union which had leverage over several Arab states. He also aspired to lead an "African" bloc critical of Arab states but only achieved limited success.

Meanwhile, Ethiopia faced Somalia on the issue of its Somali-inhabited Ogaden. In July 1977, in support of irredentist Ethiopian Somali leaders and inspired by the idea of uniting Somali people under "Greater Somalia" (*Soomaaliweyn*), the government of Somalia launched a full-scale invasion of Ogaden. Irredentist Western Somali Liberation Front (WSLF) operating in Ogaden, which Mogadishu supported, had laid the groundwork for the invasion by using the uncertainty of the political transition in Ethiopia to gain control over most of the territory.

After initial hesitation, the Somali invasion convinced Moscow to accept the Derg as part of the Soviet Bloc and rescue Ethiopia. It let go of its earlier alliance with Somalia, which in turn sought to improve its ties with the US. Saudi Arabia, a staunch US ally and a regional power, also positioned itself against Marxist Ethiopia and sought to undermine its territorial integrity by increasing its support to Sabbe's "Arabist" faction of the Eritrean liberation movement and stir Mogadishu's aspirations in the Somali-inhabited Ogaden by seeking to bolster nationalist, Islamic, and anti-Ethiopian sentiments.[51] Saudi efforts, largely through their leverage among Ogadeni Somali leaders, contributed to the nationalist current which consumed the Barre government and led to Somalia's invasion of Ethiopia.

During the brief but destructive Ogaden War (1977–8), Cuba, the Soviet Union, and the People's Democratic Republic of Yemen (PDRY or South Yemen) came decisively to Ethiopia's aid. This helped the Derg to narrowly escape defeat when Soviet military material and advisors, and a significant Cuban contingent, arrived. In response, Somali president Siad Barre, realizing that Somalia was going to lose the war, reoriented Somalia's foreign policy toward the US but was at the time unable to convince Washington to commit to supporting Somalia[52] despite receiving assistance from the Western-aligned Arab states.[53] The external support from the Soviet Bloc turned the course of the war and led to Ethiopian victory. By March 1978, the last Somali military units had abandoned Ogaden which effectively ended the war, although a low-scale WSLF insurgency in eastern Ethiopia lingered on well into the 1980s when it was replaced by the Ogaden National Liberation Front (ONLF).

Ethiopia's military victory in Ogaden put it in a powerful position relative to its neighbors. The defeat marked an end to any feasible Somali irredentist nationalist project and led to state weakness that subjected it to increasing Ethiopian influence in the coming decades. After the war, Ethiopia's foreign policy came to be characterized by the attempt to keep Somalia, which sought to rebuild its military with US support, from posing a threat to its stability and dominance in the Horn of Africa while also seeking to destabilize Sudan by supporting insurgents, especially in the southern part of the country. At the same time, in the context of Arab assistance for the Eritrean Muslim factions and Somalia, Mengistu had a significant concern over a possible Arab encroachment in Djibouti which could deprive Ethiopia of sea access through the Addis Ababa-Djibouti railway.

Having secured its territorial integrity in the east and significant Soviet support, the Mengistu government shifted from its more defensive foreign policy outlook to a more interventionist one. With Soviet inspiration and support, Ethiopia assumed a leading role in a loose network of Marxist African states but faced strengthening Eritrean armed opposition. Although Iraq and Syria, both socialist regimes, continued to support the Eritrean insurgents, Ethiopia, publicly denouncing Israel, was able to cement a partnership with Libya and PDRY in August 1981 which facilitated resources to the Somali clan-based armed opposition that it hosted.[54] The junta also reinvigorated its assistance to rebels in southern Sudan[55] in part to deter Khartoum from supporting liberation groups in its territory in addition to its endorsement of opposition formations in Somalia. The strategy toward the latter, in which Ethiopia supported and encouraged cooperation among several armed movements, aimed at maintaining Somalia from becoming a resurgent threat. The strategy was successful to the extent that allowed the Ethiopian military to move resources toward addressing its mounting internal threats and engage the Eritrean opposition with increased force to which the Soviet Union and its allies contributed. Eventually, with Siad Barre's fall becoming imminent, the Derg opted to maintain the support of Somali opposition groups which it could manipulate to maintain Ethiopian influence over Somalia.[56]

Meanwhile, the conflict in Eritrea raged on and inspired other regional liberation movements in and beyond Ethiopia. After the victory in Ogaden had neutralized Somalia as a military threat, Ethiopian leadership turned its attention toward internal dissident movements. In 1978, with Soviet support, including billions of dollars of military assistance, the army engaged in a massive campaign against the Eritrean and Tigrayan opposition forces. An attempt was made to curtail their external support through pacts with other states, but agreements with Sudan, the PDRY, and Libya, had limited impact on the Derg's military fortunes.

The war was taking its toll on the Ethiopian military and although the Derg welcomed Soviet military installations, training, and material, it needed more. The 1981 tripartite Treaty of Aden with Libya and PDRY to form a common front against US-aligned Egypt, Saudi Arabia, Somalia, and Sudan was short-lived. When Libyan leader Muammar Gaddafi, more convinced by Somalia's African Muslim credentials than the socialist ideology, began endorsing Barre's government against Ethiopian interference, the alliance failed. In these circumstances, after having briefly expelled Israelis in 1978, the Derg leadership felt obliged to count on secret Israeli military support, which became increasingly important when the Soviet assistance waned. Israel's commitment to Ethiopia fed from fending off

Arab influence in the Red Sea and to a much lesser extent from the perceived connection between Judaic religions.

Moreover, the intensification of the war in Eritrea, and its enormous humanitarian consequences especially in terms of refugees which especially affected Sudan led to numerous expressions of Arab solidarity toward the Eritrean cause. Saudi Arabia was actively providing covert support for the Eritrean liberation forces,[57] especially ELF and Osman Saleh Sabbe's right-wing breakaway group ELF-Popular Liberation Front, and funded US arms purchases for Somalia and Sudan to isolate Ethiopia and to curb Israel's influence. Even after left-wing EPLF became the dominant force in the Eritrean struggle in the 1980s, Riyadh reluctantly followed Washington's preference and continued supporting mainly splinter groups of the Muslim faction of Eritrean insurgents and the Somalian administration as a counterweight to the Mengistu regime.

In 1985, the Derg adjusted its bilateral relations due to the fall of Jaafar Nimeiri's regime (1969–85) in an army coup in neighboring Sudan. Egypt, concerned about the developments in Sudan, among which was Iran gaining an increasing foothold in the country, sought to improve ties with Ethiopia, while Ethiopia and Somalia agreed to stop assisting each other's opposition movements. In its Middle East relations, Ethiopia, however, continued to side with post-revolution Iran. In June 1989, in Sudan, a brief democratic interlude was interrupted by another military coup. Inspired by political Islam, and connected to hardliners favoring a military solution to the "southern problem" (insurgency), sections of the military-affiliated with the Islamist National Islamic Front took power. This led to the cooling of the Mengistu regime's relations with Sudan, which was consequently seen as propagating political Islam, not isolated from Salafist links to Saudi Arabia, and promoting political destabilization through violence among Ethiopian Muslims.[58] This became problematic for the incoming TPLF leadership due to the persisting self-perception of central Ethiopia constituting a Christian bastion surrounded by antagonistic Muslim populations.

Within Ethiopia, the TPLF gradually became the strongest opposition faction. From the early 1980s, its humanitarian arm Relief Society of Tigray, forming part of the Emergency Relief Desk consortium based in Khartoum supported by Scandinavian church organizations, of which the EPLF's Eritrean Relief Association formed part as well, began channeling humanitarian assistance to alleviate the effects of an ensuing famine that the Ethiopian government sought to use to subdue the TPLF. In 1989, together with the EPLF, it formed an opposition umbrella, the Ethiopian People's Revolutionary Democratic Front (EPRDF). While armed groups in Ethiopia continued receiving external support, they started making gains when the outside support of socialist states to the Derg regime began to wane. Following the failure of the economic reforms to produce a successful centrally planned economy, and increasing difficulties related to war and famine, the government made constitutional changes in 1987 by formally moving the country under civilian administration as the People's Democratic Republic. This, however, did not reduce the mounting rebel military pressure and the importance of external support which the administration heavily depended on.

Meanwhile, Mengistu continued to side firmly with the Soviet Union. Ethiopia was highly dependent on its Warsaw Pact partners. When investment for economic development was not forthcoming the situation became increasingly dire. Ethiopia also relied almost exclusively on military support from the Soviet Union and when training and arms flow began to dry out, it faced increasing difficulties keeping armed opposition at bay. This, however, along with a late attempt to denounce communism and open up the economy was not enough to remedy the decline of Soviet support on which the Ethiopian regime had so heavily relied.[59] By May 1991, the central government could no longer resist the advance of the TPLF-led EPRDF rebels and collapsed. The ideological commitment and loyalty of the Derg to the Soviet Union and its patronage had not been sufficient to meet the structural requirements for regime survival at the end of the Cold War.[60]

The TPLF Era

The EPRDF victory marked the beginning of a new era of authoritarian rule in Ethiopia. From the outset, the TPLF embarked on a mission to gain control and consolidate its power over the state apparatus. Having been dependent on its Eritrean allies, and unwilling to risk a war against the EPLF which would jeopardize its position, the TPLF reluctantly agreed to Eritrea's independence. Under the 1994 constitution, the TPLF-led government reorganized the country politically into a federal system, using ethnolinguistic criteria to justify territorial divisions to deviate from the various previous governments' commitment to the centralized state. This system was designed to reflect the realities at the end of the civil war and provide a framework for inter-ethnic cooperation through strong provisions of self-determination for ethnically defined federal regions.[61] However, this converted ethno-nationalist forces, drawing from the ethnically organized rebel moments, into political formations which became central players in the federal political system. Along with the constitutional right to secede, the allocation of ethnic "homelands" to the biggest identity groups resulted in persistent friction between the centralizing tendency of the TPLF-led federal government and the ethnically defined regional administrations. This friction strengthened due to the TPLF's consolidation efforts by using the EPRDF and its satellite parties, which conflicted with the idea of devolution through ethnic federalism and provoked claims for self-determination through wider autonomy, greater control of resources and equality between federal regions, or in some cases through outright calls for secession.[62] This tension between centralism and regional self-determination led to the imposition of central control and simultaneous marginalization of certain ethnic identity groups and epitomized the inherent weakness of the TPLF-EPRDF government.

Although experimentation with the socialist planned economic system ended during the latter stages of the Mengistu rule, the TPLF leadership was well aware of the importance of maintaining a level of control over the economy to ensure the economic power of its political elite. It also vouched for sustained economic growth and poverty reduction as a strategy for state consolidation and political stability. Inspired by China and other Asian examples, the government headed by the TPLF leader and Prime Minister Meles Zenawi put in place a type of economic system based on the idea of the developmental state in which the government was heavily involved in regulating the markets and guiding and stimulating industrialization. In this system, large state-related, or parastatal, enterprises and conglomerates dominated the country's economic organization. This led to the state, namely, the EPRDF and the prominent TPLF individuals, controlling the economy, which compromised the dynamism of the private sector by undermining its productive capacity.[63] From the beginning of the EPRDF rule, the Ethiopian economy returned to the path of sustained growth and reached double-digit numbers in its leading sectors around the mid-2000s.[64] This was despite the Tigrayan-led government and its economic system's failure to gain overwhelming political support in several federal regions, including in the major Oromo and Amhara federal states.

In December 1994, elected constitutional representatives adopted a new constitution for the Federal Democratic Republic of Ethiopia. The constitution became the fundamental tool to guide the EPRDF government's foreign policy. In Article 86, the constitution included six principles for Ethiopia's foreign relations among which the first, "protection of national interests and respect for the sovereignty of the country," was considered paramount.[65] Some of the other principles, such as "noninterference in the internal affairs of other states," were observed less rigorously or outright contradicted whenever they were seen to undermine the efforts to achieve the first principle. Building on the principles outlined in the constitution, in 2002 the EPRDF released the Foreign Affairs and National Security Policy and Strategy.

In its external relations, Ethiopia under TPLF sought to present itself as a security guarantor in the Horn of Africa. Zenawi was motivated by the interest to build hegemonic peace through which Ethiopia could ensure sea access after the independence of Eritrea in 1993. In the regional context of Ethiopia's largest neighboring states, Somalia and Sudan, embroiled in civil war made Ethiopia seem like an island of stability in the sub-region despite its own internal problems. From the early 1990s onward the Ethiopian regime portrayed itself as a bulwark against the expansion of political Islam propagated mainly by the Sudanese regime and linkages to conservative, Salafist, elements emanating from Saudi Arabia. It aligned with the US and pursued a security and stability-based regional strategy and engaged in interventionism and peacekeeping in the neighboring countries that helped to emphasize its dominant position in the Horn of Africa.

Ethiopia's foreign policy came to heavily reflect interests determined by the TPLF-EPRDF leadership which were guided by the domestic political dynamics and economic reality. Addressing threats to the governing regime, perceived to emerge mainly from internal conflicts, political instability, and poverty, became paramount in orienting the foreign policy strategy. These were to be addressed principally through a commitment to economic development and promises for democratization which were seen to bring economic growth and political stability. Ethiopia was to project its power in the region and fend off threats from the neighboring countries by taking an active role and strengthening regional organizations, particularly in the sub-regional organization IGAD in which it could seek a dominant role. This approach was motivated by the attempt to push for regional political stability and was accompanied by concrete unilateral military activity and bilateral diplomatic efforts.[66]

During the TPLF-EPRDF, Ethiopia's Foreign policy was driven mainly by Prime Minister Zenawi. Instability within the coalition government, and the resultant need to strengthen TPLF leadership over other factions, led to Zenawi dominating and monopolizing foreign policy decision-making.[67] Meanwhile, the Ministry of Foreign Affairs engaged in the everyday operation of the diplomatic service and came to emphasize results-based economic diplomacy as a central feature in diplomatic careers. Ethiopian representatives converted into instruments of "salesman diplomacy," a policy to obtain mainly financial and economic resources from abroad for regime consolidation in exchange for strategic and material assets.

As a result, for the TPLF-EPRDF regime, and the Abiy Ahmed administration which came to power in April 2018, the strategy of economic statecraft has been salient. The use of economic diplomacy as foreign policy practice is seen as crucial for regime survival and consolidation to promote the state leadership's interests. Forming part of the overall strategy, economic diplomacy has therefore formed a key technique to operationalize foreign policy and to reach the set objectives. Due to the strong economic focus in its foreign policy, Ethiopian leadership has employed economic instruments, such as contracts, land, natural resources, labor, economic presence, and political guarantees in exchange for financial and material benefits, in its engagement with foreign powers. This pragmatic and transactional approach has led to carefully thought but frequently shifting balancing between alignments with external powers. In practice, it has consisted of the exchange of local strategic assets for financial and other material resources and political, diplomatic, and military support. These transactional relations have been particularly salient in Ethiopia's relations with its Middle East partners, especially the leading Gulf States.

Early on, a defining moment for the TPLF-EPRDF's regional relations came with the souring of relations with the EPLF after Eritrean independence. Seeking partnership with the US, the TPLF decided to adhere to Washington's demand to hold an election. Eritrea did not follow the same path and the EPLF converted into the People's Front for Democracy and Justice (PFDJ) one-party government. With signs of increasing Ethiopian economic domination, the tension between the two countries heightened with Eritrea introducing its currency, *nakfa*, to replace the Ethiopian *birr* and closing the vital port in Assab to Ethiopia. Due to a perceived border encroachment, Eritrean leadership sent the military to invade the Ethiopian-held border town of Badme, which it considered legally belong to Eritrea. This led to the Ethiopian military response and the Eritrean–Ethiopian War (1998–2000), the most significant interstate conflict in the Horn of Africa since the Cold War. Although Ethiopia was able to invade part of Eritrea, it suffered a strategic defeat by not managing to regain access to Eritrea's Red Sea ports. This heightened Ethiopia's dependence on Djibouti and led up to 90 percent of its imports and exports being channeled through the country. Also, Ethiopia's regional foreign policy came to focus more on confrontation with Eritrea which sought to systematically undermine Ethiopia's TPLF-led regime and dominance in the Horn of Africa.

Before the Eritrean–Ethiopian War, a salient feature of TPLF-EPRDF's regional relations included a confrontational approach toward Sudan. Following the assassination attempt of Egyptian president Hosni Mubarak during the OAU summit in Addis Ababa in 1995, Ethiopia joined, along with Eritrea and Uganda, the US Front Line States strategy, aimed at pressuring the Islamist regime in Khartoum. It invaded al-Fashaga, Sudanese territory where Ethiopian farmers have engaged in agriculture for decades, and supported the US-aligned Sudan People's Liberation Movement/Army rebels to make territorial gains in southern Sudan.

In 1998, faced with the confrontation with Eritrea, Ethiopia finally improved relations with Sudan. The relations strengthened further after Omar al-Bashir removed Islamist ideologue Hassan al-Turabi from de facto state leadership and moved to consolidate his position. Since then, and especially after the independence of South Sudan in 2011, Ethiopia's relations with Sudan have been generally good until very recently. The new deterioration of relations came due to Sudan, and especially Egypt, being concerned about the effects of the newly built Ethiopia's Grand Ethiopian Renaissance Dam (GERD) on water availability on the Nile and more recently a land ownership dispute in al-Fashaga, as well as concerns about destabilizing cross-border effects of the Tigray conflict. While Egypt, which maintains leverage on Sudan largely through connections in the military, has been seen as influencing Khartoum's position on the Nile waters, it and the arrival of Tigrayan refugees, military, and fleeing combatants heightened tensions at the border. In the agriculturally rich al-Fashaga region, killings and clashes occurred even after the Sudanese military retook it during the early months of 2021 following Saudi Arabia's unsuccessful offer to mediate.

The Eritrean–Ethiopian War (1998–2000) marked the culmination of effective Eritrean independence and its departure from the shadow of Ethiopia's economic influence. Despite the loss of access to the Red Sea through Eritrea, the economic focus of Ethiopian foreign policy and focus on Djibouti as the import-export channel helped to sustain a high level of economic growth. Ethiopia secured financial resources to combat the chronic shortage of foreign currency and sought financial balance to maintain growth. Partnerships with Middle East actors in terms of investment, aid, and other cash flow became particularly important for the Ethiopian government to ensure a manageable financial position despite simultaneous and sustained apprehension about the intentions of Arab powers in Ethiopia and the Horn. During the 2010s, trade and investment gradually increased to surpass aid and an emerging middle class stimulated the expansion of the consumer market.[68]

The TPLF-EPRDF orchestrated developmental state policy in Ethiopia relied on state-affiliated conglomerates and the construction of strategic large-scale infrastructure to stimulate economic growth. For example, the upgraded railway connection between Addis Ababa and the Port of Djibouti, operational since 2016, and the building of the Berbera Corridor, connecting Addis Ababa with the Gulf of Aden, ensure sea access and stimulate trade. Similarly, the Lamu Port-Southern Sudan-Ethiopia Transport Corridor (LAPSSET) is envisioned to provide Ethiopia with another viable avenue to the sea. The GERD, funded in part by voluntary contribution is not only seen as a power generation facility but a source of national pride, the success of which is essential for the government. Its symbolic significance is important to show that the Ethiopian government can light up the country and supply hydropower to the neighboring states. It is therefore perceived as a symbol of Ethiopia's regional power, including toward Egypt, and, along with the transport corridors, a source of further integration in the Horn of Africa.

Under Meles Zenawi's premiership (1995–2012), the Ethiopian economy and population grew at a high rate. Although the government was successful in implementing the ideology of the developmental state to make impressive gains in economic development and sustain high levels of growth, the benefits of an improved standard of living were mainly felt in urban areas where a middle class emerged. Meanwhile, much of the gains failed to reach people in the regional peripheries. Impression of the leading figures of the ruling party, in control of the security apparatus and the economy, monopolizing political and economic power, and marginalizing others generated grievances that articulated largely in politics along ethnic lines.

This not only fed political instability at home but led to tens of thousands of Ethiopians migrating abroad. The Middle East and especially the oil-rich Gulf States became a desired destination for Ethiopian migrants. Females emigrating for domestic work became a key group moving to the Middle East where males often work in construction.[69] Many have been subjected to ill-treatment based on local perceptions and attitudes of superiority toward the "African."[70] In the Arabian Peninsula, Saudi Arabia has been the main destination for Ethiopians, who are currently estimated at 750,000, but many remain in an irregular and desperate situation and seek to return home.[71] Many migrants have transited through Yemen, where amid civil war approximately 5,000 Ethiopians are stuck.[72] Migrant remittances, however, have come to constitute an important source of income for Ethiopian families and have contributed to economic activities, lifting some out of poverty. The governments of Ethiopia and Saudi Arabia have sought to address the issue of repatriation. In 2013–14 alone, more than 160,000 Ethiopians were repatriated,[73] and by early 2019 approximately 230,000 Ethiopians had returned although migratory pressure has not seized. Migrants were detained and expelled again during the Covid-19 pandemic, and reportedly in early 2021 Ethiopia and Saudi Arabia reached an agreement for the repatriation of thousands of migrants.[74] These dynamics have the potential to strain Ethiopian-Saudi relations and undermine Saudi financial assistance and investments and diaspora remittances to Ethiopia.

In recent years, the Ethiopian government has removed barriers to diaspora remittances. In 2018 it set up a Diaspora Agency managed under the Ministry of Foreign Affairs to allow the diaspora to contribute to the economic development of the country. A system of diaspora accounts, which is in use in various African countries, has been a success and generated a high level of deposits of much-needed foreign currency. In the 2021/2022 fiscal year Ethiopia targeted USD 4 billion in remittances and at nine months the amount already stood at USD 3.8 billion.[75]

As with other states in the wider region, the TPLF-EPRDF government's early relations with Middle Eastern countries, particularly the Gulf States, were from the outset dominated by security and economic concerns. Conservative and radical religious influences, seen to emanate from the Arabian Peninsula and penetrate the Horn of Africa, as well as those propagated in Sudan, were considered a threat to highland Christian-led Ethiopia with a significant Muslim population. For example, charities and private foundations from Persian Gulf countries beyond government control channeling learning opportunities often linked to conservative doctrines and interpretations of Islam, or Sudan's support of Islamist opposition groups were not only seen to threaten the political and societal status quo but also the very ethos of the perception of Ethiopian national identity as highland Christian Orthodox-driven. This view emanated from persisting attitudes related to Ethiopian nationalism connected to the Orthodox Church and confrontations with the surrounding Muslim lowland polities.[76]

From 2001 onward, with the US pursuit of the War on Terror, the Ethiopian-American security partnership gained further strength through military and intelligence cooperation. Addis Ababa's military intervention in Somalia to bring down the Islamic Courts Union (ICU) in 2006–07, in which the US collaborated, was executed mainly due to Ethiopian leadership's insistence based on a self-generated scenario in which Somalia posed an existential threat to the Ethiopian state.[77] Although supporting the Somali Transitional Federal Government to fight back ICU's Islamic influence and Eritrean involvement in Somalia, which were seen to undermine Ethiopia, were central concerns behind the intervention, maintaining the long-established practice of destabilizing and weakening Somalia was also a factor.

However, although the ICU was successfully disbanded in December 2006, its radical splinter factions lived on and came to form persisting Islamist resistance undermining state-building in Somalia and affecting stability in eastern Ethiopia. In Somalia, Eritrea sought Qatari assistance to minimize Ethiopia's dominance in the sub-region, which led to Addis Ababa momentarily sever its ties with Doha. Addis Ababa's direct military involvement in Somalia became a persistent feature of its external relations in the Horn.

Meanwhile, the TPLF-EPRDF regime's relations with the Middle East powers came to be characterized increasingly by economic and security interconnections. While Qatar sought to profile itself as a mediator and peacemaker in the Horn, Saudi Arabia, especially after President al-Bashir prevailed in the leadership struggle in Sudan, intensified engagement with Khartoum partly in an attempt to counterbalance Iran's influence in the sub-region. Egypt and the UAE joined Saudi Arabia in this effort, especially after the Arab Spring and Riyadh and Abu Dhabi-supported return of the military at the helm of power in Cairo. Addis Ababa's alignment with the US in security affairs also facilitated Ethiopia's relations with

Saudi Arabia. However, a far more influential element in the relations between the two regimes was Saudi interest in investing in Ethiopia. Sheikh Mohammed Hussein Ali al-Amoudi drove and coordinated Saudi investment in Ethiopia. Half Ethiopian, with a Yemeni Hadhrami father and Ethiopian mother, al-Amoudi rose to prominence in Saudi Arabia due to his connections with the ruling family and the state's patronage of his business ventures. He has engaged through the Mohammed International Development Research and Organization Companies (MIDROC) Ethiopia Investment Group and Saudi Star Agricultural Development Plc. comprising ventures in various sectors of the economy. Inspired by Riyadh's concern to secure food production abroad that would be under Saudi control, he spearheaded large-scale land acquisitions.[78] In late 2021, it was announced that Ethio Agri-CEFT, part of the MIDROC group, will spend USD 1 billion to establish an edible oil processing complex for both domestic and foreign markets which is expected to significantly cut the USD 1 billion currently spent on edible oil imports[79] and help Ethiopia gain increasing revenue by exporting oil rather than raw oil seeds.

As well as in agriculture, al-Amoudi has been the channel for wide investment in the banking, real estate, construction materials, and hospitality sectors in Ethiopia.[80] He made use of close links developed with the TPLF-EPRDF government leadership, including Prime Minister Zenawi, and has sought to build close relations with the Abiy Ahmed administration since 2018. These relations have allowed al-Amoudi to buy various state-owned companies designated for privatization and provided him and the Saudi government with economic and political influence during and after the TPLF-EPRDF regime.[81] Al-Amoudi's prominent role in Ethiopia is exemplified in that in 2011, following Prime Minister Zenawi's request, he pledged approximately USD 88 million in support for the Grand Ethiopian Renaissance Dam which Egypt, a significant Saudi ally, has opposed.[82] During Zenawi's last visit to Egypt around the same time, the issue was conspicuously not discussed. After al-Amoudi was imprisoned in Saudi Arabia on corruption charges in 2017 in which Egypt was suspected to play a hand, the new Ethiopian prime minister Abiy Ahmed Ali, who has worked with Saudi Arabia and the UAE closely, sought his release. Al-Amoudi was finally released in 2019 and although a number of his investments and businesses in Ethiopia have been put under pressure, al-Amoudi and his enterprises have continued to be major economic players in Ethiopia.

As a result, al-Amoudi and his companies can be considered the most important example of the Persian Gulf economic statecraft in Ethiopia. However, although their connection with the patrons of the Ethiopian state paved the way for the unprecedented rapprochement between Addis Ababa and Asmara in 2018, for example, the Saudi influence on Ethiopia's foreign policy, sought through mainly financial and economic means, has been limited by the local power of the Ethiopian governing elite. Political decisions on Ethiopian foreign policy are made locally and ultimately according to the interests of the prime minister, often in consultation with selected members of the governing elite. Maintaining foreign partnerships simultaneously with various, including competing and contradicting external powers, Ethiopian leadership seeks to precisely limit dependence on a single foreign partner and avoid repeating the mistakes made during the Cold War. This has moderated Saudi influence despite its extensive economic and charitable engagement.

Ethiopia's relations with the Persian Gulf and Middle Eastern powers have mainly been driven by the government's chronic need for foreign currency. To increase its reserves, it has frequently offered state-guaranteed investment opportunities in various sectors. Since 2018 the economic opening and privatization have accelerated. Notably, one significant investment was the UAE's approximately USD 3 billion commitment to establish a sugar plantation in the country's Somali region in 2017 as part of a drive to reduce Ethiopia's sugar imports. Development aid from Middle Eastern states has played a much smaller role because assistance is often channeled through "Arab" or "Islamic" agencies for which largely Christian Ethiopia has not featured as an attractive destination state. In its 2002 Foreign Affairs and National Security Policy and Strategy, the EPRDF government emphasized that "Our diplomacy should be, in the main, that of economic diplomacy" and recognized that "the impact of the Middle East on Ethiopia is more prominent than that of the African countries . . . [and] . . . Directly or indirectly . . . influences our economic development in a substantial way."[83] The document went ahead to state that Ethiopia's policy toward the Middle East should seek to ensure economic development and, somewhat paradoxically, the building of a democratic political system. This way the government recognized that Ethiopia should seek to maximize the developmental benefits of its Middle East relations. While the financial power of the petroleum-rich states and their potential for investment and economic development in Ethiopia has been officially recognized, such states' prospects for serving as markets for Ethiopian agricultural exports have also been highlighted. Although important, Ethiopian labor migration to the Gulf States has received much less attention until recently. Notably, the 2002 policy and strategy document recognized the connection between the two regions in terms of peace and stability, including the fear of religious extremism emanating from the Arabian Peninsula.[84]

In Ethiopia's foreign affairs, the issue of the Nile and relations with Egypt have occupied a prominent role. At different times, Haile Selassie and Mengistu Hailemariam both sought a solution to Egypt's fears of Ethiopia's aspiration to utilize Blue Nile waters, and in the 1970s when such plans were brought to a halt due to political instability and war. The right to use the Nile waters, which Egypt (together with Sudan) has monopolized through colonial treaties, has become increasingly disputed among the upstream states. The total downstream flow of the river depends 80–90 percent on water originating from Ethiopia, while, with the construction of the GERD, the Ethiopian government has grown more assertive about using its Nile water resources to drive economic development in the largely agrarian and electricity poor country.[85] Egypt has sought to deter Ethiopia from plans to extensively use the Nile waters by securitizing the issue, presenting it as an existential threat, referring to the possible use of military force, seeking to bar external funding destined for Ethiopia's water resources development, and attempting to rally Ethiopia's opposition forces and neighbors behind its cause. These efforts have been aimed at stopping the GERD and other water projects by putting pressure on the Ethiopian administration.

The 2002 strategy and policy guidance document also points to the positive and long-standing relations with Yemen, which historically emanate from the time of the Aksum Empire and beyond, and mentions the historical relationship with Saudi Arabia. It raises Egypt's influence on the Arab states, Islamic extremism, and the Arab–Israel confrontation as key issues clouding Ethiopia's Middle East relations. Israel's role is seen as productive, and relations with Tel Aviv (currently Jerusalem) are encouraged by increasing economic and security cooperation and supporting a just solution to the issue of Palestine. In 2002 both Ankara and Tehran were also mentioned as economic partners with important but unexploited potential.[86]

The main message in the last two decades from the foreign affairs and national security strategy on Ethiopia's relations with the Persian Gulf and the wider Middle East has been the intensification of relations. It has mainly engaged in economic diplomacy, centered on attracting finance and investment for development and markets for Ethiopian goods. However, the patrons of the Ethiopian state have also recognized the need to gain an improved understanding of the realities in the Arabian Peninsula and the wider Middle East, especially related to possible national security threats such as religious extremism. The diplomatic strategy, while focusing on economic aspects, also highlights the importance of improving the image of the country among Middle Eastern states, including by clarifying Ethiopian position on the Nile and explaining its domestic inter-religious reality, while emphasizing Ethiopia's potential contribution to ensuring peace and stability in the Arabian Peninsula.[87]

Among significant foreign policy issues connecting Ethiopia with Middle East politics has been the Nile waters dispute with Egypt. The deliberately timed public announcement of the commencement of the construction of the Millennium Dam (later renamed as the GERD) in the Benishangul-Gumuz federal region near the Sudanese border in March 2011 infuriated the Egyptian leadership which was in disarray following the January 25 Revolution that had brought down the long-standing regime of President Hosni Mubarak. The USD 4.5 billion hydroelectric dam is the biggest in Africa and is expected to stimulate industrialization, economic development, electricity exportation to the region, and the approximately sixty-five million Ethiopians not connected to the electric grid. Ethiopia has also signed agreements to provide electricity to its neighboring states which is seen to buttress Ethiopia's dominant role in the Horn of Africa and accelerate regional integration. The dam is also a source of national pride and unity for many Ethiopians as it has been partly financed by their voluntary contributions. Although already envisaged during imperial times, the construction of the dam became part of Prime Minister Zenawi's strategic vision to assert cash-strapped Ethiopia's regional power by supplying neighboring states with hydropower[88] in exchange for much-needed hard currency and maintain the TPLF-led government's drive for economic growth and development. This threw Ethiopia increasingly toward the Persian

Gulf countries which have invested in the country but also provided funds to support the value of its currency and fiscal stability.

The 2011 Arab Spring, which the internationally influential Gulf monarchies considered a threat to their domestic political order, generated growing attention to the Horn of Africa from the Middle East powers. It led to increasing competition for influence in northeastern Africa and the Horn between Qatar and Türkiye on the one side and Saudi Arabia and the UAE on the other. In the regional power competition, Saudi Arabia, which grew concerned about the situation in Yemen, intensified its effort to neutralize Iranian influence in the Horn of Africa, while Türkiye gained a larger foothold in the sub-region. As Saudi Arabia and the UAE competed increasingly with Qatar, which had been particularly active in the region since the 2000s, Türkiye, which had revived its engagement through the much-publicized visit of Prime Minister Recep Tayyip Erdogan to Somalia in August 2011 and the provision of humanitarian aid, moved closer to Qatar due to a common interest in empowering religious grassroots and civil society movements often behind popular mobilization and revolutionary activity. The Arab Spring, and its effects in neighboring Bahrain and Yemen, also contributed to Saudi Arabia stepping up its effort to neutralize Iranian influence. This meant intensified engagement in the Red Sea region and the Horn of Africa.

Ethiopia took advantage of this interest and the rivalry between the Middle East powers in the Horn of Africa. By engaging in economic diplomacy Prime Minister Hailemariam Desalegn (2012–18) continued the developmental policy and engagement with the leading Persian Gulf countries and Türkiye. Hailing from a minority group, Desalegn had less internal leverage than his predecessor, Meles Zenawi, but he allowed the relationship with Türkiye to grow from the initial railroad construction contract with Yapi Merkezi in 2012 to an overall investment of at least USD 6 billion.[89] This has led Turkish companies to follow the Chinese as important employers in Ethiopia, while the countries have consolidated a bilateral trade relationship projected to reach at least USD 1 billion.[90] Symbolizing the strong relationship, in February 2021, Ethiopia's deputy prime minister Demeke Mekonnen opened a new Ethiopian embassy in Ankara ahead of Prime Minister Abiy Ahmed's visit in August to obtain Turkish armament and assistance to stop the advancing Tigray armed opposition forces and again in December for the Türkiye-Africa Partnership Summit. Abiy government's deepening partnership with Türkiye has been significant for its survival.

Meanwhile, the Saudi and UAE approach to Ethiopia was more based on security concerns and the wariness of the TPLF-EPRDF government's aspirations as the Horn sub-region's dominant state. Therefore, in the first half of the 2010s, they worked closely with Egypt, Sudan, Eritrea, Somalia, and Djibouti, until the Saudi-led intervention in the civil war in Yemen and change of leadership in Somalia and Ethiopia shook up some of the alliances in the Horn of Africa. Although Saudi and Emirati investment already became important in Ethiopia during the early decade, following Abiy Ahmed's rise in power in 2018 the relations became more intimate and particularly the UAE investment to the country grew significantly in part due to the UAE president Mohamed bin Zayed Al Nahyan's warm personal relationship with Abiy Ahmed.

In the context of Ethiopia's ties with the leading Persian Gulf countries and Türkiye, high-level careers in diplomatic service have become increasingly linked with successful economic diplomacy. One's ability to attract investment and funding is now directly linked to career success. One well-known example is Mulatu Teshome, who used his position as Ethiopia's Ambassador to Türkiye to boost Turkish investment in the country which later enabled him to become president (2013–18).[91]

The importance of this 'salesman diplomacy" as part of the economic foreign policy approach shows the critical significance of financial inflows for the Ethiopian economy to remedy the chronic shortage of foreign exchange and lack of economic development. As outlined in Ethiopia's 2002 foreign affairs strategy, economic diplomacy binds economy and regime security together and encourages economic partnership with countries such as Türkiye, Iran, and Israel, among others. The government's ability to monopolize and exert a level of control on foreign economic relations points to the strength and resilience of the Ethiopian state and its institutions relative to some of its neighbors.[92]

In 2015, Ethiopia's minister of foreign affairs, Tedros Adhanom, pointed out that from the outset the TPLF-EPRDF's foreign policy had emphasized addressing political and economic aspects of "the country's internal vulnerabilities and problems."[93] Here, the focus of the diplomatic effort became to ensure regime survival by seeking external partnerships that support economic development and poverty reduction as well as an increasingly democratic order. State strength, and its weaknesses, were seen to emerge from domestic economic and political realities, and the function of the foreign policy was to generate resources for the transformation of both. From the mid-1990s onward the leadership made a strong commitment to ensuring national security by promoting security and economic interests abroad. It endeavored to diversify Ethiopia's foreign relations and engage in partnerships with a wide variety of countries to avoid the faith of the previous Derg regime which had heavily relied on one partner. Ethiopia also renewed its commitment to international and regional multilateral organizations, and the TPLF-EPRDF regime increased its influence in the OAU and the succeeding African Union (AU) while becoming a leading state in the sub-regional organization, Inter-Governmental Authority on Development (IGAD). This approach was to ensure the domestic status quo through economic development and growth and assert Ethiopia's dominance as the guardian of security and stability in the Horn of Africa.

However, at the same time, there was a fear of domestic instability feeding from foreign sources. With the emergence of wide and persistent Oromo, and to an extent Amhara, protests, there was a rising concern of especially Sudan, Somalia, and Eritrea being used as tools for extending violent Islamist extremism in Ethiopia. This kept the TPLF-EPRDF government wary of its Arab partners despite the financial windfall and opened doors for economic engagement with other partners, especially Türkiye. With the leadership change in 2018, the limitations of economic partnerships with Arab states, including Saudi Arabia and the UAE, were eased because the incoming prime minister Abiy Ahmed required financial support from abroad to face the outgoing and politically and economically powerful TPLF, and deliver on his promise of economic reforms. Riyadh and Abu Dhabi became publicly higher profile partners especially after they were seen to have delivered the unlikely rapprochement between Ethiopia and Eritrea for which Premier Abiy was internationally celebrated. This shows the importance of economic diplomacy and foreign partnerships to obtain resources for the use of gaining an upper hand in domestic power struggles.

Early Years of the Abiy Ahmed Administration

Abiy Ahmed's ascent to power led to a shift of the domestic center of power from the TPLF to the Amhara nationalists who became Abiy's main constituency. Although his alliance with some Amhara factions is fragile, and Eritrea, which has provided Abiy critical support, has recently grown disgruntled after the Ethiopian government's ceasefire agreements with the TPLF, both the Amhara and Isaias Afwerki's Eritrea have formed an integral part of the leadership's strategy of survival. While partnering with China, the Abiy administration has engaged in close cooperation with Saudi Arabia, the UAE, Qatar, and Türkiye. In its new foreign policy strategy presented in December 2019, the Abiy government has sought to distinguish itself as different from the former TPLF-led administration by precisely emphasizing deeper cooperation with external partners beyond the pragmatic and transactional relations. Engaging through the sub-regional organization IGAD, in which Ethiopia has a significant role, it pushed increasing coordination on regional Red Sea affairs,[94] but these efforts lost importance after the launching of the Saudi-led Red Sea Council in early 2020 which, in addition to Saudi Arabia, includes the Red Sea and Gulf of Aden littoral countries Egypt, Jordan, Eritrea, Yemen, Sudan, Djibouti, and Somalia. However, in the Horn of Africa and Persian Gulf/Middle East relations, Ethiopia's multilateral efforts are shadowed by its continued focus on engaging its partners bilaterally.

Abiy's administration has therefore not engineered a major shift from the underlying principles of Ethiopian foreign policy. Securing regime survival and consolidation continue at the heart of the policy and economic diplomacy toward a spectrum of foreign partners ensures incoming financial and material resources to empower the incumbent over domestic rivals who constitute its biggest threat. Diversification of relations and reduced donor dependence are perceived essential to ensure "national" security, which is seen to depend on maintaining the domestic political and economic status quo in a region marked by insecurity, shifting alliances, and a history of difficult interstate relations. This approach emphasizes the importance of obtaining resources from the exterior, but despite the reforms effected by the Abiy administration since 2018, several barriers to investment, including limited access to foreign currency and credit, Internet, and bureaucratic and legal hindrances, still exist.

In July 2018, the Ethiopian-Eritrean rapprochement was one of the most celebrated political events in Africa and beyond. The UAE and Saudi Arabia, with active US facilitation, mediated the reconciliation by providing incentives for both parties. Leading to the agreement, in June 2018, the UAE pledged USD 3 billion in financial support and investment for Ethiopia bringing temporary financial relief. One-third of the amount was to be deposited in the Ethiopian national bank to alleviate the country's chronic need for foreign exchange. Emirati investors then embarked on a USD 1.9 billion luxury housing megaproject and other real estate endeavors in Addis Ababa [95] which strengthened Abiy's position and consolidated the relationship between the two governments. Ethiopia's Saudi relations were affected by the transition of leadership in Riyadh, and Crown Prince Mohamed bin Salman's purge among the Saudi elite. These events appear to have diminished MIDROC's role as the main coordinating body for Saudi investment in Ethiopia. In December 2019, the Saudi government granted two loans worth a total of USD 140 million for infrastructure and energy projects to the country[96] but has since been accused of favoring Egypt in the GERD dispute between its major regional partner Cairo and Addis Ababa. Recently, Saudi Arabia and Ethiopia have discussed further Saudi investments in Ethiopia's agriculture and livestock sector.

Addis Ababa's security partner, the US, was a consistent backer of the TPLF-led administration and continued the same policy with the incoming Abiy government early on. In 2016–20, until the Tigray crisis resulted in a reversal of the US policy, Washington provided Ethiopia with over USD 4.2 billion in humanitarian and development aid.[97] Its support was also instrumental in 2019 when the World Bank (WB) and the International Monetary Fund (IMF) pledged over USD 5 billion to back the Ethiopian government's economic reforms.[98] However, US-Ethiopia relations momentarily deteriorated due to the Tigray conflict.

Meanwhile, as part of a more general trend, Chinese investment in Ethiopia has decreased amid doubts about the profitability of funded projects, particularly in infrastructure. In 2018, the Chinese mission to the AU expressed that China Export and Credit Insurance Corporation was scaling back its investment in Ethiopia and in August 2021 the EximBank refused to release USD 339 million to Addis Ababa because of its increasing repayment problems related to the growing debt burden.[99] Chinese reluctance to lend to Ethiopia reflects its concern about the general problem of repayment and return to investments particularly from large infrastructure projects in Africa after its funding and lending flurry in the mid-2010s. China has been the biggest investor in Ethiopia, including in manufacturing, investing over USD 4 billion in the country during the second half of the past decade alone. Despite the outside funding, the strict financial controls and government interventions to support the value of the local currency, and other factors related to the economic model of the developmental state, have meant that the Ethiopian economy has generated a chronic need for securing foreign exchange.

In September 2020 the leaders of Eritrea, Ethiopia, and Somalia met for the third trilateral meeting to coordinate their efforts in the Horn of Africa. In the meeting, they proposed to form a new regional bloc, which has been referred to as the "Horn of Africa Cooperation," but the initiative received mixed reactions at best,[100] with some characterizing it as based on the individual ambitions of the three leaders and its overall effect as destabilizing.[101]

At the same time, within Ethiopia, the tension between the Abiy administration and the TPLF escalated due to the latter's resistance to the political reforms that pushed it aside from the center of national politics. The TPLF began to focus on the Tigray Region, strengthening the regional forces and local militias and organizing a regional election in September 2020 which the federal government deemed illegal due to the decision to postpone the general elections in the country because of the Covid-19 pandemic. The TPLF also became the main voice against replacing the EPRDF with a Prosperity Party, deemed by some as an abandonment of ethnic federalism in favor of a more centralized political system.

The tension between the government and the TPLF culminated in a military intervention in Tigray primarily to remove the TPLF-controlled regional government and to bring its senior leaders to justice. Ethiopian National Defense Force (ENDF) got support from Amhara regional forces as well as the Eritrean military, while Emirati drones from the Assab military base also attacked Tigrayan forces, driving them to the remote eastern highlands of Tigray. With the end of the UAE's alleged drone strikes due to the US pressure after President Joe Biden came to power,[102] TPLF-organized Tigray Defense Forces (TDF), which had gained wide support among the local population devastated by the ENDF and its allies' offensive, scored several victories. It drove the ENDF and its allies out of eastern and central Tigray and first advanced in Amhara and Afar region and subsequently toward Addis Ababa. The TPLF also advanced to the east, seeking to cut the government's supply route to Djibouti through which approximately 95 percent of Ethiopia's external trade passes. The TDF also sought to reach a land border for opening a route of external supply through western Tigray, ostensibly for potential Egyptian and Sudanese support, but the regional forces supported by the ENDF and Eritrea have occupied and annexed it to the Amhara region. The Tigrayan forces additionally armed ethnic minority groups, proportioning weapons captured from its opponents. Although the federal government and its allies managed to control western Tigray, their position was complicated by TDF's significant military capability further buttressed by weapons and material captured from the ENDF and regional forces. In August 2021, the Oromo Liberation Army (also known as Oromo Liberation Front/OLF-Shene), which had refused to disarm despite the OLF's 2018 peace agreement with the government, declared an alliance with the TPLF.[103] The OLA is militarily active in various parts of the federal Oromo Region and has made periodic gains in the west and southwest of the country.

In December 2021, the TDF advance toward Addis Ababa was stopped. Here, Premier Abiy's earlier efforts to secure external support for state survival were integral. In July, Ethiopia signed a defense cooperation treaty with Russia,[104] preceding Moscow's material support for the ENDF. Ethiopia also acquired Iranian drones. In August 2021 Abiy visited President Recep Tayyip Erdogan to further strengthen ties with Türkiye after having more visibly aligned with its competitor, the UAE. Turkish ties, and Ankara's strong connection with Mogadishu, brought

Abiy significant economic and military backing. In March 2022 a fragile ceasefire deal was reached after the TDF forces had been pushed back to Tigray. Fighting erupted again in August and was brought to an end in a second ceasefire agreement between the government and the TPLF under the auspices of the African Union in South Africa in early November after significant military gains by the government side backed by Eritrea and Amhara regional forces and militias. The US played a significant role in pressuring the parties to a truce, while China had also made a serious behind-the-scenes effort to mediate.

During the crisis, the Middle Eastern regional powerhouses, especially the UAE, played an important role. Notably, the Emiratis, who also have good relations with Egypt, Sudanese military leadership, Somaliland, and Eritrea, became important suppliers of military support. Although they withdrew from Assab in early 2021 (possibly due to the US pressure after their alleged use of drones in Tigray), in September the UAE established an air supply corridor of military material for the Ethiopian government of which a significant part originated from China.[105] In particular, Emirates-supplied Chinese, as well as Turkish and Iranian, drones gave the government unprecedented air-to-surface strike capacity which tipped the military balance[106] because TDF has no considerable surface-to-air capability. They helped to reverse the TDF advance and push Tigrayan forces back to the region. Abiy's efforts to engage the Middle East powers obliged them to take sides and prevented them from being seen as neutral mediators in the crisis.

In June 2021, according to predictions, Abiy scored a sweeping triumph in the general election. The TPLF, however, had its own endgame. Through significant military gains beyond Tigray, it sought anywhere between significant political concessions, including a greater degree of self-determination, and regime change. The TPLF presented its fight as one for the whole of Tigray and drew on the violence and government crackdowns to recruit fighters for the TDF. The hard-line rhetoric for outright independence at one point was toned down by those seeking external support based on the understanding that it would turn away potential foreign patrons, such as Egypt. TPLF devised its international media campaign to counter the government propaganda and not only gained Tigrayan diaspora support but notably solidarity among political voices in Washington.

Due to the conflict, the Abiy government's partnership with the US deteriorated. The US condemned the human rights violations related to the conflict and along with the UN and its Western allies advocated for greater humanitarian access in Tigray. The US administration, which in the previous five years had provided billions of dollars in development and humanitarian assistance, suspended Ethiopia from the tariff-free African Growth and Opportunity Act, froze initially the American part of a USD 850 million initial investment in its telecommunications sector (but later reversed the decision[107]), and passed an executive order facilitating imposition of targeted sanctions when deemed necessary.[108] Washington then went on to sanction Eritrean individuals and entities it saw responsible for human rights violations and escalation of the crisis while threatening the main parties to the conflict with further sanctions if they fail to comply with the conditions of the humanitarian ceasefire in place since March 2022. Other external powers, including the Abiy government's main backers China, Türkiye, and the UAE, as well as Iran and Russia, continued to support the federal government, which replaced the previous US assistance. However, after the November 2022 agreement which appears to have brought the Tigray conflict to an end Ethiopia and the US have sought to improve ties.

Since late 2020, due to the Tigray crisis and the coinciding Covid-19 pandemic, Ethiopia's public finances came under extreme pressure. Recently, this has been further compounded by the Russian invasion of Ukraine which has mainly affected food and energy prices. Foreign direct investment in Ethiopia has increased from almost USD 2.4 billion in 2020 to over USD 4.2 billion in 2021, while the country's public debt has increased from almost USD 35 billion in 2020 to over USD 44 billion in 2021 and an estimated almost USD 56 billion in 2022. It constituted over 32 percent of the GDP in 2020 and is expected to rise rapidly and top 40 percent already in 2022. Simultaneously, with the high, estimated over USD 2.5 billion price tag, of the Tigray conflict, and US pressure on the WB and IMF to withhold funding, the Ethiopian birr depreciated 12 percent against the USD in the first half of 2021 and has then continued in a trend of a longer-term decline. Ethiopia has, however, continued to experience significant annual GDP growth which according to the National Bank jumped from 6.3 percent in 2020 to 8.7 percent in 2021.

The soaring overall debt, along with Ethiopia's opaque but large debt to China, as well as the rising price of imported food and energy due to the Ukraine crisis, will exacerbate Ethiopia's need for foreign exchange. As a result, in July 2021 Abiy government sought to restructure USD 1 billion of its debt under the G-20 common framework[109] and is dependent on foreign sources of funding. Ethiopia's leadership and diplomatic corps will be more stretched to attract foreign investment, aid, and loans due to the fears of instability generated by the ongoing conflicts. As a cost-cutting measure to mitigate economic difficulties related to the Covid-19 pandemic and political instability and conflict, in early July 2021, Ethiopian leadership began a rationalization process involving its foreign missions. At least thirty of Ethiopia's fifty-nine overseas missions were to be closed and in several other missions personnel be reduced in connection to the economic crisis partly due to a shortage of foreign currency and ongoing conflicts.[110] Diplomats were called back by August 2021 for reorientation and redeployment while seeking to save money through a structural reform of the foreign ministry. Ethiopia's two missions in each, Saudi Arabia, Türkiye, and the UAE, were affected. In 2021, a 3.7 billion birr budget was allocated to the foreign ministry, of which 325 million, or almost 9 percent, was earmarked for economic and business diplomacy,[111] but it is expected that the chronic shortage of foreign exchange and the political and economic troubles will require scaling back the budget. These measures have reduced the available personnel for "salesman diplomacy" and will likely, until the effectiveness of the remaining diplomats increases, lower the capacity of Ethiopian foreign missions to engage in economic diplomacy and attract financial and material resources from abroad.

In recent years, the UAE has been particularly active in extending its presence in the Horn of Africa. Through the DP World and its military, the UAE has engaged in port development and operations and establishing military facilities, which have paved the way for partnerships with the Horn states. While falling out with Djibouti (2015) and the Farmaajo (2017–20) administration in Somalia, Abu Dhabi established itself in Eritrea's Assab (until 2021), Somaliland's Berbera, and Yemeni Socotra and Perim islands, the latter of which is strategically located at Bab al-Mandab. These footholds, along with good relations with Ethiopia and Sudan, and improving ties with Somalia (2022–), have made Abu Dhabi a significant player in the Horn. While often considered junior to Saudi Arabia, it has partnered with Egypt and recently upgraded ties with Israel (2020–) and Türkiye (2021–). The UAE has been relatively successful in balancing its great power relations with China and the US, which has elevated its status in the wider region.

In April 2018, the UAE deployed troops to Socotra Island and has since maintained a presence there. Despite claims to have withdrawn from Yemen in 2019, Abu Dhabi has remained active in the conflict and maintained an important presence in Bab al-Mandab and the Gulf of Aden. In early 2021, it came to light that the UAE had largely withdrawn its forces from its major military base in Eritrea's Assab and instead engaged in building an airbase on the Perim Island in Bab al-Mandab.[112] This indicates that the UAE seeks to maintain a central role in the Red Sea politics, secure commercial shipping lanes through its narrowest stretches, and not fully disengage from Yemen. In June, the US thanked the UAE leadership for seeking "a ceasefire and political solution" to the Tigray conflict.[113] In November 2021 Abu Dhabi crown prince Mohammed bin Zayed visited Ankara and made a USD 10 billion investment commitment from the UAE.[114] This move came amid Türkiye's economic difficulties, including currency depreciation, and appears to have ended a decade of uncomfortable relations between the two countries since the Arab Spring.

Since 2018, the UAE has aided the Ethiopian government's efforts of consolidation. Apart from the Emirati leadership using DP World to partner with Ethiopia and provide Addis Ababa alternative sea access through Berbera, it has provided support in the Tigray conflict and sought to mediate in the Ethiopia-Egypt-Sudan Nile dispute and the Ethiopia-Sudan border conflict in al-Fashaga.

In March 2018, Ethiopia became a partner in the Berbera Corridor connecting Addis Ababa to the Berbera port in Somaliland. Despite the outgoing TPLF-EPRDF government's initial preoccupation about the UAE's role, a tripartite agreement was reached in which the Ethiopian government agreed to assume a 19 percent stake, while the Government of Somaliland remained with 30 percent and DP World with 51 percent, respectively. In the original agreement with Somaliland, DP World pledged USD 442 million for the development of the port into a state-of-the-art facility. In the new deal, Ethiopia additionally committed to developing its domestic infrastructure leading to the Somaliland border. In May 2021 Ethiopia signed an agreement for DP World and its partners to invest USD 1 billion to build logistics infrastructure along the corridor, while Abu Dhabi Fund for Development and the United Kingdom Department for International Development (DFID) upgraded the road connecting the port with Ethiopia (Berbera-Wajale).[115] The first Ethiopian ships bringing foodstuffs docked at Berbera Port in July 2021, and it has recently captured the attention of logistics companies around the world. However, rifts in the tripartite partnership appeared in June 2022 when Somaliland Minister of Finance Saad Ali Shire stated that Ethiopia had lost its stake in Berbera Port due to the lack of making a financial contribution to its construction.[116] This and Ethiopia's agreement with Djibouti in July to begin using the livestock terminal at Doraleh port for exporting to the Arabian Peninsula signal a shift in Addis Ababa's strategy toward the Berbera project and preference of further strengthening ties with Djibouti and China which has a heavy logistics and military presence in Doraleh.

The Berbera Corridor supplies Addis Ababa with alternative sea access and ties Somaliland closer to Ethiopia economically and politically through the joint import-export route. As infrastructure is completed, it will increasingly compete with the Chinese-built, over USD 4.2 billion and 756-kilometer-long electric standard gauge railway between Addis Ababa and the Doraleh port in Djibouti opened in 2018. However, the Berbera Corridor, or sea access through Eritrea (Assab or Massawa), Sudan (Port Sudan), or Kenya (Lamu), is not likely to threaten Djibouti's strategic position as a channel of a large proportion of Ethiopia's imports and exports.

Another issue involving Ethiopia, the UAE, and other Middle East powers is the contentious Nile dispute featuring Addis Ababa and Cairo. Negotiations over the GERD negotiation continue uncomfortably under the auspices of the AU because although the UAE and Türkiye, among others, have offered to mediate, they are not perceived as neutral. Türkiye, for example, has been unsuccessful in mending fences with Egypt despite its recent overtures.[117] Similarly, in July 2021, Egyptian president Abdel Fattah al-Sisi and Abu Dhabi Crown Prince bin Zayed al-Nahyan inaugurated an Egyptian naval base near the Libyan border,[118] which signals a continuing significant commitment to Cairo. Meanwhile, the Ethiopian government insisted on its sovereignty in the Tigray crisis and actively lobbied for the AU, based in Addis Ababa, as the main forum for resolving the Nile water conflict.

Not entirely separate from the Nile dispute is the Sudan–Ethiopia border conflict in al-Fashaga. Belonging to Sudan, the fertile area has been mainly cultivated by farmers Ethiopian for decades with Sudanese consent. However, tension and violence in al-Fashaga escalated during the Tigray crisis which has caused instability in the Sudanese border and possibly due to Cairo's pressure on Khartoum to seek confrontation due to Ethiopia's initial rounds of filling of the GERD basin. The UAE initially played an important role in mediation on al-Fashaga but withdrew in May 2021 due to Sudan's refusal to accept the proposed terms, and the US pressure to diminish its support for the Ethiopian government. The US pressure was in part to back President al-Sisi's regime in Egypt, which heavily depends on appearing strong in the Nile negotiations[119] after being critical of Addis Ababa due to the Tigray crisis. Among regional powers, the Egyptian regime is heavily backed by Saudi Arabia and the UAE which are concerned about the Muslim Brotherhood and the possibility of a grassroots mobilization in Egypt that could extend to the Arabian Peninsula similar to the 2011 Arab Spring.

However, the recent initiation of economic cooperation between Türkiye and the UAE is a welcome step for the Abiy Ahmed administration in Ethiopia due to its strong partnership with both. This may help temper Egypt.

In July 2021, the UN Security Council (UNSC) debated about Ethiopia's second unilateral filling to increase the water level of the GERD reservoir, while Sameh Shoukry, the Egyptian foreign minister, described it as an "existential threat." Despite the Egyptian government's hopes that the UNSC would side with it due to its good relations with great powers, the Security Council threw the issue back to the AU without providing a deadline for its resolution,[120] considering the regional organization as the appropriate forum for finding a solution to the dispute. This decision can be viewed as a significant diplomatic victory for Ethiopia which hosts the AU, stands as one of its most loyal funders, and has leverage in the organization. It also deters Egypt's insinuations of military action on the GERD. More recently the UAE, which has good relations with all three parties to the dispute, has sought to assume a mediation role through informal talks but little progress has been made. Overall, however, the GERD can be seen less as a case of the absolute quantity of water reaching Egypt, and Sudan, and more as an issue of political survival of the incumbent regime in Egypt, where President al-Sisi is seen to be obliged to stand firm on the issue, and in Ethiopia, where the GERD is considered a uniting national symbol and a source of pride to which Ethiopians far and wide have contributed financially.

Despite being torn by ravaging conflict in various parts of the country, Ethiopia has continued on the path of development and impressive economic growth. This is in part driven by successful economic diplomacy resulting in diverse external partnerships and accompanying investment and financial inflow. The government's efforts to stimulate diaspora remittances also result in a significant inflow of much-needed foreign currency. Foreign exchange reserves can be used to finance trade deficits and external debt.

Although resistance to the ongoing political reforms and restructuration and armed violence and insurgencies have caused a degree of instability, they have not greatly undermined the Ethiopian government's ability to monopolize the main foreign relations and their benefits. Even in the current scenario of political fragmentation, a nuanced understanding of the configuration of political and economic power in Ethiopia reveals how power continues to concentrate on the state. The Tigray example shows that while other power centers, as a form of sub-state or non-state actors, have emerged they are not able to significantly draw on external connections in their efforts to challenge the political status quo. This is because Ethiopian leadership has actively engaged external actors through its "salesman diplomacy" and drawn them in to support the economic development and financial stability of the country, while also using its international legal status to obtain financial resources. The economic and financial relationship has steered Ethiopia's external partners toward protecting their investment and supporting the Abiy administration against potentially destabilizing non-state actors. Against the expectations of critics, the Abiy administration has been successful in selling Ethiopia's strategic market and production potential and attracted a diverse and growing foreign currency inflow from various sources that helps maintain a high level of economic growth despite local instability in various parts of the country. At the same time, by increasing the diversity of Ethiopia's external partners and sources of income, the Abiy government has created more potential for effecting shifts in foreign relations orientation and domestic policy without causing severe consequences for regime security and survival.

Conclusion

Ethiopia is the dominant state in the Horn of Africa. It is attractive to foreign powers due to its strategic importance and economic potential. Ethiopian state draws its power from capabilities related to its size, economic and coercive capacity, high population, and foreign alliances, as well as its geography and history which are central to the contextualized understanding of the Horn. In its neighborhood, the Ethiopian state is historically the most established, and its leadership projects important influence through its foreign policy and security apparatus. The country's external affairs have for a long time drawn mainly on domestic realities and its "national" interest projected in its foreign engagements continues to reflect the objectives of its governing elite and forces and constituencies behind it. Although there is a hegemonic dimension to Ethiopia's objectives owing to its central location, size, and importance in the Horn of Africa, they are intimately related to the efforts of the state patrons to conserve their domestic power and maintain a status quo by consolidating the political regimes in power. This is the case to the extent that resources extracted domestically and through extraversion from foreign partners, including in the Middle East, are in part used to fend off domestic political challengers in the continuous process of negotiating power and (re)shaping the state through coercion or by other means.

Although the Abiy administration has been criticized for using foreign alignments for economic benefit and self-consolidation, this strategy is not new or particular to the current administration. As the discussion in this chapter indicates, the strategy used today is long-established and continues to form the core of Ethiopian foreign policy. Similarly to today, previous regimes in Ethiopia engaged heavily in economic diplomacy to obtain financial and other material resources which they used to curb domestic rivals and opposition. They also sought to use the resources for generating economic development and growth to minimize potential challenges to the political status quo that could emerge among the discontented population. This strategy has affected the longevity of political regimes during the imperial, socialist, federalist, and post-TPLF eras. It has been relatively successful whenever the governments have been strong enough to centralize power and prevent other significant power centers from emerging. For example, Ethiopian regimes have been generally resistant to peripheral political instability, such as revolts and insurgencies, whenever they have been able to prevent the strengthening of the non-state actors perpetrating them. Here, thwarting their efforts to gain significant foreign backing has been fundamental as the collapse of the Derg regime has shown. Therefore, monopolization of the most important foreign relations has been a major part of the regime strategy because it has for the most part prevented non-state actors from using their own foreign connections to amass sufficient resources to challenge the patrons of the state.

In the past two decades, the interest from the Middle East, and in particular the Gulf States and Türkiye, in the Horn of Africa has greatly increased. The economic and security interests of these actors, and their financial and material resources, have provided opportunities that the previous Meles Zenawi-led TPLF-EPRDF and the current Abiy administration have sought to exploit. Whereas Meles's approach toward the regionally influential Persian Gulf countries was initially cautious but later warming, Abiy has demonstrated less apprehension and further deepened the partnership with Saudi Arabia, the UAE, Türkiye, and Qatar. In the background, however, looms the heating great power competition between the US and China in which successive Ethiopian governments have exploited both Beijing's economic and Washington's security approaches. While the TPLF-EPRDF government used the Chinese engagement to generate economic growth and the US relations to improve its security apparatus, the Abiy administration has sought to incorporate growing American economic interests more extensively to further diversify external sources of income. At the same time, in the context of the ever-present peripheral insurgencies, the government has been forced to face competition from non-state actors, particularly the former ruling party TPLF, in both domestic and foreign affairs. Such parties have sought foreign assistance beyond the state, and TPLF has been successful in gaining a modicum of foreign diplomatic and political support. Yet, this has not been enough to challenge the state which monopolizes official foreign relations and exploits significant external partnerships for its political and economic consolidation.

As indicated in the earlier discussion, the Abiy government, like its predecessors, has used economic diplomacy, and outright "salesman" policy, as part of its foreign policy strategy which aims at the administration's domestic survival and consolidation. It faces the daunting task to convert the increasing foreign power and non-state actor interest in Ethiopia to extract continuous material and political benefits. In its strategy, maintaining a position of strength relative to domestic rivals is paramount. This can be achieved, in part, by pursuing foreign partnerships which produce financial and material resources. The more diverse and widespread these partnerships and the resulting sources of financial, material, and nonmaterial (diplomatic and political) resources are, the less power an individual foreign partner has in the relationship. Therefore, pursuing diverse external relations empowers the state, or a non-state actor, and gives it space for maneuvering and shifting alignments, orientation, and concentration areas in foreign connections. While in one way or another all governments and non-state actors are constrained in their external relations, they tend to gain power and further autonomy by diversifying foreign partnerships. This is what Ethiopian administrations have tended to do. After all, fruitful management of the great and middle power relations continues to be essential for regime survival in the Horn of Africa's dominant state.

Chapter 4

SOMALIA

A BATTLEGROUND OF INTERESTS

The Somali Peninsula, the eastern stretch of the Horn of Africa protruding to the Indian Ocean and forming the southern banks of the Gulf of Aden across from the southern tip of the Arabian Peninsula, was the seat of old proto-Somali civilization already several centuries before the Common Era. In light of current historical and archeological evidence, the Somali people, ethnically categorized as Eastern Cushitic, are indigenous to the Horn of Africa at least since the second millennium AD, possibly longer. However, "Somali physical features nonetheless bear the firm imprint of the long contact of Somaliland with Arabia."[1] Already during antiquity, Somali merchants supplied the Middle East and Mediterranean empires with exotic luxury commodities. The classical Greek historical record mentions Macrobians as mighty herders and seafarers whose empire ostensibly transformed into several commercially oriented city-states, such as Opone, competing over the lucrative trade toward Europe and India. As a result, Somali people have a long history of engaging in trade and maritime activity in the Red Sea and the Indian Ocean, as well as connections with peoples beyond the two bodies of water.

Contemporary, post-1991 state collapse, Somalia has often been seen as a failed state where foreign state and non-state actors, including from the Persian Gulf, roam and sponsor local big men, clan militias, and other armed groups to advance their strategic political and economic interests. However, prominent sub-state and non-state actors in Somalia command significant local power which gives them an advantageous position to bargain with foreign players seeking to shape the local political, economic, or social reality. This gives such local actors the ability to strengthen themselves by extraverting resources from external players and partners. The discussion here seeks to highlight the local agency in Somalia in relations particularly with actors in the Persian Gulf and wider Middle East.

Yet, due to the limitations of space, the discussion here does not pretend to provide a comprehensive account of the external relations of various actors in Somalia, but to provide some examples of how economic diplomacy and political interactions have featured in the pragmatic and largely transactional relations between local Somali state and non-state actors and mainly those from the Persian Gulf, Arabian Peninsula, and elsewhere in the Middle East.

Historical Connections

Somalis were among the first to embrace Islam in Africa. Often presented evidence for this is the Labo-Qibla Mosque in Zeila built during the first Hijra, only years after the founding of the al-Sahaba Mosque in Massawa, Eritrea, and initially oriented toward Jerusalem. Somali role in the history of the expansion of Islam is a source of pride in Somalia, but a clear distinction is made between religion and other cultural and political influences. The Somalis tend to consider themselves as proudly African, as opposed to Arab, which appears to be sometimes forgotten by those in the Middle East seeking to extend political and cultural influence, and particular religious doctrines, to the Somali homeland in the Horn of Africa.

However, despite their particularities, Somalis and people from today's Yemen have a deeply intertwined social and cultural connection due to geographical proximity that has enabled continuous interaction. For example, Somalia has adopted Arabic as an official language, although most people do not have command of it, and its Hadhrami and Yemeni dialects are most prevalent in the country. Over a long period, Hadhrami migrants have also become present in other coastal Horn states Djibouti and Eritrea, as well as to some extent in contemporary Ethiopia, where their descendants who crossed Bab al-Mandab settled mainly in the Harar region.[2]

From medieval to modern times several sultanates engaging in commerce and overseas trade existed in the Somali territories. Among the powerful Gulf of Aden, coastal empires were the Ifat and Adal sultanates for which particularly Zeila,[3] as well as other port cities such as Berbera, were essential points of connection with faraway lands. Coexisting with them was the influential Indian Ocean trading empire of Ajuran which absorbed the city-states located in today's central and southern Somalia and cast influence inland toward Bale and through colonies in the Maldives and Sofala in today's Mozambique.

During the Middle Ages, followed by Egypt's Mamluk ruler al-Nasir Muhammad's persecution of Coptic Christians, several conflicts in which religion was instrumentalized took place took place in the Horn of Africa. Inspired by al-Nasir, Emir of Ifat Sultanate, Haqq ad-Din I, entered into a confrontation with Abyssinia. This led to hostilities between the two efforts by the Ifat and subsequent Adal sultanate to dominate the Abyssinian highlands. While in the course of the Abyssinian-Adal War (1529–43) Imam Ahmad ibn Ibrahim al-Ghazi occupied part of the highlands, the conflict weakened both parties which then faced Oromo migrations and Ottoman encroachment. In the fourteenth and fifteenth centuries, due to their power in the Red Sea region, Egypt and the Ottoman Empire were able to influence the most powerful sultanates in the Horn of Africa and undermine Abyssinia. But because Egypt's power in the politics of the sub-region was largely articulated through alignments with local actors often on religious grounds, and it had no significant interest or capacity to maintain permanent forces in the area, its presence and influence were limited and short-lived.

In 1517, the conquest of Mamluk Egypt converted it into an Ottoman province (*Eyalet*). As a result, Ottoman rulers became increasingly interested in securing the African littoral of the Red Sea and took control of several coastal cities. This strengthened their position in the Red Sea trade which became important for Ottoman possessions in Egypt. Subsequent extension of the Ottoman dominion to the southern coastal areas of the Arabian Peninsula led to the control of both sides of the strategic Strait of Bab al-Mandab were Ottomans could obstruct rivals from entering the Red Sea. Additionally, extending territorial control beyond the littoral was deemed necessary to safeguard the Ottoman coastal and maritime presence.

Local Muslim states benefited from the Ottoman presence in their confrontations with Abyssinia. Initially, in his conquest of Abyssinia, Imam al-Ghazi, Adal Sultanate's military commander, used the alliance with the Ottomans to gain military support which allowed him to almost conquer the whole Abyssinian Empire. Largely Argobba, Harari, and Harla, the Adal sultanate not only extended its dominion to the areas surrounding Abyssinian highlands but through military conquest came to briefly control much of the highland territory as well.

However, due to the war and intensifying Great Oromo Expansions, Adal Sultanate declined and was replaced by the Sultanate of Harar. Despite its early successes, Harar's resistance against Abyssinia was short-lived, and it was succeeded by a weaker Imamate of Aussa and subsequently the Afar Sultanate of Aussa[4] and a stronger breakaway Emirate of Harar (1647–1875) which initially extended from the strategic areas of today's Somaliland to the borders of Abyssinian highlands and controlled much of the trade between the coastal Gulf of Aden and the interior. Harar Emirate gained from its alliance with the Ottomans, which helped it to maintain a central role as an independent state. Harar Emirate endured until 1875 when it was annexed by Egypt and subsequently by Abyssinia after a treaty with the British who controlled Egypt (1882–1956) and sought assistance against the Mahdists who had expelled the Ottoman (Turco-Egyptian) rulers and established a sovereign Islamic state in Sudan in 1885.

During the eighteenth century, another sultanate composed mainly of the Somali Isaaq clan emerged in the territories of contemporary Somaliland and part of eastern Ethiopia. Its rise coinciding with increasing intrusion by European powers put it on a collision course with external interests and in particular expanding British influence. With its major trading port in Berbera, connecting the interior Horn of Africa with the Arabian Peninsula and lands across the western Indian Ocean,[5] the Isaaq Sultanate under the Guled family dynasty engaged in commerce in the Gulf of Aden, but its efforts were undermined by the British attempt to control the maritime trade. Following a blockade, the British gained forcibly access to the lucrative Berbera port in an 1827 battle. Despite an effort to seek support from the Emirati al-Qasimi dynasty, a maritime power once in control of the Strait of Hormuz in the Persian Gulf, the Isaaq Sultanate had to give way to an increasing British influence.

The Colonial Era

In 1884 the British took over the administration of coastal territories from Egypt and expanded their dominion through the mid-1880s treaties with coastal and interior Isaaq sub-clans until the establishment of British Somaliland in 1887. The agreements with the Isaaq, Issa, Gadabursi (Samaron), and Warsangali clan leaders were framed as protection treaties, but the establishment of British Somaliland was aimed at protecting the British interest to ensure the viability of its primary port in Aden.[6] Control of the Somali ports across the Gulf of Aden and protection of the overland trade routes ensured its meat supply, but the British had otherwise little interest in the interior[7] due to fierce local resistance and few foreseeable gains.

From 1899 to 1920 a powerful Somali multi-clan nationalist movement under Mohammed Abdullah Hassan waged persistent opposition against the European and Ethiopian colonial power in the Somali territories. As an influential Salihiyya Sufi Muslim figure, Sayyid Mohammed shaped his Dervish movement to have a significant revivalist religious zeal.[8] Creating a short-lived Somali state, he advocated for Somali independence from external domination until his movement suffered a military defeat. However, the Dervish movement inspired a series of anti-colonial revolts and rebellions and was followed by non-violent nationalist independence activism in the form of Haji Farah Omar's Somali Islamic Association which was founded in 1920.[9]

Meanwhile, during the early stages of the European partition of Africa, Italians extended their influence over the main trading ports Mogadishu, Merka, and Barawa of the Benadir Coast. One by one, starting with the Sultanate of Hobyo in 1888-9, areas under the Somali Majeerteen clan came under Italian domination until the establishment of the "Somalia Italiana" in 1908 comprising today's Puntland, central Somalia, and Jubaland, the latter handed over by the British in 1925 for Italy's support in the First World War. In the 1880s, Italians also extended their control over Eritrea, while the French established a colony on the African side of Bab al Mandab.

Whereas the British conformed to controlling their colonial possessions in the Horn of Africa through indirect rule, and the French governed colonial territories as an extension of France, the Italian colonial project was aimed at building "new Italies." In British Somaliland, the colonial administration used the local culture and customs by adopting and reshaping the existing system of elders. French Somaliland, on the other hand, was governed through a clear pattern of inclusion of citizens and exclusion of those considered subjects without political rights.[10] Italian colonial policy sought to establish centralized and hierarchical administration by introducing and imposing foreign institutions on a largely nomadic population with a largely horizontal societal structure. In its vertical dispensation of power, the externally imposed state came to be seen as a separate institutional organization that excluded and undermined local, culturally embedded, power structures and was effectively distinct. Prior societal institutions were abolished or deprived of their official status while new institutions were given official capacity as part of the colonial state. Among the various colonial territories inhabited by Somalis, this incompatibility came to most drastically characterize the Italian dominion.

After Italy's defeat during the Second World War, Italian Somaliland came under British military administration. During this period, an organized Somali nationalist liberation movement emerged in the form of the Somali Youth Club which soon became the Somali Youth League (SYL). Although the SYL was not the only organized political force in the Somali territories, it sought to present itself as a progressive pan-Somali liberation movement by de-emphasizing clan identity affiliations, forbidding clannishness, and advocating unification of Somali territories. Although SYL called for further development of the Somali language, it largely relied also on Arabic, which, along with Arabic being Somalia's second official language,[11] demonstrates the continuity of deep cultural connection with the Arabian Peninsula. While British Somaliland remained a protectorate until 1960, the status of French Somaliland in Djibouti changed to an overseas territory in 1946. However, in a 1958 French Somaliland referendum, marred with irregularities and manipulation by the French authorities, over 75 percent of the voter preferred a continued association with France. The former Italian Somaliland became an Italian-administered United Nations (UN) Trust Territory of Somaliland in 1950 on the condition that it would be granted independence within ten years.

Meanwhile, in 1948, Britain returned the Somali-inhabited territory of Haud it had ceded in 1897 to Ethiopia. Emperor Haile Selassie, who had reinstated his rule, absorbed the territory as an integral part of Ethiopia despite the initial condition put forth by the British that Somalis in the area should maintain autonomy. In 1956, following US pressure on Britain and the UN to make Eritrea a federal part of Ethiopia, the British attempted to buy back the ceded Haud territory from Ethiopia but without success. This, along with Haile Selassie's earlier claim in the UN for Ethiopia to annex both Eritrea and Somalia, in an attempt to quell nationalist sentiments, set the stage for a series of later confrontations between Mogadishu and Addis Ababa over the dominion of Somali-populated territories annexed to Ethiopia. As part of this contestation, external actors in Ethiopia and Somalia have since played an important role in the region's narrative and claims of belonging.[12]

European colonialism among the Somalis was divisive and undermined the formation of a coherent and functioning state in Somalia. The imposition of incisive and penetrating colonial power shaped social relations and imposed foreign political organization, institutions, and governance practices. This led to fragile hierarchical and extractive state structures which among themselves were largely incompatible due to the imposition of various types of colonialism. From the outset, the postcolonial state lacked effective hierarchical state structures with strong centralizing capacities in part due to the variable colonial experience and the incoherent imposition of foreign formal institutional structures on Somali society. The historical background of non-territorial sultanates in which fixed population centers were hardly the norm, and the cultural reality based on largely nomadic horizontal societal structure, did not favor the consolidation of a "modern" centralized state. In a sense, society and its dynamics and institutions dominated the formal configuration of the state which to an extent became a façade for the interests of societally powerful actors. This gave way to various societally based authorities and power centers (e.g., clan leaders) which appropriated parts of the state functions as a vehicle to buttress their socially acquired power. After the Ogaden War (1977–8) when external powers had increasing opportunities to empower non-state actors against the Somali central government, the societal leaders' powerful role became increasingly apparent.

Postcolonial and Cold War Dynamics

Eventually, in 1960, the colonial period in the British and Italian-dominated Somali territories came to an end. However, the merger of the former British and former Italian Somaliland was not a marriage of equals. Largely consumed by the nationalist sentiment for creating Greater Somalia, and in part as a response to Ethiopian expansionism, Somaliland legislators, under British tutelage, opted for union with the Italian Trust Territory of Somaliland. On June 27, one day after independence, Somaliland legislators approved a bill to voluntarily join Italian Somaliland upon its independence on July 1, 1960.[13] Over a year after the independence, a referendum and parliamentary ratification confirmed a new constitution which many Somalilanders opposed since it appeared to undermine their region which they considered a prominent constitutive part of the republic. The Ethiopian government sought to capitalize on this sentiment by endorsing the establishment of the North Somalia Liberation Movement (NSLM) to undermine the union.

Soon after independence, the Greater Somalia nationalist project led to Mogadishu's confrontation with neighboring states. By using the deepening animosity with Ethiopia as justification, Somali nationalists aligned with Nasser's Egypt. The initial propaganda support for the irredentist cause in eastern Ethiopia was followed by Egyptian weapons and training of the Somali military. Egypt's support formed part of President Gamal Abdel Nasser's government's attempt to undermine its regional rivals Ethiopia and Israel in the context of the Cold War great power competition in which Cairo sided with Moscow. However, Ethiopian leadership's instrumental role in the establishment and hosting of the Organization of African Unity (OAU) since 1963, and Somalia's confrontational policy with its neighbors that went against the OAU's principle of respecting colonial borders, Nasser changed his approach and while continuing to support Mogadishu, he attempted to moderate Mogadishu's foreign policy but without much tangible effect.

Somalia's confrontation with its neighbors then led to open hostilities. In 1963, a rebellion involving tax and land issues erupted in Bale Province, Ethiopia. Involving Bale and Oromo, the revolt extended among the Ogadeni Somali in eastern Ethiopia[14] and the rebels gained initially moderate assistance from Somalia.[15] The hostilities then spread across the border and contributed to a two-month border war in January 1964 after Aden Abdulle Osman Daar's government in Mogadishu signed a military assistance treaty with the Soviet Union. Although a ceasefire agreement in April 1964 ended the conflict, Somalia started receiving Soviet assistance which led to the modernization of port facilities in Berbera as part of a strategy to increase Soviet naval presence in the Indian Ocean and the Red Sea.

Meanwhile, the British government ceded the southern part of the Northern Frontier District to be administered by Kenya. This was despite the region being overwhelmingly inhabited by Somalis who overwhelmingly wished to join Somalia. Upon independence, Kenyan nationalist leaders held on to the territory against the will of the overwhelming majority of its people which contributed to the making of the irredentist Gaf Daba conflict (1963–7). The Northern Frontier District Liberation Movement (NFDLM) took arms against the government intending to secede and join Somalia and received support from Mogadishu to reach its objective. This led Kenyan leadership to sign a defense treaty with Ethiopia. However, in 1967, after Mohamed Haji Ibrahim Egal, later longtime Somaliland president who had briefly guided Somalia in July 1960, was appointed as the prime minister of Somalia for the second time, Mogadishu sought rapprochement with Ethiopia and Kenya which led to the winding down of rebellion in eastern Ethiopia, border conflict in Ogaden, and armed opposition in the Kenyan Northern Frontier District.

Also, despite the spreading nationalist sentiment among Somalis, propelled by SYL's resounding victory in Somalia's 1964 parliamentary election, the French continued to grip the strategic territory they occupied across the Strait of Bab al Mandab. In 1967 they changed the name of the Overseas Territory into the French Territory of the Afars and the Issas after a second referendum of self-determination in which Issa Somalis had expressed their will for independence and eventual unification with Somalia. Similarly to the earlier 1958 referendum, the plebiscite was marred with irregularities, and the territory continued to be associated with France until the third referendum finally led to its independence in 1977.

In its early efforts to create Greater Somalia, Mogadishu counted on Soviet support. Moscow saw Somalia as a counterweight to the Washington-aligned Ethiopia and supplied arms to maintain a strategic alliance that gave it access to the Gulf of Aden. On the other side of the crucial water body, the Soviet Union secured an alliance with South Yemen (the People's Democratic Republic of Yemen, PDRY).

On October 21, 1969, following the assassination of President Abdirashid Ali Shermarke, the military under Mohamed Siad Barre took power in Somalia. Barre's Supreme Revolutionary Council declared Somalia as a scientific socialist state, and initially deepened ties with Moscow while working with other Soviet-aligned states in the Red Sea region, including South Yemen and Sudan. After the completion of the port in Berbera, Soviet communication and naval support facilities were established along with an airbase in Hargeisa.[16] This was to an extent a countermove to the US presence in the Asmara Barracks (later Kagnew Station) since the Second World War, and Israeli presence in the Dahlak archipelago. While the Berbera base provided the Soviet Union a strategic advantage through presence on both sides of the Gulf of Aden, Soviet aid in terms of arms, materiel and training became significant for improving Somalia's military capacity.

The 1973 oil crisis hit Somalia and the other petroleum-importing nations in the Horn of Africa hard. This, along with the Barre administration's experimentation with the so-called scientific socialism, led to an economic downward spiral that, along with increasing repression after the Ogaden War (1977–8), generated emigration to the oil-rich Gulf States and elsewhere. As a result, many professionals left Somalia and settled in the main cities in Saudi Arabia and the UAE. This led to increasing connections in the Persian Gulf in which the diaspora individuals and exile organizations played an influential economic and political role.

Following the Ethiopian revolution in 1974, Somali nationalists and irredentists accelerated the effort to annex the Somali-inhabited part of eastern Ethiopia, often referred to as Ogaden. Saudi Arabia's promotion of Somali nationalism and irredentism, which formed part of Riyadh's attempt to advance its influence in the Horn, contributed to this effort and persuaded Mogadishu to join the Arab League. After securing an alliance with Mogadishu, Western-aligned Riyadh then positioned itself against Marxist Addis Ababa. Planning to annex eastern Ethiopia, the Barre government first provided support for the WSLF and promised to invade the region after WSLF had established control over a significant part of it. The WSLF also used its leverage among socialist and Arab states to gain assistance for its military operations. After negotiations between Mogadishu and Addis Ababa failed, Somali military personnel was sent to strengthen the WSLF, and the Somali National Army engaged in a build-up on the Ethiopian border.

In July 1977, after the WSLF had managed to exert control over a large part of Somali-inhabited eastern Ethiopia with the Somali Abo Liberation Front (SALF) and Harari assistance, the Somali military invaded Ethiopia. Following initial successes that led to the Somali National Army and the WSLF controlling most of eastern Ethiopia, the Soviet Union and several associated communist states, especially Cuba and South Yemen, rallied to support the Ethiopian government. This, in the absence of any comparable direct military assistance for Mogadishu, eventually produced the Somali defeat in March 1978. Despite providing approximately USD 300 million in financial assistance for the Somali war effort,[17] and counting on Egypt and Sudan's support for Mogadishu, Saudi Arabia's initial attempt to build a regional Arab alliance in the Horn of Africa and defeat communist Ethiopia and its allies had failed. Riyadh's other effort in the 1970s to turn the Red Sea into an "Arab Lake" was not much more successful largely because of being at odds with the interests of Israel and Soviet-aligned regional rivals Ethiopia and South Yemen.

Somalia's defeat in the Ogaden War paved way for the increasing US engagement in the Horn of Africa. After initial reluctance, but convinced by Riyadh, Cairo, and Khartoum, Washington began supporting Mogadishu as a counterforce to communist Addis Ababa and took over the former Soviet facilities in Berbera. What followed was Saudi Arabia initially financing Somali arms purchases and later providing aid to Mogadishu as part of an attempt to deter Addis Ababa's influence. The tripartite Ethiopia-Libya-South Yemen defense pact in August 1981 raised concerns in the US and among its allies. While the Barre administration took advantage of Western and Arab support to rebuild the Somali army, the government-linked non-state actors, such as the WSLF, also benefited from it for a limited time.

Until the early 1980s, the Somali government continued counting on the WSLF to destabilize eastern Ethiopia and allowed the military to support the movement. However, from 1978 onward WSLF atrocities against northern Somali civilians as part of a repressive government effort disillusioned its Fourth Brigade called "Afraad" composed of northern Isaaq officers. By 1980 they had begun combat operations against the WSLF mainstream and subsequently organized themselves as the core fighting force of the Somali National Movement (SNM) which was initially established in 1979 in Jeddah. Although SNM had initially strong Saudi and religious links, in 1981 its leaders relocated headquarters to London and incorporated other diaspora organizations, while claiming to be pro-Western,[18] to obtain financial, material, and nonmaterial support.

Following the defeat in Ogaden, President Barre sought to hold on to power by adopting an increasingly oppressive policy of clannism[19] and family-based nepotism. The policy of dividing the increasingly restive population and using clannism as a tool for state repression undermined the central government's legitimacy and authority. With US assistance, Barre rebuilt the army which was used mainly to suppress domestic opposition, especially targeting various externally supported clan-based armed opposition groups. During this period, Ethiopia became host to Somali armed groups as the Mengistu administration sought to capitalize on Somalia's defeat and build a network of clan-based opposition forces to destabilize the Barre regime in response to Somalia's attempt to undermine political stability in the Ogaden. In this, Mengistu drew on his partnership with the Soviet Union and regional allies. Ethiopia, together with Libya, endorsed the military formation and provided a base for the Somali Salvation Democratic Front (SSDF) established by Majeerteen (Darod) officers led by Abdullahi Yusuf Ahmed who had survived a purge after a failed coup attempt to oust Barre in 1978. Formed in Aden, South Yemen, in October 1981, from a merger of three Somali opposition organizations, the SSDF exemplifies the close relationship and continuous migration across the Gulf of Aden and between communist states in the region. Mengistu government also provided refuge and support for the Isaaq clan-based SNM, which played a role in Addis Ababa's plan to extend its influence to the shores of the Gulf of Aden in northern Somalia. This forced the US and its Arab allies to support the Somali government despite its increasing repression and prevent its collapse.

In 1982, yet another confrontation flared up on the Somalia-Ethiopia border. Somalia's continuous non-recognition of the UN-approved colonial boundary agreement, the lingering support to the insurgents in Ogaden, Mogadishu's deepening economic and more superficial military partnership with Washington, the US regional Arab allies' effort to fuel antagonism between Mogadishu and Addis Ababa each played a role in this. Particularly Somalia aligning with the US and becoming part of its Indian Ocean defense network was alarming to the Mengistu regime which as a countermove stepped up its support for the Somali armed opposition. Although an Ethiopian invasion in June 1982, to which SSDF heavily contributed, was repulsed with timely US assistance,[20] Somali-backed armed opposition in eastern Ethiopia withered and Ethiopian-supported Somali armed groups strengthened. The US, which increased its military aid to Somalia,[21] came to focus on strategically located Berbera[22] for monitoring the Gulf of Aden and entrance to Bab al-Mandab.

In 1986, Somalia and Ethiopia initiated an effort to settle their disputes over territorial boundaries. On April 3, 1988, the two leaders, Barre and Mengistu, signed a peace treaty in the last joint attempt to curb their respective armed opposition, but it came too late and the border issue remained unresolved. Proxy armed groups had otherwise become viable on their own and no longer needed either weak government as a patron. While Barre who did not have much control of the Somali armed factions active against the Ethiopian regime sought to abolish the WSLF, Mengistu was unable to honor his part of the deal because the Somali armed groups Addis Ababa had backed crossed the border to Somalia where they intensified guerrilla activity.[23] This, along with external pressure on the increasingly repressive Barre regime, which used US assistance to put down opposition on a clan basis, led to a full-blown civil war.

Despite the Ethiopian Derg regime's weakness in the face of strengthening domestic opposition, Mengistu's efforts to destabilize Somalia through the support of the armed groups as proxies were effective. It pushed the Barre administration to excessively rely on one partner, the US, for support. However, although Ethiopia's main interest was the mere weakening of the Barre regime, which its late attempt to prevent the Somali armed opposition from strengthening excessively demonstrates, the destabilization strategy had set in motion a dynamic that contributed to the eventual collapse of the Barre government.

The accelerating civil war in Somalia caused the breakdown of the central government's authority and the resulting power vacuum was filled by non-state actors. While in many areas the Barre administration was able to exert a modicum of influence though police presence and military operations, the clan-based armed opposition movements gradually gained ground and captured the hearts and minds of many who were torn between the waning and repressive government authority and the non-state forces. The emergence of the armed non-state actors also led to the decentralization of foreign connections in the country because these groups were engaged in their own external affairs. For example, the SSDF and SNM secured Ethiopian support and refuge, and, despite Addis Ababa's later efforts to restrain them and the Barre regime's attempts to confront them and coopt their leaders, these groups survived and crossed into Somalia where they became formidable forces.

Meanwhile, the SNM conducted an offensive in Somaliland which led to government reprisals and systematic atrocities against civilians. This caused an estimated almost two million people to leave their homes, many finding refuge abroad. When state sources of support grew thin, the SNM had to rely more on the Isaaq diaspora, particularly in Saudi Arabia and other Gulf States, but also in Ethiopia and other countries, for financial backing. The SNM benefited from remittances and other funds transferred by intermediaries such as Dahabshiil and developed a system of local taxation which added to the viability and strength of the movement. It, therefore, developed rather independently, albeit also being subjected to Ethiopian influence.

By the late 1980s, the ideological Cold War competition in the Horn of Africa had waned and became increasingly replaced by pragmatic considerations in interstate relations. The times of high oil prices had also passed which constrained investment and assistance from the oil-rich Persian Gulf countries. For the Somali government, this meant that with the waning of the US and Persian Gulf monarchies' commitment a need arose to look for new partnerships to ensure regime survival in an increasingly contested political context. The Barre regime established ties with states such as Libya that had been on the opposite side during the early part of the decade. This, however, was not enough to replace the declining American aid. In August 1989, in his last efforts to salvage the regime, Barre announced a political reform and establishment of a multi-party system to be implemented before 1991 but his desperation became clear when his closest associates and relatives who were also key members of the regime made their way to exile.

State Collapse and Its Discontents

In early 1991, the Barre government which had relied on narrow family and clan loyalties finally collapsed. This owed largely to the strengthening of the coalition of clan-based armed opposition movements, the regime repression which diminished its legitimacy, and the waning of its international backing. Among the armed movements, United Somali Congress (USC) based on the Hawiye clan was a significant latecomer to the fragmented stage of the civil war. Founded in 1987 in Rome, Italy, it was heavily supported by Ethiopia which provided training and resources for the movement. While other armed and non-armed movements played an important role in the initial ousting of the regime, the military successes of the military wing of USC led by Mohamed Farrah Aidid were instrumental in preventing Barre to return to power and forcing him into exile.

The collapse of central authority meant a dispersal of Somalia's foreign relations further into several non-state political authorities. Clan-based armed groups came to dominate the political and economic landscape through collaboration with local business elites. Warlords came to control territories and collect taxes, for example from imports and at checkpoints. Mogadishu, due to its importance as the capital and because of its vibrant business environment, became the grand prize. Through economic and financial connections abroad facilitated by the business community, warlords and clan militias engaged in extraversion of material and nonmaterial resources to strengthen themselves against local rivals. The division of the country among warlords and clan territories in many cases led to hybrid local governance involving various internal and external actors.[24]

The international community, preoccupied with the lack of central authority and famine-like conditions due to recurrent drought and persistent inter-clan conflict in the country, agreed on a humanitarian mission, UN Operation in

Somalia I (UNOSOM I). UNOSOM I was operational in 1992 but its struggle to sustainably provide, facilitate, and secure humanitarian relief at a large-scale was in vain. In December 1992 Unified Task Force (UNITAF) replaced UNOSOM I as an interim force that was unable to create a secure environment despite some positive impact on the security situation and the delivery of humanitarian aid. In March 1993 it was succeeded by the UN Operation in Somalia II (UNOSOM II) to which various Arab countries and Türkiye provided civilian and military personnel. Notably, the UAE sent a military contingent that cooperated closely with the US until withdrawing from Somalia in March 1994 just before the American force.[25]

During this period, clan-based movements operated by the big men[26] strengthened. They gained external resources from interaction with foreign actors. This meant that they had a stronger claim in the clan territories under their command and control of associated local resources. The armed movements used the gained financial and material resources (e.g., from the sale of local assets, aid, and weapons) to buttress their power in the contested political space that had opened up in the absence of the central government. Resources obtained through external relations could make a difference in terms of relative power between the movements. For example, Aidid's Somali National Alliance, a USC breakaway group established in June 1992 in alliance with the Darood faction of the Somali Patriotic Movement (SPM) and other groups from southern Somalia, gained Iranian and Sudanese military and financial support. This type of assistance helped strengthen its efforts to control central and southern parts of Somalia and enabled Aidid to defeat the UN and associate American intervention forces which withdrew in March 1995. Three months later, he claimed the presidency as a de facto leader of the country.

However, many did not consider Aidid's claim legitimate. This was because his rival commander and the leader of the USC mainstream, Ali Mahdi Muhammad, against who he fought over the control of the capital, had been officially declared as the president in a 1991 conference in Djibouti and subsequently internationally recognized following an initiative by Djibouti, Egypt, Saudi Arabia, and Italy. Aidid was fatally wounded in a confrontation against the USC forces in 1996, and controversy remains over his financier Osman Ali Atto's role in his death and in a possible northern Isaaq-led plot by Somaliland president Mohamed Haji Ibrahim Egal to destabilize southern Somalia.

After being driven out from its stronghold in the Puntland port city of Bosaso by Abdullahi Yusuf Ahmed's forces in 1992, Al-Itihaad al-Islamiya (AIAI), an Islamist militant group came to occupy large areas of the Gedo Region in the southwest of the country. Formed in 1984 as a merger of Salafi groups Al Jama'a Al Islamiya and Wahdat Al Shabaab Al Islam, AIAI was built around Somalis who had studied abroad and sought to create an Islamic state of Greater Somalia and East Africa based on Islamic law. The expansion of AIAI's influence in its neighborhood would be achieved by engaging in *jihad,* particularly against Ethiopian domination. By pursuing "activities in the humanitarian and social realm, providing schooling, food and health care so as to obtain the support of a Somali population exasperated by perpetual lawlessness,"[27] the group gained people's goodwill. The AIAI allegedly received funds, training, and logistical support from al-Qaeda, and financing, training, and weapons from Sudan until 1999, along with overseas "donations from diaspora communities in Europe, North America, and the Arabian Peninsula; from private financiers in Saudi Arabia and throughout the Middle East; and from organizations such as the Muslim World League, the International Islamic Relief Organization, and Al-Haramain Islamic Foundation."[28] Its leadership's connections with individuals, and charitable and relief organizations, particularly in Saudi Arabia, Yemen, and Pakistan, enabled the group to draw "advice, training, finance and military equipment."[29] The Cal Miskaad mountain range surrounding Bosaso in the Bari region turned into a stronghold for armed Islamists and the Islamic State which continue to compete in northern Puntland and cast influence on its northern shores, including the eastern borderlands of Somaliland.

In 1996 the AIAI-affiliated Islamist forces staged attacks within Ethiopia and engaged the Ethiopian military in Somalia's southwestern border region. This led Addis Ababa to support the AIAI rival group, the Somali National Front, as its proxy force in the region. These events set a precedent for occasional military incursions to various parts of Somalia in pursuit to neutralize what were considered destabilizing forces and influences emanating from Somalia. The Ethiopian government was particularly preoccupied with the Salafi Islamist ideology of the AIAI, its leaders' links to both designated terrorist organizations and regional rival states, including Arab powers, and possible destabilizing effect on Ethiopia due to its interest in the Ethiopian Somali Region. A particular concern was the AIAI's alliance with the separatist Ogaden National Liberation Front (ONLF), in line with the Ogadeni Darood origin of one of AIAI's leading figures, Hassan Abdullah Hersi al-Turki.

In opposition to the growing Salafist trend, moderate Sufi leaders in central Somalia founded the Ahlu Sunna Waljama'a (ASWJ) in 1991. ASWJ has stood against extremist interpretations, imposition of governance inspired by Wahhabism, and application of Shari'a law. Its activities, oriented against AIAI and subsequently al-Shabaab, have centered on the Galguduud region of the Galmudug federal state. The group gained importance during the civil war by supporting Aidid's clan-based forces and has since sustained itself in part through a close alliance with Ethiopia which favors the moderate Sufi movement as opposed to the Salafist jihadist actors who are considered to pose a religious radicalization and destabilization threat to Addis Ababa. In January 2018, ASWJ joined the Galmudug security forces which the federal administration declared as a boost in the war against al-Shabaab, but its relationship with regional and federal administration before and after the merger has been uneasy and caused significant periodic clashes. This has mainly owed to ASWJ leadership's discontent with local politicians[30] and disappointment with the federal efforts against al-Shabaab, while the federal administration has waged a campaign against the group accusing it of obstructing governance and destabilizing the counterinsurgency effort against al-Shabaab.[31] However, at the same time, there continue to be indications that some individuals in the federal administration and some persons and groups close to it, including some of its foreign backers, may not have distanced themselves from al-Shabaab at least when their and al-Shabaab's interests converge.[32] For example, President Farmaajo's main backer Qatar has been alleged to maintain linkages with al-Shabaab, as part of its "regular contact with Al-Qaeda and its affiliates in Syria, Iraq, Somalia and Yemen in order to exert geopolitical influence, play an intermediary role between terrorist organisations and the West, maintain Qatar's immunity to terrorist attacks, and/or show Doha's sympathy."[33]

The persisting mistrust between local leaders and communities and federal authorities explains in part the escalation of conflict between the locally powerful groups and representatives of the federal, and at times state, government as in the case of Galmudug. The federal government's absence, corruption, lack of service provision, and efforts to impose itself locally by force have alienated many local communities and undermined its legitimacy.

Following the collapse of central authority in Somalia, customary clan-based and religious leaders and institutions claimed authority. In northern Somalia, shortly after the demise of the central government, the majority Isaaq-based SNM, which had gained wide territorial control, sought peace with various smaller clans which eventually led to the revocation of Somaliland's voluntary union with Somalia and the declaration of independence ratified by the clan leaders (traditional elders) and SNM on May 18, 1991. By almost exclusively concentrating on the territory in the northwest, the SNM had gained wide acceptance among the population and independence from other armed groups contesting political power and space in central Somalia.

On May 16, 1993, Egal, a former Somali prime minister and an official of the Barre regime, was elected as the second president of Somaliland. Between 1994 and 1995 Egal consolidated his position over defiant and opposing clan forces through a carefully crafted strategy of military confrontation and cooptation which subsequently enabled him to centralize power and initiate state-building. From the outset, Somaliland's leadership sought an indigenous path to develop the political system, rejecting UN intervention and preferring to be left to its own devices. This was in part due to foreign parties' interest in a united Somalia and preference not to support Somaliland as a separate political entity. Neighboring Ethiopia, however, posed as an exception because it maintained close ties with Somaliland authorities mainly due to its interest in activating the Berbera corridor, a sea access route to the Gulf Aden, and trade that connected the two states.

On May 31, 2001, Somaliland authorities held a referendum on a draft constitution which Somalilanders confirmed along with the country's unilateral independence from Somalia. The referendum demonstrated Somalilanders' rejection of the internationally supported attempt to restore central political authority in Mogadishu that would claim jurisdiction over Somaliland. However, the Transitional Federal Government, founded in 2004, did not recognize Somaliland's de facto independence and included it as an integral part of Somalia in Article 2.3 of the 2004 Transitional Federal Charter of the Somali Republic.[34]

In the course of the 1990s, Puntland emerged as a semi-autonomous territorial unit in Somalia. Following the collapse of the central government, the SSDF, active mainly in Puntland where the Maajerteen clan is the majority, became a major force. However, a leadership feud ensued which split the movement between Chairman Mohamed Abshir Muse's political wing, which he directed largely from exile in Saudi Arabia, and his Deputy Abdullahi Yusuf Ahmed's SSDF military wing which had been instrumental in wresting control of Bosaso from the AIAI that had subsequently withdrawn to the surrounding mountain region. Abdullahi Yusuf also played a major role in the National Salvation Council which came together with the Somali National Alliance in a 1997 peace agreement in Cairo to establish a new federal structure and form a transitional government.[35]

Similarly to Somaliland where the leadership and the clan-based liberation movement played a major role in peacemaking and the birth of a new political system, Abdullahi Yusuf and the SSDF paved way for an indigenous, locally driven, peace and state-building process in Puntland.[36] In 1998, a more than three-month-long local constitutional conference took place, in the region's capital, Garowe, with hundreds of delegates from Puntland's constituent regions and the diaspora, including prominent individuals based in Saudi Arabia, the UAE, Kuwait, and Qatar. Again similarly to the process in Somaliland, the conference included important local stakeholders such as traditional clan-based elders, members of the political elite, representatives of the business community, and local intellectuals and civil society representatives, leading to the establishment of the Puntland State. With Abdullahi Yusuf as the first regional president, Puntland became a self-governing regional political entity within Somalia that engaged in security and service provision, trade facilitation, and interaction with domestic and international partners.[37] While it was decided that Puntland would remain part of Somalia, the federal state would be administered by prominent traditional elders in a clan-based political system, unlike central and southern Somalia, and pursue its foreign relations autonomously. Article 11 of the 2004 Transitional Federal Charter of the Somali Republic recognized the right of regions such as Puntland to federate as state governments within the state of Somalia.[38]

In April–May 2000 hundreds of delegates, many of them with ties to the countries in the Arabian Peninsula participated in the Somalia National Peace Conference held in Djibouti and endorsed by the UN Security Council. The conference resulted in the Arta Declaration seeking the formation of transitional political institutions aimed at preparing Somalia "for a peaceful, permanent and democratic future."[39] This led to the establishment of the Transitional National Government (TNG) and a former official of the Barre administration, Abdiqasim Salad Hassan, being elected as the president by a limited number of representatives of the Somali political elite. Despite the establishment of the major institutions of a standing government, Abdiqasim Hassan ruled until October 2004 over a weak regime that exerted fragile influence over the capital, Mogadishu, and suffered from internal fractures that led to the change of the prime minister four times. Its incapacity to raise taxes caused a shortage of resources and an inability to provide social services. As a result, Abdiqasim Hassan monopolized the decision-making power to himself, rendering public officials as locally ineffective figures of an unrealistic portrayal of a broadly representative state.[40] This, however, did not generate confidence in the TNG.

However, influential factional and regional leaders positioned themselves against the Djibouti conference and the resultant government. Some considered Djibouti's role in hosting the conference as partial because of its leaders' strong connections with politically powerful individuals in Somalia and influence over the process of making the government. Hussein Mohamed Farrah Aidid (son of Mohamed Farah Aidid), Mohamed Dhere, and Somaliland leaders headed by Egal opposed the conference. Hussein Aidid was concerned about external influence on the TNG, including Salafism emanating from Saudi Arabia and militant Islamist agitation. He subsequently established the competing Somali Reconciliation and Restoration Council (SRRC), which was also oriented against the Juba Valley Alliance (JVA) against which Aidid was contesting the control of Jubaland in southern Somalia and its strategic Juba River valley and the port of Kismayo. Various factions opposing the TNG led to an initial lack of local legitimacy despite the UN and (sub)regional organizations, the African Union (AU), and the Inter-Governmental Authority on Development (IGAD), endorsing the nascent government.

In September 2003, at the Somali National Reconciliation Conference in Nairobi which aimed at peace and state-building in Somalia, the delegates made further ground for forming a national government. With the support of the IGAD, AU, Arab League, and the UN, the conference led to reconciliation between the TNG and SRRC and the formation of the Transitional Federal Government (TFG). In October 2004, a presidential election was organized in which the candidates signed a declaration to demobilize their militias and the TFG parliamentarians voted Abdullahi Yusuf Ahmed, favored by Ethiopia and the US as a secular, anti-Islamist, alternative, as the first president of the new government. Several faction leaders and warlords, such as Hussein Aideed who doubled as the interior and deputy prime minister, gained positions. While the government formation increased the legitimacy of TFG by accommodating faction leaders, the power remained in the hands of those who maintained their militias and territorial control in various parts of the country and pursued policies and foreign relations autonomously.

Meanwhile, the Puntland administration exercised a significant degree of independence. Following Abdullahi Yusuf Ahmed's election as the president of the TFG, Puntland was led by Mohamed Hashi before the election of Mohamud Muse Hersi "Adde" as the regional president in January 2005. Adde pursued an active foreign policy for the sub-region independently from the TFG, for example engaging the UAE to fund economic development in Puntland. Using Puntland's commercial capital Bosaso's strategic location on the coast of the Gulf of Aden as an asset, Adde convinced prominent individuals in the UAE and landed various infrastructure and development projects. The UAE leaders, in turn, were interested in using petrodollars to gain further influence in the Gulf of Aden and to increase food security through rising livestock imports from Somalia, although major infrastructure investments were often considered risky. Two months in power, Adde began plans for the construction of an airport in Bosaso with foreign capital. In 2007 the airport construction got underway with funding from the UAE, and in 2008 Dubai's Lootah Group agreed to establish several companies to drive the development of the airport, the seaport, and an associated free trade zone along with providing management support for trade facilitation. This set the precedent for a close relationship between the Puntland administration and the UAE. At the occasion of announcing the deal, Ibrahim Saeed Ahmed Lootah, Chairman of Lootah Group, expressed the enterprise's commitment "to support the growth vision of his Excellency the President of the Punt Land of Somalia" as a "very privileged . . . partner with the state government."[41] More than a year earlier, Adde made a deal with a member of Ras al-Khaimah leadership in the UAE for a livestock quarantine facility. His personal economic diplomacy representing Puntland was successful in attracting Arab funding. He built a transactional relationship with the UAE in which strategic locations and local assets (e.g., livestock) in Puntland were offered for investment and development in exchange for financial gains.

In the January 2009 regional presidential election, Abdirahman Mohamud Farole emerged as the leader in Puntland. Following the example of his predecessor, Farole engaged the UAE, but also other international actors, to address Somali piracy in the Gulf of Aden and the Indian Ocean which had drastically increased in the previous year. In 2010 the regional administration passed anti-terrorism and anti-piracy laws, the latter of which paved the way for the construction of a naval base in Bandar Siyada near Bosaso. In response to the call by the UN Security Council,[42] the Puntland Maritime Police Force (PMPF) was established with the support of the UAE and states interested in establishing a local institutional anti-piracy framework. With the UAE's support, PMPF's capacity increased, allowing the expansion of its operations, which some in the UN Somalia-Eritrea Monitoring Group (SEMG) interpreted as a major threat to stability.[43] In 2012, the UAE sent forces to tackle piracy,[44] and the same year the SEMG characterized PMPF as "a highly profitable enterprise for relatives and close associates of Puntland President Faroole."[45] The UN investigation also implied that UAE's involvement in supplying the PMPF and the activities of private security company Saracen International/ Sterling Corporate Services (SCS) were violations of the UN arms embargo on Somalia and made PMPF a security threat. TFG authorities also challenged the Puntland authorities claiming that any foreign actors operating in Puntland should not violate the UN arms embargo and should be answerable to TFG.

However, despite criticism, with the PMPF and international support, piracy in Puntland drastically decreased and pirate networks shifted southward to the region of Galmudug.[46] The close relationship between Puntland leadership and the UAE also continued.[47] In April 2017, in the context of Abu Dhabi's effort to secure and expand its influence in the Gulf of Aden, Puntland leadership agreed to a USD 336 million 30-year concession deal for the Dubai Ports World (DP World) develop and operate the Bosaso port after a similar agreement with Somaliland at Berbera had been signed in the previous year.[48] This shows the relative autonomy of individuals in the Puntland leadership to pursue economic diplomacy and external relations and use the obtained foreign funding and resources to advance their interests, including strengthening their local position irrespective of the position of the central government in Mogadishu.

Migration and Diaspora Connections

In the case of Somalia, migration has also provided an important source of agency for various actors in local developments and external relations. Amid difficult conditions characterized by oppression, conflict, and insecurity over livelihoods, internal displacement and emigration have become persisting societal conditions. While internal displacement, for more than 2.6 million people[49] of the over 16 million in total, has been a survival strategy, it has also been an important source of revenue and other material resources for those who have engaged in the business of international aid and humanitarian assistance. Particularly in the 1990s, it not only enriched individuals who became stakeholders in the prevailing political constellation in the country, but led to political power through control over, or alliances with, parties using means of coercion in the absence of well-established central authority.

However, outward migration since the 1970s has resulted in approximately two million Somalis living out of the country. Initially pushed out mainly by the worsening economic conditions at home, especially during the oil crisis, and the later increasing repression under the military dictatorship, the Somali migrants were pulled in by the employment opportunities in the petroleum-rich Persian Gulf countries. Currently, the majority of the Somali diaspora population resides in the neighboring states in the Horn of Africa, Persian Gulf countries, and Yemen, but also in Western Europe and North America which host sizeable populations. Due to the widespread diaspora, these regions have served as a source of financial and material resources for the Somali-inhabited areas in the Horn of Africa.

For decades, Somalis have emigrated to the Persian Gulf countries and Egypt. Particularly Saudi Arabia and more recently the UAE host thousands of Somalis as migrant workers, while many have a deep historical connection with Yemen, including through tribal diaspora. Due to historical and contemporary linkages, the Somali and Yemeni populations have intermixed and settled in both countries. Yemen has also served as a transit country for Somalis to the Persian Gulf and beyond, which has contributed to the extension of the Somali diaspora. The Somali business community in the Gulf States has become an important player in domestic politics in Somalia. Its sheer size, estimated to be approximately 100,000 in the UAE alone, makes individuals hailing from the expatriate business community significant in the relationship between the two countries. Located in the UAE Somali businesses can cater to the Somali market by offering financial services or re-exportation of goods, sometimes by using intermediaries.[50]

In many parts of the world, Somali immigrants have struggled, but some have also gained affluent livelihoods and even ascended to politically and economically prominent positions in the host societies. However, their connection and commitment to Somalia often remain strong, which has translated into up to USD 1 billion in diaspora remittances in terms of money and resources back to Somalia in a given year. The success of many diaspora individuals has inspired young Somalis to migrate, institutionalizing *tahriib* (illegal migration) over the years into a widely aspired practice, particularly among the disenfranchised youth.[51]

Many diaspora individuals have become prominent back home through their wealth and ideas acquired abroad. They have been active and powerful in politics at the national and sub-national levels, as well as in Somaliland, and among non-state actors such as Islamist movements. Their activities have included peacemaking, state-building, investment, trade, and development activities. The Salafist diaspora leaders related to the Islamist movement in Somalia, as well as some of the prominent members of the federal and regional governments, have mainly come among those who migrated to countries such as Saudi Arabia and Qatar, or other Gulf monarchies, Egypt, and Sudan, where they were exposed to Salafist teachings and Wahhabist practices. The Persian Gulf and Middle East linkages of more secular or moderate prominent individuals have tended to come through business connections in countries such as the UAE and Türkiye. Local politicians have also benefited from diaspora remittances, which have strengthened their position in the domestic political landscape and have had both stabilizing and destabilizing effects[52] depending on their and their partners' interests and behavior.

Another Unraveling: Islamic Courts Union and al-Shabaab

Meanwhile, since the 1990s, the warlords dominating Mogadishu had become increasingly compromised and were eventually overwhelmed by the Islamic Courts Union (ICU). Having changed from claimed representatives of clan interests into security providers for the highest bidder, proportioning security for taxes for big businessmen who made fortunes by channeling international aid,[53] they were increasingly challenged and unable to impose law and order. Lacking resources to uphold their legitimacy, they had fragmented into smaller forces. The ICU, an aggrupation of Sharia courts emerging from the clan-based political dynamics in Mogadishu dominated by various sub-section of the Hawiye, came to control the capital in June 2006. This had alarmed the US, which as part of its War on Terror staged covert operations to neutralize prominent religious leaders suspected of terrorist connections and worked with those warlords who opposed the ICU to form the Alliance for Restoration of Peace and Counter-Terrorism. With US funding, the warlords strengthened their position but were no match to the ICU which used both local and international connections to obtain financial and material resources. The ICU, a network of Islamist organizations, which in part due to its increasing competitiveness in "selling security"[54] had become a viable security provider for influential businesses in Mogadishu, benefited from its relationship with local businessmen and used the al-Shabaab Salafi youth militia associated with some of the former AIAI leaders to defeat the warlord alliance and drive it out of the city. As the main enforcer of the rule of law, relying on clan-based militias, it was able to stabilize the city and enforce security.[55]

After the ICU takeover of the capital, the international community became increasingly alarmed. This was because the ICU's rapid extension in the central and southern parts of the country threatened the authority of the internationally backed TFG which relied on Ethiopian support and still had limited territorial

control in and around Baidoa. On July 20, 2006, the Ethiopian military entered
the country by the apparent invitation of TFG, and Addis Ababa justified the
invasion as self-defense, preventive action against a terrorist threat, and to secure
the country's territorial integrity.[56] The following day, the ICU declared Jihad, a
holy war, against Ethiopia. By October, the ICU and Ethiopian-backed TFG were
at full-scale war and Ethiopia conducted military operations in defense of the
latter. In November, the UN released a confidential report which pointed fingers
at Hezbollah, an organization designated as a terrorist, as well as Eritrea, Iran,
Syria, Libya, and Egypt, as supporters of Somali Islamists, and warned about the
possibility of relapse to war between Eritrea and Ethiopia and Somalia becoming
consumed by Islamist insurgency and terrorism.[57] When AIAI leader Sheikh
Hassan Dahir Aweys wowed that "We will leave no stone unturned to integrate
our Somali brothers in Kenya and Ethiopia and restore their freedom to live with
their ancestors in Somalia,"[58] fears in the region about the resurgence of Somali
nationalism and territorial expansionism grew. Particularly Ethiopian and the US
administrations were worried about spreading instability due to the leading figures
of AIAI, including Sheikh Aweys and al-Turki who had participated in the Ogaden
War, playing leading roles in the ICU. They feared that ICU agitation could have a
radicalizing effect among Ethiopian Muslims and strengthen the separatist ONLF
insurgency in eastern Ethiopia.[59]

In December, the military escalation culminated in the Battle of Baidoa. In the
six-day confrontation, the combined Ethiopian and TFG forces, with US special
operations support, overran the ICU defenses. Forces from the autonomous
territories of Galmudug, Puntland, Southwestern Somalia, and Jubaland joined
them to take Mogadishu largely unopposed two days later. As the ICU disintegrated,
many fighters continued to be active in the resulting splinter groups. The Islamist
forces withdrew to southern Somalia near the Kenyan border which converted
into a major stage of armed confrontation in the following years. Meanwhile, in
January 2007, the TFG relocated to Mogadishu, and the same month the AU's
Peace and Security Council established the AU Mission in Somalia (AMISOM)
which was subsequently approved by the UN Security Council.

In September 2007, resisting TFG's takeover, leaders of the disintegrated ICU
and displeased former TFG officials formed a political party, Alliance for the
Re-liberation of Somalia (ARS), in Asmara.[60] Claiming broad-based support in
Somalia, they sought to overthrow the TFG which they portrayed as a foreign
agent that is heavily influenced and dependent on anti-Islamic and anti-Somali
nationalist external actors, such as the US and Ethiopia, and forming part of
Addis Ababa's machinations to maintain Somalia weak. Politicizing this viewpoint
enabled anti-TFG and anti-Ethiopia sentiments to thrive and facilitate recruitment
to oppose the new government. Radical Islamist groups, initially operating mainly
in the south, gained strength. Among them was al-Shabaab, the former radical
youth organization within the ICU, which developed into a Salafi jihadist group
of its own, espousing violent Wahhabism and positioning itself against TFG, its
foreign allies, and the majority Sufi Muslims in the country. Although a peace
conference in Djibouti in May–June 2008 produced an agreement between the

ARS and TFG, it did not please all leaders and the armed radical Islamist groups remained the main violent opposition.

In January 2009, former ICU leader, Sharif Sheikh Ahmed, was elected and sworn in as the president in Djibouti. Realizing the growing strength of al-Shabaab under the leadership of the former ICU executive council member Ahmed Abdi Godane and the dire security situation in the country, he began rallying for support and resources for the TFG in the Arab League and the UN. Although with the support of the AMISOM, the TFG drove al-Shabaab out of Mogadishu, in 2009 it became indisputably the most powerful armed opposition force with a stronghold in the southern part of the country. During this period, the US continued air strikes which it had commenced in 2007 against what it considered al-Qaeda-associated Islamists. Al-Shabaab defeated and eventually absorbed the Hizbul Islam, a rival Islamist force that combined Al-Turki's Ras Kamboni Brigades with other Islamist groups, such as a faction of the ARS based in Asmara under Sheikh Aweys who defied the Djibouti peace agreement. In 2009–10 it became increasingly apparent that Godane pursued a transnational agenda by first seeking to move against UN World Food Program and Western humanitarian agencies and sidelining more nationally focused leaders such as Hassan Aweys, and also pledging allegiance to al-Qaeda and Osama bin Laden several times. Illustrating his attempt to internationalize the struggle before his death in a US airstrike in September 2014,[61] Godane stated that "The aim of the (foreign) invasion is to divide the remaining Somalia between Kenya and Ethiopia under the cover of the establishment of Somali states" and that "Somalis, your religion has been attacked, your land divided, your resources looted directly and indirectly through the puppet government - our victory lies in Jihad."[62] While this alienated some of those who felt that the movement should have only a national cause, it inspired foreigners to join the organization and attracted financial resources from individuals and conservative and radical circles in the Middle East and among the diaspora.

Over the years, al-Shabaab's campaigns for foreign recruitment have been successful in gaining the movement international publicity. Through the effective use of online and audiovisual media, al-Shabaab has been successful in recruiting Somali and Muslim youth from faraway places, such as Europe, North America (e.g., the US and Canada), and Asia (e.g., Afghanistan, Bangladesh, Malaysia, and Pakistan), although many recruits have come from the nearby states, including Kenya, Sudan, and Yemen. Saudi individuals, especially Shaykh Muhammad Abu Fa'id in his role as a financier, have played an important role in the movement. This has enabled the use of foreign linkages for obtaining resources to strengthen the position of the leading individuals and the movement as a whole. Although its much-publicized allegiance to al-Qaeda in the early 2010s, and later to the Islamic State of Iraq and the Levant (ISIL) in 2015, brought a rift between "internationalists" and "nationalists" within the movement, it has maintained al-Shabaab's international profile and appeal to foreign recruits. Al-Shabaab has also engaged in selling charcoal to Persian Gulf countries and channeling sugar from the Gulf States to Kenya, through its influence in Kismayo while maintaining profitable commercial relations also with the Kenyan contingent of the AMISOM.[63]

In 2018 the UN Security Council pinpointed the UAE and Iran as being involved in such trade,[64] although Abu Dhabi, which Mogadishu had engaged in 2014 to support Somalia's reconstruction,[65] designated al-Shabaab as a terrorist group and engaged in efforts against violent non-state actors by assisting Somali PMPF and security forces. Despite the UAE's recent history of complicated official relations with Somalia due to its perceived favoring of sub-state units and non-state actors during the Mohamed Abdullahi Mohamed "Farmaajo" presidency (2017–22), the Somali diaspora, and especially migrant workers and businesses, have buttressed strong economic and social connections making the UAE as one of Somalia's main trading partners and links to the world.[66] These international connections, along with a domestic system of taxation, including road tolls, port duties, religious payments, and taxation of businesses, agriculture, and livestock sustain al-Shabaab,[67] and mafia-like tactics of intimidation often oblige individuals and organizations doing business around the country to engage it.

Together with its fundraising mechanisms, al-Shabaab has obtained resources from foreign sources which have contributed to its strength. It has reached out to financiers particularly in the Middle East, where Saudi, Iranian, Egyptian, Libyan, Syrian, Qatari, and Yemeni individuals and groups have been accused of providing it funding, while also engaging in fundraising in Europe, North America, and Asia. This has resulted in al-Shabaab running a significant economic and financial enterprise which has strengthened the movement and allowed it to defy the government and its international backers' state-building effort.

The internationally supported federal government and AMISOM attempt to defeat al-Shabaab has suffered from fractured local elites and their contradicting interests. For example, there have been individuals forming part of the federal state establishment who see more benefit in efforts to extravert resources from the public office for private ends than building a coherent front against violent opposition that uses tactics of extortion targeting also state employees and businesses. While some would like to see the central government gain strength, its perpetual weakness continues to favor power centers around prominent individuals, groups, and sub-state actors. When challenging the government, some of these local actors wield coercive force, extract resources locally, and engage in external relations through which to gain resources and strength.

Similarly, al-Shabaab leadership has been able to market itself as a major coercive political player to external parties interested in influencing the political dynamics in Somalia. However, although having developed links to powerful Persian Gulf countries such as Saudi Arabia, UAE, Iran, and Qatar, it has pursued its agendas independently from these and other external actors with which it has maintained connections. In terms of power, al-Shabaab has been able to secure the continuity of its coercive force through a flow of weapons from the federal government and black market intermediaries, and by arms brought from Yemen through Puntland[68] where local businessmen have been linked to the suspected weapons deals which have also allegedly involved Yemeni national and al-Qaeda financier, Sayf Abdulrab Salem Al-Hayashi, and his proxies.[69] Such financial and material resources improved al-Shabaab's operational and destructive capacity, and until today it has remained a nationally significant actor with a presence not only in southern and south-central Somalia but also in highlands in Puntland and Somaliland border areas. Al-Shabaab has gained resources by reaching out to external actors and maintaining international networks for example with the al-Qaeda of the Arabian Peninsula. Its shadowy economic diplomacy has involved attracting financiers and recruits to its cause by using physically delivered, online, and media propaganda as well as engaging in lucrative economic activities such as taxation and trade. Although weakened by the AMISOM, Somali army and militias, and regional militaries and their allies, until recently al-Shabaab has continued to be active especially in Bay, Lower Shabelle, and northern Bari regions, and areas in and surrounding Mogadishu and feeds from external linkages which strengthen it in its domestic activities. In an attempt to curb al-Shabaab's estimated USD 100 million annual revenue, the US Department of Treasury has imposed targeted sanctions on a number of its leading individuals, including Abdullahi Jeeri, Khalif Adale, Hassan Afgooye (a reward of up to USD 5 million for information), Abdikarim Hussein Gagaale, Abdi Samad, Abdirahman Nurey, Mohamed Hussein Salad, Ahmed Hasan Ali Sulaiman Mataan, and Mohamed Ali Badaas involved either in domestic and international fundraising activities or weapons trafficking mainly in Yemen and Somalia. US Treasury sees particularly Afgooye's extensive overseas and local financial network, involving charities, companies, fundraising, racketeering, and kidnapping as key to financing al-Shabaab's operations.[70]

Post–Arab Spring Realities

The Arab Spring pitted Persian Gulf monarchies seeking to maintain the domestic status quo in the Middle East against those states that favored political transformation from the grassroots. In this context, the Horn of Africa, with fragile authoritarian states and an important Muslim population, became a battleground for Middle Eastern interests. While Saudi Arabia, alarmed by the deteriorating political situation in Yemen, accelerated the effort to neutralize Iranian presence in the Red Sea region, Türkiye and Qatar became increasingly involved particularly in Somalia. Instrumentalizing humanitarian concerns as a vehicle in its opening up to Africa policy, in 2011 Ankara entered into increasing cooperation with Mogadishu amid a ravaging famine following several years of drought. Qatar had engaged in mediation on the African side of the Red Sea for a number of years and had developed relationships with Islamist leaders and grassroots movements. For Somalia, Türkiye quickly became an indispensable humanitarian, development, and security provider, taking over airport and port operations in Mogadishu, capacitating the federal military and securing its presence in Mogadishu by founding a military base and elaborate embassy, and providing investment and importing Turkish goods. In a short period of time, Ankara, through the ruling Turkish Justice and Development Party leadership, which saw Somalia as the initial testing ground of its Africa policy, established itself as a major partner of the Mogadishu political elite and prominent businessmen closely related to the presidency. Through its support of the federal government, Ankara has sought to build a modicum of stability that should enable it to obtain even greater proceeds from the unequal partnership. Reportedly, Turkish enterprises have engaged in corrupt practices and siphoning of funds from airport and port operations, while its intelligence service has allegedly maintained a close relationship with al-Shabaab.[71] Ankara supported Hassan Sheikh heavily during his first presidential term (2012–17) and vouched for his reelection to secure a continued central role in Mogadishu, but his successor, Mohamed Abdullahi "Farmaajo" (2017–22), also decided to work closely with Türkiye. Hassan Sheikh benefited enormously from Turkish involvement and built his individual political and economic power by using Turkish resources, while also seeking to benefit from warm Emirati and Qatari relations. During Hassan Sheikh's first tenure, various corruption scandals emerged, including top officials being implicated in the embezzlement of public funds from the central bank and Mogadishu port for private means. This resulted in economic resources for leading individuals in the Somali government which enabled them to buttress their social position and political prominence.

Qatar, on the other hand, was already increasingly involved in Somalia before the turn of the decade. It developed a pattern of financially assisting its favored presidential candidates as in the case of Hassan Sheikh[72] and his successor Farmaajo. While Farmaajo also received financial endorsement from Doha's Persian Gulf rivals and made his first foreign visit in February 2017 to Riyadh, weighing his options, he continued to favor alignment with Qatar which would serve his political project that emphasized nationalist rebuilding and re-strengthening of central authority. The eruption of the Qatar diplomatic crisis in June 2017, which coincided with Farmaajo's first year in office, and to which the competition over Somalia may have somewhat contributed, made Mogadishu initially isolated because of its significant connections to the leading Persian Gulf countries. To diversify cooperation with external powers, Farmaajo then began emphasizing relations with Türkiye and Ethiopia. However, formal and informal connections to the Persian Gulf remained strong.

Through its support during the Farmaajo presidency, Doha made an important contribution to the political dynamics in the country. It provided financial resources to prominent individuals and groups. In the 2008–12 period, and again during the diplomatic crisis, Qatar was accused of supporting al-Shabaab, but any close linkages are unlikely and not qualitatively distinct from other Persian Gulf monarchies' "tactical alliances with hard-line militants" or their struggles "to clamp down on donations to extremists by wealthy individuals."[73] Recognizing the interests and funding potential of external financiers, presidential candidates, high-profile officials, and business leaders have frequently sought to tap into such opportunities by emphasizing their religious credentials and commitment to Islam as a building block for a "new" Somalia. This was the case with Farmaajo's election in 2017 in which his campaign manager and Doha's proxy, Fahad Yasin Haji Dahir, a Salafist and former AIAI member, played an important role. Funds channeled through Fahad Yasin were instrumental in coopting individuals working in, or who were knowledgeable of, Hassan Sheikh's administration, including Hassan Ali Khaire, who served as the prime minister between 2017 and 2020.

However, although this has bought Qatar a modicum of influence, its attempts at economic statecraft have rested on the fickle personal positions and alignments with the prominent individuals and groups willing to take advantage of support in their domestic struggles. This leads to a bargaining game in which such individuals and groups use their foreign connections as leverage and engage in personalized economic diplomacy to "sell" their local political and economic assets, including influence and (non)material resources, but maintaining a significant degree of power in such arrangements due to their local prominence. Qatar has been accused of meddling in Somali politics and causing instability through its backing of the Farmaajo administration's efforts to advance its influence. Some are convinced that Doha was behind the impasse over the postponed presidential election which finally took place in 2022, supporting the federal government and al-Shabaab activity against the federal states,[74] and engineering attacks on its rivals, such as the UAE's DP World in Bosaso.[75]

Similarly to Qatar and Türkiye, Saudi Arabia and the UAE have also been active in attempting to influence Somali politics. While Saudis have mainly been concerned with curtailing Iranian influence by offering financial incentives,[76] the UAE, especially since 2017, has been more preoccupied with internal politics in part because of its emphasis on the political rift between federal states and the central government. As a major regional player, Saudi Arabia has approached Somalia largely from the perspective of containing Iran. While emphasizing cooperation on religious and cultural grounds, Riyadh has used economic means for political persuasion. As with other states in the Horn of Africa, the Saudi attempt at economic statecraft has included direct funding, such as investments, transfers, and financial support, as well as trade. These means have been used with variable success at best to influence election results and sway Mogadishu to align with its interests, recently in its military alliance in Yemen and confrontation with Qatar.

However, it was Somali president Hassan Sheikh's visit to Saudi Arabia in October 2015 which initiated deeper cooperation between the two states. After a Saudi delegation visited Mogadishu later the same year, and Riyadh executed a well-known Shia cleric in January 2016 which prompted angry mobs to attack Saudi missions in Iran, the Somali government agreed to end diplomatic ties with Iran in exchange for a USD 50 million pledge of aid from the Saudi Development Fund.[77] This set a precedent for Saudi attempts to influence Somali governments for relatively small sums of money, which in the case of the Qatar diplomatic crisis failed to persuade the Farmaajo government to cut ties with Doha. Multilaterally, Saudi Arabia hosts the Islamic Development Bank which engages projects in the member countries, including Somalia, which is part of the Organization of Islamic Cooperation. In the private sector, Saudi Arabia has served as the primary market for Somali livestock, the bulk of which originates from the Ethiopian Somali Region. This has made Somaliland and Puntland particularly vulnerable to any market disruptions caused by occasional livestock import bans and quarantines.[78] Saudi Arabia has also been implicated as a recipient in the charcoal trade from

Kismayo port, and at least one individual has been linked to al-Shabaab through financial contributions and ideological affinity.[79] Still, Saudi attempts to influence Somali political actors have fallen short of achieving control of Somali external relations. Instead, various Somali actors have exploited linkages to Saudi Arabia economically to a variable degree, resulting in equally variable power locally.

Abu Dhabi's involvement in Somalia intensified after the Arab Spring in an attempt to counter Turkish and Qatari overtures. Already during Hassan Sheikh's first presidential term (2012–17), the UAE had also taken up training and partial responsibility over the Somali federal army salaries, but the pay hardly reached the units. This gave incentive for soldiers to engage in criminal activities and coerced exploitation of civilians to ensure their livelihoods, including selling weapons in the black market. The year before the presidential election marked a peak of corruption, eroding the government's legitimacy, and "extortion, robbery, murder, and torture" largely attributed to the security forces.[80] Although some effort in establishing an institutional framework capable of holding leaders accountable was made during President Farmaajo's tenure, including the establishment of the Judicial Service Commission and the Anticorruption Commission, President Hassan Sheikh Mohamud dismantled the two institutions after returning to power in 2022 because their creation had not been approved by the federal parliament's senate.[81] This reflects endemic corruption and perpetuation of the deeply engrained practice of using public resources, offices, and institutions for personal gain which ties in external actors and their resources.

In response to Somalia's deeper partnership with its rival Qatar, but also Türkiye, during the Farmaajo presidency, the UAE began favoring the sub-state actors over the federal government. During the Farmaajo years, it mainly engaged in a rivalry with Qatar, "each providing weapons or military training to favored factions, exchanging allegations about bribing local officials, and competing for contracts to manage ports or exploit natural resources."[82] At the same time, the leaders of the Somali federal states took advantage of UAE's interest and its failed attempts to gain significant influence in Mogadishu after the 2017 presidential election. This leveraged them and strengthened their autonomous, or outright independent, position relative to the central government. For example, Somaliland's leadership, in its increasingly sophisticated foreign policy, reached out to the UAE and then several other states to consolidate separate foreign relations from Mogadishu. Its main stated objective has been to gain international legal recognition, which would unlock funding from international financial institutions, but Hargeisa, unlike Mogadishu, has also moved from the peace and state-building stage into propelling development. While Somaliland's limited ability to use economic diplomacy has fluctuated depending largely on the individual agency of each president, Hargeisa has sought to use its relations with the UAE and other states as leverage.

In the first part of June 2015, less than two months after Abu Dhabi fell out with Djibouti, Ahmed Mohamed Mohamud "Silanyo," the president of Somaliland, visited the UAE. His visit can be seen as an opportunistic foreign policy move in the changing circumstances in regional politics. Silanyo's delegation discussed development projects and humanitarian issues regarding Yemeni refugees and agreed to the Emirati conglomerate DP World to engage in port development and operation in Berbera,[83] which not only buttressed Silanyo's personal position but also initiated a drive for the development of the Berbera Corridor linking to Addis Ababa and elevated Somaliland's geopolitical and strategic importance. Silanyo's visit has been interpreted as Abu Dhabi's attempt to persuade the Somaliland leadership for military cooperation, including establishing a base and training Somaliland security forces,[84] and to use the port and the Soviet-era airfield in Berbera as staging grounds for operations in Yemen. On May 10, 2016, President Silanyo's USD 442 million landmark deal with DP World for the development and operation of the Port of Berbera for thirty years was made public. It was followed by an agreement for the UAE to build a military base in early 2017[85] and a deal in 2018 for Abu Dhabi to train Somaliland forces. The operations for the upgrading of the Berbera Port began in March 2017, and its development has greatly improved its capacity and efficiency. According to the DP World Group chairman and CEO Sultan Ahmed Bin Sulayem, "It will be a viable, efficient and competitive option for trade in the region, especially for Ethiopian transit cargo."[86]

In March 2018, the announcement that Ethiopia would become a partner in the deal with a 19 percent stake infuriated Mogadishu leadership. Hargeisa–Mogadishu relations deteriorated further, and armed confrontations in Somaliland's eastern border with Somalia's Puntland federal state, which had first started after an unannounced Mogadishu minister of planning's visit in the area in January, continued intermittently throughout the year.

The UAE's presence in Berbera complemented its efforts to increase its geostrategic influence in the Gulf of Aden, which has also included garrisoning the islands of Socotra and Perim (Mayyun). Although aware of discussions that led to the deal, Hassan Sheikh having silently accepted the UAE–Somaliland deal, Farmaajo leadership aligned with Qatar vehemently objected to Abu Dhabi's presence in Somaliland and sought Saudi assistance to convince the UAE to withdraw its plans for the military base[87] in part because this was seen to increase Hargeisa's power and independence relative to Mogadishu. Although investing heavily in the Berbera port and transport corridor to Addis Ababa, the UAE eventually abandoned the plan for setting up a military base and prepared the Berbera airfield for civilian use. In early 2021, Abu Dhabi withdrew from Eritrea's Assab but has opted to otherwise maintain a presence in the strategic coastal and island locations in the Red Sea and the Gulf of Aden.[88]

The port deal was part of a larger strategic calculation for activating the Berbera Corridor serving as an alternative sea route from Somaliland's "traditional" ally Ethiopia which has envisaged for decades to diminish its dependence on Djibouti. It also enabled UAE's DP World, which was expelled from Djibouti in favor of a Chinese port operator, to opt for an alternative logistics route to the Ethiopian market. In another development in 2019, Mohamed Saeed Guedi, a prominent business leader in Somaliland, the Horn of Africa, Dubai, and the Middle East,[89] heading the MSG Group of Companies active in various sectors, struck a joint venture for a USD 40 million grinding unit with the main Omani cement producer Raysut Cement Company.[90] Raysut had initially announced an investment in

Somaliland in 2013 but had been caught in the middle of Hargeisa's effort to wrest increasing control of economic activity from the local clan-affiliated businessmen and consolidate its authority in Berbera. Hargeisa also debunked Turkish, and subsequent Ethiopian and Somalia's other international backers' efforts to mediate in its dispute with Mogadishu. This is because Somaliland authorities have considered as biased and a threat to its sovereignty. In December 2021 Taiwanese state oil company CPC Corporation entered into an agreement with the UK-based Genel Energy for future drilling in onshore blocks in central Somaliland, where the latter had been awarded an exploration license in 2012. Somaliland government's relations with the UAE, the United Kingdom, and the United States, and recent dealings with Taiwan, for example, mirror its interest to become an increasingly assertive regional actor through domestic economic development and increasing defense capacity aimed against potential destabilization attempts by Islamist militants or Somali government agents.

Although Farmaajo leadership in Mogadishu was forced to tolerate Abu Dhabi's continued support of Puntland, it condemned what it viewed as the UAE's subversive involvement in Somaliland and the federal states. This owes in part to the 2017 presidential election, in which the UAE supported Farmaajo's rivals, including Prime Minister Omar Abdirashid Ali Sharmarke, who was seen as the best option to compete against Turkish and Qatari economic and Islamic influence.[91] Farmaajo's close relations with the UAE's major regional rival Qatar fed the condemnation of the UAE's dealings because they were seen as undermining the power of the federal government relative to the federal states and Somaliland, although the previous president Hassan Sheikh who had used both Abu Dhabi and Ankara for patronage and advancing national reconciliation had silently accepted the UAE's direct business with Hargeisa.

The UAE and Ethiopia had merging interests in Somalia, and they drew closer ahead of the change of leadership in Addis Ababa and its reconciliation with Asmara in 2018. Ethiopian leadership has a long-term objective to maintain Somalia weak and divided to minimize the possibility of the re-emergence of nationalism that could threaten Ethiopia's stability and territorial integrity. It has maintained a significant military presence in Somalia through the AMISOM (since April 2022 the African Union Transition Mission in Somalia, ATMIS) and otherwise. Until recently, Ethiopia's interest has been compatible with the UAE's efforts to work with the federal states and Somaliland and maintain Mogadishu weak because of its regional rivalry with the Farmaajo government's close allies Qatar and Türkiye. However, with the return of Hassan Sheikh to power, Mogadishu's relationship with Abu Dhabi, as well as with other Arab powers active in the Red Sea region which defied the previous administration, is set to improve.

Farmaajo Presidency

From early on, President Farmaajo's tenure became affected by the Qatar diplomatic crisis. Perceived to have obtained the presidency with Qatari support, Saudi

Arabia and the UAE put pressure on the Somali leadership to cut ties with Doha or leave office. While Djibouti and Eritrea joined the boycott, prompting Qatar to withdraw its peacekeeping force monitoring their disputed border, Farmaajo rejected Riyadh's alleged USD 80 million offer to become part of the effort to isolate Doha.[92] His decision went against many local politicians, leaders of federal states, and business elite with ties to the Emirates and Saudi Arabia. Farmaajo's decision shows that while the connections between prominent local individuals and groups and their Persian Gulf partners are pragmatic and transactional, the local actors maintain considerable power in the relationship. Through selective external alignments, they can advance their interests and consolidate their position against local rivals. More potential foreign partners these local actors can attract, the more avenues for gaining external resources they have. This also enables them to have more space for foreign policy maneuvering. Their local power, enhanced through foreign sources, enables them to position themselves according to their interests that may or may not go against the aspirations of what appear as internationally more powerful actors.

In April 2018, Somali authorities confiscated USD 9.6 million that UAE officials were bringing in through Mogadishu Airport.[93] The seizure of funds, which took place amid the Qatar diplomatic crisis and after Ethiopia joined the Somaliland Berbera Port project, was accompanied by accusations that Emirati cash payments such as the one confiscated could stir instability. The UAE officials claimed that the funds were for training activities they were conducting for Somali security forces, and Abu Dhabi subsequently withdrew its diplomats and overall assistance to the Somali federal government. The UAE also abandoned its plans for a military base, suspended its training activities and salary support to the Somali army, and closed a hospital it had constructed in Mogadishu. President Farmaajo, in turn, used the crisis to leverage his administration's position against the legislature, allegedly supported by Abu Dhabi to oust him,[94] with the assistance of Qatar's ally Türkiye and by extension Ethiopia. While Emirati meddling became a pretext for the government to do away with rivals, prominent individuals and federal states aiming to strengthen themselves relative to the federal government sought to use the opportunity to further benefit from connections with the UAE and Saudi Arabia. This brought the two external actors on a collision course. Abu Dhabi accused Ankara of manipulation of the political and economic landscape in Somalia due to its close partnership with the Farmaajo government, and Ankara blamed Abu Dhabi for providing support to al-Shabaab.[95] This demonstrates the complexity of relationships that local actors maintain with external parties in their attempts to benefit from the aspirations of the latter.

The connections of the Somali state and sub-state actors to the Gulf countries and Türkiye have led to political rivalries in the Middle East resonating within Somalia. For example, with the worsening rift among the GCC in mid-2017 in the context of Saudi Arabia, the UAE, Bahrain, and Egypt severing diplomatic relations with Qatar, the relations between the Somali federal government and the federal state governments were affected. Although President Farmaajo fended off the pressure to join the boycotting states, three federal states, Galmudug,

Puntland, and Hirshabelle, defied the federal government and took a stand with the Saudi–Emirati coalition, which led Mogadishu to state that it alone exercised authority to make statements about Somalia's foreign relations.[96] In the ensuing parliamentary wrangling, which led to the resignation of the Speaker of the Lower House and Farmaajo opponent, Mohamed Osman Jawari, one legislator admitted that "the overlap between parliamentary infighting and the Gulf powers' rivalry has increased opportunities for patronage."[97] The mounting tension was manifested in early 2018 when relations between Mogadishu and Hargeisa plummeted after Ethiopia joined the DP World–led Berbera Port consortium. This was compounded by the UAE government's decision to withdraw support from the Somali federal government after Somali authorities confiscated funds from the UAE representatives at Mogadishu Airport. Meanwhile, Abu Dhabi deepened its collaboration with Hargeisa, continued to assist the Puntland state administration, and envisaged a port development in Kismayo, Jubaland,[98] a lucrative trading hub connecting southern Somalia to the UAE.

Although not significant parties to the Qatar crisis, neighboring states, Ethiopia and Kenya, have been heavily involved in Somalia as part of AMISOM, and otherwise, following their respective unilateral military interventions in 2006 and 2011. Both have sought to influence Somali politics. Despite the initial disaffection by the outgoing TPLF-EPRDF administration, the new incoming premier Abiy strongly supported the Farmaajo leadership and brought it into a tripartite alliance with Addis Ababa and Asmara. Ethiopia's policy to endorse the Somali federal government has changed from previous support for decentralization, although there is still apprehension in Ethiopia about the possible resurgence of Somali nationalism and irredentism. Kenya entered Somalia in 2011 and has since joined AMISOM, but its activities, involving al-Shabaab and support of former prominent ICU member Sheikh Ahmed Madobe's leadership in Jubaland resulted in frosty relations with Farmaajo leadership which sought to expand its authority in southern Somalia. Madobe's clan connections stretching to Ethiopia's Somali Region and his relationship with the Jigjiga regional government during the TPLF-EPRDF have undermined his relationship with the post-transition regional administration under Mustafa Muhumed Omer which maintains strong relations with the Abiy central government. Mustafa abolished the controversial and violence-prone regional Liyu police force which may have opened new space for armed groups, including al-Shabaab. In 2019, the Farmaajo administration unsuccessfully supported a rival candidate in the Jubaland election to replace Madobe, which strained Somalia–Kenya relations along with Kenya's activities in Jubaland and the maritime dispute which the International Court of Justice resolved in Somalia's favor in October 2021.

Late in his term, President Farmaajo further strengthened the alliance with Ethiopia and Eritrea. The tripartite alignment between Addis Ababa, Asmara, and Mogadishu in 2018, soon after Abiy Ahmed's rise to power, envisaged reshaping the political and economic landscape in the Horn and neutralizing sub-state and non-state rivals of the respective leaders. With Ethiopian, Qatari, and Turkish support, the Farmaajo administration was able to gain ground in its internal wrangling against federal state and non-state actors, including Jubaland and Puntland administrations and al-Shabaab, but because of the intensification of conflict in Ethiopia's Tigray such assistance was increasingly compromised. In 2021 claims emerged, which were given credence by the abduction and disappearance of Ikran Tahlil Farah, a National Intelligence and Security Agency (NISA) employee who was believed to be in possession of sensitive information, that Somali recruits were trained in Eritrea and deployed in the Tigray conflict. The NISA had clandestinely trained recruits in Somalia who after the Addis Ababa–Asmara rapprochement were relocated to Eritrea with promises to be trained in Qatar. NISA chief Fahad Yasin, with the assistance of his deputy Abdullahi Kulane, appears to have been the main architect of the move which seemingly had President Farmaajo's blessing and Doha's support. The troops were then reportedly used in the Tigray conflict with devastating consequences under Abdirizak Mohamud Haji Muhumud, who has strong links to Eritrea.[99] This shows how the Somali leadership colluded with its regional allies to strengthen its domestic position and participated in the effort to eliminate the TPLF as a significant political force in Ethiopia and the sub-region.

In his final speech as president, Farmaajo admitted to having secretly agreed to a three-year training program of 5,000 recruits in Eritrea under the coordination of the NISA. He, however, failed to comment on accusations by the UN and survivors[100] of their use in Tigray despite the desperation of family members who had lost contact with their loved ones for answers.[101] President Farmaajo hindering investigation caused a rift with Prime Minister Mohammed Hussein Roble and put increasing international pressure on the president. The mounting burden to which the issue of recruits contributed forced an end to Farmaajo's attempt to obstruct the presidential election until securing a favorable environment for his reelection. The election which was conducted indirectly through electors finally took place in May 2022 and resulted in the former president Hassan Sheikh Mohamud (2012–17) securing his second term in office. He has since steered the return of the recruits after they have completed their training in Eritrea, and overseen their incorporation into the Somali military which toward the end of 2022 escalated its operations against al-Shabaab and expected to defeat it in the coming months.[102]

Through his business ventures, President Farmaajo was also able to influence Somalia's relations with the neighboring countries. For example, Farmaajo and a family associate have a significant stake in the lucrative *khat* business. He was able to use it as leverage, especially against Somalia's major *khat* suppliers Ethiopia and Kenya. Due to deteriorating relations with Kenya, Farmaajo locked Nairobi out by using Covid-19 as a pretext, and let Ethiopian associates supply *khat*[103] from eastern Ethiopia. The maritime boundary dispute between Somalia and Kenya, involving oil and gas interests and fishing rights, further inflamed the relationship even after the October 2021 International Court of Justice ruling in favor of Mogadishu. In February 2020, Farmaajo signed a law that disenfranchised the federal member states from oil exploration and concentrated power over the deals to the central government.[104] By August, the Somali government had begun to issue exploration licenses in which politically and economically influential local individuals, connected to the Farmaajo administration, sought to partner with foreign companies, including Gulf States and Türkiye. This shows how the Somali leadership has been able to privatize the state's foreign relations, and at times its public assets, for personal benefit. While direct material gains from relations with sub-regional actors such as Ethiopia and Kenya often do not match those from more powerful states such as those in the Middle East, their security support and economic dealings often allow the local big men to strengthen their domestic position.

Recent Dynamics

Historically, Somalia's strategic location has attracted the interest of foreign powers. The region connecting the Red Sea and the Indian Ocean drew attention already in ancient Egypt and has since then been in the interest of various European, Middle Eastern, and other internationally powerful states.

In the past decade, the leading Gulf States and Türkiye have intensified their strategically driven engagement in the Horn of Africa with Somalia as one of their focal points. This is largely because of Somalia's geopolitical importance and close cultural and economic connections with the Arabian Peninsula, but also due to its fragility which enables foreign powers to pursue their interests both within and outside the control of the central authority in Mogadishu. As discussed earlier, the leading Persian Gulf governments and Ankara have sought to achieve their security, political, and economic objectives through strategies of economic statecraft, which have mainly involved their financial, and at times other material, assets. In part due to the political instability and armed conflict, financial efforts to affect Somali politics have been more prominent than permanent profit-oriented investments in the country. The Middle Eastern external actors have generally limited their investments to strategic and securable fixed assets, such as logistics hubs.

On the other hand, the foreign involvement and rivalries among the external actors have opened space for local individuals and groups to choose between foreign partners to exploit their financial and material resources in the local political and economic competition. In return, the local actors have made promises of political alignments and decisions involving political, security, and economic affairs. In a transactional manner, in exchange for money or other material benefits that allow local actors to strengthen themselves, they have provided access to strategic and economic material and nonmaterial assets, such as advantageously located land, infrastructure operation and development, investment and trade partnerships, and natural resources. This has resulted in two forces based on the interests of the local actors; efforts to build peace and effective central authority or preference for perpetual fragmentation and significant power of federal states or non-state actors relative to the federal administration. Although it has been argued that in this interaction the local actors have mainly sought to maximize material benefits in the short term,[105] the stability and shifts of local actors' foreign alignments have been characterized by both their own short- and long-term interests and aspirations that often consist of a combination of political, economic, and social objectives.

Recently, with the easing of the Qatar diplomatic crisis, the Gulf States and Türkiye have toned down their rivalry in Somalia. Since 2021, Türkiye, partly driven by its currency crisis, has sought to improve ties with the UAE and Saudi Arabia,[106] Riyadh already having been the top investor in Türkiye before the Qatar diplomatic crisis.[107] Ankara has also aspired to further diversify its economic partnerships in the Horn of Africa, but the Somali government has managed to maintain a significant position in the Turkish strategy. This largely owes to Somalia's leverage due to a decade of increasingly established economic, humanitarian, and security cooperation, as well as to some extent to migration and economic ventures of the Somali population in Türkiye. During the June 18–20, 2021, Antalya Diplomacy Forum, the Turkish investment Authority and Somalia Investment Promotion Authority (SOMINVEST), which has taken the lead as an institution pursuing economic diplomacy and seeking foreign funds for the state, signed a Memorandum of Understanding "boosting cooperation on investments, promoting collaborative ventures, and providing technology transfer between the two countries."[108]

In January 2020, it was reported that Moscow had been eying on a Russian military base in Berbera,[109] but, despite initial traction, such plans were not taken seriously in Hargeisa due to Somaliland's recent attempts to get closer to Washington. Meanwhile, Moscow has sought implementation of the deal it struck with the previous Omar al-Bashir government in Sudan for establishing a Russian naval base in Port Sudan. It has forged close ties with Sudan's generals, who have received Russian assistance against the pro-democracy movement through the Wagner Group in exchange for gold[110] and appear committed to upholding the naval base agreement. This, along with Moscow's close relations with the al-Sisi administration in Cairo and Afwerki government in Asmara, would ensure its maritime presence in the Red Sea and generate wealth amid Western sanctions imposed due to its invasion of Ukraine. Russia's attack has contributed to increasing fuel prices, and it has complicated Somalia's food crisis due to the country's high dependence on Ukraine and Russia for cereals.

After significant delays, in May 2022 presidential election took place and led to the return of Hassan Sheikh to power. His election should complement Mogadishu's existing firm alignment with Türkiye by improving relations with Saudi Arabia and the UAE, which, if successful, should generate new resources for the federal government and generate unity among regional leaders of Somalia's constituent parts. Some indication of this has been the Hassan Sheikh administration's apology to the Emiratis and returning the funds confiscated in the April 2018 incident, the president's first trip in office to the UAE with which he had forged strong ties during his first tenure, and a large Somali delegation visiting Saudi Arabia as part of the *Hajj* which included the now lower house Speaker Madobe and former prime minister Roble. Improved ties with the UAE and Saudi Arabia should result in financial resources and aid to strengthen the response to the current famine and enhance the government's capacity to provide security. With the active support of the two Gulf monarchies, Somalia could also follow Ethiopian leadership's strategy and seek to implement a more centralized model of governance which would empower the central government over the federal states.

For Somaliland, however, Mogadishu's improved relations with Riyadh and Abu Dhabi, and continued close collaboration with Addis Ababa, could be unfavorable and undermine its ultimate political objective; the gaining of international recognition. For Qatar, the UAE's major rival in Somalia and the Horn, Mogadishu's warmer relations with Abu Dhabi and Riyadh are likely to be detrimental despite the formal end of the embargo in early 2021 that surprisingly appeared to have a strengthening effect on the Qatari economy and its independence from the GCC.[111] Doha has since replaced its long-serving ambassador to Somalia under Farmaajo, which signals an attempt for a fresh start.

Since 2021, the Somaliland leadership has increased its effort to gain growing international recognition. After making clear not to associate with China, Hargeisa has consistently worked with its partners in the West and the Persian Gulf toward closer partnership. Somaliland's increasingly assertive foreign policy, also engaging Taipei, has triggered Beijing to focus on its ties with Mogadishu and to lure Abu Dhabi and Addis Ababa, somewhat unsuccessfully, to weaken ties with Hargeisa, while it has fed intense debate in Washington for a deeper relationship at a time when clear US allies in the Horn of Africa have been growing thin. For Hargeisa, the Berbera Corridor has been the financially and strategically most important foreign investment and places it in direct competition with Djibouti, and its close partner China, which has supplied Ethiopia with goods through its Red Sea port facilities.

In June 2021, the first phase of the Berbera Port expansion was inaugurated with the finishing of the upgraded container terminal. The DP World also went ahead to invest in an accompanying Free Economic Zone and the Berbera transport corridor connecting the port with Ethiopia. The road leading from the port to the Ethiopian border has also been upgraded by Abu Dhabi Fund for Development and the UK Department for International Development (DFID), while Ethiopia struck a deal with DP World for it and its partners to invest up to USD 1 billion over the next decade to develop supply chain infrastructure, including dry ports, reefer depots, and warehouses along the corridor.[112] Hargeisa bypass, constructed with the support of the UK,[113] is set to further facilitate the flow of traffic, trade, and aid. However, in June 2022 it came to light that Ethiopia missed the deadline for acquiring its shares in the Berbera Port project and lost its 19 percent stake for not having contributed financially to its construction.[114] This may be related to Addis Ababa's financial difficulties or strategic calculation to favor China which has a privileged role in the key logistics route between Ethiopia and Djibouti through which the vast majority of its imports and exports pass.

In 2022, Somalia continues to face significant challenges for peace and state-building. Part of the country suffers from continuing drought and food shortages which may escalate into famine and high-profile Al-Shabaab attacks have continued, including attempts to expand activities to Ethiopia, while the rift with Somaliland has deepened due to the strengthening of the centralist sentiment in Mogadishu. There is also an attempt to reconcile with federal administrations to bring them to the fold and seek ways to resume negotiations with Hargeisa. Hassan Sheikh's administration, therefore, faces a complex set of problems. Mogadishu needs to maximize benefits for its regional partnerships, but so far heavy leaning toward the UAE, Saudi Arabia, and, to some extent, Kenya in regional relations is likely to come at the expense of other relationships, especially with Qatar.

Conclusion

The Somali people have thousands of years of history in the Horn of Africa. They also have deep-rooted connections to the Arabian Peninsula. These relations are manifested today in genetic and cultural linkages, as well as through political, economic, and migratory interaction. As a state in the Horn of Africa, Somalia is unique. The state collapse in 1991 and partial territorial disintegration were followed by a period of intense peace and state-building which involved a variety of local and foreign actors. Continuing lack of peace, security, and state authority has caused perpetual weakness and opened space for sub-state and non-state actors to compete against the central government. This has invited external players, especially from the Persian Gulf, and led local actors to forge foreign ties to strengthen themselves in the domestic political and economic competition.

In these transactional relations, the local state, sub-state, and non-state actors gain power through control of formal state structures, informal local institutions, economic and strategic assets, territory, or local communities. They engage outside players pragmatically through extraversion to gain resources for extending their local political and/or economic power relative to their competitors. Without centralized state control, Somalia's foreign relations have fragmented and are driven both by patrons of the state and sub-state and non-state actors. Despite the attempt to build centralized power, sub-state and non-state actors have the capacity to locally challenge the federal state in part because of their ability to use their foreign relations to strengthen themselves financially, materially, and militarily in various parts of the state territory.

This has clear implications for foreign policy because the federal government does not have a monopoly on external relations. The local power realities reduce the government into just one player among several competing sub-state and non-state actors. The federal administration's lack of relative power over other domestic actors diminishes its political and economic control and undermines its capacity to monopolize the most significant bilateral foreign relations with certain partners. As one example, in recent years Puntland administration's relations with the UAE have in many ways surpassed those of the federal government. In the prolonged condition of the absence of a strong central authority, local actors have appropriated foreign discourses for strengthening their domestic position. Imported discourses, such as religious doctrines or those related to state-building and stabilization, have been adapted to improve the standing of the "big men."[115] In most cases, they involve a strong pragmatic and transactional material dimension. Somali leaders' have developed remarkable versatility to adopt local, national, and foreign roles to strike partnerships and benefit from external alignments. This is demonstrated by many such leaders playing a key role in politics at the local or national level and then transitioning into regional leaders or vice versa. It has allowed leading Somalis to use their individual, community, and territorial assets and resources for pursuing foreign relations autonomously from the state particularly during periods when the central authority has been weak. Meanwhile, sections of the Somali business elite have strongly embraced Salafism[116] which has increased their legitimacy among foreign and local Islamists and produced opportunities, including obtaining resources through Islamist networks abroad and collaborating locally with clan militias or Islamist militants such as al-Shabaab for material benefits.

The enduring violence and conflict have provided opportunities for the enrichment and consolidation of personal and group power. While government officials have engaged in rhetoric of state-building and stability which has helped them to materially gain from external assistance and investment, a study from 2020 shows that employing coercive force by the federal and state militaries, as well as al-Shabaab, as a strategy to obtain bribes has recently increased in the country.[117] Although in Somaliland, with relatively strong and accountable state institutions, this was less the case, in the federal government-held areas, for example, the high level of extortion owes to endemic corruption and relates to the necessity for individuals in the security forces, which often rely on foreign actors for salaries, to ensure their livelihoods. Much of external investment and aid go to buttress the position of the patrons of the central government or politically prominent individuals who control the state instead of building government legitimacy and accountability. This local conflict and security entrepreneurs' use of their coercive capacity to sell security to their clients as a business continues to perpetuate the securitization of the political and economic landscape.

Due to the emphasis on their foreign connections to generate income and material resources, local Somali actors often engage in economic diplomacy. Somalia's official foreign policy is dictated by the president's office which uses the federal government's legal status for economic diplomacy and extraversion. However, it has been limited by the federal government's perpetual inability to control the territory and population, which has diminished its legitimacy and authority relative to sub-state and non-state actors. Particularly Somaliland has pursued independent and increasingly assertive foreign policy despite its international non-recognition, and Puntland, despite its commitment to the federation, has engaged external parties autonomously while also making strides in building its local political system.[118] Economic diplomacy has featured strongly in the external relations of both polities, and in the nonofficial foreign connections of prominent individuals, particularly because foreign investment, trade, and joint business ventures have been prioritized as avenues for private wealth and more general economic development and well-being. Similarly, non-state actors, including al-Shabaab which in recent years has been in retreat in terms of territorial control, have managed to engage in foreign economic activity which has contributed to sustaining their organizations and operations. Connections and activities in business hubs such as Dubai have been facilitated by the widespread diaspora and local contacts and the various Somali money-sending services. Therefore, in the external relations strategies of Somali sub-state and non-state actors, connections with Middle Eastern players, both public and private, from the Arabian Peninsula and Türkiye in particular, remain extremely important.

In their pragmatic and transactional foreign affairs with their Middle Eastern counterparts, Somali authorities, and non-state actors, have also sought to capitalize on strategic assets. These include political goods, such as alignment and/or decisions in favor of certain external actors, handing over control of geopolitically or geo-economically significant locations and infrastructure (e.g., land and ports of entry), and providing access to natural resources in exchange for financial, economic, and material benefits. Somalia's strategic position on the shores of the Indian Ocean and the Gulf of Aden and its largely unexploited offshore oil reserves have been of interest to its Middle Eastern partners. For example, in January 2020 Turkish president Erdogan explained that Ankara would embrace the invitation from Somalia to explore oil offshore,[119] while Somali authorities have vowed to uphold old exploration and extraction agreements made before the state collapse. Similarly, port authorities in Mogadishu have used the government's partnership with the Albayrak Group, linked to the Turkish leadership, to embezzle funds from port operations. This shows how Somali officials utilize their position as legally recognized authorities to exchange the country's strategic assets for personal financial gain. While it is difficult to determine how large proportion of the money will end up in private use, given widespread corruption and the established practice of bribery and kickback payments it is safe to assume that financial and material resources from external powers are widely used for strengthening prominent and politically influential individuals' personal position.

However, the influence of the external partners, including the Persian Gulf countries and Türkiye, has been limited to partnerships with local actors who have used alignments for gaining financial and other material assets and advancing their agendas. Aware of the rivalries among these foreign players, the local actors often seek to benefit from more than one side, as during the Qatar diplomatic crisis, by diversifying their external relations. Such individuals, and sub-state, and non-state actors have tapped into the interest of Gulf monarchies and Türkiye in gaining influence in Somalia, by exercising their bargaining power. They offer local assets under their control, such as political influence, strategically located land, or resources in exchange for financial and other material benefits and nonmaterial support.

This has generated a distorted image of the overall power relations because of the lack of understanding of how local power and influence play out in international interactions and exchanges. While the Persian Gulf and Turkish actors have used mainly their financial and material resources to seek power, the level of influence they are able to exert is much lower than international relation analysis depicts because in most cases these players are unable to control the behavior of local actors. Instead, local players use foreign alignments for gaining resources to strengthen themselves mainly against domestic rivals and often shift such external partnerships or strike simultaneous deals with the external players' competitors. This makes pragmatic and transactional foreign connections often short-lived and unpredictable. As a result, although at the interstate level power appears heavily tilted toward the Middle East actors, a deeper look into the political and economic dynamics of these relationships, as in the case of external involvement in Somalia, reveals that power at the local level in the Horn of Africa lies largely with local actors.

Chapter 5

ERITREA

THE FICKLE ALLY

Eritrea is the newest internationally recognized state in the Horn of Africa. Emerging from a devastating and protracted war of liberation, it became a centralized one-party state in which its patrons' socialist ideological convictions of self-sacrifice for a common good came to characterize the essence of the independent country. The liberation era leadership's strong grip on power has meant that it has continued to dominate Eritrea's political and economic life. The government has been able to prevent other power centers from emerging and challenging the political status quo, and it is in control of the main foreign connections in the country. Unlike in Somalia, for example, the Eritrean government's ability to exert extensive control has prevented non-state actors from emerging and developing substantial external connections to challenge its supreme political power.

As a state Eritrea is small, but it commands considerable influence in the Horn of Africa. This is largely because the Eritrean leadership has successfully used the country's strategic location at the Red Sea and international connections in particular with Arab countries, Israel, and Iran as an asset in its foreign relations. Despite Eritrea's small population and limitations in terms of territory and resources, the country and its leadership are intimately connected to neighboring Ethiopia, the dominant state in the sub-region, and Sudan, through ethnic and cultural linkages and political and economic dealings. Although Eritrean mainstream history is closely connected to that of Ethiopian Christian highlands and culture, its coastal lowland extensions, notably including the Dahlak Archipelago, have strong Muslim traditions in connection with the Arabian Peninsula and Sudan.[1] In its foreign relations, Eritrean leadership has preferred frequently changing emphasis and shifting alignments, but its overall connections with Arab countries have been among its most enduring external linkages.

Ancient and Historical Linkages

During antiquity, lands that form part of today's Eritrea were host to various civilizations and likely formed part of what Egyptians called the Land of Punt.[2] Several archeological sites on both sides of the current Eritrea–Ethiopia border indicate the existence of the Kingdom of D'mt predating Aksum. It is believed that D'mt, extending over the Tigrayan Plateau and in control of the ancient trading port of Adulis near today's Massawa, was modestly influenced by the Sabaean Kingdom established in the lands of modern-day Yemen in southern Arabia. While the Sabaean Kingdom declined due to competition over leadership among Yemeni dynasties, the Kingdom of Aksum emerged on the other side of the Red Sea as a powerful trading empire. In the sixth century following King Kaleb's punitive expedition against King Dhu Nuwas, who was persecuting Christians, Aksum came to briefly dominate southern Arabia as its protectorate. However, it soon lost the Yemeni territories as a result of the expansion of the Sasanian Empire, which took control of the territory of what constituted contemporary western Yemen until being overwhelmed by the expansion of Islam.

The close connection between the peoples of Eritrea and Ethiopia and those of the southern Arabian Peninsula is also evidenced in the debate over the origin of the highland Habesha people. Linguistically, the Habesha are commonly seen as a sub-branch of the Semitic strand with Yemeni influence,[3] but there are also some remnants of the Abyssinian presence in Yemen. This shows that economic and political connections were accompanied by the spread of ideas and cultural influences on both sides of the Red Sea and the Gulf of Aden.

The Kingdom of Aksum which emerged in the second century encompassed much of today's Eritrea. Among the great religions, Aksum first embraced Christianity during Ezana's reign in the fourth century and hosted companions of Prophet Muhammad during the First Hijra which led to the arrival of Islam. Al-Sahaba Mosque in Massawa, which points toward Jerusalem and is commonly considered the first mosque in Africa, is believed to have been built during this time[4] when the coastal peoples, such as sections of the Tigre and Afar, converted to Islam. With the new religion came the Arabic language, which became important in the Eritrean Muslim lowlands. In the early medieval period, in Muslim coastal extensions of today's Eritrea, various sultanates emerged, including in the Dahlak Islands, coinciding with the highland Zagwe Kingdom and later with the Adal and associated Afari, or Danakil, sultanates. The Afar people, who now mainly inhabit the territory commonly known as the Afar Triangle in the borderlands of northeast Ethiopia, southern Eritrea, and Djibouti, importantly contributed to Adal's power and formed the Danakil sultanates. The coastal extensions of the Afar land in the current Eritrea and Djibouti have for long been strategically important connecting the Horn of Africa to the southern Arabian Peninsula at Bab al-Mandab, the narrowest stretch of the Red Sea. The strait has historically been a route for migration and cultural influences, as well as an area over which various powers have sought to project influence and control.[5]

With the demise of the Aksum Empire, its northern part extending from the highlands of today's Eritrea to the Red Sea coast became the Kingdom of Mehri Badri. Established in the area of Bahr, Buri, Bogos, Serawye, and Hamassien, it laid north of the Zagwe Dynasty but became an Abyssinian tributary in the fifteenth and early sixteenth centuries. As part of the Christian highlands, Mehri Badri allied with the Portuguese and initially engaged in resistance during Imam Ahmad ibn Ibrahim al-Ghazi's Conquest of Abyssinia (1529–43), but then aligned with the Adalites in an attempt to break from Abyssinian domination.

By the mid-fifteenth century, the Sultanate of Adal had emerged as eminent in the Red Sea littoral of the Horn of Africa. Following the end of the Walashma dynasty, various sultans expanded the Adalite territories and were able to exert a measure of influence over the Horn of Africa's Red Sea trade. However, after the Conquest of Abyssinia, the ensuing Oromo raids, and infighting, the sultanate went into decline until its capital was moved from Harar to Aussa where the Afar established an Imamate. The Imamate was succeeded by the Afari Sultanate of Aussa which during the late nineteenth century controlled the southern Red Sea littoral of Eritrea, as well as most of Djibouti, until agreeing to Italian protection during Benito Mussolini's invasion of Abyssinia (1935–7). In the early 1940s, it was forced to become part of liberated Ethiopia.

Modern Era

By the sixteenth century, in the area of modern northern Eritrea, local peoples formed a confederation of tribes led by a ruling class, Beni Amer, descendants of Amir Kunu whose name came also to describe the people they ruled.[6] The other groups within the Beni Amer denomination hail from the Hedarab, Hadendowa, and Tigre,[7] while some see them as a sub-group of the Beja people. Dominant in the lowland extensions between the Nile and the Red Sea from modern Egypt and Sudan to Eritrea, sub-sections of the Beja reached up to the Eritrean highlands. Some Beja appear to have mixed with highlanders and others with Yemeni migrants of Arab origin, forming the Belew people who were prominent in northern Eritrea until being overwhelmed by the Funj from Sudan and giving way to the Ottomans.

The Ottoman influence, which in the sixteenth century extended into the territory of what constitutes contemporary Eritrea, was largely limited to the coastal lowlands. Ottoman conqueror and administrator, Özdemir Pasha, seeking to establish a new province, began an invasion in 1557-1558 by first fortifying Massawa and Hirghido but after a brief occupation of highland Barnagash, Bahr Negus Yeshaq, who led an Abyssinian army, defeated his forces in Kebessa.[8] However, the Ottomans consolidated power over the Red Sea islands which led to their control of a number of ports and the surrounding coastal extensions. Notable among these were the Sanjaks (districts) of Sawakin, Hargigo (Arkiko), Massawa, and Zayla (Zeila) which came to form part of the Ottoman Habesh Eyalet (province). In the sixteenth century, several Ottoman attempts were made to invade the Christian Abyssinian highlands, which led to their control of some localities, such as Hamasien (the area surrounding modern-day Asmara) for several years, but all were eventually unsuccessful and their forces were driven back to the coast. Notably, in the 1570s Yeshaq invited the Ottomans to back his rebellion against the Abyssinian Emperor as he tried to extend his power by invading Tigray. But Yeshaq was eventually defeated and killed in 1578[9] and Ottomans again retreated to the lowlands. In a final attempt to conquer Abyssinian highlands in 1588–9, Ottomans allied with a local rebel commander in Hamasien but were once more pushed back to the lowlands once. There they mounted a successful defense against the Ethiopian invasion which enabled the Ottomans to maintain a longer-term presence in the coastal lowlands and their ports. Ottomans remained in areas surrounding the Red Sea ports until the nineteenth century when the British gained control over Egypt and its possessions and Italians began actively seeking presence in the Red Sea. The story of Yeshaq, and other local leaders using alignments with external powers, epitomizes resistance and attempts by local actors to use temporary alliances for strengthening their position against local rivals.

Colonial Eritrea

The European Scramble for Africa eventually led to the establishment of Eritrea as an Italian colony. Italian ambitions were initially marked by a monk, Giuseppe Sapeto, who had previously advocated French to establish themselves in the Red Sea region. Sapeto then served as a front for the Societa Rubattino shipping company, purchasing land in 1869 from the Ankala Afar chiefs, Sultan Ibrahim Ahmed and Sultan Hassan Ahmed,[10] in the desolate coastal area around Assab with a plan to establish a coaling station to support Italian shipping through the Suez Canal. However, while this gave Italians a foothold in the Red Sea region, it was not until the 1880s after the Italian state had taken over the possession of the infant colony from the shipping company that more elaborate plans for establishing a colony were made.

Italian expansionist plans were facilitated by the failed Turco-Egyptian Ottoman invasion of Abyssinia and the establishment of the Mahdist Islamic revivalist state in Sudan which diminished Egypt's influence in the region. Turco-Egyptian forces had engaged Abyssinians from the 1860s and gained control of its northern Bogos province in 1868, where from 1872 they garrisoned Sanhit (later Keren),[11] but a campaign ordered by Khedive Ismail in 1875–6 led to the decisive defeat of King Yohannes IV and his generals, notably Ras Alula. However, less than a decade after, the Mahdist revolution sweeping over Sudan caused Ottoman Egypt to lose its most prized possession with an exception of Sawakin, which it continued to garrison with British assistance. The conflicts against Muslim invaders from the north kept the Abyssinian crown occupied and depleted its resources in continuous military campaigns.

As a result, Italians found space to expand their dominion. The British supported their plans out of concern regarding the potential expansion of the French colony in Djibouti. There was little interest in enforcing the tripartite Treaty of Adwa (1884) between Abyssinia and Egypt in which the former had been ensured free transit of merchandise through Massawa port under British supervision. Mainly preoccupied with the French, the British government allowed Italians to occupy Massawa, violating the treaty. They hoped that rapid Italian expansion would stop the French, who, as part of their strategy to weaken British hold over Egypt had occupied Tadjoura in 1884 immediately after Ottoman Egyptian withdrawal and in the following year signed a treaty with the Somali Issa chiefs to make the southern part of the Bay of Tadjoura a protectorate.

Meanwhile, in 1882, Italy established the colony of Assab and sought to expand its colonial possessions from the coast by sending an army contingent inland. It faced stiff Abyssinian resistance and was forced to take a defensive position at Saati, but when Abyssinian commander Ras Alula annihilated a relief force in Dogali the Italians were pushed back to the coast. However, the sudden demise of Emperor Yohannes IV in 1889 in a battle against the Mahdists in Metemma, and the ensuing power struggle in Abyssinia, led Italians to attempt another invasion of the interior highlands. In Abyssinia, King Menelik of Shewa equally exploited the power vacuum and took power. In Wuchale (1889), he then made peace with Italians who accepted territory in exchange for recognizing his rule, provisioning Ethiopia with financial assistance, and allowing it continued access to European arms. Subsequently, Menelik embarked on defeating the remaining internal rivals and consolidating his power. Although the Wuchale treaty shows how Menelik used external alignments to gain resources and strengthen himself against domestic competitors, it also demonstrates the confusion of signing treaties in two distinct languages. While the Italian version implied that Menelik had accepted Abyssinia to become an Italian protectorate, the Amharic version was interpreted differently. This led to an increasing confrontation in the 1890s.

In the second half of the nineteenth century, in the highlands of today's Eritrea, resistance to the Abyssinian occupation continued. For example, already in the 1870s Bahta Hagos, a Tigrayan, became one of the leaders of the struggle against Ras Alula, who decisively defeated the Turco-Egyptian forces in 1876 in Gula and then sought to subdue the local tribal leaders. This prompted Raesi Woldemichael Solomon of Hamasien, the king of the autonomous Medri Bahri, to mount an insurgency and align with the Turco-Egyptians (Ottomans). Emperor Yohannes IV appointed Alula as the governor of the region,[12] and in 1879 Alula betrayed and detained Solomon and had his forces occupy Mehdi Badri. Having lost his ally, Hagos then joined the Turco-Egyptian garrison in Sanhit in 1880 before its defeat. Following the departure of the Egyptians, Hagos took the opportunity to align with the Italians with the hope to gain a degree of local autonomy under Abyssinian domination. Alula moved the capital of Abyssinia's northern possession to Asmara and inflicted a defeat on the Italians who had advanced to the highlands in Dogali in 1887, but his resistance was severely weakened after the sudden death of Emperor Yohannes IV in the Battle of Metemma.[13] Hagos provided important support to the Italian advance to Gura in 1889 and occupied Akele Guzai, controlling highland territory that became part of the Italian colony of Eritrea established after the occupation of Asmara in 1889. However, Hagos soon became disappointed in the behavior of Italian occupiers and turned against them in 1894 and was killed, but his brother continued the struggle against Italians who pushed further in the highlands culminating in the Battle of Adwa in 1896.[14] Bahta Hagos's story again exemplifies the importance of the big men in understanding local actors' relations with external parties. It shows how the power of such actors at the local level is significant and how they have been able to use connections with external parties to improve their position in the local context. In this case, entering into a game of strategic alignments by creating and using connections with external actors that were competing for influence allowed Hagos to obtain political (such as prestige and reputational) and material resources which enabled him to gain prominence and advance his position in the local political context. His prominence and strength, on the other hand, made him an attractive local partner for external parties. This dynamic resembles the situation today in the Horn of Africa–Middle East relations in which prominent local actors remain powerful and attractive partners for foreign powers.

Having gained control of roughly the territorial extension of today's Eritrea, Italians embarked on strengthening their position and developing their prized possession. They built a railroad from Massawa to Asmara and then onward to Bisha and invested in industries and agriculture. Locals were employed extensively in construction, production facilities, and law enforcement as well as recruited to fight in Italy's colonial wars in which the Eritrean Ascari played an important role as part of advancing Italy's imperialist ambitions. Eritrea was considered the most advanced of the Italian colonies in Africa and thousands of Italians settled there creating an extensive community of locals of Italian origin. Although the Italians suffered a severe blow to their plans to conquer Abyssinia in the Battle of Adwa in 1896 and were subsequently forced to recognize their defeat, they scored a strategic win in the subsequent agreement that recognized the Eritrean border with Abyssinia. This recognition allowed them to further consolidate their rule over Eritrea. However, the Italian defeat opened space for other European powers, and Ethiopia and France negotiated an alliance in 1897 which gave impetus to the French dream of establishing a string of connected colonial territories from Senegal to Djibouti. Meanwhile, the Italian defeat prompted the British, who feared French expansion, to secure the Nile River and concretize their plan of claiming colonial territories from Cairo to Cape Town.

The rise of fascism in the 1920s laid the ground for the desire for further expansion of Italy's colonial dominion in Africa. With a pretext of a "civilizing mission," in 1935 Italian forces invaded Ethiopia from Eritrea and Italian Somaliland and conquered the country despite stiff resistance that continued after the fall of Addis Ababa in May 1936.[15] Soon after dictator Benito Mussolini declared the founding of an Italian Empire in which Italian East Africa and its crown jewel, the industrial hub Eritrea, played an important role. Although Asmara had become a buzzing "Italian" city during this period, its development came to a halt with the British invasion and occupation of Eritrea in 1941. The British administrators then imposed a colonial policy of cultural segregation based on language and religion which heightened the division between highland Christians and lowland Muslims. For more than two years, Italians and their Eritrean associates engaged in guerrilla resistance to the British occupation, which in some ways laid the foundation for the later Eritrean independence struggle symbolized by much-celebrated liberation fighter Hamid Idris Awate, a Tigre who had made his career as an Ascari. When Italians were forced to accept the end of Eritrea's status as a colony in 1947, Italian influence over the Eritrean independence movement withered away despite the important foreign presence in Asmara, including the European, Eritrean Muslim, and Yemeni merchants' continuing domination of commerce in the capital. While the strong Italian influence through figures such as Vincenzo Di Meglio in the initial stages of the independence movement has led to arguments about external origins and the "imported" nature of the Eritrean identity and struggle for freedom, such arguments often fail to account for the motivations, strategy, and actions of local actors in their attempts to fight off foreign domination.

Annexation to Ethiopia and Early Struggle for Liberation

In 1942 Ethiopian sovereignty was restored and Emperor Haile Selassie began advocating for territorial expansion in part aimed at gaining sea access. Selassie skillfully exploited his position as a US partner to argue for Ethiopia's claims over the disputed Ogaden and the need for direct access to the sea through historical connections between his state and Eritrea. Although until the 1947 peace treaty Italians sought to maintain a grip on Eritrea by arguing that it should become an Italian protectorate, Ethiopia's claims of annexation were considered more significant. In the following year, Selassie persuaded the great powers to agree to the annexation Ogaden region, and then lobbied successfully to have the US and the United Nations (UN) agree on Eritrea's federation into Ethiopia as its autonomous part in 1950.[16]

Meanwhile, Eritrean leaders had already formed organizations that began advocating for independence. In the late 1940s, many Eritreans wanted independence either under Italian tutelage or without, which led to the founding of the Independence Bloc in 1949. But especially after Eritrea passed from being a British protectorate to an autonomous region of imperial Ethiopia, pro-independence Eritreans were intimidated and terrorized by unionists supported by Addis Ababa and its state-aligned Orthodox Church.[17] Eritrea's faith was ultimately sealed by great power calculations, including fears that its independence would cause a wave of resistance and instability in colonial Africa. In the process, Selassie successfully advanced his interest in obtaining sea access by exploiting his partnership with Washington in the early days of the Cold War.

The decision within the Eritrean resistance movement to engage in a liberation struggle fermented in the context of the Ethiopian annexation of Eritrea. However, those advocating for independence were forced to work in secret. Although Eritrea was to maintain a degree of regional autonomy,[18] it soon became clear that Haile Selassie's centralized and repressive Ethiopia would not respect the agreed arrangement. As the emperor's son-in-law, Andargachew Messai, became the supreme administrator of Eritrea who actively undermined its federal status,[19] the Chief Executive of the Eritrean Legislative Assembly, Ato Tedla Bairu, implemented the Ethiopian crown's policies. Eritreans protested in the UN and advocated for a referendum of self-determination but to no avail.

On May 22, 1954, amid deteriorating conditions and a threat to the federation posed by the Chief Executive's actions, the Eritrean Legislative Assembly, largely with the initiative of the Muslim representatives, passed two motions that denounced Ethiopian actions in Eritrea.[20] This contributed to an increasing confrontation between Tedla Bairu and the suppressed pro-independence leaders. In August of the following year, Haile Selassie replaced Bairu and the Chairman of the Assembly, Ali Musa Radai, with Asfaha Woldemichael and Idris Mohammed Adam to deepen Ethiopian control and end Eritrea's federal status. This was accompanied by a wave of repression, including an attempt to impose Amharicization against the two previously agreed official languages, Arabic and Tigrinya, and to suppress Eritreans' other identities. However, the repression and stripping of Arabic and Tigrinya of their official status led to the spread of nationalist sentiment.

The cultural divisions between highlands and lowlands, and the official weakening of the status of the Arabic language, led to grievances and heightened the nationalist sentiment among Eritrean Muslims. In 1957, Adam, a Tigre-speaking Beni Amer, who was increasingly at odds with Woldemichael's repressive policies, resigned and fled to exile in Cairo, where a small group of Eritrean activists under Egyptian protection already existed since 1955. Cairo's importance as a refuge for Eritrean Muslims drew on its religious importance and the government providing a relatively hospitable environment for dissidents and freedom fighters. By 1959 Ethiopia had assumed administrative and judicial control of Eritrea and then forced the Eritrean Legislative Assembly to change the name of the government to "Eritrean Administration" ahead of its dissolution and declaration of Eritrea as an Ethiopian province on November 14, 1962.

Meanwhile, in November 1958, individuals from mainly eastern coastal Eritrea founded the Eritrean Liberation Movement (ELM) in Port Sudan as a moderate and inclusive opposition group. However, the movement was soon supplanted by the Eritrean Liberation Movement (ELF) founded on July 10, 1960, by students and graduates under Adam's leadership in Cairo, where, at the time, political agitation among Eritrean exiles was tolerated. The ELF Central Committee consisted of eleven members. Adopting a hard-line stand, the ELF pursued Eritrean independence by organizing an armed struggle which Adam delegated to Beni Amer religious leader Sayedna Mohamed Ibn Dawd who agitated against the perceived rivals, prepared groundwork for the rebellion, and invited Hamid Idris Awate to start a holy war against Ethiopia. Beni Amer, mostly living in Eritrea, became initially an important constituency for the armed resistance largely based in Kassala, Sudan, the home of the Mirghaniyya Sufism. From the outset, Eritrean resistance was able to use Sudan as an important base and this was possible throughout the liberation struggle despite periodic restrictions and enforcement attempts at the porous border. The fluid and expansive frontier between the two states has enabled migration, smuggling, and activities by dissident groups to continue.

In December 1960, Adam visited Saudi Arabia. However, the ELF's first foreign mission failed to secure immediate support from King Saud in part because of the inconsistency of its position due to Adam's disagreement with Sheikh Ibrahim Sultan, an Eritrean veteran politician who had accompanied him on the trip.[21] Yet, Adam soon returned to Saudi Arabia to rally support among the growing Eritrean diaspora and met Osman Saleh Sabbe, who later became a prominent figure in securing external assistance for the movement. Together they proceeded to Somalia where a covert office for the Eritrean cause was established and Sabbe became the ELF Liaison Officer.[22] In September 1961, armed with a few old firearms, the ELF began its armed resistance by attacking several police posts in western Eritrea. Meanwhile, the Eritrean Liberation Movement sought to compete with the ELM by adopting a military strategy, but the ELF's effort to eliminate the ELM as a rival was successful. When the ELM went defunct in 1965 the ELF absorbed much of the ELM's remaining force but continued to maintain the religious divide between Muslims and Christians.[23] ELF leadership's favoritism of Muslim members had far-reaching consequences in the 1970s and beyond.

The ELF developed extensive links in the Middle East which it used for strengthening and widening its activities. From early on, Adam toured the Middle East, paying visits for example to Bahrain, Kuwait, Lebanon, Saudi Arabia, and Syria. In 1962 Adam (chairman), Osman Saleh Sabbe (foreign relations), and Idris Osman Galadewos (military organization) established the group's executive, the Supreme Council, according to their agreement in Cairo. Then a Revolutionary Command was established in Kassala under Eritrean officers previously employed in the Sudanese army as the armed wing of the movement, the Eritrean Liberation Army (ELA). But when President Gamal Abdel Nasser abandoned Egypt's strategy of undermining rival governments including Ethiopia, which was seen as a threat in case it would disturb the flow of the Nile waters, after the founding conference of the Organization of African Unity in 1963, and when Sudan's president Ibrahim Abboud followed suit, the ELF began facing increasing pressure.

During the ELF's foundational years under the Nasser administration's patronage, the leadership, as well as some of those who had studied in Egypt, portrayed their struggle as a Muslim cause. In some ways, this reflected the religious divide between highland and lowland Eritrea and explains in part attitudes toward Christian recruits. They adopted an Arab outlook which facilitated flirtation with the pan-Arabist idea promoted ardently by their early patron, President Nasser. The use of Arabic language was central to the ELF leadership for asserting the group's pan-Arabist and pan-Muslim credentials. This enabled the ELF leadership to sell the liberation project in Cairo and elsewhere in the Middle East as a Muslim struggle against the expansionist and oppressive Christian empire of Ethiopia. Aimed at invoking the sentiments of solidarity to address historical and current injustices against Muslims, the strategy associated power competition in the Horn of Africa with religious undertones. In response, various Arab states showed solidarity toward the ELF as a movement for the liberation of Eritrean Muslims and some portrayed the struggle as pan-Arabist. From the early 1960s onward, Sudan's limited, erratic, and shifting support became vital for the ELF,[24] while financial contributions from the Eritrean diaspora in Saudi Arabia initially facilitated modest weapons acquisition.

Meanwhile, the ELF leaders approached Middle Eastern governments, as well as other states. In the Middle East, they resorted to Islam as a major justification for the liberation struggle. The ELF established a presence in Jeddah where it sought Saudi diplomatic and material support while also raising funds among the Eritrean diaspora community which had developed in the country since the 1950s.[25] The ELF leadership also gained sympathy from the Arab Socialist Ba'ath Party, which had taken power in Syria after a coup that had led to the breakup of its union with Egypt in 1961, and embraced relations with the Syrian government. Syrian Ba'athist government was ready to support the ELF as an extension of the pan-Arabist revolutionary cause, which it often justified as opposition to Zionism. In the case of Eritrea, Ethiopia came to be deemed as a Christian imperial power collaborating with Israel to oppress Eritrean Muslims that had a just cause for liberation. In Damascus, the ELF, still largely drawing on the Beni Amer as its main constituency, was compelled to also emphasize its "Arab" credentials in which presenting the Ethiopian empire as a repressive Christian ally of the Zionist cause was useful. Israel, on the other hand, exploited ELF's "Arab association" and deepened cooperation with Ethiopia in the late 1960s by providing support, both military and intelligence, against ELF and allegedly establishing bases and radar facilities in the Dahlak Islands.[26]

ELF's main support base in Damascus was invaluable for the early struggle. Initially, from 1963, the Syrian government provided funding, weapons, and training for the ELF, which, however, did not convert the group into a large guerrilla force.[27] Following the 1967 Arab–Israeli War, Syrian and other Arab assistance diminished considerably, and although it lingered on until the mid-1970s, the ELF leadership felt obliged to look for new patrons. In July 1968 another Ba'athist coup took place, this time in Iraq. The ELF leadership immediately seized the opportunity to open an office in Baghdad, which along with Damascus considered ELF as an Arab liberation movement.[28] The ELF maintained support offices in Damascus, Mogadishu, and above all in Kassala where the behind-the-border organization of the insurgency took place. There, the Eritrean refugee community grew from 28,000 in 1967 to over 50,000 by the early 1970s partly due to the intensification of the armed struggle.

In the 1960s, along with Syria, Iraq provided training and assistance to the ELF. It also obtained support from Algeria, China, Cuba, Libya, and the Palestinian liberation movement. In 1965, following the revelation of a large clandestine weapons shipment in Khartoum,[29] Sudan purged the ELF momentarily, but Saudi Arabia, South Yemen, and Somalia allowed the movement to use their territories as weapons supply routes.[30] In 1967 in Damascus, Adam, in agreement with the Chinese authorities, sent five ELF members, among them Isaias Afwerki, to China for guerrilla training that included ideological indoctrination but Beijing then ended its support in 1970. However, the Chinese training had far-reaching consequences because Afwerki used it in the 1970s to define his military command as a popular front while building his image as a cult figure relying on popular support within the ranks and adopting an autocratic leadership style based on purging rivals.

Other Arab states also provided aid. For example, the radical regime in Libya did so,[31] but in the aftermath of the 1967 Arab–Israeli War Arab support of the ELF increasingly reflected preoccupation to curb Israeli influence in the southern Red Sea which was deemed to emanate in part from Ethiopia. In this context, South Yemen (People's Democratic Republic of Yemen, PDRY) converted into a major conduit for material assistance and training until the mid-1970s.

By the late 1960s, the ELF had grown into a more considerable force. The modest Syrian and South Yemeni assistance had allowed the movement to establish a capable fighting force[32] and enabled it to implement organization into zonal commands. This eventually led to zonal commanders becoming powerful and largely autonomous actors largely separate from the overall command structure of the movement. Rivalries emerged between the largely ethnically and religiously based zonal commands. In these circumstances, Sabbe abolished the Supreme Council in an attempt to exert his influence over the movement and recover it as a coherent force. Against Adam and Galadewos, he then, in early 1970, orchestrated a takeover of part of the field command from a new base in Beirut by airlifting fighters from Kassala to Aden. From Aden, they later sailed to the Dahlak Islands and onward to the Eritrean southern coastal region where they formed a new command, Popular Liberation Forces (PLF), under Mohammed Ali Umero and with fighters from the Semhar area.[33] After a brief dispute within the PLF factional command, a new leadership under Chinese-trained Romedan Mohammed Nur was formed. Romedan, Umero, and others who went to South Yemen were "exposed to numerous left and Arab nationalist political movements and governments" which inspired their discussions about forming a political party.[34] During their time in South Yemen, with Sabbe's lead, the Eritrean fighters also improved their logistical support linkages across the Red Sea which enhanced the movement's ability to take on the Ethiopian military.

Factionalism and Rise of Eritrean People's Liberation Front

In 1970, two more splits in the movement took place. As the continued persecution of Christian elements in the ELF exacerbated divisions, the Ala group of fighters from the Christian highlands had become increasingly dissatisfied with the central command. Despite its leader Abraham Twelde initially seeking to negotiate, the group eventually broke away under Tigrinya-speaking, primarily orthodox Christian leadership. After Twelde died on May 17, 1970, he was succeeded by Isaias Afwerki. In the following year, the group established the Eritrean Freedom Party headed by Afwerki over a council of five. Later its name was changed again to the Popular Liberation Forces in a move that attracted Mesfin Hagos, a Syrian trained commander, and fighters of Christian highland origin, to abandon Sabbe's faction. Another defection in the ELF was orchestrated in November when a group of Beni Amer established a separate command called Obel.

In October–November 1971 long-awaited first congress of the ELF was held at Arr. It issued an ultimatum to the two Muslim factions (Sabbe and Beni Amer) to reincorporate into the main ELF or face military measures, while the Afwerki-led Christian Ala group was invited to negotiate. However, the Ala group refused and responded by issuing its first manifesto which appears to have drawn on Afwerki's personal experience and sentiments toward the ELF mainstream.[35] The manifesto, leaning on Marxist revolutionary ideas for social and political change, conformed to a similar ideological orientation as many other liberation movements at the time, based its accusation on ELF's sectarian nature and portrayal of itself as an "Arab" and "Muslim" movement, rather than an "Eritrean" liberation force, oriented against Christian Ethiopia. It further explained that the struggle would be for the whole Eritrean nation irrespective of religion and that Arab support was welcome for strategic reasons but not because Eritreans were either Arab or Muslim.[36]

Following the congress, the three breakaway groups deepened their cooperation to face the mainstream ELF and ensure their respective survival while the mainstream organization sought to neutralize them. After a tripartite deal in Beirut in February 1972 which was followed by an agreement on a joint military command, Sabbe, who utilized his extensive network of contacts and support in the Arab countries, initially took over the foreign linkages and patronage of the three factions. In a swift military action, the ELF defeated the Obel group (Beni Amer) and then engaged the Sabbe and Afwerki factions, which precipitated their merging and led to the formation of the Eritrean People's Liberation Forces (EPLF) in August 1974. A few months after, in part due to the civilian pressure, ELF and EPLF signed a ceasefire and again concentrated their efforts on the struggle against Ethiopia despite Addis Ababa's offer to restore Eritrea's federal status in the aftermath of the military takeover.

In 1974–5 ELF and EPLF sought to take advantage of the confusion after the regime change in Ethiopia and launched a successful offensive on Asmara and in other areas of Eritrea. In this effort, the EPLF supported the emerging Ethiopian opposition formation, the Tigray People's Liberation Front (TPLF), a Christian highland movement hailing from the same Tigrayan ethnolinguistic cultural group as its leadership but from the other side of the Eritrea–Ethiopia colonial border.

However, Ethiopian forces, aided by external allies, staged an unprecedented counteroffensive that targeted not only the rebels but also the civilian population suspected of collaborating with them. The indiscriminate and widespread killings led to a growing number of Eritreans gravitating toward the ELF and EPLF. Ethiopia drew on Israeli support and employed anti-Muslim propaganda which along with the perceived weakening of Ethiopia after the revolution may have motivated an increase in the generally modest Arab material support for the Eritrean resistance.[37]

In 1975, Alimirah Hanfare, the Afar sultan of Aussa, went to exile in Saudi Arabia after a firefight that ensued when the Ethiopian Derg government sought to arrest him. While there, he was in contact with the ELF and established the Afar Liberation Front. His son, Hanfare Alimirah, organized the Afar movement initially with Somali assistance. However, following Somalia's defeat in the Ogaden War (1977–8), the movement eventually disintegrated into small factions some of which gained momentary support from the US-aligned Saudi Arabia as part of its effort to destabilize what it viewed as Marxist and Christian opponents in Eritrea and Ethiopia. Hanfare's efforts were crucial for securing the Afar people a federal region in Ethiopia after the collapse of the Derg in May 1991.

In the course of the 1970s, the revolutionary and secular governments promoting pan-Arabism gave way to more conservative right-wing and at times religion-associated regimes in the Middle East. This led to the waning of Western-aligned Arab governments' interest in the Eritrean struggle. For example, Saudi Arabia, which backed Eritrean (Muslim) resistance and Somali nationalism as counter-forces to communism and actively promoted radical interpretations of Islam in the Horn countries as part of an attempt to expand its influence was opposed to the Marxist ideological current adopted by the EPLF and ended its assistance to the group. This followed Riyadh's policy to form an alliance based on pan-Arab solidarity against communist expansion in the Horn of Africa, which culminated in its support for Somalia in the Ogaden War.[38] While other Western-aligned Arab states, such as Egypt, also had assisted Somalia and supported Eritrean opposition, opaque Saudi involvement appeared as the most extensive.

In these circumstances, the Eritrean exile leadership's ability to obtain external support came increasingly under stress. In the early 1970s, South Yemen became the main lifeline for weapons and supplies for the Eritrean factions but two years after the Ethiopian revolution the assistance had all but ceased. Moving to Saudi Arabia, Adam, one of the founders of the ELF, sought to maintain a level of prestige and visibility of the Eritrean Muslim cause. But swayed by the ideological currents emanating from the oil-rich Persian Gulf countries he turned increasingly toward political Islam and could not recover control of a significant fighting force within the movement.

Sabbe, on the other hand, sought single-handedly to reconcile with the ELF mainstream, while his connections to the Middle East continued to yield a vital flow of weapons and supplies especially through South Yemen. Although after joining the EPLF Sabbe became largely responsible for its foreign mission and obtaining funds and material support from abroad,[39] he also negotiated with the ELF in Beirut and Baghdad without consulting the EPLF leadership and reached an agreement with ELF leadership in Khartoum in September 1975 to merge the two movements. This angered the EPLF field command which rejected the agreement and broke off relations with Sabbe in March 1976.[40] Sabbe then went on to establish his own group, the Eritrean Liberation Front–People's Liberation Forces (ELF-PLF) which the ELF command endorsed until mid-1977 as an associated minor force. However, with the support of Sudanese president Gaafar Nimeiri, a merger of ELF and EPLF was reached in Khartoum and the ELF-PLF was left out. Although Sabbe's organization was later invited to join the ELF-EPLF, he refused due to the likelihood of further weakening of his personal power base. Sabbe's agency, economic diplomacy, and extensive networks were important for securing vital external support for Eritrean liberation in the Middle East.

In January 1977 the EPLF held its foundational congress. During the proceedings, which were observed by representatives of several Arab states such as Iraq, Libya, and Syria, Romedan Mohammed Nur and Isaias Afwerki, leftist radical leaders, were confirmed in the leading positions. Meanwhile, the leadership of a political formation accompanying the group had been handed over to Haile Woldense and Alamin Mohammed Seid. Afwerki then played a leading role in the negotiations leading to EPLF's merger with ELF. However, joining the two groups was met with obstacles, including the ELF leadership's continued disdain of Christian fighters which had led some to defect and form the Eritrean Democratic Front. Similarly, a short-lived Islamic ELF faction under Said Hussein emerged with Sudanese and Yemeni support which was put down in 1978. The defeat of these forces weakened the ELF, while an increasing number of Christian fighters joining the EPLF strengthened the latter. Simultaneously, the ELF mainstream suppressing Islamic elements turned away important external financiers, such as Iraq, which saw it as an expression of the movement's declining Islamic credentials. Instead, in the late 1970s climate of expanding conservative political Islam which consumed much of the Horn of Africa, Arab states became inclined to support more conservative ELF elements. At the same time, South Yemen aligning with communist Ethiopia put it in confrontation with a group of Western-oriented Arab countries headed by Saudi Arabia. These circumstances favored the EPLF over its rival groups and contributed to its emergence as the leading force of the Eritrean liberation struggle.

The Liberation

Following Somalia's defeat in the Ogaden War, the Ethiopian government put its attention on defeating the Eritrean liberation movement. With Soviet and Cuban assistance the superior Ethiopian military made important gains, but its attempt to deliver the final blow to the Eritrean resistance failed. Soviet presence in Eritrea, including in Dahlak Islands, alarmed the Western-aligned Arab states, which in turn increased their support mainly for the conservative elements of the ELF. Under increasing pressure, the ELF came to EPLF's aid to organize the defense of its sanctuary in the highland Sahel region after the latter's offensive which culminated in the failed siege of Massawa. However, efforts of the Ethiopian government and its partners, as well as Arab states such as Iraq which supported various ELF factions, further undermined the coherence of the ELF and again led to the deterioration of its relations with the EPLF. In June 1980 the ELF abandoned the defense of the Sahel and the EPLF subsequently leaned on the TPLF for assistance to defeat the ELF. Already weakened by factionalism and defections, and the struggle against the Ethiopian forces, the ELF eventually collapsed and withdrew to Sudan, where its main military force became largely inactivate in 1981. Thousands of Eritrean Muslims, particularly ELF leaders and from coastal areas in and near Massawa, fled to Saudi Arabia, especially Jeddah,[41] where a diaspora community of Eritreans had existed for decades. The remnants of the ELF found some sympathy from post-revolution Iran which was keen to support a Muslim liberation movement, but this did not resuscitate the movement. Neither did the Saudi efforts to reconcile among the various splinter factions.

In the early 1980s, the Eritrean struggle for independence entered a new phase with the EPLF as its dominant force. Arab states such as Algeria, Kuwait, Saudi Arabia, Syria, and the UAE made statements in support of the Eritrean cause, and multilateral Arab and Islamic organizations demanded that the Ethiopian government negotiates with the liberation movement, while approximately half a million Eritreans had taken refuge in Sudan.[42] Although the ELF had waned militarily, the EPLF had gained strength which strained ties with conservative Arab regimes. In addition, EPLF's socialist Arab backers, namely, Libya and South Yemen, signed a tripartite defense pact with Ethiopia in August 1981. These developments curtailed EPLF's external support and forced it to emphasize self-sufficiency as a survival strategy.

Due to the EPLF's Marxist profile, Saudi Arabia engaged in a modest effort to counter the EPLF's dominant position in the Eritrean struggle. It propelled Islamization, particularly Wahhabism, as an alternative ideological posture to Marxism among Muslim elements in the Eritrean armed resistance. The wider effort to propel Wahhabi fundamentalism eventually inspired, with Sudanese support, the creation of the Eritrean Islamic Jihad Movement (EIJM)[43] aiming to overthrow the EPLF and establish an Islamic caliphate in Eritrea.[44] Saudi ally Egypt also shared Riyadh's apprehension toward the Christian-led and Marxist-inspired EPLF,[45] which, both feared, could develop into another South Yemen around the strategic Red Sea choke point at Bab al-Mandab. Having tolerated EPLF's representation on its soil for several years, Riyadh finally closed its office in Jeddah in 1985.

In the 1980s the sectarian rift in the Eritrean independence movement remained. The religious rift among its social constituencies fed from mistrust and the Saudi and Sudanese support for Islamism among lowland Muslims. The EPLF, seen as a highland Christian force especially due to its leadership, began dictating the Eritrean cause, and Afwerki's coercive control of the movement buttressed his position. It permitted him to dictate the movement's ideological and political agenda, often according to his personal preferences. In 1987 Afwerki was made the secretary general of the EPLF, which consolidated his position as the movement's undisputed figurehead.

In the course of the 1980s, the EPLF's network of foreign relations became narrower and support was drying up. This was despite extensive visits by EPLF delegations in the Persian Gulf countries, with a notable exception of Iran,[46] which was at war with Iraq. This led to a growing focus on self-reliance as an ideology and strategy, with a pretext of minimizing foreign influence, although the movement had been mainly self-sustaining for most of its armed struggle. Following the military defeat of the ELF, the Ethiopian army engaged in campaigns in 1982 and 1983 against the EPLF during which hundreds of thousands of Eritreans fled over the border to Sudan[47] and beyond, but the Ethiopian regime failed to defeat the movement.

Meanwhile, the EPLF consolidated its position as a ruling force in the hardtop access areas under its control. It engaged in political, socioeconomic, and development activities through political indoctrination, education, provision of health services, land reform, and organizing agricultural activity. During the devastating famine in 1983–5, the EPLF's humanitarian office, the Eritrean Relief Association, supported by Scandinavian church organizations and diaspora, played a major role in feeding the population with limited resources until international agencies would step up their aid. In the early 1980s military strategy and ideological differences, including the type of warfare to be waged, the issue of self-determination, and the idea of pan-Tigrinya, led to a brief confrontation between the EPLF and the TPLF as the two movements competed for aid. The EPLF momentarily blocked the TPLF's access to the humanitarian lifeline from Sudan through Eritrea but the TPLF seemingly accommodated by separating itself from the Eritrean cause and agreeing to disassociate Eritrea from Ethiopian ethnopolitics. By the end of the decade, the two movements had rekindled their relationship. To an extent, the EPLF's experience of self-reliance and diaspora support served as an inspiration for the post-independence national development strategy and the system of obligatory diaspora remittances used for financing the state.

Toward the end of the decade, with the increasing prospects for the failure of the communist project, there was an increasing impetus for moderating the rigid Marxist ideological propositions of the struggle. Consequently, they were shaped into a more pragmatic version of socialism that the EPLF leadership deemed more suitable for the Eritrean reality. Reflective of the increasing emphasis on nationalism over the Marxist ideological tenets was the 1989 decision to transform EPLF in due time into a mass movement, the People's Front for Democracy and Justice (PFDJ).

In March 1988, the Ethiopian army suffered its biggest defeat in the Battle of Afabet. Supported by Soviet advisors, a planned offensive turned into a disaster when the EPLF ambushed and annihilated three Ethiopian divisions and captured a large amount of military material. While the Battle of Afabet did not end the war, it was symbolically significant and demonstrated that the EPLF had grown into a formidable force.

The experience of the Eritrean war of liberation shows how various leaders and factions dictated the foreign relations of the liberation forces. A salient figure among them, Osman Saleh Sabbe, who passed away in 1987 in Cairo, created a network of contacts in the Middle East which was crucial for sustaining various groups during the struggle. He, and Idris Mohammed Adam, used skillful diplomacy to secure funding, training, weapons, and supplies for the liberation movement without which it could have not succeeded. They exploited the sentiments of pan-Arabism and Islamic solidarity and used the opportunity provided by the radical political tide to obtain support from regimes and organizations in the Middle East. Although Afwerki's Ala group had denounced these actions in its initial manifesto, it benefited from the external resources. The story of the active and incessant efforts and agency of individuals such as Sabbe and Adam in foreign relations is often lost in the dominant state-based narratives of the Middle East–Horn of Africa relations, especially when they are observed from the perspective of what are deemed as more powerful states.

Independence

After the fall of the Ethiopian Derg regime, Eritrea went through turbulence related to the consolidation of the EPLF provisional government. Saudi Arabia, concerned about the socialist Christian highland movement becoming the governing force in Eritrea, sought to bring the remaining ELF splinter groups together in Jeddah under the National Pact Alliance. Riyadh also advised Eritreans in the country not to vote in the self-determination referendum, but then shifted its position and began supporting Eritrea's independence as a counterweight to increasingly Iranian-influenced Sudan.

Eritrea gained independence two years after the collapse of the Ethiopian Derg regime. It was preceded by a referendum that produced an overwhelming 99.83 percent vote for self-determination. This left little doubt about the will of the majority of Eritreans after the long and arduous war of liberation. EPLF's strategic partner, the TPLF, dictated the political transition in Ethiopia and its leadership reluctantly upheld its earlier promise to the EPLF that Eritrea would gain independence after the Derg's defeat. The US played an important role in pushing for Eritrean independence and its Arab allies followed suit.

In 1994 the EPLF had its final congress in Asmara where it converted into the PFDJ. With independence, the PFDJ, the liberation movement turned government, adopted a policy recognizing all languages spoken in the country. However, Tigrinya and Arabic remained as dominant working languages. Approximately 700,000 Eritreans had resided in Arabic-speaking countries during the war which led returnees to propel the Arabic language, but although the language was both officially and unofficially endorsed, it came to suffer from a chronic lack of capacity in its administrative and educational use.[48]

Although the overwhelming majority of Eritreans celebrated the opportunity to reconstruct the country and build their own sovereign state, the liberation did not address some minority groups' political concerns. For example, among the Afar people, the struggle for liberation from Eritrea, Ethiopia, and Djibouti continued. In 1991–3 pan-Afar liberation movement based in Assab Sahrir and among the diaspora took advantage of Saudi interest in advancing its political Islamist project and gained support from the country for its attempt to create a self-governing Afar region. Around the same time sections of the Afar coalesced into the Afar Revolutionary Democratic Unity Front (ARDUF), which positioned itself against Eritrea and successfully established an autonomous ethnic federal region for the Afar people within Ethiopia However, Afar-inhabited parts in southern Eritrea remained administratively separate due to the international border.

The conversion of the EPLF into the government of Eritrea allowed its leadership to monopolize power over the newly created institutions. From the outset, Isaias Afwerki, the EPLF supreme leader, exercised power behind the formal governing institutions. In this, he drew on a personality cult built during the liberation struggles which portrayed him as an icon of the Eritrean liberation. In May 1993 the PFDJ National Assembly elected Afwerki as the country's president, which enabled the consolidation of associating the state with his person.

Since then, President Afwerki's personal decisions, drawing on his experiences, education, and socialization, dictate state policy. Marxist-communist ideology, which he was educated on during his training in China, appears to still play an important role in influencing the governance and state development strategy as does self-reliance and engaging the diaspora which both became a necessity in the absence of sustained and reliable external backing during the war of liberation. Despite the initial receptiveness to cooperate with the TPLF-led government in Ethiopia and the strong lobbying to host a US military base after the Eritrean–Ethiopian War (1998–2000), Eritrean leadership did not deviate from its hard-learned ideologies and practices. Instead, against the post–Cold War tide of waning past ideologies and further extension of Western liberal democracy and free market capitalism, the Eritrean government consolidated an ideologically driven political system somewhat resembling the North Korean "Juche," in which individual's self-sacrifice for the state and its sovereignty, as well as its self-reliance, is emphasized. External ideological influences, such as personal political freedoms and liberties, have been minimized to ensure the continuity of people's belief in the highly hierarchical power structure in which the state, as a common good won through a hard-fought independence struggle, supersedes the individual.

President Afwerki's personal behind-the-scenes diplomacy and maneuvers have played a salient role in Eritrea's foreign policy. Therefore, similarly to other highly hierarchical states with a narrow concentration of power, the "national" interest is defined based on the state leader and his close advisors' views. Although often opaque, Afwerki's foreign policy approach, with an important emphasis on economic diplomacy, has been pragmatic, opportunist, and versatile, and largely aimed at obtaining resources for the government from various external sources. Emphasizing relations with several states and non-state actors simultaneously, irrespective of their ideological orientations, mutual animosity, or behavior toward other states, and, more importantly, preferring opaque and unstable short-term alignments over long-term alliances, has allowed Afwerki to maintain obscure behind-the-scenes linkages with various external actors and reinforced his government with financial and material resources from foreign partners. According to a former Eritrean official, "Issayas would ally himself . . . with both Libya and Israel at the same time . . . to get his way . . . [and] . . . sought to ally with the US by playing on an Islamist threat within Eritrea, and then got on supporting Islamists in Somalia."[49] This points to Afwerki's highly pragmatic approach in dictating Eritrea's foreign affairs according to the so-called "forward policy"[50] which he has pursued systematically by engaging in shuttle diplomacy oriented toward the regionally powerful states.

After independence, Afwerki forged ties with regional powers to gain resources for state-building and implementing the forward policy. Indebted to the Israelis who successfully treated him for cerebral malaria, Afwerki developed opaque, but lasting, relations with Tel Aviv which included Israeli presence in Eritrea and monitoring of the Red Sea. Although Israel had initially opposed Eritrean independence, Afwerki engaged in a working relationship with Tel Aviv to balance Eritrea's foreign relations and to avoid developing an overreliance on the regionally influential Arab states. The orientation toward Israel, Saudi Arabia, and Iran was therefore a largely pragmatic effort to advance Eritrean leadership's domestic and regional interests by taking advantage of the external powers' ambition to control the narrowest part of the Red Sea. From early on, Eritrea's strategically located long coastline stretching toward Bab-al-Mandab became an asset in its foreign relations, and the Afwerki government has sought to utilize it for improving its domestic and regional position.

In the early 1990s, Saudi Arabia, Egypt, and Israel were preoccupied with Iran's involvement in Sudan, which Cairo and Riyadh consider part of their sphere of influence. Seeking increasing influence to counter the Iranian presence, the Saudi government provided humanitarian aid for Eritrea and promised USD 35 million for improving its energy development capacity.[51] In the second half of the 1990s, Riyadh and Cairo sought Asmara's assistance to weaken the National Islamic Front government in Sudan, which, relying on the teachings of ideologue Hassan al-Turabi, had some years earlier aspired to become the international beacon of revolutionary political Islam. Challenged by Iran's collaboration with the Sudanese "national salvation" (*Irghaz*) regime, which also gained support from Beijing, Saudi Arabia, Egypt, and Israel, and their great power partner, the US, engaged Eritrea as a bulwark against the Sudanese threat. Outside powers considered Eritrea, with a significant Muslim population, to be vulnerable to the expansion of the Sudanese Islamist project, which the Afwerki government sought to take advantage of by fanning the fears of potential destabilization by the Khartoum-linked EIJM. Israel provided weapons and military advisors, and Saudi Arabia sent aid to Eritrea, but Asmara's relations with Riyadh continued to be marred by the legacy of Saudi support of Muslim factions during the liberation struggle as well as its track record of promoting Wahhabism.[52]

Post-Independence Foreign Relations

Since independence, as part of its forward policy, Eritrea has intervened in or confronted a number of its neighboring countries. This includes the Yemeni Hanish Islands conflict (1995), two joint operations with Ethiopia in Sudan and the Democratic Republic of Congo (1996–8), destabilization attempts of Ethiopia through Somalia (from 1998 until the mid-2000s), border conflict with Djibouti (2008–18), support of the Saudi-led coalition in Yemen (2015–21), and the Ethiopian Tigray conflict (2020–). This shows that Eritrea has been militarily active in the greater Horn of Africa and the surrounding regions since its independence, in most cases to advance its influence either through involvement in other states or by seeking modest but strategically significant territorial expansion.

Asmara's most significant confrontation has been with Addis Ababa. From 1998 to 2000 it fought a devastating war against the TPLF-led Ethiopia, and soon after sought to destabilize it through the neighboring countries, namely, Somalia. Since the normalization of relations in 2018 after the emergence of new leadership in Ethiopia, Asmara's battle against the TPLF has culminated in the Tigray conflict in which it has sided with the Ethiopian government.

Eritrean leadership's animosity toward the TPLF owes to a sentiment of betrayal. In the 1974–5 period, the EPLF supported the emerging movement, but soon after its 1976 founding manifesto expressed an aspiration to establish an independent "Republic of Greater Tigray" by annexing southern Eritrea to secure sea access and western Ethiopia to control water resources and rich agricultural land[53] which displeased the EPLF leadership. Although the 1983 TPLF manifesto shifted the movement's objectives from secessionism to "the elimination of national oppression," and to the support "the struggle of the Eritrean people for self-determination and national independence,"[54] this appears to have been a pragmatic shift due to the realization that the TPLF needed the EPLF as a partner in its struggle to defeat the Ethiopian regime and that with EPLF's assistance this began to seem increasingly possible. However, TPLF's modification of its stated objectives did little to deter Eritrean suspicion, particularly when the TPLF leadership, in seeming reluctance despite facing American, other international, and Eritrean pressure, reluctantly accepted Eritrean independence in 1993. The continued fear for the TPLF's true plans clashes with Afwerki's ambition to have Eritrea play a leading role in uniting the Horn of Africa.

Soon after independence, with the rise of internal political dilemmas associated with state leadership's monopolization and consolidation of power, Afwerki externalized Eritrea's political problems through confrontation with neighboring states. Already in 1994, after previously lodging an official complaint at the United Nations Security Council (UNSC), Asmara broke relations with Khartoum which supported the EIJM as part of its regional policy of promoting political Islam. In a countermove, the Eritrean government began hosting the National Democratic Alliance (NDA) opposition umbrella organization, particularly the Beja Congress, and actively assisted in the NDA's political agitation and military efforts. Two years later, in April 1996, Djibouti accused Eritrea of a military incursion in Ras Doumeira but retracted when the alleged Eritrean troops withdrew.

Meanwhile, Eritrean claim on the strategically located Hanish Islands in the narrow southern stretches of the Red Sea led to a confrontation with Yemen. Both governments were motivated to control the islands due to maritime resources, namely, fishing, and prospective oil deposits, and because of their tourism potential, while they were also ideal from a geopolitical perspective for monitoring the southern Red Sea. Despite initial attempts to find a diplomatic solution in late 1995, Yemen sent reinforcements to secure a German company's investment to build a tourist complex. This sparked Eritrean military action despite Yemen's claim to the islands.[55] Although Eritrea argued that its liberation fighters had used the islands during the struggle, Yemen stated that they had done so temporarily with Aden's consent. Eritrea's claim came as a surprise to several Arab states which interpreted it as part of an Israeli plan to use the country to establish a base to monitor the southern Red Sea and its vital shipping lanes. Saudi Arabia, with a complex and obscure relationship with Israel, is engulfed in competition with Iran and drawn to a border dispute in the northern Shia-inhabited region of Yemen which was obscurely supported by Eritrea.[56] Egypt and the Arab League sought to mediate, while several Arab states blamed Israel. In December, the crisis escalated into a short-lived armed conflict when Eritrean troops invaded and occupied the largest island, Hanish al-Kabir. Both belligerents looked toward Washington to assume a greater role in the security of the southern Red Sea, but the US was inclined to have France, with a stronghold in Djibouti, "to act as the primary guardian of the southern Red Sea and the Bab al-Mandab."[57] Approximately six months later, the parties agreed to an arbitration process which took place in October 1998, the Permanent Court of Arbitration (PCA) awarding the main islands to Yemen and small southwestern islets to Eritrea.[58] In November, Yemeni troops arrived and Eritreans withdrew from Hanish al-Kabir.

In May 1998, another dispute, this time on the border between Eritrea and Ethiopia, somewhat accidentally[59] triggered an armed confrontation that then escalated into a full-blown interstate war. Although often debated, the causes of the war are well documented. They included political and economic factors, including Eritrean fears of Ethiopian economic domination and its introduction of the national currency, Nakfa, in 1997, which was subsequently pegged to the USD, as well as disagreement on boundary demarcation and ownership of border territories. [60]

The devastating war came to an end in a cessation of hostilities in June 2000 after much devastation and loss of thousands of lives on both sides. Although Ethiopia made some territorial gains during the war, Eritrea held on and secured relatively opportune terms of peace. Notably, the Eritrea-Ethiopia Boundary Commission was put in charge to demarcate the border, and the PCA that decided on the boundary gave the disputed area around Badme to Eritrea. A temporary 25-kilometer security zone was established on the Eritrean side of the border which was monitored by the United Nations Mission in Eritrea and Ethiopia.

The Eritrean–Ethiopian War generated efforts by both governments to undermine each other. Asmara used the two-year conflict to reconcile with Sudan and deepen ties with Egypt and Yemen. The Eritrean government also lobbied strongly to establish good relations with the US by emphasizing its importance in the war against terrorism in the strategic Red Sea region. By pegging its currency to the USD it not only aimed at fiscal stability but also to edge closer to Washington and its Middle East allies. However, Asmara could not convincingly argue for its strategic importance over Ethiopia, especially after the Eritrean–Ethiopian War, and Washington turned toward Addis Ababa. In the decision, Ethiopia's importance as the dominant state in the Horn of Africa, including its size and potent military and intelligence apparatus, played a determining role. Consequently, with an active effort by Ethiopia's TPLF-led government to undermine the Eritrean administration and major powers supporting Addis Ababa, Asmara became increasingly portrayed as a regional pariah.

However, in turn, the Eritrean leadership engaged in coercive efforts to further concentrate power domestically and continued to engage in the "forward policy" with an emphasis on destabilizing Ethiopia. Eritrean leadership's efforts to limit Addis Ababa's regional dominance included escalation of border confrontation with Ethiopia's vital partner Djibouti, and support of Afar factions in Ethiopia, Islamist factions in Somalia, and Ethiopian opposition groups, the Oromo Liberation Front (OLF) and Ogaden National Liberation Front (ONLF). This earned Eritrea growing Western and international condemnation.

Eritrea's border confrontation with Djibouti in 2008 was initially used to justify the international criticism of Asmara. In April Djibouti expressed concern about Eritrean encroachment and wrote to the UNSC requesting intervention. Nearly two months later, the militaries of the two states clashed in Ras Doumeira after Djibouti accused Eritrea of territorial encroachment. The Arab League condemned Eritrea's action, and the African Union encouraged dialogue between the warring parties. The following year the UNSC urged dialogue and welcomed Djibouti's withdrawal of forces back to the pre-conflict position. Eritrea and Djibouti then agreed for Doha to step in to mediate and establish a buffer zone monitored by Qatari peacekeepers. In June 2017, Doha withdrew the peacekeeping force in the context of Eritrea and Djibouti's support of the Saudi and Emirati-led embargo of Qatar. More than a year later, in September 2018, Eritrea and Djibouti normalized relations after the reconciliation between Asmara and the new Abiy Ahmed leadership in Addis Ababa.

However, above all, Eritrea's assistance to the ICU as a countermove to the Ethiopian-supported Transitional Federal Government (TFG) in Somalia came with international repercussions. Eritrea briefly assisted Somali Islamists and anti-TFG groups, which drew on a perception of the TFG as a foreign powers' imperialist project. Some of these groups had connections to Ogaden in eastern Ethiopia and also to opposition movements such as the OLF and ONLF which set up offices in Asmara. During the war with Ethiopia, the Afwerki government used these groups to create another front through southern Somalia, and the Eritrean support continued in the postwar situation in which both parties continued to use proxies to undermine each other. Even after the Ethiopian invasion and disintegration of the ICU in 2006–7, Asmara ostensibly continued to briefly assist the radical splinter group al-Shabaab as a tactical move against Addis Ababa.[61] This led the UNSC to impose sanctions on Eritrea based on evidence of arming and financing anti-government groups in Somalia. It established the UN Monitoring Group on Somalia and Eritrea as Ethiopia's Western allies put pressure on the UN to actively work for Asmara's isolation. The UNSC Resolution 1907 (2009)[62] imposed an arms embargo, travel restrictions, and asset freezes on Eritrean political and military leaders because of Asmara's perceived involvement in Somalia and unwillingness to withdraw troops from Djiboutian territory until 2010. A later UNSC Resolution 1916 (2010) extended and expanded the mandate of the Somalia monitoring mission.[63]

In Eritrea, the measures to isolate the country propelled a sentiment of international betrayal. This was particularly the case after the release of the UN Monitoring Group report in 2010 claiming Eritrea's continued support for rebels in Somalia, which Asmara rejected.[64] A year after, the group's report claimed Asmara had been financially supporting al-Shabaab, but its 2012 report no longer presented evidence of such activity. Meanwhile, however, the US government imposed targeted sanctions on high-ranking Eritrean officers for allegedly promoting armed opposition, including al-Shabaab, in Somalia. The multilateral UN sanctions on Eritrea were finally removed after its reconciliation with Ethiopia in 2018,[65] but in November 2021 the US imposed new targeted sanctions due to Eritrea's involvement in the conflict in Ethiopia's Tigray.[66]

Eritrean leadership has deplored what it considers as the lack of international understanding of its need to adopt an active and interventionist foreign policy in the sub-regional context dominated by Ethiopia. During the UN sanctions regime, Asmara considered that mitigating the effects of increased isolation required deeper relations with regionally powerful states, namely, Iran, which in turn raised further concern from Saudi Arabia and its regional and international partners in the context of the escalating Yemen crisis.[67] Confrontation with Djibouti and involvement in Somalia were costly for Eritrea, but it could be argued that Asmara's approach was a necessary response to the wider political constellation in the Horn of Africa emphasizing Djibouti's strategic importance for Ethiopia and the US and geared toward deepening isolation of Eritrea.[68]

The sanctions regime, effective until 2018, had a crippling effect on Eritrea's forward policy. It generated a sentiment within Asmara leadership that the international community had again failed Eritrea. Seeking to mitigate the financial shortfall, the Afwerki government embraced tighter self-reliance, a policy that had helped the EPLF survive during the liberation struggle. Increasingly desperate for inward financial flows, Eritrea maintained the policy of taxing its sizable diaspora, one-third of the country's population and over one million in the Arab states alone. In this way, the Eritrean government continued to channel to its citizens in exile state-financing and welfare responsibilities in exchange for providing crucial documents necessary for residence permits.[69] In addition, to alleviate its financial distress, Eritrea struck a deal with the EU to work together to decrease the exodus of Eritreans leaving the country for Europe. Young Eritreans pushed to emigrate due to the lack of jobs, economic opportunities, and prospects, as well as the long periods of national service as a sacrifice for the state. In recent years, they have constituted a major segment of the overall migration from the Horn of Africa to Europe. The deal with the EU brought in some financial aid and other assistance, but the EU's condemnation of Asmara's support of the Ethiopian government in the military operation in Tigray and pressure to undermine Eritrea's regional position have soured relations.

The sanctions also pushed Eritrea to look for external partnerships. Following the Arab Spring, Asmara took advantage of the Gulf monarchies' insecurity and edged closer to Saudi Arabia and the UAE which sought to neutralize Iranian influence and extend their power in the Red Sea and Gulf of Aden region. Pushing Iranian relations aside, but not fully discarding their use as a potential future bargaining tool, Afwerki concentrated on reaping the benefits of alignment with Riyadh and Abu Dhabi. The relations culminated in the UAE's establishment of a military base in Assab in 2015 and Eritrea's participation in the Yemen conflict on the side of the Saudi-led coalition after having previously been accused of supporting the Houthi movement.

At the same time, the Eritrean administration has drawn financial inflow from long-established personal relationships and individual networks the government officials maintain in the GCC states. These linkages with individuals in Saudi Arabia and the UAE, in particular, as well as the obligatory diaspora contributions, have provided a significant source of income channeled through the Persian Gulf financial hubs for regime survival. This opaque economic diplomacy and financial extraversion from foreign partners has continued to secure the external economic means for ensuring the viability and continuity of the Afwerki government.

As a result, Eritrea's relations with Arab states have been characterized by opaque and personalized connections. The ideological foreign partnerships that might have been important in the early days of the liberation struggle have become less significant because Eritrea's relations with external parties are mainly pragmatic and oriented to serve the domestic power of the narrow leadership and its security apparatus and political base. While self-reliance and self-preservation have led the Afwerki government to pursue widespread foreign relations, including simultaneously with states that between them are adversaries, this has been less the case in Eritrea's recent relations with the Persian Gulf countries because connections with Iran and Qatar have been compromised by the closer association and alignment with Saudi Arabia and the UAE.

The more persistent links characterizing Eritrea's relations with the Persian Gulf countries are through prominent individuals and diaspora communities in the Arabian Peninsula. These connections go back to the times of the early liberation struggle and persevere today. Since independence, however, the human element of Eritrean foreign relations is overshadowed by the state's institutionalized system of resource extraction from the diaspora population to secure financial means for regime survival. Eritrea has an extensive diaspora community estimated at one-third of its total population. While the neighboring countries Sudan and Ethiopia host the largest Eritrean exile communities, North America and a number of Western European states also have sizable Eritrean exile populations. Over one million Eritreans reside in Arab states, with Saudi Arabia alone hosting more than 100,000 Eritreans followed by smaller populations in the UAE, Kuwait, Qatar, Bahrain, and Yemen.[70] The diaspora in the Persian Gulf countries is an important source of income for the Eritrean state which facilitates work-based migration and imposes a 2 percent diaspora tax on all income and benefits from other remittances. Although the government reaches outside its borders, particularly in Sudan where Eritreans maintain rather unrestricted access, active opposition elements are also present in the diaspora.

The Eritrean government seeks to control the diaspora. It seeks to restrict space for expressing political opinions abroad and monitors opposition individuals while expecting demonstrations of loyalty through participation in activities organized by Eritrean missions as it engages in propaganda to justify the need for obligatory financial contributions and uses families of diaspora individuals at home as collateral.[71] In addition, the Eritrean administration's efforts to monitor and control the diaspora community in the Arab states include educational and social activities, such as running Eritrean schools and organizing social gatherings in Riyadh and Jeddah,[72] while its intelligence and security services are also active among the communities. Since Eritreans in the Gulf States are mainly considered migrant workers, they depend on valid Eritrean passports and consequently on the state authorities.[73] The involuntary and voluntary financial flows from the diaspora are often channeled through the Gulf States. They are received by prominent individuals linked to the state administration, or by government-related companies, and stored in financial hubs such as Dubai where official Eritrean missions, often under orders of high-ranking military officers, administer and channel them onward for strategic purposes.[74]

The strategic elements of Eritrea's foreign partnerships with the Arab states are characterized by transactional relations. In these exchanges Eritrean leadership, according to its view of what constitutes its subjective "national" interest, has used local assets in its possession toward external actors as a bargaining chip. Eritrea's strategic location along the narrowest stretches of the Red Sea has been one such strategic element. As the Yemen conflict has shown, this has played a major role in its relations with Arab states but since the withdrawal of the UAE from Assab in early 2021, and the Russian invasion of Ukraine one year later, the Eritrean leadership has sought closer ties with China and Russia which eye on growing presence on the Red Sea coast. Again, this is due to its pragmatic approach to foreign relations to ensure diplomatic and material support for survival.

Eritrea, similarly to other Horn states, has suffered from a chronic shortage of foreign exchange. This has mainly owed to Asmara's international isolation and resulted in a lack of investments, loans, and grants, and diminished options for business and commerce. The Eritrean government has sought to remedy the shortage of official foreign currency inflow through opaque sources of money and emphasizing obligatory diaspora remittances (taxes) and self-sufficiency with variable success. However, financial inflows have been essential for backing the political structure, state finances, the currency, and paying for exports. Afwerki administration has pursued a fiscal policy based on pegging its currency to the USD which has facilitated foreign financial connections particularly in the US and with its partners across the Red Sea.

Emphasizing economic diplomacy, the government sought to obtain funds and investment through selective foreign partnerships in the context of international isolation. Efforts to obtain foreign exchange through transactional relations have included the mining sector as a local source of revenue generation while the government has also established a free trade zone in Massawa and commercialized Eritrea's two main, strategically located, ports (Massawa and Assab). Following the escalation of the war in Yemen, Eritrea's main sea linkage became the Saudi Arabian port of Jeddah. By 2011 Eritrea attracted foreign mining investors and founded the gold-focused Bisha mine operated by Canadian Nevsun Resources Ltd. with a 60 percent stake and Zara Mining Share Company, in which Chinese Shanghai Corporation for Foreign Economic and Technological Co-operation (Sfeco) holds the same share. Bisha mine quickly became an important source of export revenue, while Zara's Koka Gold Mine, which began production in 2016, also started production. Chinese companies, spearheaded by Sichuan Road and

Bridge Group which has mainly engaged in infrastructure improvement, have come to dominate the main mining operations for gold, copper, zinc, and silver in the country. In the 2015–18 period, Chinese companies acquired Canadian possessions Sunridge Gold and Nevsun,[75] to monopolize the sector which has cemented Asmara's ties with Beijing in recent years. It has also further consolidated the Afwerki government's foreign policy strategy to exchange Eritrea's resources and strategic location for financial, material, and diplomatic support. Although the mining exports have helped to somewhat alleviate Eritrea's chronic foreign exchange shortage, the leadership has been obliged to engage in wider economic diplomacy to diversify its external sources of financial and material resources and focus in its foreign policy alignment and partnerships on those states and non-state actors which are willing to work with it.

Asmara's Recent Foreign Relations Orientations

After the Ethiopian intervention and the removal of the ICU in Somalia, and faced with growing international isolation, Eritrea reached out to the regionally powerful states to alleviate its immediate need for foreign partnerships. In 2008 President Afwerki engaged in economic diplomacy to obtain Saudi investment, but slim prospects of profit and potential reputational consequences associated with involvement in a sanctioned country watered down the initiative as Eritrea faced pressure from the US, Riyadh's major partner. Afwerki subsequently approached Iran, which Washington considered another pariah. In May 2008 he visited Tehran[76] which led to an agreement of cultural, scientific, and educational cooperation, and Iran to renovate the Assab oil refinery as well as providing other support. The transactional nature of the relationship was exemplified by Eritrea's public defense of the Iranian nuclear program, and, according to some allegations, allowing Tehran to use the Port of Assab to exert control over the Bab al-Mandab and provide training and channel arms to the Houthi rebels in Yemen.[77] At the same time, however, Asmara reportedly engaged in relations with Iran's rival Israel, which, despite Eritrean denial, was alleged to maintain a naval presence in the Dahlak Archipelago and Massawa, and a listening post at Amba Soira, to monitor Iran's activities from the strategically significant Red Sea state.[78] For the Eritrean government, the strategy to pursue diverse external relations, including simultaneously with competing states such as Iran and Israel, and to use such relations to generate interest of other rival states such as Saudi Arabia, has been beneficial. This approach, also implemented by the Horn of African states during the Cold War, has generated invaluable financial, economic, and military resources to sustain the political status quo in the country.

In the second half of the 2000s, Eritrea also edged closer to Qatar. More significantly than Iran, which continued to focus on neighboring Sudan, Doha became Asmara's partner for foreign economic support. Despite maintaining ties with China, Israel, Libya, and Russia, for the Eritrean government, Qatar's economic endorsement and provision of financing through personal networks with Eritrean officials and high-profile individuals became essential. In exchange, Asmara allowed Doha access to its strategic Red Sea coast, and, for example, permitted the Qatari royal house to build a resort in Dahlak Kebir, the largest island of the Dahlak archipelago.[79] Since the 1990s, the Qatari government has sought to profile itself as a peacemaker in the Horn of Africa. It used its leverage to mediate a settlement in the armed border confrontation between Eritrea and Djibouti in 2010 and dispatched a peacekeeping force to monitor the area.

However, while Eritrea's relations with Iran and Qatar were aimed at mitigating the effects of its international isolation, the honeymoon was short-lived. Eritrean leadership found the alignment with Tehran worrisome due to meager economic and financial returns relative to the risk of further isolation. With Iran's interest in controlling Bab al-Mandab and supporting the Houthi in Yemen and the threat this posed to Saudi Arabia, Afwerki saw an opportunity to improve his government's position by engaging with other regional allies, namely, Riyadh and Abu Dhabi, for potentially higher returns. In the case of Qatar, Asmara grew wary of Doha's profile as a supporter of grassroots movements in the context of the Arab Spring and its aspirations as a peacemaker and good relations with Addis Ababa which could potentially undermine Eritrea's "forward strategy" and its "cold war" with Ethiopia. A few years after the Arab Spring, Eritrea's interests came to align with those of Saudi Arabia and the UAE which undermined its relations with Qatar.

Alarmed by Iranian, Qatari, and Turkish influence in the Horn of Africa during the Arab Spring, the leading Persian Gulf monarchies, Saudi Arabia and the UAE, worked increasingly in tandem to gain influence in the Red Sea/Gulf of Aden region. Concerned about Turkish and Qatari support for religious groups, such as the Muslim Brotherhood, and fearing the effects revolutionary sentiments might have at home, Saudi Arabia and the UAE sought to thwart the spread of grassroots movements. Also, governments associated with such ideas and movements, especially those linked to the Muslim Brotherhood or Iran, became targets of Saudi and Emirati influencing attempts. The main triumph of this policy was the support of the successful military takeover in Egypt, while both states embarked on an active propping up of the existing authoritarian governments in the Red Sea region. These actions brought Riyadh and Abu Dhabi into an increasing confrontation not only with Tehran but also with Doha and Ankara, giving rise to a new constellation of geostrategic competition among regional powers in Northeast Africa. The Eritrean government aspired to exploit this strategic rivalry by engaging in cooperation and alignments which would benefit its leadership most in terms of domestic power and advancing its regional aspirations.

Driven by the leadership's interest, and reduced options due to international isolation, Eritrea consequently edged closer to Saudi Arabia and the UAE. This way the Eritrean leadership exploited the legacy of past connections and current linkages with the Persian Gulf countries to push its domestic and regional agenda. In 2015, during the early days of the Saudi-led coalition's intervention in the war in Yemen, President Afwerki took the opportunity of the collapse of Djibouti's relations with the UAE and Saudi Arabia to offer the Port of Assab for the use of the Saudi-led coalition. He signed a thirty-year lease agreement with the UAE for the management and development of the port and establishment of a military base in Assab that included revamping the airfield and the associated facilities. On April 29, the day Djibouti evicted Saudi and Emirati troops, Afwerki met with Saudi king Salman bin Abdel Aziz in Saudi Arabia and signed a previously prepared partnership agreement for security and military cooperation[80] which served him to ensure the Saudi government that Eritrea had moved away from the Iranian orbit. Through strategic alignment, Afwerki had again exploited the interest of external powers in Eritrea's strategic position in the Red Sea.

In a pragmatic and transactional manner, Afwerki offered a strategic presence in Eritrea, access to the Eritrean Hanish Islands to monitor the Strait of Bab al Mandab, and support in the military intervention in Yemen. In exchange, the Eritrean government received financial assistance,[81] fuel supplies, infrastructure development, possible investment, and crucial diplomatic support.[82] While UAE established a military base in Assab, from where it launched Yemen operations and where it trained thousands of Yemeni troops, Eritrea was suspected of sending hundreds of troops to contribute to the Saudi-led coalition intervention against the Houthi.[83] These developments demonstrated Asmara's policy reversal, but, at the same time, the new alignment somewhat undermined Eritrea's aspiration to maintain diverse foreign relations because it alienated some of Asmara's previous associates and resulted in a degree of subordination to the financial power of the new partners.

Meanwhile, the UAE established a presence in the Yemeni Socotra and Perim (Mayyun) islands in the Gulf of Aden and the Red Sea, respectively. In 2018, the UAE, which had been training troops in Socotra, deployed forces on the island.[84] This led to conflict with Abdrabbuh Mansur Hadi's government in Yemen and crispation with Riyadh, Abu Dhabi's senior partner, which maintained troops on the island until it was forced out in May 2020 by the forces of the UAE-backed Yemeni separatist Southern Transitional Council (STC).[85] Soon after Saudi withdrawal, the Yemeni separatists took over administration of the island,[86] and following the UAE's normalization of ties with Israel, Saudi Arabia appears to have tacitly accepted the STC and UAE's control and an alleged Israeli presence in a joint intelligence base on the island.[87] In addition, the UAE's presence in Perim Island,[88] at Bab al-Mandab on the Yemeni coast, forms part of its continued involvement in Yemen as the island now hosts a strategically located base. Emirati presence in Socotra and Perim enhances Abu Dhabi's ability to secure sea trade through the Gulf of Aden and Bab al-Mandab, and monitor weapons smuggling to and from Yemen, elevating its importance as a strategic partner for major powers in the Red Sea region.[89] Since the UAE's withdrawal from Assab in early 2021, and its consequent divestment from relations with Eritrea,[90] Abu Dhabi seeks to use the Perim Island for a similar purpose it used Assab, enabling it to maintain an eye on Eritrea, which had been allegedly involved in facilitating weapons to the Houthi during its alignment with Iran.

As with Tehran, Asmara's closer relations with Riyadh and Abu Dhabi generated increasing tension toward Doha. As a result, in sync with the Saudi and Emirati efforts to weaken Qatar's influence in the Horn of Africa, in mid-2017 Asmara downgraded relations with Doha[91] and Qatar withdrew its Eritrea–Djibouti border peacekeeping force.[92] The deeper cooperation with Saudi Arabia and the UAE also yielded rapprochement with Ethiopia, which Afwerki used to advance his personal influence in Eritrea's immediate neighborhood in the Horn.

In early 2018, the political situation in Ethiopia changed rapidly due to internal rifts in the EPRDF government and its inability to quell the continuous protests. The incoming new prime minister Abiy Ahmed Ali was receptive to reconciliation with Eritrea, which counted on its Arab allies and American facilitation to engage in negotiations to end the almost two-decades-long "cold war" between the two countries. The mutual interest in sidelining Ethiopia's former ruling party, the TPLF, facilitated a renewed relationship. As part of the agreement, Eritrean-hosted Ethiopian armed opposition movements, namely, the OLF and ONLF, agreed to negotiate with the Ethiopian government, lay down their weapons (the OLA "Shene" as an exception), and return to the country. Air travel was resumed and the land border between the two countries was briefly opened.

The process brought much-needed relief to Eritrea's financial difficulties and international isolation. In the initial stages, the US[93] played a role in bringing Eritrean and Ethiopian representatives together, but the UAE and Saudi Arabia, which had developed strong relations with Eritrea since 2015, took the opportunity provided by the new leadership in Ethiopia to broker an agreement. This formed part of Eritrea's Arab allies' attempt to gain further leverage over Ethiopia, the most powerful state in the Horn of Africa, and take advantage of opportunities brought by economic liberalization advocated by the new prime minister. As an incentive, before the deal, Afwerki obtained a pledge from the UAE for widespread investment in Eritrea,[94] and Abu Dhabi granted USD 3 billion to Ethiopia, depositing USD 1 billion in the central bank and pledging USD 2 billion in investments.[95] The agreement inked on July 9, 2018, could be seen as an extension of President Afwerki's strategy to present Eritrea as a strong sub-regional actor that is equal, if not superior, to Ethiopia, and Addis Ababa's further opening to Saudi and Emirati influence, the latter also envisaging a possibility to play a major role in rebuilding logistics linkages between Addis Ababa and Eritrean ports to counter the Ethiopian Chinese-dominated import-export route through Djibouti. Eventually, Saudi and Emirati investment was mainly geared toward Ethiopia due to its central and strategic position and size. Ethiopia's attractiveness to the Persian Gulf powers is increased by its potential future markets and investment opportunities in various sectors, including food production, manufacturing, telecommunications, and hospitality, as they face increasing pressure to invest their hydrocarbon proceeds productively and profitably.

However, the much-publicized rapprochement provided an opportunity for Afwerki to strengthen the Eritrean government's position through new financial and diplomatic support, exert influence on Ethiopia's new leadership, and show goodwill that would persuade the international community to end the sanctions regime. Behind the agreement laid a pact between Ethiopian prime minister Abiy Ahmed Ali and President Afwerki on phasing out the TPLF as a major political force in Ethiopia TPLF's weakening was important for Abiy's consolidation, while

Afwerki's animosity toward the organization goes back to the Eritrean liberation struggle. Somali president Farmaajo was also quickly included in the tripartite pact for crafting a new political landscape in the Horn of Africa. This gave Eritrea a central role in the calculations for the future coordination of affairs in the sub-region.

Eritrean leadership's keenness to neutralize the TPLF has owed to an uneasy and often confrontational relationship originating in the 1970s. According to some observers, TPLF's minority position and suspected links and subordination to Eritrea led to a chronic lack of its domestic legitimacy in Ethiopia,[96] which President Afwerki may have aspired to use to increase Eritrea's influence. It appears that during the TPLF period in Ethiopia, claiming Eritrean superiority over the movement and pushing substantial weakening of the TPLF-embodied Tigrayan nationalism enabled the Eritrean, largely Tigray-speaking and Christian-highland-based, leadership to further differentiate itself from the neighboring Ethiopian Tigray and to minimize what it perceives an expansionist threat. After TPLF's removal from power in Ethiopia, and the concentration of its forces across the border in Tigray, Eritrea participated in the "law enforcement operation" and conflict in Tigray to secure its southern border from the threat posed by the TPLF. Partnering with the new leadership in Addis Ababa has allowed President Afwerki to seek to neutralize the TPLF and exert unprecedented influence on the federal government in Ethiopia. Although some see the recent peace agreement between the Ethiopian government and the TPLF as disadvantageous for Asmara because it may bring the conflict to an end without fully eliminating the TPLF as a political force, the significant weakening of the organization will strengthen Eritrea's position. TPLF's continued existence may force the current leadership in Addis Ababa to continue to rely on Asmara which would elevate Eritrea's position in Ethiopia and the Horn sub-region.

Eritrea's stand on regional organizations reflects its leadership's renewed assertiveness. Having left the main sub-regional and regional organizations, the Inter-Governmental Authority on Development (IGAD) and the African Union (AU), in 2007, Asmara has continued to focus mainly on bilateral relations. Its exit was largely due to Ethiopia's influence in the two bodies, but after the change in leadership in Addis Ababa, the Afwerki government has resumed regional cooperation arguably from a more prominent position. Although Eritrea has paid lip service to the idea of returning to the IGAD and the AU, the main manifestation of its regional cooperation has until recently been the tripartite agreement, "Joint Declaration on Comprehensive Cooperation between Ethiopia, Somalia and Eritrea" between the leaders of the three countries in September 2018. This deal between the three leading figures of the respective governments went much beyond the official statements and was largely opaque and highly personalized. The agreement, which was further strengthened through several tripartite meetings in 2020 and joint action in the Tigray war, was essentially a coordinated effort to consolidate the three leaderships against domestic and regional rivals. It allowed President Afwerki to assume an important role in influencing regional strategy for the Horn of Africa. While some might assert that Afwerki holds a grandiose vision of his role as the center of power in the Horn of Africa, another reading based on the observation of continued pragmatism in Eritrea's foreign policy would suggest that any calculation about Eritrea's future must continue to recognize the overwhelming importance of its relationship with the sub-regions dominant state, Ethiopia.

On January 6, 2020, another regional forum, a treaty for the formation of the Council of the Arab and African Countries of the Red Sea and the Gulf of Aden, or the Red Sea Council, was launched. Saudi Arabia had adopted the initiative from Egypt largely because of its security concerns regarding the strategically vital water body. Eritrea, along with Djibouti, Egypt, Jordan, Somalia, Sudan, and Yemen, joined the organization. However, in the talks leading to the later launching of the new organization, Eritrea's delegation, consisting of Presidential Adviser Yemane Ghebreab and Head of PFDJ Economic Affairs, Hagos Ghebrehiwet, expressed that "The geo-strategic and geo-political importance as well as complexity and sensitivity of the Red Sea are too evident . . . [and that the] . . . important maritime route had sadly become a theatre for reckless regional and international interferences in the past thirty years largely due to misguided exogenous agendas,"[97] reflecting Eritrea's suspicion about Riyadh's intention to use the organization to gain an advantage in its Middle East rivalries. This shows Eritrea's continued assertiveness and wariness toward regional initiatives and organizations in which it does not play a major role, as well as the regional instability to which external actors are seen to contribute.[98] In its foreign relations, Asmara, therefore, continues to prefer a pragmatic and often transactional bilateral approach.

Although President Afwerki mended ties with Ethiopia and Farmaajo-led Somalia (until 2022) to promote common interests among the leaders in the three states, Eritrea failed to escape its reputation. Asmara siding with Addis Ababa in the conflict in Ethiopia's Tigray region, which at some point had the potential to become an existential struggle for the Ethiopian government, has again put Eritrea in the spotlight among Western powers as a sub-regional pariah. This is largely because of the continuity of its assertive foreign policy that often collides with Western interests, in particular, and due to some of its policies which may be seen to contradict international norms that are promoted as universal. However, this has had less impact on Asmara's relations with a number of its non-Western partners. Although Eritrea's military intervention in northern Ethiopia has generated an uproar in the West, Asmara's relations with some of its Arab partners, China, and Russia, for example, appear to have been less affected. While, in association with its stated pulling back in the Yemen war the UAE withdrew from Assab in early 2021[99] and established a presence in the Perim Island, which may to some extent have been linked to Western pressure, the UAE has at the same time supporting the Ethiopian government, Asmara's ally, by providing drones support[100] and engaging in a continuous channeling of military material.[101]

Asmara leadership pursues foreign relations and alignments with the principal objective to maintain the domestic status quo and secondarily to assert Eritrea's importance in the sub-region. A crucial part of this endeavor is to ensure widespread external relations to obtain financial and economic resources for regime survival. Eritrea's economic diplomacy has oriented mainly toward pursuing pragmatic and transactional relations with non-democratic powers that do not criticize the country's domestic politics or foreign aspirations. By engaging with Eritrea, these states, therefore, provide tacit support for Asmara to maintain the existing state of affairs and adopt an assertive stand in its neighborhood. Here, especially the wealthy countries of the Persian Gulf and their strategic and security interests in the Red Sea have played a significant role. However, because of Eritrean leadership's domestic strength, and ability to pursue diverse foreign relations to avoid dependency on few allies despite somewhat limited options for external alignments, the Persian Gulf countries' attempts to assert influence on Eritrea have gained limited success when compared with its neighbors. The Eritrean government has cashed in on its strategic location and other assets, including natural resources and the diaspora, and continues to attract foreign financing and investment from various sources while carefully balancing and periodically shifting between external partners to control the influence.

Deemed overreliance on a few partners prompted Asmara to return to a wider focus on foreign partnerships. Since the mid-2010s Saudi Arabia and the UAE showed some promise to become the external guarantors of the continuity of the Afwerki government, but relying on the two states excessively became insufficient and risked dependency. As a result, Asmara pursued a wider spectrum of foreign alignments and gained funding from the EU due to Brussels's interest in curbing the migration crisis that has in part emanated from Eritrea. It has also sought to deepen relations with Beijing which in recent years has made overtures toward the Red Sea and Gulf of Aden littoral states. In late November 2021, shortly after Beijing failed to convince Western-aligned Hargeisa of a partnership, Eritrea joined the Belt and Road Initiative.[102] This could be seen as China's move to exploit the Western rupture with Eritrea over Tigray and further reinforce its relationship with Asmara and Mogadishu to complement strong relations with Addis Ababa and Djibouti. China recently appointed a Special Envoy for the Horn of Africa which reflects intensified efforts to engage the states in the sub-region for increasing economic interdependence and political and security cooperation.[103]

Eritrean leadership has also considered Russia, which has eyed on growing military presence in the Red Sea and held discussions with various coastal states, as a partner as long as cooperation with Moscow can produce tangible benefits. In 2018 Asmara and Moscow planned a Russian logistics center in an Eritrean port,[104] in addition to the ongoing project for a Russian naval support base and gold extraction in Sudan,[105] and they are likely to partner in other projects in the context of Moscow's attempt to circumvent Western sanctions since its 2022 invasion of Ukraine.

Securing Chinese and Russian political support in the UN Security Council is an important calculation for the leadership in Asmara. It has sought to do so by allowing Chinese industries to monopolize mineral extraction and siding with Moscow in international fora during Russia's invasion of Ukraine. Asmara has reportedly also agreed with Moscow to allow Russia strategic presence in the Red Sea through the establishment of a naval base near Massawa in exchange for "kamikaze" drones[106] presumably oriented toward tackling the looming threat from Tigray. In the end, despite Eritrea's constrained space for foreign partnerships, and troubling domestic economic situation, Asmara has sought to maintain its strategy of pursuing diverse external relations and avoid excessive reliance on a reduced number of partners. For the time being this has been sufficient for maintaining the domestic status quo and projecting a level of influence in its neighborhood.

Conclusion

For centuries, foreign powers have recognized the importance of the strategically located shorelines of the southern Red Sea. In the sixteenth century, increasing competition against the Portuguese over access to the western Indian Ocean and its lucrative trade contributed to the motivation for Ottoman expansion around both sides of the narrow stretches of Bab al-Mandab. In the Horn of Africa, the Ottomans gained control over several seaports and narrow lowland territories and sought to use them as a springboard to compete against regional rivals. They formed alliances with local polities, most notably the Adal Sultanate, to defeat the highland Christian Abyssinia but often faced significant local resistance and failed to expand their dominion to the interior highlands. On the other hand, Ethiopian emperors aspired to control the coastal lowlands to ensure access to the Red Sea and the crucial maritime commerce which had ensured the prosperity of ancient highland kingdoms. The arrival of Italians in the nineteenth century, and the establishment of Eritrea as the crown jewel of Rome's African possessions after the inauguration of the Suez Canal, again reflected the strategic importance of southern Red Sea coastal areas. Decades later, Emperor Haile Selassie's ambition to annex Eritrea and gain control of a seaport reflected this legacy.

This mainstream narrative however, fails to capture the agency of local actors in the region who collaborated with and resisted external players. They gained and maintained power locally in part through foreign connections and often fought for local autonomy. As the earlier discussion has indicated, resisting external powers was often more difficult than collaboration, but when successful it often ensured a level of independence from foreign domination. Faced with the interests of external powers, local leaders found themselves between the rock and the hard place and tended to enter into fickle alliances and alignments. For example, local leaders such as Bahta Hagos entered into strategic alignments with foreign players that competed for influence and gained political and material resources which enabled him to gain prominence and advance his position in the local political context. This dynamic is still relevant today when local actors approach external powers to gain an edge in their local rivalries.

The Eritrean liberation struggle emerged in conditions of direct external domination and repression by imperial Ethiopia. Early on, it also drew on Italian-encouraged sentiment of identity difference from highland Ethiopia and Muslim lowlanders' marginalization. Some of those who were culturally different, and appeared most severely marginalized, became the bulwark of the early opposition.

As a result, Eritrean Muslims, particularly among the Beni Amer, played an important role in the organization and operationalization of the early armed liberation.

The early Eritrean liberation movement used its Muslim credentials to attract Arab support amid Cold War rivalries. The ELF forged and exploited relations with external powers for diplomatic, political, financial, material, and training support. A number of these were Arab and considered the Eritrean plight as a pan-Muslim (and pan-"Arab") struggle against Zionism, Israel's regional ambitions, and Christian, and in the 1970s and 1980s communist, Ethiopia's domination of the surrounding Muslim lowland peoples. Saudi Arabia's emergence as a regional power by the 1970s put further emphasis on political manifestations of Islam as an ideological counterforce for communism, which was manifested in some Muslim ELF splinter sections attracting funding and support despite the organization's military defeat and the Christian-led Marxist-Leninist EPLF's monopolization of the Eritrean armed struggle. However, throughout most of the struggle, external material assistance was not significant and not a key factor in its eventual success. Rather, in the late 1970s, the heterogeneous movement developed into a largely self-reliant and self-supplying entity mainly relying on Christian highlanders and its resilience depended on local support, security, development, and service provision, and captured war material from Ethiopian forces.

The transition from national liberation into independence did not lead to a major political transformation. The EPLF leadership consolidated its power as the PFDJ forming the political structure and system and shaping the economic and social order of the newly independent state based on its ideological groundings that emanated from the liberation period.

President Isaias Afwerki, the figurehead of the former EPLF, surrounded by a small group of advisors,[107] has dictated Eritrean foreign policy since the country's independence. He shapes the country's "national interest" according to his personal perception of the needs of the state of Eritrea, which puts strengthening the top administration and Eritrea's domestic and regional influence in the foreground. Asmara's assertive stand and competition with Addis Ababa in regional affairs have often resulted in confrontation against external powers siding with its neighbors, which has convinced the Eritrean government to maintain the policy of self-sufficiency emanating from the hard years of the EPLF struggle and pursue diverse foreign relations including with authoritarian and competing partners. Ideologically, the Eritrean leadership has continued to subscribe to the liberation logic and the paramountcy of the state, and the importance of the individual's self-sacrifice for it.

Eritrea's foreign policy, therefore, emphasizes national pride and preserving hard-won statehood and territorial integrity while gaining regional influence. This is pursued through diverse external partnerships while asserting the right to defend one's interests internationally under international law despite pressure and imposition of constraints by great and regional powers. Although Christian highland identity elements have featured in the government's national project, a modest, albeit pragmatic, effort has been made to reengage with the idea of

Eritrea's unique multiethnic identity, including coastal lowland and northern cultures and highlighting the connections across the Red Sea and the Arab world. Eritrean leadership recognizes that, as currently with China, the linkages with the Arab world, and particularly regional power Saudi Arabia, were crucial during the liberation struggle and continue to play an important role in the country's foreign policy orientation today.

Another lesson emanating from the liberation struggle is the need to continue pursuing pragmatic and diverse foreign relations, sometimes even simultaneously with opposing forces. This has been an important remedy for obtaining crucial financial and other material resources and vital diplomatic support from abroad. The fact the Eritrean government has been able to prevent other power centers from emerging and challenging the political status quo shows that it is in control of the main foreign connections in the country and that any sub-state or non-state actors have not been able to develop such substantial foreign connections through which they would obtain sufficient resources to emerge as challengers to the government's political power and authority.

Economic diplomacy, using diplomatic and political relationships with foreign partners to gain economic resources, has formed part of Eritrean foreign policy for a long time. As with most of Eritrea's other external partners, these pragmatic engagements with the Persian Gulf powers have been mainly transactional and unpredictable. For example, in its approach toward Arab and other foreign powers, Eritrea has exchanged its political, strategic, and economic assets, namely, its location near Bab al-Mandab in the southern Red Sea and its natural resource base, mainly for financial, development, and other material as well as nonmaterial diplomatic, political, and reputational benefits. Eritrean leadership carefully weighs the benefits of its foreign partnerships and is known to quickly change orientation and alignments when more attractive offers from potential external partners surface. Over time, its approach of shifting political orientation and alignments with foreign powers has provided the Eritrean government with vital resources for survival and has made it a key player in the politics of the southern Red Sea and the Horn of Africa. The Eritrean leadership's tested foreign policy approach is not likely to change in the near future as it navigates through the murky waters in its neighborhood.

CONCLUSION

Regional relations between peoples of the Horn of Africa, the Arabian Peninsula, the Persian Gulf, and the wider Middle East date back thousands of years. During this time, individuals, goods, ideas, and cultural influences have traveled both ways through commerce, migration, and at times domination and conquest. However, while the interaction has been mutual, scholarly Politics and International Relations literature in particular has often depicted it as a largely one-way movement of influence from the Middle East to the Horn of Africa. An essential part of this determination is a relatively recent and narrow perception of power emanating from the International Relations discipline in which the Persian Gulf and Middle East states are considered more capable and influential than their counterparts in the Horn of Africa. This view largely owes to scholars subscribing to the "realist" interpretation of power as relative between unitary state actors and is often applied to understanding great powers and their relations with lesser states in the international system.

Caveats of the Mainstream Analysis in the Horn–Gulf Relations

In the realist International Relations literature state power plays a crucial role in understanding interstate relations. This research and policy focus was initially heavily influenced by the interest in analyzing hegemons, great powers, and strong nation-states and oriented toward examining these perceivably more powerful states' relations with lesser states. The realists view states as unitary actors and what they see as stronger, more capable, states projecting power and influence on weaker ones to achieve their national interest. This is understood as uneven relations between states in which relative power difference plays a vital role. International Relations literature on the Persian Gulf and the Middle East–Horn of Africa relations is mainly based on a strategic and security analysis that applies a realist lens and assumes the superiority of the states in the former over the latter. The Persian Gulf powers are expected to exert their influence on the states in the Horn of Africa by using mainly their financial capabilities. Persian Gulf countries most intensely involved in relations with the Horn of Africa are often considered to have regional or middle power status and able to exercise power over the fragile states in the Horn of Africa.

However, this widely held view based on the realist interpretation simplifies reality. It considers both the Persian Gulf/Middle East and the Horn of Africa players as unitary state actors and restricts the relative power to such monolithic states. Rooted in the conceptualization of the state according to the Western experience as a Westphalian nation-state prototype, this viewpoint fails to account for the complexity of interstate and interregional relations and the significance of non-state actors, particularly in fragile, multinational, states. Considering power merely as relative between monolithic state actors recognizes neither the agency of multiple state, sub-state, and non-state actors nor the importance of local power particularly in the so-called fragile states that do not adhere to the nation-state archetype. This is particularly relevant in the relations between the Horn of Africa and the Persian Gulf/Middle East because the central governments, particularly in the former, do not tend to have a comprehensive monopoly of foreign relations, but rather compete against several locally powerful societal actors (e.g., individuals and groups) who maintain their independent foreign connections through which they garner resources and grow their local power. In such local- and national-level rivalries, various actors may challenge the state leadership which can produce internal and extraterritorial (e.g., cross-border) instability, as often is the case in the Horn of Africa. As a result, despite its extensive use in the Horn of Africa–Middle East relations, the realist approach based on monolithic states and a narrow conception of relative interstate power is ill-equipped for analyzing these interactions. This is because various governments in the Horn, and to an extent in the Persian Gulf/Middle East, are unable to monopolize foreign relations and face significant domestic challenges from local actors who maintain their autonomous external partnerships.

By focusing on states as unitary entities pursuing their "national interest," the realist analysis does not take into account the broad landscape of competing political actors in fragile states and the complexity of their relationships both domestically and regionally. Adopting the monolithic view, it fails to consider the importance of a network of multiple relationships between state, sub-state, and non-state actors, and their separate agencies and interests. Therefore, the realist analysis alone does not provide an adequate theoretical framework to produce reliable analysis or findings, especially in the case of foreign relations of fragile and largely authoritarian states, such as those in the Horn of Africa, where the leadership pursues its own or a narrow ruling elite's interests (as opposed to general "national" interest) but is often unable to monopolize foreign relations, allowing sub-state and non-state actors to pursue their interests through autonomous external connections. This not only results in various actors' separate external linkages but also affects the state's overall relations, which are a collection of such external relationships, and has an effect on all interacting parties. For example, people migrating from the Horn of Africa to the financially affluent Gulf States affect the relations between the countries involved as might simultaneous foreign linkages of a particular sub-state administration, insurgent group, or individual leader or official. The state's overall relations in the Horn's fragile states should then be determined by a combination of a web of relationships involving the most powerful state, sub-state, and non-state actors. In these relations, the central government tends to be the most influential actor as in the case of Ethiopia and Eritrea, but this is much less the case in the weaker states such as Somalia. While the government would dictate most official relations, the combination of semi-official or informal relationships may become more important in determining the true nature of the overall relationship. For example, while official relations might be cordial, issues such as smuggling, human trafficking, religious propagation, or other external involvement in local affairs may sour the behind-the-scene relations between states. Therefore, opaque, highly personalized, pragmatic, and transactional relationships often taking place behind the scenes characterize the Horn of Africa–Persian Gulf/Middle East relations.

Similarly, the realist understanding of power as relative between two unitary state entities fails to provide a nuanced analytical frame for interpreting the Horn of Africa–Persian Gulf/Middle East relations. Instead, any serious inquiry should consider local power within states as part of the analysis of foreign relations. This is crucial because locally powerful state-related and societal actors in the Horn of Africa engage in domestic competition for resources and influence, and often challenge the government's power locally. Such actors gain power through control of local assets and resources and utilize external parties seeking influence in the sub-region to advance their own interests which are in most cases related to domestic or cross-border rivalries. Empowered by their control and influence in the local setting, the domestic actors limit the reach and influence of their external partners. Such local power, arising from the control of material and reputational (nonmaterial) resources, results in the local actors' influence on the external players who seek to achieve their objectives in the Horn of Africa. These relationships, involving multiple actors and power considerations, shape the overall relations between the interacting states. The realist interpretations of international relations based on a simple view of unitary states and relational power between them is inept to provide in-depth analysis and nuanced findings of such relationships. This is mainly because the realist paradigm does not address the complexity of actors and interests or the multiple dimensions of power involving the local level.

The Importance of Agency and Local Power

The extensive use of the realist framework in the Persian Gulf/Middle East–Horn of Africa relations has resulted in disregarding the significant agency and local power the actors from the Horn exercise in relations with their Persian Gulf and Middle Eastern counterparts. When such analyses refer to instability, for example, they often explain that this is merely due to intense external involvement. However, the simplistic analysis is blinded from a more nuanced understanding of the complex relationships joining external players and powerful local actors, both seeking to advance their interests. A more in-depth understanding reveals that it is not the mere external involvement but the clashing local-level interests and rivalries in which local actors play a key role that leads to instability.

As a result, there is a necessity for the studies of Horn of Africa–Persian Gulf/ Middle East relations to engage in a more profound and pluralistic analysis. This study has emphasized the need to account for mutual relationships and influences among multiple actors, both state and non-state. This enables reaching beyond the consideration of states simply as monolithic and the only significant actors in strategic and security analysis of international relations, and consequently steering away from observing power as a concept that manifests itself solely between such unitary states. As has been argued in the in-depth chapters of this volume, several sub-state and non-state actors exercise various types and degrees of agency and local power related to the formal and informal foreign relations in the fragile Horn of African states. Therefore, the significant local agency makes the outcomes of external powers' approach toward the Horn countries consequential, unpredictable, and often locally destabilizing.

Generally, various state and non-state actors in the Horn states, political and societal alike, seek to engage their foreign counterparts to gain resources for survival in the domestic power rivalries. Such material and nonmaterial resources (e.g., money, weapons, or diplomatic support) can make an important difference in their domestic competition and may provide an upper hand against political rivals in fragile state settings. Although governments in the Horn tend to be the most significant actors in external relations at the national level and use their foreign policy to strengthen their position against domestic challenges, they often face significant local rivals, such as sub-state administrations, non-state entities and groups, and powerful individuals who can challenge their power locally. The most glaring example is Somalia, where, for instance, federal states such as Puntland and Jubaland, al-Shabaab, and various clan leaders and militias, and powerful businessmen maintain their own foreign connections and challenge the federal government, which in the past decades has had little power beyond the capital, Mogadishu. Similarly, in the Horn of Africa's regionally most powerful state, Ethiopia, the federal government has faced challenges above all from ethno-nationalist forces. Even in Djibouti, there have been sporadic challenges from groups opposing the government, such as a splinter organization of the Front for the Restoration of Unity and Democracy (Front pour la Restoration de l'Unité et de la Démocratie, FRUD),[1] which draw resources through their foreign linkages. In Eritrea, despite some limited challenges from organizations such as the EIJM, the government's dominant role and extensive societal control appear to have allowed it to maintain more exclusive control of the overall external relations.

In the largely authoritarian states of the Horn, as in their counterparts in the Middle East and the Persian Gulf, the leaders and governing elites generally seek to advance their interests and use the state to maintain the political, economic, and social status quo that benefits them. The challenges they face tend to come from non-state, and at times sub-state, actors who may have sufficient autonomy from the state to pursue their own foreign connections beside it. These may empower them to challenge the state leadership and the governing elite in a power competition which in turn is likely to create turbulence. Thus, political upheaval and instability emerge from local realities and are fueled by the local protagonists' use of external sources for strengthening themselves.

The foreign relations of the fragile Horn of Africa countries overall are a collection of the state's more official foreign connections and sub-state and non-state actors' autonomous linkages with a variety of external players. The domestic actors in the Horn seek to minimize constraints in their external relations and maintain simultaneous partnerships with various foreign actors to maximize benefits from diverse external sources. Their local power gives Horn actors leverage in their foreign relationships and ensures that they can engage in careful balancing between various external partners.

External Rivalries and Overall Foreign Relations

Entwined strategic, security, and economic dimensions are crucial aspects of geopolitical competition among great and middle powers in the Red Sea region and the Horn of Africa. The rise of China as an international economic powerhouse that influences both sides of the Red Sea has led to increasing attention on geo-economic rivalries among external powers and drawn in Persian Gulf/Middle East regional powers and their junior partners. While for the proximate states, such as Saudi Arabia and the UAE, security aspects in the Red Sea region have continued to be significant, for most regional and extra-regional actors economic interests in terms of investment for extraction and market access have become increasingly important in the context of the rapidly developing region. Employing economic statecraft as a means to achieve strategic objectives through increasing political influence, and the associated economic and security benefits, has formed an important part of their overall foreign policy.

However, the economic aspects of external relations are also crucial for the state and non-state actors in the Horn of Africa. Chronic foreign currency shortages in most countries in the sub-region motivate governments, sub-state administrations, and non-state actors to seek external financing and investment to fund political power competition and economic activity and development. Therefore, they tend to engage in transactional relations in which they exchange local material or nonmaterial assets and resources for financial benefits. Mainstream theories would argue that while this allows such local actors to access much-needed funding from abroad, it constrains their space for foreign relations and compromise their sovereignty. Yet, most state and non-state actors in the Horn seek to mitigate dependence on single foreign partners and practice careful balancing between various partners, who themselves are sometimes rivals, to maximize benefits and maintain wider space for foreign policy maneuvering. For this, they use mainly personalized high-level interactions and covert diplomacy.

Moreover, when the domestic actors in the Horn engage in transactional relations in the international sphere, they do so on pragmatic person-to-person grounds. These actors also seek to ensure that they exercise an important degree of local power over their foreign partners because of their local position and status.

Their control of the domestic assets and resources gives them a strong position relative to their external partners. This applies to transactional dealings related to critical infrastructure, such as ports and airports, as well as other strategic assets and resources, including political influence and natural resources. For example, when the government of Eritrea and the Somaliland authority entered into a deal with the UAE on port and airport development, or the Ethiopian administration agreed to land and construction deals with Saudi and UAE investors, they maintained an important degree of power over the process and had leverage to arbitrarily modify or abrogate the agreement due to their local power. Similarly, a given high-level Somali federal or state-level official, or a clan leader, could obtain financial or other material benefits from an external partner in exchange for promises to influence decision-making in the national or local political institutions but in this case, it is largely up to the leader in question to decide whether to honor the agreement or not. This puts the foreign financier in a vulnerable position due to significant uncertainty over the success of his/her investment. Yet, such risk has not significantly deterred the wealthy Persian Gulf individuals, groups, and governments who have used their financial power in an attempt to buy strategic political and economic influence in the Horn of Africa.

For several decades, state and non-state actors in the Horn of Africa have targeted the Middle East and the Persian Gulf for financial resources and material, political, or diplomatic support. This, along with outward migration from the Horn mainly to the Persian Gulf, has led to intimate political and societal relations in which financial and economic aspects have gained importance. As a result, the Horn actors have engaged increasingly in the personalized, pragmatic, and transactional practice of economic diplomacy. That is, they often orient their official diplomatic, business, and informal efforts toward extracting economic and financial benefits from their foreign partners through the use of transactional noncoercive instruments (e.g., by exchanging economic, strategic, or nonmaterial assets for financial assets). These resources allow them to improve their local social, economic, and political standing.

Meanwhile, the Horn actors' financially affluent Persian Gulf/Middle East partners often have more ambitious designs to influence the political reality in the sub-region. In their strategies, these regionally powerful states tend to engage in economic statecraft and also practice economic diplomacy mainly through noncoercive instruments (e.g., investment, financial injections, aid, and trade). In this way, they differ from the great powers which are more prone to engage in coercive action in the Horn of Africa (e.g., armed interventions and sanctions), although they are not strangers to applying economic and diplomatic pressure to advance their interests. The significant economic and security interests in the Horn of Africa often oblige the Middle Eastern regional powers and their junior partners to engage in an elaborate strategy to gain political influence in which economic statecraft plays an important role. This differs from the approaches of the state and non-state actors in the Horn which center on economic diplomacy for gaining material resources and nonmaterial support mainly for domestic purposes. Overall in these opaque, personalized, pragmatic, and transactional regional relations, partnerships and alignments tend to be volatile and depend on the foreign partners' ability and willingness to deliver the desired resources.

Due to the Horn governments' limited capacity to monopolize the countries' overall external relations, they should be considered as fragmented and not as monolithic manifestations of the national interest of unitary states. Although the central government leadership often drives the states' official relations according to its interests, the countries' overall foreign connections should be viewed as a combination of governments' foreign relations and the locally significant sub-state and non-state actors' external linkages. This is because, as noted earlier, the Horn governments' capabilities in controlling the overall foreign connections vary significantly. For example, while in Somalia the largely autonomous sub-state and non-state actors play a greater and more autonomous role in the country's international connections, especially in terms of informal relations, in Eritrea the government has been able to maintain control over the main foreign linkages and prevent other power centers from emerging that could challenge the political status quo. Whereas in Somalia sub-state and non-state actors maintain their own significant foreign linkages and exercise sufficient local power to challenge the central authority in various parts of the country, in Eritrea sub-state or non-state actors have not been able to develop such substantial external connections which would generate sufficient resources to convert them into challengers of the central government's domestic political power and authority. Meanwhile, in Ethiopia, the Horn of Africa's most powerful state, the institutionalized ethnic federal system has consolidated strong ethnic-regional identities which have paved the way for regional ethnopolitical dynamics. The federal government's lack of capacity to fully control significant foreign linkages has allowed some ethno-nationalist movements to develop their own external connections which have permitted them to accumulate resources and stage local challenges to the central authority. These observations demonstrate the need to reach beyond the blanket conceptualizations and categories, such as those advocated in the mainstream realist International Relations theory, to facilitate nuanced analysis and generate accurate findings regarding the Horn of Africa–Middle East/Persian Gulf relations.

NOTES

Introduction

1 *Encyclopaedia Britannica Online*, s.v. "Bab el-Mandeb Strait," accessed on May 10, 2022, https://www.britannica.com/place/Bab-El-Mandeb-Strait.

2 In the 2000–2015 period wheat imports alone to the Middle East and North African countries passing through Bab al-Mandab saw a 98 percent increase. See Rob Bailey and Laura Wellesley, *Chokepoints and Vulnerabilities in Global Food Trade* (London: Chatham House, 2017), 10–11, 16.

3 "إنفوغرافيك.. أهمية باب المندب ومخاطر تهديدات الحوثي," *Sky News Arabia*, July 26, 2018, https://www.skynewsarabia.com/middle-east/1167884.

4 United States Energy Information Administration, Maritime Chokepoints Critical to Petroleum Markets, March 2, 2021, https://www.eia.gov/todayinenergy/detail.php?id=330.

5 GlobalSecurity.org, "Bab al-Mandab Strait," accessed May 11, 2022, https://www.globalsecurity.org/military/world/yemen/bab-al-mandab.htm.

6 United States Energy Information Administration, "The Bab el-Mandeb Strait Is a Strategic Route for Oil and Natural Gas Shipments," August 27, 2019, https://www.eia.gov/todayinenergy/detail.php?id=41073.

7 Using the term "fragile" in association with states this study indicates state weakness in terms of the lack of capacity, authority, and legitimacy in terms of government–society relations. It is used descriptively and does not refer to the politicization of the term. For more on the politicization and instrumentalization of state fragility, see the thematic issue of the *Third World Quarterly*, "Fragile States: A Political Concept" (vol. 35, no. 2, 2014). Sonja Grimm, Nicolas Lemay-Hébert, and Olivier Nay, "'Fragile States': Introducing a Political Concept," *Third World Quarterly* 35, no. 2 (2014): 197–209.

8 On weak states and their leadership, see e.g. parts one and three in Joel S. Migdal, *Strong Societies and Weak States: State-Society Relations and State Capabilities in the Third World* (Princeton: Princeton University Press, 1988).

9 The literature on African victimhood in international relations is extensive. Some salient works that deal with various aspects of it include Walter Rodney, *How Europe Underdeveloped Africa* (Dar es Salaam: Tanzania Publishing House, 1972), and Patrick McGowan, Scarlet Cornelissen, and Philip Nel, eds., *Power, Wealth and Global Equity: An International Relations Textbook for Africa* (Cape Town: University of Cape Town Press, 2006).

10 See e.g. Tandeka C. Nkiwane, "Africa and International Relations: Regional Lessons for a Global Discourse," *International Political Science Review* 22, no. 3 (2001): 279–90.

11 See Mel Bunce, Suzanne Franks, and Chris Paterson, eds., *Africa's Media Image in the 21st Century From the "Heart of Darkness" to "Africa Rising"* (Abingdon: Routledge, 2017), and Ashutosh Pandey, "Is Africa a Victim of Bias by International

Investors?," *Deutsche Welle*, August 14, 2020, https://www.dw.com/en/africa-imf-bias -discrimination-debt-international-investors/a-54564359.

12 See e.g. Oluseyi Adegbola, Jacqueline Skarda-Mitchell, and Sherice Gearhart, "Everything's Negative about Nigeria: A Study of US Media Reporting on Nigeria," *Global Media and Communication* 14, no. 1 (2018): 47–63, Morten Bøås and Kathleen M. Jennings, "Insecurity and Development: The Rhetoric of the 'Failed State'," *European Journal of Development Research* 17, no. 3 (2006): 385–95, and Grimm, Lemay-Hébert, and Nay, "'Fragile States': Introducing a Political Concept," 197–209.

13 See e.g. Edward V. K. Jaycox, "Sub-Saharan Africa: Development Performance and Prospects," *Journal of International Affairs* 46, no. 1 (1992): 85–95, Jack Spence, "Africa: What Does the Future Hold?," *Strategic Review for South Africa* 19, no. 2 (2000): 1–14, "Hopeless Africa," *The Economist*, May 11, 2000, https://www .economist.com/node/333429, and Nicolas van de Walle, *African Economies and the Politics of Permanent Crisis, 1979-1999* (Cambridge: Cambridge University Press, 2001).

14 These include, for example, variations of dependency theory and the world-systems approach. See e.g. Paul A. Baran, *The Political Economy of Growth* (New York: Monthly Review Press, 1957), Andre Gunder Frank, *The Development of Underdevelopment* (New York: Monthly Review Press, 1966), and Terence K. Hopkins and Immanuel Wallerstein, *World-Systems Analysis: Theory and Methodology* (Beverly Hills: Sage, 1982).

15 See various aspects of the "rising Africa" narrative in "Africa Rising," *The Economist*, December 3, 2011, https://www.economist.com/leaders/2011/12/03/africa-rising, Brahima Sangafowa Coulibaly, "In Defense of the 'Africa Rising' Narrative," *Africa in Focus*, June 27, 2017, https://www.brookings.edu/blog/africa-in-focus/2017/06 /27/in-defense-of-the-africa-rising-narrative/, Tony Ansah, "The Narrative of Africa Rising," October 23, 2018, https://www.sdgphilanthropy.org/The-Narrative-of-Africa -Rising, and the United Nations, "Africa Rising in Business, Trade, Innovation, Deputy Secretary-General Says at Harvard Event, Urging Lifting of Barriers to Create Equal Opportunity," January 21, 2020, https://press.un.org/en/2020/dsgsm1384.doc .htm.

16 See Christopher Clapham, *Africa and the International System: The Politics of State Survival* (Cambridge: Cambridge University Press, 1996), William Brown and Sophie Harman, eds., *African Agency in International Politics* (Abingdon: Routledge, 2013), Ronald Chipaike and Matarutse H. Knowledge, "The Question of African Agency in International Relations," *Cogent Social Sciences* 4, no. 1 (2018), https://doi.org/10.1080 /23311886.2018.1487257.

17 For more discussion on asymmetric power and the shortcomings of the realist interpretations of international relations in the Horn of Africa–Persian Gulf interactions, see Aleksi Ylönen, "A Critical Appraisal of Realist International Relations Concepts in the Horn of Africa – Persian Gulf Relations: The State, Power, and Agency," *Cadernos de Estudos Africanos* 43 (2023), https://journals.openedition .org/cea/.

18 See William Brown, "A Question of Agency: Africa in International Politics," *Third World Quarterly* 33, no. 10 (2012): 1889–908.

19 For more holistic studies, see e.g. Roberto Aliboni, *The Red Sea Region: Local Actors and the Superpowers* (Abingdon: Routledge, 1985), Haggai Erlich, *Ethiopia and the Middle East* (Boulder: Lynne Rienner, 1994), Anoushiravan Ehteshami and Emma C. Murphy, *The International Politics of the Red Sea* (Abingdon: Routledge, 2011),

and Robert Mason and Simon Mabon, eds., *The Gulf States and the Horn of Africa: Interests, Influences and Instability* (Manchester: Manchester University Press, 2022).

20 This literature is vast and growing. Some works representing this perspective include Asteris Huliaras and Sophia Kalantzakos, "The Gulf States and the Horn of Africa: A New Hinterland?," *Middle East Policy* 24, no. 4 (2017): 63–73, Harry Verhoeven, "The Gulf and the Horn: Changing Geographies of Security Interdependence and Competing Visions of Regional Order," *Civil Wars* 20, no. 3 (2018): 333–57, Brendon J. Cannon and Federico Donelli, "Asymmetric Alliances and High Polarity: Evaluating Regional Security Complexes in the Middle East and Horn of Africa," *Third World Quarterly* 41, no. 3 (2019): 505–24, Zach Vertin, *Red Sea Rivalries: The Gulf, the Horn and New Geopolitics of the Red Sea* (Doha: Brookings Doha Centre, 2019), Abdinor Hassan Dahir, *Foreign Engagements in the Horn of Africa: Diversifying Risks and Maximising Gains* (Istanbul: TRT World Research Centre, 2019), Tamara Naidoo, "The Grand Game: Gulf Interests in the Horn of Africa," *The Horn Bulletin* 3, no. 2 (2020): 1–9, Federico Donelli, *Turkey in Africa: Turkey's Strategic Involvement in Sub-Saharan Africa* (London: IB Tauris, 2021), Federico Donelli and Ariel Gonzalez-Levaggi, "Crossing Roads: The Middle East's Security Engagement in the Horn of Africa," *Global Change, Peace & Security* 33, no. 1 (2021): 45–60, and Viktor Marsai and Máté Szalai, "The 'Borderlandization' of the Horn of Africa in Relation to the Gulf Region, and the Effects on Somalia," *Journal of Borderlands Studies* (2021), https://doi.org/10.1080/08865655.2021.1884118.

21 See e.g. Mohammed Ayoob, "Inequality and Theorizing in International Relations: The Case for Subaltern Realism," *International Studies Review* 4, no. 3 (2002): 27–48.

22 Kevin C. Dunn and Timothy M. Shaw, eds., *Africa's Challenge to International Relations Theory* (London: Palgrave Macmillan, 2001).

23 See e.g. Agustina Giraudy, Eduardo Moncada, and Richard Snyder, "Subnational Analysis: Theoretical and Methodological Contributions to Comparative Politics," *Revista de Ciencia Política* 41, no. 1 (2021): 1–34.

24 Although examples of these actors are numerous, particularly important players in this sense have been groups such as the Tigray People's Liberation Front (TPLF) and Eritrean People's Liberation Front (EPLF) in Ethiopia and Eritrea, leaderships of federal states in Jubaland and Puntland, socially and politically powerful individuals in Somalia, and various political actors of the *de facto* independent state of Somaliland. See more on these and other actors' engagement in foreign relations in the corresponding country chapters.

25 Cannon and Donelli, "Asymmetric Alliances," and Donelli and Gonzalez-Levaggi, "Crossing Roads."

26 The narrow delimitation of the Horn of Africa normally includes Djibouti, Eritrea, Ethiopia, and Somalia, while a wide conception of the "Greater" Horn of Africa includes the above countries and their direct neighbors Kenya, South Sudan, Sudan, and at times by extension Uganda. The principal sub-regional organization in the Horn of Africa, the Inter-Governmental Authority on Development (IGAD), consists of all the above states but classifies South Sudan and Sudan as Nile Valley states and Kenya and Uganda as Great Lakes states. Eritrea suspended its IGAD membership in 2007.

27 Niccolo Machiavelli, *The Prince* (New York: Oxford University Press, 1984), 66. See also Martin Wight, "Why is There No International Theory?," in *Diplomatic*

Investigations: Essays in the Theory of International Politics, eds. Herbert Butterfield and Martin Wight (London: Allen & Unwin, 1966), 12–33.

28   Anna M. Agathangelou and L. H. M. Ling, *Transforming World Politics: From Empire to Multiple Worlds* (Abingdon: Routledge, 2009), 15.

29   Machiavelli, *The Prince*, 66.

30   See e.g. Edward H. Carr, *The Twenty Years' Crisis, 1919-1939: An Introduction to the Study of International Relations*, 2nd ed. (London: Macmillan, 1946) and Hans J. Morgenthau, *Politics Among Nations: The Struggle for Power and Peace* (New York: Alfred A. Knopf, 1948).

31   See e.g. Robert Keohane and Joseph Nye, *Power and Interdependence: World Politics in Transition* (New York: Little, Brown, and Co., 1977).

32   See e.g. Joseph Nye, *Bound to Lead: The Changing Nature of American Power* (New York: Basic Books, 1990), Joseph Nye, *Soft Power: The Means to Success in World Politics* (New York: Public Affairs, 2004), Joseph Nye, *The Future of Power* (New York: Public Affairs, 2011).

33   John R. P. French and Bertram Raven, "The Bases of Social Power," in *Studies in Social Power*, ed. Dorwin Cartwright (Ann Arbor: University of Michigan Press, 1959), 259–69.

34   See for example Morgenthau, *Politics among Nations*, Kenneth Waltz, *Man, the State and War* (New York: Columbia University Press, 1959), and Kenneth Waltz, *Theory of International Politics* (New York: McGraw-Hill, 1979).

35   See e.g. Keohane and Nye, *Power and Interdependence*, Robert Keohane, *After Hegemony: Cooperation and Discord in the World Political Economy* (Princeton: Princeton University Press, 1984), Charles Lipson, "International Cooperation in Economic and Security Affairs," *World Politics* 37, no. 1 (October 1984): 1–23.

36   Robert Powell, "The Problem of Absolute and Relative Gains in International Relations Theory," in *Cooperative Models in International Relations Research*, eds. Michael D. Intriligator and Urs Luterbacher (Boston: Springer, 1994), 127–50.

37   See e.g. Hedley Bull, *The Anarchical Society: A Study of Order in World Politics* (London: Macmillan, 1977); Martin Wight, *Systems of States* (Leicester: Leicester University Press, 1977), and Alexander Wendt, *Social Theory of International Politics* (Cambridge: Cambridge University Press, 1999).

38   Nye, *Soft Power*, 15, 111.

39   On personal relationships which can be perceived to resemble bilateral interstate relations, see Laura K. Guerrero, Peter A. Andersen, and Walid A. Afifi, *Close Encounters: Communication in Relationships*, 5th ed. (Thousand Oaks: SAGE, 2018), 481–3.

40   On relational power between people, see e.g. Stephanie A. Goodwin, "Impression Formation in Asymmetrical Power Relationships: Does Power Corrupt Absolutely?" (Master's Thesis, University of Massachusetts Amherst, 1993), https://scholarworks .umass.edu/cgi/viewcontent.cgi?article=3371&context=theses.

41   See e.g. Brantly Womack, *Asymmetry and International Relationships* (Cambridge: Cambridge University Press, 2016).

42   For example, Lenin's explanation of imperialism, as well as dependency and world systems theory, build on Marxist structuralism. See e.g. Vladimir Ilyich Lenin, *Imperialism, the Highest Stage of Capitalism* (Petrograd: Life and Knowledge Publishers, 1917), Baran, *The Political Economy of Growth*, Frank, *The Development of Underdevelopment*, and Immanuel Wallerstein, *The Politics of the World-Economy: The States, the Movements and the Civilizations* (Cambridge: Cambridge University Press, 1984).

43 See e.g. Klaus Knorr, *The Power of Nations: The Political Economy of International Relations* (New York: Basic Books, 1975).
44 Susan Strange, "What Is Economic Power, and Who Has It?," *International Journal* 30, no. 2 (1975): 216–23.

Chapter 1

1 Not all scholars use the terms "middle power" and "regional power" interchangeably. Some perceive middle powers to have more global reach than regional powers. See e.g. Şuhnaz Yilmaz, "Middle Powers and Regional Powers," *Oxford Bibliographies*, last modified September 27, 2017, https://www.oxfordbibliographies.com/view/document/obo-9780199743292/obo-9780199743292-0222.xml. However, this study makes no specific distinction between them because its focus is not on studying such differences.
2 The term "small states" does not refer to the size of the state in terms of geography, economy, or population, for example, but rather to its international reach. Some small states, such as Finland, are often referred to as "punching above their weight" in international affairs which indicates that their international influence is perceived to outweigh their relative size as a state.
3 Examples of this include successful resistance during major conflicts such as the Second World War as in the case of Finland's defense against the Soviet invasion in 1939–40.
4 The four BRICS countries, Brazil, Russia, India, and South Africa, as well as Türkiye, Saudi Arabia, Iran, Nigeria, Egypt, and Ethiopia, pose as examples.
5 For example, Iran has challenged the US in the Middle East, while India has to an extent helped the US to limit the extension of Chinese influence in South Asia. Türkiye has also seemingly sought to challenge the prevailing order in the Caucasus and Eastern Mediterranean and become a major player in the Horn of Africa.
6 One important example of this is regionalism in Africa. The attempts to build a continent-wide free trade zone, African Continental Free Trade Area (AfCFTA), has brought sub-regional powers Egypt, Ethiopia, and Nigeria to challenge South Africa's position.
7 See e.g. Annette Baker Fox, *The Power of Small States: Diplomacy in World War II* (Chicago: University of Chicago Press, 1959), Trygve Mathisen, *The Functions of Small States in the Strategies of the Great Powers* (Oslo: Universitetsforlaget, 1971), 181–9, Christine Ingebritsen et al., eds., *Small States in International Relations* (Seattle: University of Washington Press, 2012), Yee-Kuang Heng and Syed Mohammed Ad'ha Aljunied, "Can Small States be More than Price Takers in Global Governance?," *Global Governance* 21, no. 3 (2015): 435–54.
8 Abu Dhabi's recent economic, diplomatic, and military involvement in the Red Sea region and the Horn of Africa shows its financial and coercive power in its neighborhood, while Doha's repertoire for regional influence has included the extension of soft power through peacemaking and media. See more on Robert Mason, "Small-State Aspirations to Middlepowerhood: The Cases of Qatar and the UAE," in *Unfulfilled Aspirations: Middle Power Politics in the Middle East*, ed. Adham Saouli (Oxford: Oxford University Press, 2020), 157–82.
9 Crystal A. Ennis, "Reading Entrepreneurial Power in Small Gulf States: Qatar and the UAE," *International Journal* 73, no. 4 (2018): 574.

10 For a brief explanation of the development of the concept of "fragile states," see e.g. Peter Albrecht and Maria-Louise Clausen, *Fragile States* (Copenhagen: Danish Institute for International Studies, 2022).

11 Waltz, *Theory of International Politics*, 194–5.

12 See e.g. Migdal, *Strong Societies and Weak States*.

13 Somalia in the late 1980s is an excellent example of this process.

14 For more on the connection between states' international objectives and domestic goals see e.g. Michael Mastanduno, David A. Lake, and G. John Ikenberry, "Toward a Realist Theory of State Action," *International Studies Quarterly* 33, no. 4 (December 1989): 457–74.

15 See e.g. Robert H. Jackson, *Quasi-States: Sovereignty, International Relations and the Third World* (Cambridge: Cambridge University Press, 1993), Clapham, *Africa and the International System*, and Jean-François Bayart and Stephen Ellis, "Africa in the World: A History of Extraversion," *African Affairs* 99, no. 395 (2000): 217–67.

16 Somalia gained coercive force due to its superpower alliance with the United States and in the 1960s and 1970s sought to extend its sphere of influence by creating "greater Somalia" at expense of respecting the territorial integrity of neighboring Kenya and Ethiopia. The Ethiopian government capitalized on having gained a strong position in the Horn of Africa following its war with Eritrea and used its foreign relations to strengthen domestically and exert international influence in its neighborhood. Ethiopian leadership has also sought to use the country's sizable population, central location, market potential, and Christian religious orientation, to highlight its importance and attract external partners.

17 See e.g. Michael I. Handel, *Weak States in the International System*, 2nd ed. (London: Frank Cass, 1990).

18 Snyder, *Myth of Empire*, 317–18.

19 For an analysis of small states in Europe, see Peter Katzenstein, *Small States in World Markets: Industrial Policy in Europe* (Ithaca: Cornell University Press, 1985).

20 See e.g. Michael C. Desch, "War and Strong States, Peace and Weak States?," *International Organization* 50, no. 2 (April 1996): 237–68, John J. Mearsheimer, *The Tragedy of Great Power Politics* (New York: WW Norton & Company, 2001), and Anthony Payne, "Small States in the Global Politics of Development," *The Round Table: The Commonwealth Journal of International Affairs* 93, no. 376 (2004): 623–35.

21 See more in the *Cambridge Review of International Affairs* thematic issue "The Foreign Policy Power of Small States" (vol. 23, no. 3, 2010). Alan Chong and Matthias Maass, "Introduction: The Foreign Policy Power of Small States," *Cambridge Review of International Affairs* 23, no. 3 (2010): 381–2.

22 More on this discussion can be found in Rory Miller and Harry Verhoeven, "Overcoming Smallness: Qatar, the United Arab Emirates and Strategic Realignment in the Gulf," *International Politics* 57, no. 1 (2020): 1–20.

23 See e.g. Colin S. Gray, *The Geopolitics of Super Power* (Lexington: University Press of Kentucky, 1988), Jakub J. Grygiel, *Great Powers and Geopolitical Change* (Baltimore: Johns Hopkins University Press, 2006), and C. Dale Warton, *Geopolitics and the Great Powers in the Twenty-First Century* (Abingdon: Routledge, 2007).

24 See for example Christopher Gogwilt, *The Fiction of Geopolitics: Afterimages of Culture, from Wilkie Collins to Alfred Hitchcock* (Stanford: Stanford University Press, 2000), 35–6, and Jason Dittmer and Joanne Sharp, eds., *Geopolitics: An Introductory Reader* (London: Routledge, 2014).

25 For an overview that conceptualizes Geo-economics, see Edward N. Luttwak, "From Geopolitics to Geo-Economics: Logic of Conflict, Grammar of Commerce," *The National Interest*, no. 20 (1990): 17–23.

26 For an excellent literature review pointing to the distinction between the two concepts, see Mikael Mattlin and Mikael Wigell, "Geoeconomics in the Context of Restive Regional Powers," *Asia Europe Journal* 14, no. 2 (2016): 125–34.

27 Sören Scholvin and Mikael Wigell, "Geo-economic Power Politics: An Introduction," in *Geo-economics and Power Politics in the 21st Century: The Revival of Economic Statecraft*, eds. Mikael Wigell, Sören Scholvin, and Mika Aaltola (Abingdon: Routledge, 2019), 2.

28 Braz Baracuhy, "Geo-economics as a Dimension of Grand Strategy: Notes on the Concept and Its Evolution," in *Geo-economics and Power Politics in the 21st Century: The Revival of Economic Statecraft*, eds. Mikael Wigell, Sören Scholvin, and Mika Aaltola (Abingdon: Routledge, 2019), 15.

29 See e.g. Sami Moisio, "Towards Geopolitical Analysis of Geoeconomic Processes," *Geopolitics* 23, no. 1 (2018): 22–9.

30 See Mikael Wigell, "Conceptualizing Regional Powers' Geoeconomic Strategies: Neo-Imperialism, Neo-Mercantilism, Hegemony, and Liberal Institutionalism," *Asia Europe Journal* 14, no. 2 (2016): 135–51, and Sören Scholvin and Mikael Wigell, "Power Politics by Economic Means: Geoeconomics as an Analytical Approach and Foreign Policy Practice," *Comparative Strategy* 37, no. 1 (2018): 73–84.

31 Wigell and Scholvin, "Geo-economic Power Politics," 1, 5.

32 Richard Youngs, "Geo-economic Futures," in *Challenges for European Foreign Policy in 2012: What Kind of Geo-Economic Europe?*, eds. Ana Martiningui and Richard Youngs (Madrid: FRIDE, 2011), 14.

33 See Matthew Sparke, "Geoeconomics, Globalisation and the Limits of Economic Strategy in Statecraft: A Response to Vihma," *Geopolitics* 23, no. 1 (2018): 30–7.

34 Blackwill and Harris argue that geo-economics is "the systematic use of economic instruments to accomplish geopolitical objectives." Robert D. Blackwill and Jennifer M. Harris, *War by Other Means: Geoeconomics and Statecraft* (Cambridge, MA: Harvard University Press, 2016), 1. See also Friedrich Wu and Koh De Wei, "From Financial Assets to Financial Statecraft: The Case of China and Emerging Economies of Africa and Latin America," *Journal of Contemporary China* 23, no. 89 (2014): 781–803. Economic diplomacy and economic statecraft are also not universally defined concepts and can be understood in various ways. However, they can be differentiated from each other to gain analytical significance and explanatory power as argued later in this chapter.

35 See e.g. Charles F. Hermann, Charles W. Kegley Jr., and James N. Rosenau, eds., *New Directions in the Study of Foreign Policy* (London: Allen & Unwin, 1987).

36 Margaret G. Hermann and Charles F. Hermann, "Who Makes Foreign Policy Decisions and How: An Empirical Inquiry," *International Studies Quarterly* 33, no. 4 (December 1989): 362.

37 See e.g. Waltz's seminal neorealist work *Theory of International Politics*, Mearsheimer's *The Tragedy of Great Power Politics*, and Fareed Zakaria, "Realism and Domestic Politics: A Review Essay," *International Security* 17, no. 1 (Summer 1992): 177–98.

38 See e.g. Richard Rosencrance and Arthur A. Stein, eds., *The Domestic Bases of Grand Strategy* (Ithaca: Cornell University Press, 1993), Jack Snyder, *Myths of Empire: Domestic Politics and International Ambition* (Ithaca: Cornell University Press, 1991), and Laura Neack, Jeanne A. K. Hey, and Patrick J. Haney, eds., *Foreign Policy Analysis:*

Continuity and Change in Its Second Generation (Englewood Cliffs: Prentice Hall, 1995).

39   See e.g. Vendulka Kubálková, ed., *Foreign Policy in a Constructed World* (Armonk: M.E. Sharpe, 2001), David Patrick Houghton, "Reinvigorating the Study of Foreign Policy Decision Making: Toward a Constructivist Approach," *Foreign Policy Analysis* 3, no. 1 (January 2007): 24–45, Roxanne Lynn Doty, "Foreign Policy as Social Construction: A Postpositivist Analysis of U.S. Counterinsurgency Policy in the Philippines," *International Studies Quarterly* 37, no. 3 (September 1993): 297–320, and Christopher S. Browning, *Constructivism, Narrative and Foreign Policy Analysis: A Case Study of Finland* (Frankfurt am Main: Peter Lang, 2008).

40   See e.g. Kenneth Waltz, "The Emerging Structures of International Politics," *International Security* 18, no. 2 (Fall 1993): 79, and William Curtis Wohlforth, *The Elusive Balance: Power and Perceptions during the Cold War* (Ithaca: Cornell University Press, 1993) and Fareed Zakaria, *From Wealth to Power: The Unusual Origins of America's World Role* (Princeton: Princeton University Press, 1998) for more extensive explanations.

41   See Hermann and Hermann, "Who Makes Foreign Policy Decisions"; Alex Mintz and Karl DeRouen, *Understanding Foreign Policy Decision Making* (Cambridge: Cambridge University Press, 2010), 57–67, Stephen Quackenbush, "The Rationality of Rational Choice Theory," *International Interactions* 30, no. 2 (2004): 87–107, and Frank C. Zagare, "Reconciling Rationality with Deterrence," *Journal of Theoretical Politics* 16, no. 2 (2004): 107–41.

42   Bruce Bueno de Mesquita, "Foreign Policy Analysis and Rational Choice Models," *Oxford Research Encyclopedia of International Studies*, January 11, 2018, accessed December 30, 2022, https://oxfordre.com/internationalstudies/view/10.1093/acrefore /9780190846626.001.0001/acrefore-9780190846626-e-395.

43   See Joshua S. Goldstein and John R. Freeman, "U.S.-Soviet-Chinese Relations: Routine, Reciprocity, or Rational Expectations?," *The American Political Science Review* 85, no. 1 (March 1991): 17–35, Eric Stern and Bertjan Verbeek, eds., "Whither the Study of Governmental Politics in Foreign Policymaking? A Symposium," *Mershon International Studies Review* 42, no. 2 (1998): 205–55, and Nelson Michaud, "Bureaucratic Politics and the Shaping of Policies: Can We Measure Pulling and Hauling Games?," *Canadian Journal of Political Science* 35, no. 2 (2002): 269–300.

44   Graham T. Allison, "Conceptual Models and the Cuban Missile Crisis," *American Political Science Review* 63, no. 3 (September 1969): 689–718, and Graham T. Allison, *Essence of Decision: Explaining the Cuban Missile Crisis* (Boston: Little, Brown, and Co., 1971).

45   Christopher M. Jones, "Bureaucratic Politics and Organizational Process Models," *Oxford Research Encyclopedia of International Studies*, November 20, 2017, accessed December 30, 2022, https://oxfordre.com/internationalstudies/view/10.1093/acrefore /9780190846626.001.0001/acrefore-9780190846626-e-2.

46   Qingshan Tan, "Explaining U.S.-China Policy in the 1990s: Who Is in Control?," *Asian Affairs: An American Review* 20, no. 3 (1993): 143–60.

47   Roger Hilsman, *The Politics of Policy Making in Defense and Foreign Affairs* (New York: Harper & Row, 1971).

48   These include "examination of cognitive and personal characteristics of leaders, small group dynamics, organizational process, bureaucratic politics, domestic political contestation, national culture, and economic considerations, … [and] … broader regional and international systemic forces." Valerie M. Hudson, "Foreign Policy

Analysis Beyond North America," in *Foreign Policy Analysis Beyond North America*, eds. Klaus Blummer and Valerie M. Hudson (Boulder: Lynne Rienner, 2015), 2.

49 See e.g. Douglas T. Stuart, "Foreign-Policy Decision-Making," in *The Oxford Handbook of International Relations*, eds. Christian Reus-Smit and Duncan Snidal (Oxford: Oxford University Press, 2010), 576–93.

50 Hudson, "Foreign Policy Analysis," 2.

51 See e.g. Jonathan Fisher and David M. Anderson, "Authoritarianism and the Securitization of Development in Africa," *International Affairs* 91, no. 1 (January 2015): 131–51.

52 This is manifested in a flurry of recent publications and the new edition of William A. Baldwin's seminal work *Economic Statecraft* (Princeton: Princeton University Press, 1985).

53 Geoff R. Berridge and Alan James, *A Dictionary of Diplomacy* (Basingstoke: Palgrave MacMillan, 2003), 81.

54 Morton A. Kaplan, "An Introduction to the Strategy of Statecraft," *World Politics* 4, no. 4 (July 1952): 548.

55 See Baldwin, *Economic Statecraft*, and Robert F. Zimmerman, *Dollars, Diplomacy, and Dependency: Dilemmas of US Economic Aid* (Boulder: Lynne Rienner, 1993).

56 As an indicator of the uncommon use of coercion especially in the bilateral diplomatic practice, some authors refer to it as "coercive diplomacy." In these cases, it can be seen as an instrument of the foreign policy strategy of statecraft. See e.g. Thomas Schelling, *Arms and Influence* (New Haven: Yale University Press, 1966), Paul Gordon Lauren, "Ultimata and Coercive Diplomacy," *International Studies Quarterly* 16, no. 2 (June 1972): 131–65, and Jack S. Levy, "Deterrence and Coercive Diplomacy: The Contributions of Alexander George," *Political Psychology* 29, no. 4 (August 2008): 537–52.

57 Michael Mastanduno, "Economic Statecraft, Interdependence, and National Security: Agendas for Research," *Security Studies* 9, no. 1–2 (1999): 288–316.

58 On sanctions as instruments of economic statecraft, see e.g. Daniel W. Drezner, *The Sanctions Paradox: Economic Statecraft and International Relations* (Cambridge: Cambridge University Press, 1999).

59 Baldwin, *Economic Statecraft*, and Jean-Marc F. Blanchard and Norrin M. Ripsman, "A Political Theory of Economic Statecraft," *Foreign Policy Analysis* 4, no. 4 (October 2008): 371–98.

60 Tony Wayne, "What Is Economic Diplomacy and How Does It Work?" *Foreign Service Journal*, January/February 2019, https://www.afsa.org/what-economic -diplomacy-and-how-does-it-work.

61 See e.g. Patricia A. Davis, *The Art of Economic Persuasion: Positive Incentives and German Economic Diplomacy* (Ann Arbor: University of Michigan Press, 1999).

62 See e.g. Benn Steil and Robert E. Litan, *Financial Statecraft: The Role of Financial Markets in American Foreign Policy* (New Haven: Yale University Press, 2006), and Leslie Elliott Armijo and Saori N. Katada, eds., *The Financial Statecraft of Emerging Powers Shield and Sword in Asia and Latin America* (Basingstoke: Palgrave MacMillan, 2014).

63 The term "dollar diplomacy" is associated with the effort of the Taft administration (1909–13) to exercise economic power by extending the international use of the US dollar by issuing and guaranteeing dollar-denominated loans to foreign countries.

64 See e.g. Qingxin Ken Wang, "Recent Japanese Economic Diplomacy in China: Political Alignment in a Changing World Order," *Asian Survey* 33, no. 6 (1993): 625–41.

65 Kevin P. Gallagher, "Yuan Diplomacy," *Aljazeera*, February 29, 2012, https://www
.aljazeera.com/opinions/2012/2/29/yuan-diplomacy/.

66 See e.g. Yi Li, "Saudi Arabia's Economic Diplomacy through Foreign Aid: Dynamics,
Objectives and Mode," *Asian Journal of Middle Eastern and Islamic Studies* 13, no. 1
(2019): 110–22.

67 See Charles Clover and Michael Peel, "China Tries Chequebook Diplomacy in
Southeast Asia," *Financial Times*, November 7, 2016, https://www.ft.com/content/
abb35db2-a4cc-11e6-8b69-02899e8bd9d1.

68 Philippe Le Corre, "What China's Checkbook Diplomacy Means for Europe," *Politico*,
May 12, 2016, https://www.politico.eu/article/what-chinas-checkbook-diplomacy
-means-for-europe/, and Soren Patterson and John Custer, "Six Deep Dives into
China's Checkbook Diplomacy," *AIDDATA*, January 23, 2018, https://www.aiddata
.org/blog/six-deep-dives-into-chinas-checkbook-diplomacy.

69 "Commentary: The Myth about China's 'Chequebook Diplomacy'," *Xinhua*, May 12,
2017, http://www.xinhuanet.com/english/2017-05/12/c_136277532.htm.

70 Keith Johnson, "Trump Reaches for Checkbook Diplomacy to Counter China,"
Foreign Policy, October 8, 2018, https://foreignpolicy.com/2018/10/08/trump-reaches
-for-checkbook-diplomacy-to-counter-china/.

71 Aleksi Ylönen, "The Dragon and the Horn: Reflections on China–Africa Strategic
Relations," *Insight on Africa* 12, no. 2 (2020): 145–59.

72 See Zaw Thiha Tun, "How Petrodollars Affect the U.S. Dollar," Investopedia, accessed
December 30, 2022, https://www.investopedia.com/articles/forex/072915/how
-petrodollars-affect-us-dollar.asp.

73 See e.g. Lina Khatib, "Qatar's Foreign Policy: The Limits of Pragmatism," *International
Affairs* 89, no. 2 (2013): 417–31, Karen E. Young, "A New Politics of GCC Economic
Statecraft: The Case of UAE Aid and Financial Intervention in Egypt," *Journal of
Arabian Studies* 7, no. 1 (2017): 113–36, Li, "Saudi Arabia's Economic Diplomacy,"
and Miller and Verhoeven, "Overcoming Smallness."

74 See e.g. Wolfram F. Hanreider, "Dissolving International Politics: Reflections on the
Nation-State," *American Political Science Review* 72, no. 4 (December 1978): 1276–87,
and Edward L. Morse, "The Transformation of Foreign Policies: Modernization,
Interdependence and Externalization," *World Politics* 22, no. 3 (1970): 371–92.

75 The general Horn of Africa–Persian Gulf/Middle East relations are discussed further
in the next chapter. On the recent intensification of relations, see e.g. International
Crisis Group, *Intra-Gulf Competition in Africa's Horn: Lessening the Impact* (Brussels:
International Crisis Group, 2019), Dahir, *Foreign Engagements in the Horn of Africa*.

76 For example, while Djibouti's government has extensively used its geostrategic
location in its foreign relations to gain resources for regime sustenance, Ethiopia's
leadership has sought to capitalize on its large population size, emerging consumer
market, and agricultural potential.

77 See e.g. *Democracy Index* (https://www.eiu.com/n/campaigns/democracy-index
-2021/), *Freedom in the World* (https://freedomhouse.org/report/freedom-world), and
The Human Freedom Index (https://worldpopulationreview.com/country-rankings/
freedom-index-by-country).

78 This is particularly the case when governments' decision-making is not separated
from political lobbies and their constituent identity (e.g., ethnic, tribal, clan, or
kinship) groups. See more in Yaacov Y. Vertzberger, "Bureaucratic-Organizational
Politics and Information Processing in a Developing State," *International Studies
Quarterly* 28, no. 1 (1984): 69–95, and Baghat Korany and Ali E. Hillal Dessouki, *The*

Foreign Policies of Arab States: The Challenge of Change, 2nd ed. (Boulder: Westview Press, 1991).

79 Hermann has further suggested that examining decision units in foreign policy should take into account their dynamics in which factors such as a predominant leader, single group, and a coalition play a role. See e.g. Margaret G. Hermann, "How Decision Units Shape Foreign Policy: A Theoretical Framework," *International Studies Review* 3, no. 2 (2001): 47–81.

80 See *Fragile States Index* (https://fragilestatesindex.org/).

81 See e.g. Clapham, *Africa and the International System*. Clapham overwhelmingly uses the term "state" when referring to the governments and their foreign policy approaches. Here, we prefer more specific terms "government" and "regime" referring to the general bodies of the state in charge of foreign policy. In this study, more specific references to individuals, groups, and coalitions are made when deemed necessary for clarity and advancing the overall argument.

82 This does not only involve proxy warfare but also attempts to influence political dynamics through direct intervention or support of politically relevant individuals and groups inside or outside of the country. Since the Cold War, Ethiopia has maintained important influence in Somalia and Somaliland and Eritrea has sought to weaken Ethiopia by using such measures.

83 For example, in recent years Ethiopia's role in the sub-regional organization Inter-Governmental Authority on Development (and to an extent the African Union which it physically hosts) has been notable. This has contributed to Eritrea's boycott of a selection of regional institutions.

84 De Waal has described this as an economic marketplace. Alex de Waal, *The Real Politics of the Horn of Africa: Money, War and the Business of Power* (Cambridge: Polity, 2015).

85 This has been the case with Djibouti, Asmara, and Hargeisa engaging the UAE's Dubai Ports World (DP World) which Abu Dhabi uses as an extension of its foreign policy. DP World's long-term port development and management contracts have been lucrative for the Horn governments.

86 These have been particularly salient, albeit expensive, part of the "sticks and carrots" approach of economic statecraft in the US foreign policy. Military interventions and sanctions, as in the case of Iraq and Libya, are salient examples of harnessing military power in service of economic statecraft. Similarly, the leading Gulf States have used military power (Yemen) and embargos (Qatar) to achieve their foreign policy objectives. Therefore, although the military enterprise is primarily a costly coercive foreign policy tool, it is also capable of generating economic benefits.

87 See, e.g., Donelli, *Turkey in Africa*, and Yunus Turhan, "Turkey's Foreign Aid to Africa: An Analysis of the Post-July 15 Era," *Journal of Balkan and Near Eastern Studies* 23, no. 5 (2021): 795–812. Turkish foreign policy toward the Horn of Africa has a significant humanitarian and cultural soft power dimension. It has benefited from people-to-people interactions which have helped to consolidate relationships to achieve economic and political objectives.

88 See e.g. Jos Meester, Willem van den Berg, and Harry Verhoeven, *Riyal Politik: The Political Economy of Gulf Investments in the Horn of Africa*, CRU Report (Den Haag: Clingendael, Netherlands Institute of International Relations, 2018), and Khalid S. Almezaini and Jean-Marc Rickli, eds., *The Small Gulf States: Foreign and Security Policies before and after the Arab Spring* (London: Routledge, 2017).

Chapter 2

1   See e.g. Lina Khatib, "Qatar's Foreign Policy," F. Gregory Gause III, *Beyond Sectarianism: New Middle East Cold War* (Doha: Brookings Doha Center, 2014), and Miller and Verhoeven, "Overcoming Smallness."

2   For analysis on recent Turkish involvement in the Horn of Africa, see e.g. Zach Vertin, *Turkey and the New Scramble for Africa: Ottoman Designs or Unfounded Fears?* (Doha: Brookings Doha Center, 2019), and Donelli, *Turkey in Africa*.

3   See e.g. Erlich, *Ethiopia and the Middle East*.

4   Ludovic Orlando, "Back to the Roots and Routes of Dromedary Domestication," *Proceedings of the National Academy of Sciences of the United States of America* 113, no. 24 (2016): 6589.

5   See e.g. David W. Phillipson, *Foundations of an African Civilisation: Aksum & the Northern Horn 1000 BC - AD 1300* (London: James Currey, 2012).

6   Ali Mazrui, "The Black Arabs in Comparative Perspective: The Political Sociology of Race Mixture," in *The Southern Sudan: The Problem of National Integration*, ed. Dunstan M. Wai (London: Frank Cass, 1973), 47–81.

7   See e.g. Murray Gordon, *Slavery in the Arab World* (New York: New Amsterdam, 1989), and Yusuf Fadl Hasan, "Some Aspects of the Arab Slave Trade from the Sudan, 7th-19th Century," *Sudan Notes and Records* 58 (1977): 85–16.

8   See e.g. Dunstan M. Wai, "African-Arab Relations: Interdependence or Misplaced Optimism?," *The Journal of Modern African Studies* 21, no. 2 (1983): 189–92, and Dunstan M. Wai, "African-Arab Relations from Slavery to Petro-Jihad," *A Journal of Opinion* 13 (1984): 9–10, 13. For examples of Arab-Muslim dominated social hierarchy and "social race" in Sudan, which exemplifies persisting attitudes, see Francis Mading Deng, *War of Visions: Conflict Identities in Sudan* (Washington: The Bookings Institution, 1995), 369–400, 484–5, Jok Madut Jok, *War and Slavery in Sudan* (Philadelphia: Pennsylvania Press, 2001), 21, and Aleksi Ylönen, *On State, Marginalization, and Origins of Rebellion: The Formation of Insurgencies in Southern Sudan* (Trenton: Africa World Press, 2017), 11, 19, 36–40.

9   Frank L. James, *The Unknown Horn of Africa: An Exploration from Berbera to the Leopard River* (London: George Philip & Son, 1890), 327.

10 James C. Prichard, *Researches into the Physical History of Mankind: Ethnography of the African Races* (Sherwood: Gilbert & Piper, 1837), 160.

11 Abdisalam M. Issa-Salwe, *The Collapse of the Somali State: The Impact of the Colonial Legacy* (London: Haan Associates, 1996), 34–5.

12 After the collapse of the Ottoman Empire, the Turkish War of Independence (1919–23) kicked off a stream of newly independent states in the Middle East. In the Horn of Africa, Sudan (1956) was the first to join the never-colonized Ethiopia as an independent state. It was followed later by Somalia (1960), Djibouti (1977), and Eritrea (1993). Somaliland declared independence in 1991, but it has so far not been formally recognized by any United Nations member state.

13 John Howell, "Horn of Africa: Lessons from the Sudan Conflict," *International Affairs* 54, no. 3 (July 1978): 421–36, and Ylönen, *On State, Marginalization, and Origins of Rebellion*.

14 For Ethiopia's efforts to deepen its partnership with the US during this period, see Jeffrey A. Lefebvre, *Arms for the Horn: U.S. Security Policy in the Horn of Africa, 1953-91* (Pittsburgh: University of Pittsburgh Press, 1991), 75–110.

15 See more in Chapter 5, which focuses on Eritrea.

16 In the 1960s Israel engaged in technical assistance and military support to African governments and liberation movements which gave it increasing influence in the continent. However, by the early 1970s, most African states had turned their backs on Israel and begun supporting the Arab cause. See e.g. Ali A. Mazrui, "Black Africa and the Arabs," *Foreign Affairs* 53, no. 4 (1975): 728–30.

17 See Jeffrey A. Lefebvre, "Middle East Conflicts and Middle Level Power Intervention in the Horn of Africa," *Middle East Journal* 50, no. 3 (1996): 393, and J. Bowyer Bell, *The Horn of Africa: Strategic Magnet in the Seventies* (New York: National Strategy Information Center, 1973), 31–2.

18 Lefebvre, "Middle East Conflicts," 394.

19 Federal Research Division, *Ethiopia: A Country Study*, 4th ed. (Washington: Library of Congress, 1993), 300–1.

20 Colin Legum and Bill Lee, *Conflict in the Horn of Africa* (New York: Africana Publishing, 1977), 5.

21 Aliboni, *The Red Sea Region*, 95–6.

22 Aliboni, *The Red Sea Region*, 99.

23 Mazrui, "Black Africa," 731–9.

24 See e.g. Peter Schwab, "Cold War on the Horn of Africa," *African Affairs* 77, no. 306 (1978): 6–20.

25 Gilles Kepel, *Jihad, on the Trail of Political Islam* (Boston, MA: Harvard University Press, 2002), 180.

26 Kepel, *Jihad*. See also e.g. Gabriel Warburg, *Islam, Sectarianism and Politics in Sudan since the Mahdiyya* (London: Hurst & Co., 2003).

27 Imperial Ethiopia had already made plans to build a dam on the Blue Nile and conducted an eight-year survey (1956–64) to that effect. However, it was not until 2011 that the construction of the Millennium Dam (later known as the Grand Ethiopian Renaissance Dam, GERD) got underway. The Ethiopian government announced the beginning of the construction during political turbulence caused by the Arab Spring when its major rival, Egypt, with which it shares an interest in the Blue Nile waters, was in political turmoil.

28 The "Greater Somalia" nationalist ideal emerged in the 1960s and sought to expand Somalia's borders to northern Kenya, eastern Ethiopia, and Djibouti to bring Somali people living in those territories under the rule of one Somali state. However, in 1977 the Somali regime recognized the independence of Djibouti and established relations with it.

29 Somali opposition organizations sought support from other states. For example, the Somali National Movement (SNM) which became the main liberation movement among the Isaaq in Somaliland was founded and initially funded by members of the diaspora in Saudi Arabia and was later backed by Ethiopia. Other important rebel groups, the United Somali Congress (USC) and Somali Salvation Democratic Front (SSDF), based on Darod clan affiliation were founded in Ethiopia which was their biggest supporter until the late 1980s. Leftist Arab countries, such as Libya and the People's Democratic Republic of Yemen, also played a role in supporting Somali rebels.

30 Up to over 20,000 Cuban and over 2,000 Yemeni troops may have been involved in the conflict. Approximately USD 1 billion of Soviet military aid was airlifted mainly through South Yemen.

31 It provided approximately USD 300 million for the war effort. See Ehteshami and Murphy, *The International Politics*, 52.

32 By the early 1980s, the Eritrean People's Liberation Front, an offshoot group composed largely of Christian highlanders, had become the dominant faction among the Eritrean liberation forces after pushing its predecessor, a primarily Muslim Eritrean Liberation Front, out of Eritrea to Sudan.

33 While most states aligned with the West, Iran's friends in the wider region included Libya, PDRY, and Syria.

34 For more on the politics surrounding the Aden Treaty, see e.g. Central Intelligence Agency, *The Aden Treaty: Implications for Warning* (Washington: Strategic Warning Staff, 1981), https://www.cia.gov/readingroom/docs/CIA-RDP83B01027R000 300150004-8.pdf.

35 Bruce D. Porter, *The USSR in Third World Conflicts: Soviet Arms and Diplomacy in Local Wars 1945-1980* (Cambridge: Cambridge University Press, 1984), 213.

36 Such "arms for access" treaties were used by the Carter and Reagan administrations for gaining strategic access and alliances and fending off Soviet influence as part of the US foreign policy.

37 Oman showed the way during the first oil crisis in 1973, and other hydrocarbon-rich Arab states, including Bahrain (1980), Jordan (1995), the UAE (1997), Qatar (2001), and Kuwait (2003–7), also pegged their currencies to the USD.

38 See e.g. Mikael Wigell, Sören Sholvin, and Mika Aaltola, eds., *Geo-economics and Power Politics in the 21st Century: The Revival of Economic Statecrafts* (Abingdon: Routledge, 2019).

39 This has been particularly the case with Islamists, most notably in Somalia, where effective central authority is still being rebuilt.

40 International Crisis Group, *The United Arab Emirates in the Horn of Africa* (Brussels: International Crisis Group, 2018), 3.

41 See e.g. Muhammad Fraser-Rahim, "In Somalia, Iran Is Replicating Russia's Afghan Strategy," *Foreign Policy*, July 17, 2020, https://foreignpolicy.com/2020/07/17/iran -aiding-al-shabab-somalia-united-states/, and Katherine Houreld, "Iranian-Supplied Arms Smuggled from Yemen into Somalia, Study Says," *Reuters*, November 10, 2021, https://www.reuters.com/world/iranian-supplied-arms-smuggled-yemen-into -somalia-study-says-2021-11-10/.

42 Kristian Coates Ulrichsen, "The Geopolitics of Insecurity in the Horn of Africa and the Arabian Peninsula," *Middle East Policy* 18, no. 2 (2011): 120.

43 See more in Khalil al-Anani, "Upended Path: The Rise and Fall of Egypt's Muslim Brotherhood," *The Middle East Journal* 69, no. 4 (2015): 527–43.

44 Michael Peel, Camilla Hall, and Heba Saleh, "Saudi Arabia and UAE Prop Up Egypt Regime with Offer of $8bn," *Financial Times*, July 10, 2013, https://www.ft.com/ content/7e066bdc-e8a2-11e2-8e9e-00144feabdc0.

45 Saudi and Emirati troops intervened in 2011 to maintain the status quo in Bahrain, and the Saudi-led coalition entered the civil war in Yemen in defense of the government overthrown by the Houthi militia.

46 Tintswalo Baloyi, "What on Earth is Djibouti Doing?," *CAJ News Africa*, March 19, 2019, https://allafrica.com/stories/201903200216.html.

47 See e.g. Daniel Maxwell and Merry Fitzpatrick, "The 2011 Somalia Famine: Context, Causes, and Complications," *Global Food Security* 1, no. 1 (2012): 5–12.

48 See e.g. Salem Solomon, "Observers See Several Motives for Eritrean Involvement in Yemen," *Voice of America*, January 9, 2016, https://www.voanews.com/a/observers -see-several-motives-eritrean-involvement-yemen/3138689.html, and UN Tribune, "UN Report: UAE, SAUDI Using Eritrean Land, Sea, Airspace and, Possibly, Eritrean

Troops in Yemen Battle," November 2, 2015, http://untribune.com/un-report-uae
-saudi-leasing-eritean-port-using-eritrean-land-sea-airspace-and-possibly-troops-in
-yemen-battle/.

49 "Arab States Issue 13 Demands to End Qatar-Gulf Crisis," *Aljazeera*, July 12, 2017,
https://www.aljazeera.com/news/2017/7/12/arab-states-issue-13-demands-to-end
-qatar-gulf-crisis.

50 "UAE Denounces Seizure of Cash and Plane in Somalia," *Reuters*, April 10, 2018,
https://www.reuters.com/article/us-somalia-politics-emirates-idUSKBN1HH21V.

51 Godfrey Ivudria, "Legal Tussle over Dolareh Port Escalates as DP World Demands
Djibouti to Respect Concession Agreement," *EABW News*, December 7, 2020, https://
www.busiweek.com/legal-tussle-over-dolareh-port-escalates-as-dp-world-demands
-djibouti-to-respect-concession-agreement/.

52 See e.g. Baloyi, "What on Earth Is Djibouti Doing?," Ivudria, "Legal Tussle over
Dolareh," and Aleksi Ylönen, "External Power Competition in the Horn of Africa:
Somaliland's Quest for International Recognition and Development," *RUSI Journal*
166, no. 6–7 (2022): 77.

53 Mohamed Olad Hassan, "Somalia Releases Nearly $10M Seized from UAE Plane Four
Years Ago," *Voice of America*, May 19, 2022, https://www.voanews.com/a/somalia
-releases-nearly-10m-seized-from-uae-plane-four-years-ago/6580817.html#:~:text
=The%20Somali%20government%20has%20released,a%20low%20point%20ever
%20since.

54 Individual states may also privilege their relationships with prominent non-state
actors or multilateral organizations. While a state has a superior position relative
to a non-state actor in terms of international law, in the case of international
organizations states can be members but still deal directly with other member states.
A state can also remain outside of a multilateral institution but still deal bilaterally
with states that are members. Also, non-state actors may use already existing
interstate relations as leverage in their dealings with states.

55 "Bigmanism" is associated with authoritarian neo-patrimonial states in which a single
person or various big men dominate politics through informal patronage networks
which they use to control and distribute public and private resources. See more in
Ilmari Käihkö, "Big Men Bargaining in African Conflicts," in *African Conflicts and
Informal Power: Big Men and Networks*, ed. Mats Utas (London: Zed Books, 2012),
181–204.

56 In the Horn of Africa, major invasions and interstate conflicts have been between
the neighboring states themselves. External powers have often provided support,
including by applying coercive force.

57 See Christopher Clapham, "The 'Longue Durée' of the African State," *African Affairs*
93, no. 372 (1994): 435. Clapham provides an excellent review of Jean-François
Bayart, *The State in Africa: The Politics of the Belly* (London: Longman, 1993).

58 See Bayart, *The State in Africa*, and Bayart and Ellis, "Africa in the World."

59 For example, European kingdoms and aristocratic polities, major predecessors of
modern states, used this logic to deal with each other and other polities.

60 Especially the interests of powerful member states tend to dictate, or at least heavily
influence, the nature, dynamics, and conduct of such organizations. Realists would
argue that powerful states create such organizations to consolidate their power over
other states (e.g., hegemonic stability theory). An example of this would be the Red
Sea Council which Saudi Arabia created in January 2020 together with most littoral
countries (Djibouti, Egypt, Eritrea, Jordan, Somalia, Sudan, and Yemen) to strengthen

its position in the affairs of the region surrounding the strategically important water body.

61 The same can be argued about non-state actors which often conduct their affairs bilaterally with state and other non-state actors.

62 See e.g. Vertin, *Red Sea Rivalries*, 2.

63 "New Era Heralded as Turkey-UAE Ink Dozens of Investment Deals," *Daily Sabah*, November 24, 2021, https://www.dailysabah.com/business/economy/new-era -heralded-as-turkey-uae-ink-dozens-of-investment-deals.

64 "Saudi Crown Prince to Visit Turkey in Move to Boost Ties, Erdogan Says," *Reuters*, June 17, 2022, https://www.reuters.com/world/middle-east/saudi-crown-prince-visit -turkey-june-22-erdogan-2022-06-17/.

65 "Erdogan Says Saudi Crown Prince MBS to Visit Turkey Next Week," *Aljazeera*, June 17, 2022, https://www.aljazeera.com/news/2022/6/17/erdogan-says-saudi-crown -prince-mbs-to-visit-turkey-next-week.

66 "Somali President Makes His First Foreign Trip to UAE," *Hiiraan Online*, June 19, 2022, https://www.hiiraan.com/news4/2022/Jun/186693/somali_president_makes _his_first_foreign_trip_to_uae.aspx.

Chapter 3

1 Robert D. Kaplan, "Ethiopia's Problems Aren't Postcolonial," *Foreign Policy*, July 9, 2021, https://foreignpolicy.com/2021/07/09/ethiopias-problems-arent-postcolonial/.

2 Mordechai Abir, *Ethiopia and the Red Sea: The Rise and Decline of the Solomonic Dynasty and Muslim European Rivalry in the Region* (Abingdon: Frank Cass, 1980), 25.

3 Richard Pankhurst, *The Ethiopian Borderlands: Essays in Regional History from Ancient Times to the End of the 18th Century* (Lawrenceville: The Red Sea Press, 1997), 40–1.

4 There is some divergence among sources about the date of these events. See e.g. J. Spencer Trimingham, *Islam in Ethiopia* (Oxford: Oxford University Press, 1952), 74, note 4, and Paul Henze, *Layers of Time: A History of Ethiopia* (New York: Palgrave, 2000), 67.

5 Pankhurst, *The Ethiopian Borderlands*, 279–307.

6 Salih Özbaran, *The Ottoman Response to European Expansion: Studies on Ottoman-Portuguese Relations in the Indian Ocean and Ottoman Administration in the Arab Lands during the Sixteenth Century* (Istanbul: The Isis Press, 1994), 95, 108.

7 It is important to note that Ethiopia has never been considered a nation-state due to this ethnic diversity. This, combined with the exclusive and authoritarian nature of its regimes based on certain identity groups, has led the patrons of the Ethiopian state to persistently dictate the state's "national" interest based on their own ambitions and objectives.

8 See e.g. Frederick Myatt, *The March to Magdala: The Abyssinian War of 1868* (London: Leo Cooper, 1970), and Volker Matthies, *The Siege of Magdala: The British Empire Against the Emperor of Ethiopia* (Princeton: Markus Weiner, 2010).

9 For a brief discussion on the invading Ottoman Egypt's turning fortunes, see e.g. Czeslaw Jesman, "Egyptian Invasion of Ethiopia," *African Affairs* 58, no. 230 (1959): 75–81.

10 See e.g. Krishnamurthy V. Ram, *Anglo-Ethiopian Relations, 1869 to 1906: A Study of British Policy in Ethiopia* (New Delhi: Concept Publishing, 2009).

11 For more on Sudan under Mahdism, see Peter M. Holt, *The Mahdist Sudan, 1881-1898: A Study of Its Origins, Development, and Overthrow* (Oxford: Clarendon, 1958). For a more concise account, see Ylönen, *On State, Marginalization, and Origins of Rebellion*, 90–6.

12 John Young, "Regionalism and Democracy in Ethiopia," *Third World Quarterly* 19, no. 2 (1998): 192.

13 See Richard Caulk, *Between Jaws of Hyenas: A Diplomatic History of Ethiopia (1876-1896)* (Wiesbaden: Harrassowitz Verlag, 2002).

14 See "Treaty of Wuchale," May 2, 1889, accessed January 4, 2023, https://africanlegends.files.wordpress.com/2016/10/ethiopie_traite-de-wuchale.pdf.

15 For more on Menelik's strategy, see George N. Sanderson, "The Foreign Policy of the Negus Menelik, 1896-1898," *The Journal of African History* 5, no. 1 (1964): 87–97, and Harold G. Marcus, "The Foreign Policy of the Emperor Menelik 1896-1898: A Rejoinder," *The Journal of African History* 7, no. 1 (1966): 117–22.

16 See e.g. Donald L. Donham, "Old Abyssinia and the New Ethiopian Empire: Themes in Social History," in *The Southern Marches of Imperial Ethiopia: Essays in History and Social Anthropology*, eds. Donald L. Donham and Wendy James (Cambridge: Cambridge University Press, 1986), 3–48.

17 Harold G. Marcus, *The Life and Times of Menelik II: Ethiopia 1844-1913* (Lawrenceville: Red Sea Press, 1995), 241–81.

18 The circumstances of Empress Zewditu's death have been surrounded by some controversy.

19 "Ethiopian Constitution of 1931," July 16, 1931, accessed January 4, 2023, https://www.abyssinialaw.com/laws/constitutions/the-1931-ethiopian-constitution-english-version/download.

20 Aleksi Ylönen and Alexander Meckelburg, "Ethiopia: Between Domestic Pressures and Regional Hegemony," in *Africa's Thorny Horn: Searching for a New Balance in the Age of Pandemic*, ed. Giovanni Carbone (Milan: Ledizioni, 2021), 124.

21 As part of the defense agreement, the US set to strengthen the Ethiopian military. In 1943 Americans began operating a radio communications and listening center from an old Italian naval radio station, "Radio Marina," in Asmara. In a form of an expanded military base, it came to be known as the Kagnew Station in 1953. The station operated until 1977, when the new Ethiopian government forced its closure after aligning with the Soviet Union.

22 United Nations General Assembly, *Eritrea: Report of the United Nations Commission for Eritrea; Report of the Interim Committee of the General Assembly on the Report of the United Nations Commission for Eritrea*, Resolution A/RES/390(V)A-B, December 2, 1950, accessed January 4, 2023, https://undocs.org/en/A/RES/390(V).

23 United Nations General Assembly, *Eritrea: Report of the United Nations Commissioner in Eritrea*, Resolution A/RES/617(VII), December 17, 1952, accessed January 4, 2023, https://undocs.org/en/A/RES/617(VII).

24 See e.g. Leo Silberman, "Ethiopia: Power of Moderation," *Middle East Journal* 14, no. 2 (1960): 141–52.

25 For a brief period, Egypt supported Somali irredentism and Eritrean Liberation Front. See e.g. Lefebvre, "Middle East Conflicts," 391–2.

26 Belete Belachew Yihun, "Ethiopian Foreign Policy and the Ogaden War: The Shift from 'Containment' to 'Destabilization,' 1977–1991," *Journal of Eastern African Studies* 8, no. 4 (2014): 683–4.

27 See e.g. Richard Sherman, *Eritrea: The Unfinished Revolution* (New York: Praeger, 1980), Andargatchew Tiruneh, "Eritrea, Ethiopia, and Federation (1941-1952)," *Northeast African Studies* 2/3, no. 3/1 (1980–1/1981): 99–119, and Semere Haile, "The Origins and Demise of the Ethiopia-Eritrea Federation," *Issue: A Journal of Opinion* 15 (1987): 9–17.

28 Martin Plaut, *Understanding Eritrea: Inside Africa's Most Repressive State* (Oxford: Oxford University Press, 2016), 70.

29 Bahru Zewde, *A History of Modern Ethiopia* (Oxford: James Currey, 2001), 220–6.

30 See e.g. Peter Schwab, "Rebellion in Gojam Province, Ethiopia," *Canadian Journal of African Studies / Revue Canadienne des Études Africaines* 4, no. 2 (1970): 249–56, and Gebru Tareke, *Ethiopia: Power and Protest* (Lawrenceville: Red Sea Press, 1996), 160–95. There were recurrent revolts from the 1940s onward faced by the central government which sought consolidation by broadening its tax base and settling Amhara administrators in the provinces.

31 Marina Ottaway and David Ottaway, *Ethiopia: Empire in Revolution* (New York: Africana, 1978), 92, 93.

32 Roy Pateman, "Eritrea, Ethiopia, and the Middle Eastern Powers: Image and Reality," *Northeast African Studies* 8, no. 2/3 (1986): 25–6.

33 See e.g. Pateman, "Eritrea, Ethiopia, and the Middle Eastern Powers," 23–39.

34 Pateman, "Eritrea, Ethiopia, and the Middle Eastern Powers," 24–5.

35 Roy Pateman, *Eritrea: Even the Stones Are Burning* (Lawrenceville: Red Sea Press, 1998), 96–7.

36 Ylönen, *On State, Marginalization, and Origins of Rebellion*, 184, 205.

37 The Assembly of Heads of State and Government meeting in the First Ordinary Session of the Organization of African Unity, July 17–21, 1964, in Cairo. See Organization of African Unity, *Border Disputes among African States*, AHG/Res. 16(I), July 17–21, 1964, Article 2. For more on the Organization of African Unity's settling on post-colonial African borders and its role in territorial dispute resolution, see e.g. Saadia Touval, "The Organization of African Unity and African Borders," *International Organization* 21, no. 1 (1967): 102–27.

38 United States Department of State, *290. Circular Airgram From the Department of State to Certain African Posts*, CA-9629, March 21, 1964, accessed January 8, 2023, https://history.state.gov/historicaldocuments/frus1964-68v24/d290.

39 Madan M. Sauldie, *Super Powers in the Horn of Africa* (New York: APT Books, 1987), 100–1.

40 See Ylönen, *On State, Marginalization, and Origins of Rebellion*, 214, and Haggai Erlich, *The Struggle over Eritrea* (Stanford: Hoover Institution, 1983), 79–84.

41 Amare Tekle, "The Determinants of the Foreign Policy of Revolutionary Ethiopia," *The Journal of Modern African Studies* 27, no. 3 (1989): 484.

42 It did, however, until Haile Selassie's pact with Sudanese president Jaafar Nimeiri, reinforce the southern insurgents with Israeli assistance as a response to Sudan's support of Eritrean freedom fighters. Sudan also channeled assistance to the Tigray People's Liberation Front which emerged in the mid-1970s.

43 Getachew Metaferia, *Ethiopia and the United States: History, Diplomacy, and Analysis* (New York: Algora, 2009), 72.

44 Although there has been some controversy about Haile Selassie's death, evidence has shown that the military junta ordered his assassination. See e.g. Ismail Akwei, "The Real Story of the Last Days of Emperor Haile Selassie of Ethiopia - Face2Face Africa," Face2Face Africa, accessed January 8, 2023, https://face2faceafrica.com/article/the-real-story-of-the-last-days-of-emperor-haile-selassie-of-ethiopia.

45 See e.g. Robert G. Patman, "Soviet–Ethiopian Relations: The Horn of Dilemma," in *Troubled Friendships: Moscow's Third World Ventures*, ed. Margot Light (London: British Academic Press, 1993), 110–39.

46 Patman, "Soviet–Ethiopian Relations," 112–14.

47 See Aregawi Berhe, "The Origins of the Tigray People's Liberation Front," *African Affairs* 103, no. 413 (2004): 569–92, and Aregawi Berhe, *A Political History of the Tigray People's Liberation Front (1975-1991): Revolt, Ideology and Mobilisation in Ethiopia* (Los Angeles: Tsehai, 2009).

48 Tekle, "The Determinants of the Foreign Policy," 479.

49 To an extent, this attitude drew from the experience during the imperial times. See e.g. Tim Carmichael, "Bureaucratic Literacy, Oral Testimonies, and the Study of Twentieth-Century Ethiopian History," *Journal of African Cultural Studies* 18, no. 1 (2006): 37.

50 Tekle, "The Determinants of the Foreign Policy," 496–8.

51 See Haggai Erlich, *Saudi Arabia and Ethiopia: Islam, Christianity, and Politics Entwined* (Boulder: Lynne Rienner, 2007), 144–8.

52 See e.g. Donna R. Jackson, "The Ogaden War and the Demise of Détente," *The Annals of the American Academy of Political and Social Science* 632, no. 1 (2010): 26–40.

53 Particularly Saudi Arabia, Egypt, Sudan, and Iran sought unsuccessfully to convince the Carter Administration. See Lefebvre, *Arms for the Horn*, 175–96.

54 See e.g. Daniel Compagnon, "The Somali Opposition Fronts: Some Comments and Questions," *Horn of Africa* 13, no. 1–2 (1990): 29–54. The Somali Salvation Democratic Front (SSDF), formed in 1978 in Ethiopia and associated with the Majerteen clan and Puntland, was the first such group. Another important group was the Somali National Movement which emerged in 1981 and represented the Isaaq, a dominant clan in former British Somaliland.

55 Ylönen, *On State, Marginalization, and Origins of Rebellion*, 266–7 and 288–9.

56 Yihun, "Ethiopian Foreign Policy and the Ogaden War," 684–5.

57 Erlich, *The Struggle over Eritrea*, 70.

58 See more in e.g. Erlich, *Saudi Arabia and Ethiopia*.

59 See e.g. Henze, *Layers of Time*, and Zewde, *A History of Modern Ethiopia*.

60 Edmond J. Keller, "The Politics of State Survival: Continuity and Change in Ethiopian Foreign Policy," *The Annals of the American Academy of Political and Social Science* 489, no. 1 (1987): 76–87.

61 See e.g. Marco Bassi, "The Relativistic Attitude in Development: Reflections on the Implementation of the Ethiopian Multinational Constitution," *Archivio Antropologico Mediterraneo* 22, no. 21 (2) (2019), http://journals.openedition.org/aam/2319.

62 For the case of the Ogaden National Liberation Front, see Aleksi Ylönen, "Positivism or Understanding? The Complexity of Analyzing the Objectives of Armed Opposition Groups," *Critical Review* 33, no. 1 (2021): 128–44.

63 See e.g. Christopher Clapham, "The Ethiopian Developmental State," *Third World Quarterly* 39, no. 6 (2018): 1151–65, and Ha-Joon Chang and Jostein Hauge, "The Concept of 'Developmental State' in Ethiopia," in *The Oxford Handbook of the*

Ethiopian Economy, eds. Fantu Cheru, Christopher Cramer, and Arkebe Oqubay (Oxford: Oxford University Press, 2019), 824–41.

64 Fantu Cheru, Christopher Cramer, and Arkebe Oqubay, "Introduction," in *The Oxford Handbook of the Ethiopian Economy*, eds. Fantu Cheru, Christopher Cramer, and Arkebe Oqubay (Oxford: Oxford University Press, 2019), 4.

65 Article 86 of the 1994 Ethiopian constitution wows to "promote policies of foreign relations based on the protection of national interests and respect for the sovereignty of the country," "promote mutual respect for national sovereignty and equality of states and non-interference in the internal affairs of other states," "ensure that the foreign relation policies of the country are based on mutual interests and equality of states as well as that international agreements promote the interests of Ethiopia," "observe international agreements which ensure respect for Ethiopia's sovereignty and are not contrary to the interests of its Peoples," "forge and promote ever growing economic union and fraternal relations of Peoples with Ethiopia's neighbours and other African countries," and "seek and support peaceful solutions to international disputes." See "Constitution of the Federal Democratic Republic of Ethiopia," December 8, 1994, accessed January 11, 2023, https://www.refworld.org/docid /3ae6b5a84.html.

66 Harry Verhoeven, "Africa's Next Hegemon," *Foreign Affairs*, April 12, 2015, https://www.foreignaffairs.com/articles/ethiopia/2015-04-12/africas-next -hegemon.

67 Mehari Taddele Maru, *A Regional Power in the Making: Ethiopian Diplomacy in the Horn of Africa*, Occasional Paper 261 (Johannesburg: South African Institute of International Affairs, 2017), 8.

68 Maru, *A Regional Power in the Making*, 27.

69 Katie Kuschminder, Lisa Andersson, and Melissa Seigel, "Migration and Multidimensional Well-Being in Ethiopia: Investigating the Role of Migrants Destinations," *Migration and Development* 7, no. 3 (2018): 325.

70 This attitude emanates from the historical experiences related to the Arab slave trade and the relatively recently formally abolished slavery in the Arabian Peninsula. In most cases, this took place in the second half of the twentieth century.

71 International Organization for Migration, "Funding Needed to Assist over 100,000 Ethiopian Migrants Returning from the Kingdom of Saudi Arabia," March 30, 2022, accessed January 11, 2023, https://www.iom.int/news/funding-needed-assist-over -100000-ethiopian-migrants-returning-kingdom-saudi-arabia.

72 InfoMigrants, "Thousands of Ethiopian Migrants Stuck in Yemen, IOM," September 8, 2021, accessed January 11, 2023, https://www.infomigrants.net/en/post/34921/ thousands-of-ethiopian-migrants-stuck-in-yemen-iom.

73 Marina de Regt and Medareshaw Tafesse, "Deported before Experiencing the Good Side of Migration: Ethiopians Returning from Saudi Arabia," *African and Black Diaspora: An International Journal* 9, no. 2 (2015): 228, and Clara Lecadet and Medareshaw Tafesse Melkamu, "The Expulsion of Ethiopian Workers from Saudi Arabia (2013–2014): The Management of a Humanitarian and Political Crisis," *Annales d'Ethiopie* 31 (2016): 225.

74 Zecharias Zelalem and Will Brown, "First Migrants Released from Saudi Detention Centres Arrive Home after Telegraph Investigation," *The Telegraph*, January 27, 2021, https://www.telegraph.co.uk/global-health/climate-and-people/first-migrants -released-saudi-detention-centres-arrive-home/.

75 "Remittance from Ethiopians Living Abroad Reaches $3.8 Billion," *Ethiopian Monitor*, April 21, 2022, https://ethiopianmonitor.com/2022/04/21/remittance-from-ethiopians-living-abroad-reaches-3-8-billion/.

76 See more at Patrick Desplat and Terje Østebø, eds., *Muslims in Ethiopia: The Christian Legacy, Identity Politics and Islamic Reformism* (New York: Palgrave Macmillan, 2013).

77 See e.g. Katharina M. B. Newbery, "State Identity Narratives and Threat Construction in the Horn of Africa: Revisiting Ethiopia's 2006 Intervention in Somalia," *Journal of Eastern African Studies* 15, no. 2 (2021): 255–73.

78 For example, Saudi Star purchased 139,000 hectares of farmland in the Gambella region on which it has primarily cultivated rice for exportation. See e.g. Ojot Miru Ojulu, "Large-Scale Land Acquisitions and Minority/Indigenous Communities' Rights under Ethnic Federalism in Ethiopia: A Case Study of Gambella Regional State" (PhD Diss., Bradford University, 2013), 205, http://hdl.handle.net/10454/6291, and GRAIN, *SEIZED! The 2008 Land Grab for Food and Financial Security*, Briefing (Rome: GRAIN, 2008), https://grain.org/article/entries/93-seized-the-2008-landgrab-for-food-and-financial-security.

79 "Midroc Investment Group to Beef up Ethiopia's Edible Oil Processing Capacity with US$1 Billion Planned Investment," *Food Business Africa*, November 2, 2021, https://www.foodbusinessafrica.com/midroc-investment-group-beefs-up-ethiopias-edible-oil-processing-capacity-invests-us1-billion-in-new-facility/.

80 Clapham, "The Ethiopian Developmental State," 1159.

81 See e.g. Meester, van den Berg and Harry Verhoeven, *Riyal Politik*, 52–3.

82 Daniel Berhane, "Ethiopia: Al-Amoudi Pledges 1.5 Billion Br. for Renaissance Dam," *Horn Affairs*, September 12, 2011, https://hornaffairs.com/2011/09/12/ethiopia-al-amoudi-pledges-1-5-billion-br-for-renaissance-dam/. Egypt seeks to secure sufficient Nile water flow for agricultural production and public consumption. Its government considers the Nile a critical national security issue.

83 The Government of Ethiopia, *The Federal Democratic Republic of Ethiopia Foreign Affairs and National Security Policy and Strategy* (Ministry of Information, November 2002), 24, 111, 116.

84 The Government of Ethiopia, *The Federal Democratic Republic of Ethiopia*, 130.

85 The Nile treaties of 1929 and 1959 allocated a lion's share of its waters to Egypt and excluded Ethiopia. For the Nile water dispute, see e.g. Aleksi Ylönen, "Talking Nile: Historical Aspects, Current Concerns, and the Stalemate in Grand Ethiopian Renaissance Dam Negotiations," *The Horn Bulletin* 3, no. 4 (2020): 1–10.

86 The Government of Ethiopia, *The Federal Democratic Republic of Ethiopia*, 136.

87 The Government of Ethiopia, *The Federal Democratic Republic of Ethiopia*, 131.

88 See e.g. Harry Verhoeven, *Black Gold for Blue Gold? Sudan's Oil, Ethiopia's Water and Regional Integration*, Chatham House Briefing Paper (London: Chatham House, 2011), 6, and Medhane Tadesse, *Turning Conflict to Cooperation: Towards an Energy-Led Integration in the Horn of Africa* (Addis Ababa: Friedrich-Ebert Stiftung, 2003), 123, 124.

89 The total amount is quoted in Turkish sources. See e.g. Seleshi Tessema, "Mutual Growth Drives Turkish Investment in Ethiopia," *Anadolu Agency*, January 17, 2020, https://www.aa.com.tr/en/africa/mutual-growth-drives-turkish-investment-in-ethiopia/1705411.

90 Addis Getachew, "Turkey Seeks Preferential Trade Deal with Ethiopia," *Anadolu Agency*, February 15, 2021, https://www.aa.com.tr/en/economy/turkey-seeks -preferential-trade-deal-with-ethiopia/2145955.

91 Meester, van den Berg, and Verhoeven, *Riyal Politik*, 61.

92 As explained in the next chapter, in Somalia, permitted by state weakness, individual leaders and sub-state actors often use their personal or group-based foreign linkages for obtaining resources that boost their local personal financial, economic, and political power and at times enable them to challenge the central authority and contest state power.

93 See Tedros Adhanom, *Ethiopia's Foreign Policy: Regional Integration and International Priorities*, Africa Program Meeting Transcript (London: Chatham House, 2015).

94 Matthias E. Leitner, "Conflict Resolution in Northern Ethiopia and Geopolitics," International Institute for Middle East and Balkan Studies, December 27, 2020, accessed January 13, 2023, https://www.ifimes.org/en/researches/conflict-resolution -in-northern-ethiopia-and-geopolitics/4713#_ftnref3.

95 "News: After the Launch of La Gare Downtown Luxury Complex Addis Abeba City Poised to Build at Least Four Similar Joint Projects," *Addis Standard*, November 20, 2018, https://addisstandard.com/news-after-the-launch-of-la-gare-downtown -luxury-complex-addis-abeba-city-poised-to-build-at-least-four-similar-joint -projects/.

96 "Ethiopia to Get $140 Mln in Loans from Saudi Arabia," *Reuters*, December 19, 2019, https://www.reuters.com/article/ethiopia-economy-idUKL8N28T2EG.

97 Jeffrey Feltman, "A Perspective on the Ethiopian-U.S. Relationship after a Year of Conflict," United States Special Envoy for the Horn of Africa, United States Department of State, November 1, 2021, https://www.state.gov/a-perspective-on-the -ethiopian-u-s-relationship-after-a-year-of-conflict/.

98 Embassy of Ethiopia, "WB, IMF Pledge Over $5b For Ethiopia's Economic Reform," December 11, 2019, https://ethiopianembassy.org/wb-imf-pledge-over-5b-for -ethiopias-economic-reform-december-11-2019/.

99 "China's EximBank Withholds $339 Mln in Funds to Ethiopia, Cites Debt Repayment Pressures," *Reuters*, August 16, 2021, https://www.reuters.com/article/ ethiopia-debt-idAFL8N2PN47O.

100 Ingo Henneberg, "Horn of Africa Cooperation: Mixed Responses to New Regional Bloc," *The Africa Report*, September 9, 2020, https://www .theafricareport.com/40994/horn-of-africa-cooperation-mixed-responses-to -new-regional-bloc/.

101 Goitom Gebreluel, "The Tripartite Alliance Destabilising the Horn of Africa," *Aljazeera*, May 10, 2021, https://www.aljazeera.com/opinions/2021/5/10/the -tripatriate-alliance-that-is-destabilisng-the-horn-of-africa.

102 Declan Walsh, "Foreign Drones Tip the Balance in Ethiopia's Civil War," *The New York Times*, December 20, 2021, https://www.nytimes.com/2021/12/20/world/africa/ drones-ethiopia-war-turkey-emirates.html.

103 Cara Anna, "Ethiopia Armed Group Says It Has Alliance with Tigray Forces," *AP News*, August 11, 2021, https://apnews.com/article/africa-only-on-ap-ethiopia-b28 0e6622d66b7e7f9b12cd1d0041ae8.

104 "Russia, Ethiopia Ink Military Cooperation Agreement," *Anadolu Agency*, July 12, 2021, https://www.aa.com.tr/en/africa/russia-ethiopia-ink-military-cooperation -agreement/2302337.

105 See e.g. Stijn Mitzer and Joost Oliemans, "UAE Air Bridge Supports Ethiopian Military in Tigray War," *Oryx*, October 8, 2021, https://www.oryxspioenkop.com /2021/10/uae-air-bridge-supports-ethiopian.html.

106 Walsh, "Foreign Drones Tip the Balance."

107 Patrick Alushula, "US Sanction Waiver Saves Safaricom Ethiopia Deal," *Business Daily*, June 22, 2021, https://www.businessdailyafrica.com/bd/corporate/companies/ us-sanction-waiver-saves-safaricom-ethiopia-deal-3445994.

108 The White House, "Executive Order on Imposing Sanctions on Certain Persons with Respect to the Humanitarian and Human Rights Crisis in Ethiopia," September 17, 2021, https://www.whitehouse.gov/briefing-room/presidential-actions/2021/09/17 /executive-order-on-imposing-sanctions-on-certain-persons-with-respect-to-the -humanitarian-and-human-rights-crisis-in-ethiopia/.

109 Samuel Gebre and Alonso Soto, "Ethiopia in Talks to Restructure $1 Billion More of Debt," *Bloomberg*, July 7, 2021, https://www.bloomberg.com/news/articles /2021-07-07/ethiopia-in-negotiations-to-restructure-1-billion-more-of-debt -kqte6iuj.

110 "Ethiopia Recalls Dozens of Diplomats, Closes Consulates in Various Countries," *Addis Standard*, July 8, 2021, https://addisstandard.com/breaking-ethiopia-recalls -dozens-of-diplomats-closes-consulates-in-various-countries/.

111 Samuel Bogale, "Ethiopia Recalls All Diplomats but Ambassadors, Finance Heads," *Fortune*, July 24, 2021, https://addisfortune.news/ethiopia-recalls-all-diplomats-but -ambassadors-finance-heads/.

112 "UAE: Withdrawal from Assab, Build-Up on Perim," *Gulf States Newsletter*, Issue 1122, March 18, 2021, https://www.gsn-online.com/article/uae-withdrawal-assab -build-perim, and "Yemen: Mysterious Airbase Gets Built on Mayun Island," *Aljazeera*, May 25, 2021 https://www.aljazeera.com/news/2021/5/25/yemen -mysterious-airbase-gets-built-on-mayun-island.

113 The White House, "Statement by NSC Spokesperson Emily Horne on National Security Advisor Jake Sullivan's Call with His Highness Sheikh Mohammed bin Zayed Al Nahyan, The Crown Prince of Abu Dhabi," June 30, 2021, https://www .whitehouse.gov/briefing-room/statements-releases/2021/06/30/statement-by-nsc -spokesperson-emily-horne-on-national-security-advisor-jake-sullivans-call-with -his-highness-sheikh-mohammed-bin-zayed-al-nahyan-the-crown-prince-of-abu -dhabi/.

114 "New Era Heralded."

115 Deepthi Nair, "Dubai's DP World and Ethiopia Strike $1bn Deal to Develop Trade and Logistics Corridor," *The National*, May 6, 2021, https://www.thenationalnews .com/business/markets/dubai-s-dp-world-and-ethiopia-strike-1bn-deal-to-develop -trade-and-logistics-corridor-1.1218039.

116 Tesfa-Alem Tekle, "Ethiopia Loses Its 19pc Stake in Berbera Port: Somaliland Minister," *The East African*, June 11, 2022, https://www.theeastafrican.co.ke/tea/rest -of-africa/ethiopia-stake-in-port-of-berbera-3845366.

117 Hisham A. Hellyer and Ziya Meral, "Will the Page Turn on Turkish-Egyptian Relations?," Commentary, Carnegie Endowment for International Peace, March 19, 2021, accessed January 13, 2023, https://carnegieendowment.org/2021/03/19/will -page-turn-on-turkish-egyptian-relations-pub-84124.

118 Aidan Lewis, "Egypt's Sisi Opens Naval Base Close to Border with Libya," *Reuters*, July 4, 2021, https://www.reuters.com/world/middle-east/egypts-sisi-opens-naval -base-close-border-with-libya-2021-07-03/.

119 See a critical reflection of external interests in Nemo Semret, "Pay Any Prize, Bear Any Burden," EthioReference, June 5, 2021, accessed January 13, 2023, https://ethioreference.com/archives/28349.

120 "Ethiopia Claims Victory over Security Council's Support for African Mediation in Nile Dam Row," *The Arab Weekly*, July 10, 2021, https://thearabweekly.com/ethiopia-claims-victory-over-security-councils-support-african-mediation-nile-dam-row.

Chapter 4

1 Ioan M. Lewis, "The Somali Conquest of the Horn of Africa," *The Journal of African History* 1, no. 2 (1960): 214 (pp. 213–30).

2 Abir, *Ethiopia and the Red Sea*, xvii–xviii.

3 The first written records mentioning Zeila are from the first century BC, but according to the archeological record the port could have been initially established much earlier.

4 This was initially a collection of smaller states which later gave way to the consolidation of the Sultanate of Aussa under the Mudaito Dynasty.

5 See e.g. Richard Pankhurst, "The Trade of Southern and Western Ethiopia and the Indian Ocean Ports in the Nineteenth and Early Twentieth Centuries," *Journal of Ethiopian Studies* 3, no. 2 (1965): 37–74.

6 Peter Woodward, *The Horn of Africa: State, Politics and International Relations*, 2nd ed. (London: I.B. Tauris, 2002), 26.

7 Abdi Ismail Samatar, *The State and Rural Transformation in Northern Somalia, 1884–1986* (Madison: University of Wisconsin Press, 1989), 31, 42.

8 Mohamed-Rashid S. Hasan and Salada M. Robleh, "Islamic Revival and Education in Somalia," in *Educational Strategies among Muslims in the Context of Globalization: Some National Case Studies*, eds. Holger Daun and Geoffrey Walford (Leiden: Brill, 2004), 143, 146–8, 150–2.

9 See Abdi Sheik-Abdi, "Somali Nationalism: Its Origins and Future," *The Journal of Modern African Studies* 15, no. 4 (1977): 657–65.

10 Samson A. Bezabeh, "Citizenship and the Logic of Sovereignty in Djibouti," *African Affairs* 110, no. 441 (2011): 592–3.

11 This is, however, not the case in the self-declared independent Republic of Somaliland, where English has the status of second official language.

12 Tobias Hagmann, "The Somali Region of Ethiopia Must Write Their Own Narrative," *The Africa Report*, March 11, 2021, https://www.theafricareport.com/71431/the-somali-region-of-ethiopia-must-write-their-own-narrative/.

13 Victor Anant, "The Colony that Rejected Freedom," *Daily Herald*, June 29, 1960.

14 For more on the early political confrontations in the Ogaden, see e.g. Tibebe Eshete, "The Root Causes of Political Problems in the Ogaden, 1942-1960," *Northeast African Studies* 13, no. 1 (1991): 9–28.

15 Ottaway and Ottaway, *Ethiopia*, 92.

16 Schwab, "Cold War on the Horn," 12.

17 According to Ehteshami and Murphy, *The International Politics*, 52.

18 For more on the origins of SNM, see e.g. Marleen Renders, *Consider Somaliland: State-Building with Traditional Leaders and Institutions* (Leiden: Brill, 2012), 64–70.

19 Hussein M. Adam, "Formation and Recognition of New States: Somaliland in Contrast to Eritrea," *Review of African Political Economy* 21, no. 59 (1994): 21–38.

20 Alan Cowell, "Ethiopian Drive against Somalia Bogs Down," *The New York Times*, October 8, 1982, Section A, Page 1.

21 Somalia received nearly USD 800 million in economic and military aid from Washington in the 1980-1991 period. See e.g. Ehteshami and Murphy, *The International Politics*, 57.

22 Peter J. Schraeder, *United States Foreign Policy toward Africa: Incrementalism, Crisis and Change* (Cambridge: Cambridge University Press, 1994), 183.

23 For SNM, see e.g. Adam, "Formation and Recognition of New States," 29.

24 See Ken Menkhaus, "Governance without Government in Somalia: Spoilers, State Building, and the Politics of Coping," *International Security* 31, no. 3 (2007): 74–106.

25 William A. Rugh, "The Foreign Policy of the United Arab Emirates," *Middle East Journal* 50, no. 1 (1996): 69.

26 These big men have popularly been called warlords. They often led clan- or sub-clan-based militia forces and used coercive power to extract economic rents through mafia-like strategies such as the provision of protection, extortion, and illicit taxation. This increased their personal wealth and social standing and helped to sustain the forces under their command.

27 Berouk Mesfin, "Ethiopia's Role and Foreign Policy in the Horn of Africa," *International Journal of Ethiopian Studies* 6, no. 1/2 (2012): 106.

28 Center for International Security and Cooperation, "Al Ittihad Al Islamiya," Stanford University, accessed January 13, 2023, https://cisac.fsi.stanford.edu/mappingmilitants/profiles/al-ittihad-al-islamiya.

29 Mesfin, "Ethiopia's Role and Foreign Policy," 106.

30 "Ahlu-Sunna Waljama'a: State Minister and Goobaale Are Leading Soldiers Fighting against Us," *Goobjoog*, February 13, 2015, https://goobjoog.com/english/ahlu-sunna-waljamaa-state-minister-and-goobaale-are-leading-soldiers-fighting-against-us/.

31 "Death Toll Hits 120 from 3-Day Fighting in Central Somalia," *Garowe Online*, October 26, 2021, https://www.garoweonline.com/en/news/somalia/death-toll-hits-120-from-3-day-fighting-in-central-somalia.

32 Guled Ahmed, "As Farmaajo Digs In with Qatari Backing, Somalia's Election Crisis Grows Worse," Middle East Institute, February 9, 2021, https://www.mei.edu/publications/farmaajo-digs-qatari-backing-somalias-election-crisis-grows-worse.

33 Engin Yüksel and Haşim Tekineş, *Turkey's Love-In with Qatar: A Marriage of Convenience*, CRU Report (Den Haag: Clingendael, Netherlands Institute of International Relations, 2021), 20.

34 See "The Transitional Federal Charter of the Somali Republic," February 2004, article 2.3, accessed January 13, 2023, https://www.ilo.org/dyn/travail/docs/2177/Transitional%20Federal%20charter-feb%202004-English.pdf.

35 See e.g. Research Directorate of the Immigration and Refugee Board of Canada, "Somalia: The 22 December 1997 Peace Accord in Mogadishu and Subsequent Developments," SOM29118.E, April 1, 1998, https://www.refworld.org/docid/3ae6ab53c.html.

36 See e.g. Hassan Adan Mohamed and Amina Abdulkadir M. Nur, *The Puntland Experience: A Bottom-Up Approach to Peace and State Building* (Garowe: Puntland Development Research Center, 2008), https://www.interpeace.org/wp-content/uploads/2008/07/2008_SomF_PDRC_Interpeace_A_Bottom_Up_Approach_To_Peace_And_Statebuilding_EN.pdf.

37 Mohamed and Nur, *The Puntland Experience*, Annex 4.

38 See "The Transitional Federal Charter of the Somali Republic," article 11.

39   "Declaration of National Commitment (Arta Declaration)," May 5, 2000, accessed
     January 16, 2023, https://www.peaceagreements.org/viewmasterdocument/1682.
40   See e.g. Andre Le Sage, "Somalia: Sovereign Disguise for a Mogadishu Mafia,"
     Review of African Political Economy 29, no. 91 (2002): 132–8.
41   Dr Ligle, "Bossaso: A Somali Success Story . . . PICS," Somalia Online, September 4,
     2009, https://www.somaliaonline.com/community/topic/34066-bossaso-a-somali
     -success-story-pics/?do=findComment&comment=511436.
42   United Nations Security Council, *Resolution 1846*, S/RES/1846, December 2, 2008,
     accessed January 16, 2023, https://digitallibrary.un.org/record/642811/files/S_RES
     _1846%282008%29-EN.pdf?ln=en.
43   Robert Young Pelton, "Puntland Marine Police Force Enter Eyl," *Somalia Report*,
     March 2, 2012, https://piracyreport.com/index.php/post/2978/Puntland_Marine
     _Police_Force_Enter_Eyl_#:~:text=At%20the%20request%20of%20the,piracy
     %20program%20to%20the%20townspeople.
44   Ronen Bergman and David D. Kirkpatrick, "With Guns, Cash and Terrorism, Gulf
     States Vie for Power in Somalia," *The New York Times*, July 22, 2019, https://www
     .nytimes.com/2019/07/22/world/africa/somalia-qatar-uae.html.
45   United Nations Security Council, *Report of the Monitoring Group on Somalia and
     Eritrea Pursuant to Security Council Resolution 2002*, S/2012/544, July 13, 2012, 200,
     https://www.undocs.org/S/2012/544.
46   Denys Reva, *Ten Years on, Is Somali Piracy Still a Threat?*, ISS Today (Pretoria:
     Institute for Security Studies, 2018), https://issafrica.org/iss-today/ten-years-on-is
     -somali-piracy-still-a-threat.
47   "Somalia: UAE Pledges Continued Support for Puntland Marine Forces," *Horseed
     Media*, March 28, 2014, https://horseedmedia.net/somalia-uae-pledges-continued
     -support-puntland-marine-forces-146629, and "Somalia: UAE Confirms to
     Continue Supporting Puntland Troops," *Garowe Online*, April 14, 2018, https://
     www.garoweonline.com/en/news/puntland/somalia-uae-confirms-to-continue
     -supporting-puntland-troops.
48   "Somalia: Puntland Signs Deal to Develop Bosaso Port with Dubai's P&O Ports,"
     Garowe Online, April 6, 2017, https://www.garoweonline.com/en/news/puntland/
     somalia-puntland-signs-deal-to-develop-bosaso-port-with-dp-world.
49   United Nations Office for the Coordination of Humanitarian Affairs, *2021 Somalia
     Humanitarian Needs Overview*, March 9, 2021, 7, https://reliefweb.int/attachments
     /3faf9fa4-3879-3a53-ab25-a093731a7bae/20200903_HNO_Somalia.pdf.
50   See more at Embassy Nairobi, "Somalia - Political Perspectives from Dubai,"
     Wikileaks Cable: 08NAIROBI2619_a, November 20, 2008, https://wikileaks.org/
     plusd/cables/08NAIROBI2619_a.html.
51   See e.g. Nimo-ilhan Ali, *Going on Tahriib: The Causes and Consequences of Somali
     Youth Migration to Europe* (London: Rift Valley Institute, 2016).
52   See e.g. Markus V. Hoehne, et al., *Differentiating the Diaspora: Reflections on
     Diasporic Engagement 'for Peace' in the Horn of Africa*, Working Paper 124 (Max
     Planck Institute for Social Anthropology: Halle, 2010).
53   Tobias Hagmann, *Stabilization, Extraversion and Political Settlements in Somalia*
     (London: Rift Valley Institute, 2016), 29–32.
54   See e.g. Aisha Ahmad, "The Security Bazaar: Business Interests and Islamist Power
     in Civil War Somalia," *International Security* 39, no. 3 (2014/15): 89–117.
55   Cedric Barnes and Harun Hassan, "The Rise and Fall of Mogadishu's Islamic
     Courts," *Journal of Eastern African Studies* 1, no. 2 (2017): 154.

56 See e.g. Zeray W. Yihdego, "Ethiopia's Military Action against the Union of Islamic Courts and Others in Somalia: Some Legal Implications," *The International and Comparative Law Quarterly* 56, no. 3 (2007): 667, 668.

57 Colum Lynch, "U.N. Report Cites Outside Military Aid to Somalia's Islamic Forces," *The Washington Post*, November 15, 2006, A13.

58 Mohamed Olad Hassan, "Islamic Leader Urges Greater Somalia," *AP News*, November 18, 2006, https://www.hiiraan.com/news2/2006/nov/islamic_leader _urges__greater_somalia__.aspx.

59 Barnes and Hassan, "The Rise and Fall," 155.

60 See "New Somali Alliance Threatens War," *BBC*, September 12, 2007, http://news .bbc.co.uk/2/hi/africa/6990928.stm.

61 Michael Martinez, "Top Somali Militant Killed in U.S. Operation, Pentagon Says," *CNN*, September 5, 2014, https://edition.cnn.com/2014/09/05/world/africa/somali -militant-killed/index.html.

62 Abdi Sheikh, "Al Shabaab Leader Urges Somalis to Battle Old Enemy Ethiopia," *Reuters*, March 11, 2014, https://www.reuters.com/article/us-somalia-alshabaab -leader-idUSBREA29IOL20140310.

63 See Ben Rawlence, *Black and White: Kenya's Criminal Racket in Somalia* (Nairobi: Journalists for Justice, 2015).

64 Jennifer Peltz, "UN Report: Banned Somali Charcoal Exports Pass through Iran," *AP News*, October 13, 2018, https://apnews.com/article/united-nations-ivory-coast-us -news-global-trade-al-qaida-9b0bcd2c5b354e83b2882cd147e17385.

65 In March 2014 Somali prime minister Abdiweli Sheikh Ahmed visited Abu Dhabi to convince the UAE to increase its support for the Somali federal government. This reflected warm ties between Abu Dhabi and Mogadishu until the Doha-aligned Mohamed Abdullahi Mohamed "Farmaajo" presidency (2017–21). See e.g. "Somalia: Prime Minister of Somalia Meets with UAE's Deputy PM, Discuss Increased Support to Somalia," *Radio Dalsan*, March 4, 2014, https://allafrica.com/stories /201403041646.html.

66 See e.g. "Somalia: Former PMPF Director Lauds UAE's Support for Puntland," *Garowe Online*, April 28, 2018, https://www.garoweonline.com/en/news/puntland/ somalia-former-pmpf-director-lauds-uaes-support-for-puntland.

67 Michelle Nichols, "Iran Is New Transit Point for Somali Charcoal in Illicit Trade Taxed by Militants: U.N. Report," *Reuters*, October 9, 2018, https://www.reuters .com/article/us-somalia-sanctions-un-idUSKCN1MJ158. In 2011, the UN Monitoring Group on Somalia and Eritrea estimated that "Al-Shabaab generates between $70 million and $100 million per year, from duties and fees levied at airports and seaports, taxes on goods and services, taxes in kind on domestic produce, *jihad* contributions, checkpoints and various forms of extortion justified in terms of religious obligations, or *zakat*." United Nations Security Council, *Report of the Monitoring Group on Somalia and Eritrea Pursuant to Security Council Resolution 1916*, S/2011/433, July 18, 2011, 27, https://www.undocs.org/S/2011 /433.

68 United Nations Security Council, *Report of the Panel of Experts on Somalia Submitted in Accordance with Resolution 2444*, S/2019/858, November 1, 2019, 30–1, 33–4, http://undocs.org/S/2019/858.

69 Jay Bahadur, *Following the Money: The Use of the Hawala Remittance System in the Yemen-Somalia Arms Trade* (Geneva: The Global Initiative Against Transnational Organized Crime, 2020), 11–14.

70 On October 17, 2022, the US Department of Treasury issued a press release announcing the sanctions and indicating that "Al-Shabaab generates around $100 million per year through multiple funding streams, including extortion of local businesses and individuals, collections of fees on goods, as well as the facilitation of illicit trades." See United States Department of Treasury, "Treasury Designates al-Shabaab Financial Facilitators," October 17, 2022, accessed January 17, 2023, https://home.treasury.gov/news/press-releases/jy1028.

71 Guled Ahmed, "Far from a Benefactor, the Turkish Government Is Exploiting Somalia's Fragility," Middle East Institute, October 21, 2021, https://www.mei.edu/publications/far-benefactor-turkish-government-exploiting-somalias-fragility.

72 Mohamed Husein Gaas, "Qatari Involvement in the Horn of Africa: A Kingmaker and a Successful Mediator?," in *Religion, Prestige and Windows of Opportunity?*, ed. Stig Jarle Hansen (Aas: Norwegian University of Life Sciences, Noragric Working Paper no. 48, 2013), 54.

73 Bergman and Kirkpatrick, "With Guns, Cash and Terrorism."

74 Guled Ahmed, "As Farmaajo Digs In."

75 Bergman and Kirkpatrick, "With Guns, Cash and Terrorism."

76 Meester, van der Berg, and Verhoeven, *Riyal Politik*, 28.

77 "Somalia Received Saudi Aid the Day It Cut Ties with Iran: Document," *Reuters*, January 17, 2016, https://www.reuters.com/article/us-somalia-saudi-iran-idUSKCN0UV0BH.

78 See e.g. Ahmed M. Musa, Oliver Vivian Wasonga, and Nadhem Mtimet, "Factors Influencing Livestock Export in Somaliland's Terminal Markets," *Pastoralism* 10, no. 1 (2020), https://doi.org/10.1186/s13570-019-0155-7.

79 United Nations Security Council, *Report of the Monitoring Group on Somalia and Eritrea*, 181–2.

80 Marqaati, *2016 State of Accountability in Somalia: Unrestrained Corruption* (Mogadishu: Marqaati, 2017), 2.

81 Marqaati, *Five Years of Stasis: Accountability in Somalia* (Mogadishu: Marqaati, 2022), 1–2.

82 Bergman and Kirkpatrick, "With Guns, Cash and Terrorism."

83 Somaliland minister of foreign affairs and international cooperation Mohamed Bihi Yonis explained to the media afterward that "We and UAE officials discussed ways of strengthening of trade cooperation including the issue of expansion and upgrading of the facilities at the Berbera port by the Dubai Ports Authority a subsidiary of the Dubai world. We also discussed matters regarding ongoing development projects and proposed new projects . . . and providing much needed resources to deal with the ever surging influx of Yemeni Refugees." Goth Mohamed Goth, "Somaliland: President Silanyo Concludes 8 Days Working Visit to the U.A.E," *Somaliland Current*, June 14, 2015, https://www.somalilandcurrent.com/somalilandpresident-silanyo-concludes-8-days-working-visit-to-the-u-a-e/. See also Ylönen, "External Power Competition in the Horn of Africa," 74–82. For decades the Berbera Corridor had posed as an alternative option to Djibouti for Ethiopia's sea access, but the uneasy Hargeisa-Mogadishu relations and questions about the international standing of Somaliland weighed against its development until recently.

84 "Somaliland UAE Military Base to Be Turned into Civilian Airport," *Reuters*, September 15, 2019, https://www.reuters.com/article/us-somalia-emirates-idUSKBN1W00FI.

85   "Somaliland Agrees to UAE Military Case in Berbera," *BBC*, February 13, 2017, https://www.bbc.com/news/world-africa-38956093.

86   "DP World and Somaliland Open New Container Terminal in Berbera Port," *Port Technology*, June 24, 2021, https://www.porttechnology.org/news/dp-world-and -somaliland-open-new-container-terminal-in-berbera-port/.

87   "Somalia: Farmaajo Seeks Saudi Arabia Intervention in Controversial Berbera UAE Military Base," *Radio Dalsan*, February 24, 2017, http://allafrica.com/stories /201702240588.html.

88   While the UAE maintained a presence in Assab until early 2021 and has continued its activities in Bosaso, Berbera, and Socotra, it has reportedly built a base also in Perim (Mayyun) Island. See e.g. Jon Gambrell, "UAE-Backed Yemen Leader Says His Troops at Island Air Base," *AP News*, June 15, 2021, https://apnews.com/article/ yemen-middle-east-business-628ae4a2d20e074e7e5f43fda2df46b6.

89   "Mohamed Said Guedi: Businessman with a Midas Touch," *Arabian Post*, November 8, 2019, https://thearabianpost.com/mohamed-said-guedi-businessman-with-a -midas-touch/.

90   "Omani-Somaliland Joint Venture to Establish Cement Factory in Berbera," *Somaliland*, July 19, 2019, https://www.somaliland.com/business/omani-somaliland -joint-venture-to-establish-cement-factory-in-berbera/.

91   Brendon J. Cannon, "Foreign State Influence and Somalia's 2017 Presidential Election: An Analysis," *Bildhaan: An International Journal of Somali Studies* 18, no. 1 (2019): 36.

92   Diana Alghoul, "Somalia Rejects Secret $80m Bribe to Stand against Qatar in Ongoing Boycott," *The New Arab*, June 12, 2017, https://www.newarab.com/news/ revealed-somalia-rejects-secret-80m-qatar-blockade-bribe.

93   "Somalia Seizes $9.6m from UAE Plane in Mogadishu," *Aljazeera*, April 9, 2018, https://www.aljazeera.com/news/2018/4/9/somalia-seizes-9-6m-from-uae-plane-in -mogadishu.

94   International Crisis Group, *Somalia and the Gulf Crisis* (Brussels: International Crisis Group, 2019), 8.

95   "Turkey Accuses UAE of Financing Terrorists in Somalia," *Garowe Online*, May 1, 2020, https://www.garoweonline.com/en/news/somalia/turkey-accuses-uae-of -financing-terrorists-in-somalia.

96   "Somalia Chides Its Regions for Cutting Ties with Qatar," *Aljazeera*, September 22, 2017, https://www.aljazeera.com/news/2017/9/22/somalia-chides-its-regions-for -cutting-ties-with-qatar.

97   International Crisis Group, *Somalia and the Gulf Crisis*, 9.

98   International Crisis Group, *The United Arab Emirates in the Horn*, 6.

99   "EXCLUSIVE: Top Officials behind Missing Soldiers in Eritrea Exposed," *Garowe Online*, June 13, 2021, https://www.garoweonline.com/en/editorial/exclusive-top -officials-behind-missing-soldiers-in-eritrea-exposed.

100 Garowe Online, "UN Report: Somali Soldiers in Eritrea Took Part in Tigray Genocide," June 8, 2021, https://www.garoweonline.com/en/featured/un-report -somali-soldiers-in-eritrea-took-part-in-tigray-genocide; Lucy Kassa, "Somali Troops Committed Atrocities in Tigray as New Alliance Emerged, Survivors Say," *The Globe and Mail*, January 20, 2022, https://www.theglobeandmail.com/world/ article-somali-troops-committed-atrocities-in-tigray-as-new-alliance-emerged/.

101 Hiiraan Online, "Farmaajo Confirms Somali Troops Trained in Eritrea during Final Speech as President," May 23, 2022, https://www.hiiraan.com/news4/2022/May

/186315/farmajo_confirms_somali_troops_trained_in_eritrea_during_final_speech
_as_president.aspx.

102 "General Tahalil: Most of Eritrean-Trained Soldiers Returned to Somalia," *Garowe Online*, January 1, 2023, https://www.garoweonline.com/en/news/somalia/general
-tahalil-most-of-eritrean-trained-soldiers-returned-to-somalia.

103 "Ethiopian Khat Triggers Farmaajo's Dispute with PM Roble Ahead of Nairobi Trip," *Garowe Online*, August 8, 2021, https://www.garoweonline.com/en/news
/somalia/ethiopian-khat-triggers-farmaajo-s-dispute-with-pm-roble-ahead-of
-nairobi-trip.

104 Aggrey Mutambo, "Disputed Oil Blocks at Stake as Law Gives Somalia Power to Sell," *The East African*, February 18, 2020, https://www.theeastafrican.co.ke/tea/
news/east-africa/disputed-oil-blocks-at-stake-as-law-gives-somalia-power-to-sell
-1436974.

105 See e.g. Marsai and Szalai, "The 'Borderlandization' of the Horn of Africa."

106 "Erdogan Calls on UAE Businesses to Invest in Turkey," *France 24*, February 15, 2022, https://www.france24.com/en/live-news/20220215-erdogan-calls-on-uae
-businesses-to-invest-in-turkey, and "'A New Era': Saudi Arabia's MBS in Turkey as Nations Mend Ties," *Aljazeera*, June 22, 2022, https://www.aljazeera.com/news/2022
/6/22/saudi-crown-prince-mbs-visits-turkey-as-countries-normalise-ties.

107 See e.g. Imtilak Real Estate, "Saudi Arabia Tops the List of Foreign Investments in Turkey," July 5, 2022, accessed January 18, 2023, https://www.imtilak.net/en/articles/
saudi-arabia-tops-list-foreign-investments-turkey.

108 "Turkey, Somalia Sign MoU to Boost Cooperation on Investments," *Horn Diplomat*, June 22, 2021, https://www.horndiplomat.com/2021/06/22/turkey-somalia-sign
-mou-to-boost-cooperation-on-investments/.

109 Odindo Ayieko, "Russia Finalizes Plans to Set Up Naval Base in Somaliland," *EABW News*, January 31, 2020, https://www.busiweek.com/russia-finalizes-plans-to-set-up
-naval-base-in-somaliland/.

110 Nima Elbagir, et al., "Russia is Plundering Gold in Sudan to Boost Putin's War Effort in Ukraine," *CNN*, July 29, 2022, https://edition.cnn.com/2022/07/29/africa/sudan
-russia-gold-investigation-cmd-intl/index.html.

111 Nader Kabbani, "The Blockade on Qatar Helped Strengthen Its Economy, Paving the Way to Stronger Regional Integration," The Brookings Institution, January 19, 2021, https://www.brookings.edu/blog/order-from-chaos/2021/01/19/the-blockade
-on-qatar-helped-strengthen-its-economy-paving-the-way-to-stronger-regional
-integration/.

112 Nair, "Dubai's DP World and Ethiopia Strike $1bn Deal," and "DP World Inaugurates New Container Terminal at Berbera," *The Maritime Executive*, June 28, 2021, https://maritime-executive.com/article/dp-world-inaugurates-new-container
-terminal-at-berbera.

113 British Embassy Mogadishu, "UK Ambassador Launches Construction of the Hargeisa Bypass," May 4, 2021, https://www.gov.uk/government/news/uk
-ambassador-launches-construction-of-the-hargeisa-bypass.

114 Tekle, "Ethiopia Loses Its 19pc Stake."

115 In Somalia, these "big men" include politically prominent individuals, business leaders, clan elders, and religious figures. Many also double in such roles. For a deeper understanding of the role of "big men" in African politics see e.g. Mats Utas, ed., *African Conflicts and Informal Power: Big Men and Networks*, London: Zed Books.

116 See e.g. Roland Marchal and Zakaria M. Sheikh, "Salafism in Somalia: Coping with Coercion, Civil War and Its Own Contradictions," *Islamic Africa* 6, no. 1–2 (2015): 135–63.

117 The remaining paragraph is heavily based on research by Marqaati. See Marqaati, *State of Accountability in Somalia in 2020: Towards Authoritarianism* (Mogadishu: Marqaati, 2020).

118 Yaxy Bisle Suuley, "Op-Ed: The Dawn of Democracy in Puntland: A Promising Start and a Hopeful Future," *Garowe Online*, October 25, 2021, https://www.garoweonline .com/en/opinions/op-ed-the-dawn-of-democracy-in-puntland-a-promising-start -and-a-hopeful-future.

119 "Erdogan Says Somalia Invited Turkey to Explore for Oil Offshore," *Aljazeera*, January 21, 2020, https://www.aljazeera.com/economy/2020/1/21/erdogan-says -somalia-invited-turkey-to-explore-for-oil-offshore.

Chapter 5

1 See e.g. Jonathan Miran, "Mapping Space and Mobility in the Red Sea Region, c.1500-1950," *History Compass* 12, no. 2 (2014): 197–216.

2 The location of the Land of Punt is debated. It may have begun south of Egypt's sphere of influence in the Abyssinian highlands, and extended to both sides of the southern Red Sea, the northern shores of today's Somalia, and the southwestern Arabian Peninsula.

3 For evidence on this, see e.g. Siegbert Uhlig, Alessandro Bausi, and Baye Yimam, eds., *Encyclopaedia Aethiopica*, vol. 4 (Wiesbaden: Harrassowitz Verlag, 2010), 449.

4 See e.g. Madain Project, "as-Sahaba Mosque," accessed January 21, 2023, https:// madainproject.com/as_sahaba_mosque_(massawa).

5 Yasin Mohammed Yasin, "Political History of the Afar in Ethiopia and Eritrea," *Africa Spectrum* 43, no. 1 (2008): 41–4.

6 Andrew Paul, *A History of the Beja Tribes of the Sudan* (Cambridge: Cambridge University Press, 2012), 86–8.

7 James S. Olson, *The Peoples of Africa: An Ethnohistorical Dictionary* (London: Greenwood, 1996), 89–90.

8 Tom Killion, *Historical Dictionary of Eritrea* (London: Scarecrow, 1998), 413.

9 Richard Pankhurst, *An Introduction to the Economic History of Ethiopia, from Early Times to 1800* (Woodford Green: Lalibela House, 1961), 327.

10 Yasin, "Political History of the Afar," 55.

11 Jesman, "Egyptian Invasion of Ethiopia," 78.

12 Haggai Erlich, *Ras Alu'a and the Scramble for Africa: A Political Biography: Ethiopia & Eritrea 1875-1897* (Lawrenceville: Red Sea Press, 1996), 13.

13 Killion, *Historical Dictionary*, 70.

14 Killion, *Historical Dictionary*, 107.

15 Denis Mack Smith, *Mussolini* (New York: Alfred A. Knopf, 1982), 200.

16 See United Nations General Assembly, *Eritrea* (A/RES/390(V), 1950).

17 Michael Weldeghiorghis Tedla, "The Eritrean Liberation Front: Social and Political Factors Shaping Its Emergence, Development and Demise, 1960-1981" (Master's Thesis, Leiden University, 2014), 24, 26, https://hdl.handle.net/1887/32998.

18 Eritrea was given the right to a flag, judicial structure, police, and local administration, as well as the right to exercise control over its domestic affairs, including taxation. However, the Ethiopian government controlled its finances, defense, and foreign affairs. See e.g. Bereket Habte Selassie, *Eritrea and the United Nations and Other Essays* (Trenton: Red Sea Press, 1989), 41–2.

19 Dan Connell and Tom Killion, *Historical Dictionary of Eritrea*, 2nd ed. (Plymouth: Scarecrow, 2011), 70–1.

20 Tekeste Negash, *Eritrea and Ethiopia: The Federal Experience* (Uppsala: Nordic Africa Institute, 1997), 95–100.

21 Tedla, "The Eritrean Liberation Front," 40.

22 Tedla, "The Eritrean Liberation Front," 40, 42.

23 Aleksi Ylönen, "Eritrea: A Sub-Regional Menace?," in *The Horn of Africa since the 1960s: Local and International Politics Intertwined*, eds. Aleksi Ylönen and Jan Záhořík (Abingdon: Routledge, 2017), 91.

24 Sherman, *Eritrea*, 74.

25 Killion, *Historical Dictionary*, 369.

26 Pateman, "Eritrea, Ethiopia, and the Middle Eastern Powers," 26.

27 Pateman, "Eritrea, Ethiopia, and the Middle Eastern Powers," 25.

28 Lefebvre, "Middle East Conflicts," 392.

29 Pateman, "Eritrea, Ethiopia, and the Middle Eastern Powers," 26.

30 Tedla, "The Eritrean Liberation Front," 70–1.

31 Aryeh Y. Yodfat, "The Soviet Union and the Horn of Africa," *Northeast African Studies* 1, no. 3 (1979–80): 11.

32 By the second half of the 1960s, the ELF had become a relatively modern force. See e.g. Erlich, *The Struggle over Eritrea*, 21.

33 Shumet Sishagne, *Unionists and Separatists: The Vagaries of the Ethio-Eritrean Relation, 1941-1991* (Hollywood: Tsehai Publishers, 2007), 153, and Connell and Killion, *Historical Dictionary*, 207–8.

34 Dan Connell, "Inside the EPLF: The Origins of the 'People's Party' & Its Role in the Liberation of Eritrea," *Review of African Political Economy* 28, no. 89 (2001): 351.

35 Connell, "Inside the EPLF," 347, 348.

36 Tedla, "The Eritrean Liberation Front," 102.

37 Pateman, "Eritrea, Ethiopia, and the Middle Eastern Powers," 29.

38 Aliboni, *The Red Sea Region*, 108–11.

39 Erlich, *The Struggle over Eritrea*, 88.

40 Erlich, *The Struggle over Eritrea*, 89.

41 Killion, *Historical Dictionary*, 369.

42 Pateman, "Eritrea, Ethiopia, and the Middle Eastern Powers," 34.

43 In 2003, Eritrean Islamic Jihad Movement (EIJM) changed its name to the Eritrean Islamic Reform Movement, EIRM (also known as the Eritrean Islamic Salvation Movement). See more on the movement in Angel Rabasa et al., *Beyond Al-Qaeda: Part 2, The Outer Rings of the Terrorist Universe* (Arlington: RAND Corporation, 2006), 44–9.

44 See more in Erlich, *Saudi Arabia and Ethiopia*, 203–4.

45 Erlich, *The Struggle over Eritrea*, 67–96, 115.

46 Lefebvre, "Middle East Conflicts," 399.

47 By January 1982 there were 550,000 Eritrean refugees in Sudan. See e.g. Gaim Kibreab, *African Refugees: Reflections on the African Refugee Problem* (Trenton: Africa World Press, 1985), 30.

48 Killion, *Historical Dictionary*, 77–8.

49 Berouk Mesfin, *The Eritrea-Djibouti Border Dispute*, Situation Report (Addis Ababa: Institute for Security Studies, 2008), note 18, 17–18.

50 Mesfin, *The Eritrea-Djibouti*, 5.

51 Killion, *Historical Dictionary*, 370.

52 Lefebvre, "Middle East Conflicts," 402, 403.

53 See "TPLF-Manifesto -1963 E.C," February 1978, accessed January 23, 2023, https://tassew.wordpress.com/tplf-manifesto-1968-e-c/. For more information and discussion, see "TPLF MANIFESTO," ገለጻ የድረጅት ኃይስጥ, September 25, 2016, accessed January 23, 2023, https://www.goolgule.com/tplf-manifesto/.

54 "People's Democratic Programme of the Tigray People's Liberation Front (TPLF)," May 1983, accessed January 23, 2023, https://www.marxists.org/history/erol/ethiopia/tigray-program.pdf.

55 Jeffrey Lefebvre, "Red Sea Security and the Geopolitical-Economy of the Hanish Islands Dispute," *Middle East Journal* 52, no. 3 (1998): 373–5.

56 Killion, *Historical Dictionary*, 370.

57 Lefebvre, "Red Sea Security," 385.

58 See e.g. Manickam Venkataraman and Solomon Mebrie, "Eritrean-Yemeni Relations," in *Regional Security in the Post-Cold War Horn of Africa*, eds. Roba Sharamo and Berouk Mesfin (Addis Ababa: Institute for Security Studies, 2011), 281–307.

59 Neither party appears to have initially expected a full-scale war.

60 See e.g. Ylönen, "Eritrea," 98.

61 Tanja Müller, "Representing Eritrea: Geopolitics and Narratives of Oppression," *Review of African Political Economy* 43, no. 150 (2016): 661.

62 See United Nations Security Council, *Resolution 1907*, S/RES/1907, December 23, 2009, accessed January 23, 2023, https://digitallibrary.un.org/record/673859/files/S _RES_1907%282009%29-EN.pdf?ln=en.

63 United Nations Security Council, *Resolution 1916*, S/RES/1916, March 19, 2010, accessed January 23, 2023, https://daccess-ods.un.org/tmp/3024535.17913818.html.

64 Jeremy Clarke, "Eritrea Rejects U.N. Report It Backs Somali Rebels," *Reuters*, March 16, 2010, https://www.reuters.com/article/idUSLDE62F297.

65 United Nations Security Council, *Resolution 2444*, S/RES/2444, November 14, 2018, accessed January 23, 2023, https://digitallibrary.un.org/record/1652454/files/S_RES _2444%282018%29-EN.pdf.

66 "Eritrea Condemns New U.S. Sanctions," *Reuters*, November 13, 2021, https://www .reuters.com/article/uk-ethiopia-conflict-idUKKBN2HY09G.

67 Eritrea sided with the Houthi during the early Yemen conflict mainly because of its good relations with Iran at the time. Similar features can be observed with the Eritrean government's opportunistic foreign policy approach in the context of Russia's invasion of Ukraine.

68 On Djibouti, see Tanja Müller, "Assertive Foreign Policy in a 'Bad Neighbourhood': Eritrean Foreign Policy Making," in *2016 International Conference on Eritrean Studies*, eds. Zemenfes Tsighe et al. (Asmara: National Higher Education and Research Institute, 2016), 643–4.

69 For more on the diaspora, see e.g. Nicole Hirt and Abdulkader Saleh Mohammad, "The Lack of Political Space of the Eritrean Diaspora in the Arab Gulf and Sudan: Torn between an Autocratic Home and Authoritarian Hosts," *Mashriq & Mahjar: Journal of Middle East Migration Studies* 5, no. 1 (2018): 101–26.

70 Hirt and Mohammad, "The Lack of Political Space," 102.

71 Hirt and Mohammad, "The Lack of Political Space," 113–15.

72 Hirt and Mohammad, "The Lack of Political Space," 113, 114.

73 Hirt and Mohammad, "The Lack of Political Space," 103.

74 United Nations Security Council, *Resolution 1916*, 106–8.

75 "Sunridge Gold Sold Its 60% Share in Eritrea Mine to China," *TesfaNews*, November 6, 2015, https://tesfanews.net/sunridge-gold-sold-its-eritrea-mine-to-china/, and James Poole and Laura Millan Lombrana, "Nevsun Finds a White Knight in Zijin With $1.41 Billion Deal," *Bloomberg*, September 5, 2018, https://www.bloomberg.com/news/articles/2018-09-05/zijin-mining-to-buy-nevsun-resources-for-1-41-billion-in-cash.

76 "Eritrea: President Isaias Arrives in Tehran on Official Working Visit to Iran," Eritrean Ministry of Information, May 18, 2008, accessed January 25, 2023, https://allafrica.com/stories/200805191594.html.

77 It has not been clearly established to what extent in reality Eritrea might have assisted the Iranian-supported Houthis. On some of these allegations, see e.g. Yasser Seddiq, "Iranian Support to Houthis via Eritrea: Reality or Myth?," *Ahram Online*, June 15, 2015, https://english.ahram.org.eg/NewsContent/2/8/132655/World/Region/Iranian-support-to-Houthis-via-Eritrea-Allegations.aspx.

78 "Israel Using Eritrean Bases to Spy on Iran," *Ynet News*, November 12, 2012, https://www.ynetnews.com/articles/0,7340,L-4318720,00.html, and "Eritrea: Another Venue for the Iran-Israel Rivalry," *Stratfor*, December 11, 2012, https://worldview.stratfor.com/article/eritrea-another-venue-iran-israel-rivalry.

79 See more on recent Eritrea–Qatar relations in Armin Rosen, "What Is an Expensive, Idyllic Resort Doing in Eritrea?," *The Atlantic*, March 23, 2013, https://www.theatlantic.com/international/archive/2013/03/what-is-an-expensive-idyllic-resort-doing-in-eritrea/274424/.

80 Alex Mello and Michael Knights, "West of Suez for The United Arab Emirates," *War on the Rocks*, September 2, 2016, https://warontherocks.com/2016/09/west-of-suez-for-the-united-arab-emirates/.

81 Saudi Arabia used "investments, loans and central bank to central bank transfers" to persuade Eritrea, Sudan, and Somalia to align with it. See e.g. Meester, van den Berg, and Verhoeven, *Riyal Politik*, 28.

82 According to a UN Monitoring Group source, 400 Eritrean troops were engaged in Yemen. See e.g. Solomon, "Observers See Several Motives for Eritrean Involvement in Yemen."

83 Solomon, "Observers See Several Motives."

84 "UAE Forces 'Occupy' Sea and Airports on Yemen's Socotra," *Aljazeera*, May 4, 2018, https://www.aljazeera.com/news/2018/5/4/uae-forces-occupy-sea-and-airports-on-yemens-socotra.

85 "Saudi Withdraws Its Troops from Yemen's Socotra," *Middle East Monitor*, May 7, 2020, https://www.middleeastmonitor.com/20200507-saudi-withdraws-its-troops-from-yemens-socotra/.

86 Mohammed Mukhashaf, "Yemen Separatists Seize Remote Socotra Island from Saudi-Backed Government," *Reuters*, June 21, 2020, https://www.reuters.com/article/us-yemen-security-separatists-idUSKBN23S0DU.

87 See e.g. Giorgio Cafiero, "The UAE's Expansionist Agenda in Yemen Is Playing Out on Socotra," *DAWN MENA*, April 8, 2022, https://dawnmena.org/the-uaes-expansionist-agenda-in-yemen-is-playing-out-on-socotra/, and Najla M. Shahwan,

"UAE-Israel Intelligence Base on Yemeni Island of Socotra," *Daily Sabah*, September 5, 2020, https://www.dailysabah.com/opinion/op-ed/uae-israel-intelligence-base-on -yemeni-islandof-socotra/amp.

88 John Gambrell, "Mysterious Air Base Being Built on Volcanic Island Off Yemen," *AP News*, May 25, 2021, https://apnews.com/article/mysterious-air-base-volcanic-island -yemen-c8cb2018c07bb5b63e1a43ff706b007b.

89 Gambrell, "Mysterious Air Base."

90 Abu Dhabi's abandonment of the operations in Assab was in part motivated by its strategic priority in securing bases in strategic Yemeni islands to monitor the Red Sea and the Gulf of Aden and the lack of near-future prospects of reinstating a logistics route to Ethiopia due to the Eritrean government's wariness because of its persisting confrontation with Tigray.

91 Conor Gaffey, "Eritrea Becomes Latest African Nation to Side with Saudi Arabia in Spat with Qatar," *Newsweek*, June 14, 2017, https://www.newsweek.com/qatar-crisis -eritrea-saudi-arabia-625356.

92 Malak Harb and Elias Meseret, "Qatar Pulls All Its Troops from Djibouti-Eritrea Border," *AP News*, June 14, 2017, https://apnews.com/article/243ba2f8ef5841a5a2e eeb3c9e6edccf.

93 Maggie Fick and Alexander Cornwell, "In Peace between Ethiopia and Eritrea, UAE Lends a Helping Hand," *Reuters*, August 8, 2018, https://www.reuters.com/article/ us-ethiopia-eritrea-emirates-insight-idUSKBN1KT1QX. See also Aaron Maasho, "UAE to Give Ethiopia $3 Billion in Aid and Investments," *Reuters*, June 16, 2018, https://www.reuters.com/article/ozabs-uk-ethiopia-emirates-idAFKBN1JC07G -OZABS.

94 Daniel Mumbere, "Eritrea President Discusses Regional Developments, Investment with UAE Crown Prince," *AfricaNews*, July 4, 2018, https://www.africanews.com /2018/07/04/eritrea-president-discusses-regional-developments-investment-with -uae-crown//.

95 Fick and Cornwell, "In Peace between Ethiopia and Eritrea."

96 Medhane Tadesse and John Young, "TPLF: Reform or Decline?," *Review of African Political Economy* 30, no. 97 (2003): 398.

97 "Eritrea's Statement at the Meeting of High - Level Officials of Red Sea and Gulf of Aden," *Madote*, April 22, 2019, http://www.madote.com/2019/04/eritreas-statement -at-meeting-of-high.html.

98 This preoccupation goes back to the more general sentiment in the Horn of Africa about the destabilizing effect of Arab actors dating back to the Cold War. See e.g. Aliboni, *The Red Sea Region*, chapter 5.

99 Jon Gambrell, "UAE Dismantles Eritrea Base as it Pulls Back After Yemen War," *AP News*, February 18, 2021, https://apnews.com/article/eritrea-dubai-only-on-ap -united-arab-emirates-east-africa-088f41c7d54d6a397398b2a825f5e45a.

100 See e.g. Stijn Mitzer and Joost Oliemans, "Secretive UAE Air Force Aircraft Deployed To War-Torn Ethiopia," *Oryx*, December 30, 2021, https://www .oryxspioenkop.com/2021/12/secretive-uae-air-force-aircraft.html.

101 "UAE Air Bridge Provides Military Support to Ethiopia Gov't," *Aljazeera*, November 25, 2021, https://www.aljazeera.com/news/2021/11/25/uae-air-bridge-provides -military-support-to-ethiopia-govt.

102 Chris Devonshire-Ellis, "Eritrea Joins The Belt and Road Initiative," Silk Road Briefing, November 28, 2021, accessed February 3, 2023, https://www. silkroadbriefing.com/news/2021/11/28/eritrea-joins-the-belt-and-road-initiative/.

103 Aggrey Mutambo, "China's Version of Mediation for the Horn of Africa," *The East African*, March 21, 2022, https://www.theeastafrican.co.ke/tea/news/east-africa/china-s-version-of-mediation-for-the-horn-of-africa-3754916.

104 Salem Solomon, "Russia-Eritrea Relations Grow with Planned Logistics Center," *Voice of America*, September 2, 2018, https://www.voanews.com/a/russia-eritrea-relations-grow-with-planned-logistics-center/4554680.html.

105 Jennifer Holleis and Kersten Knipp, "Sudan Snubs UN, Opens Arms to Russia," *Deutsche Welle*, April 21, 2022, https://www.dw.com/en/sudan-cold-shoulder-for-un-warm-embrace-for-russia/a-61526111.

106 Angelo Gardarello, "Russia Supplies Eritrea with New Drones-Kamikazes, and Could Open a Base on the Red Sea," *Meridiano 42*, May 8, 2022, https://www.meridiano42.it/en/2022/05/08/russia-supplies-eritrea-with-new-drones-kamikazes-and-could-open-a-base-on-the-red-sea/.

107 Recently, president Afwerki's official diplomatic visits have often been substituted by delegations headed by the country's foreign minister Osman Saleh Mohammed and presidential advisor and PFDJ's head of political affairs Yemane Gebreab.

Conclusion

1 Aljazeera, "'Odious acts': 7 Djibouti Soldiers Killed in Armed Group Attack," October 8, 2022; Eelco Kessels, Tracey Durner, and Matthew Schwartz, "Violent Extremism and Instability in the Greater Horn of Africa: An Examination of Drivers and Responses," Global Center of Cooperative Security, April 2016, 9–13.

BIBLIOGRAPHY

"'A New Era': Saudi Arabia's MBS in Turkey as Nations Mend Ties." *Aljazeera*. June 22, 2022. https://www.aljazeera.com/news/2022/6/22/saudi-crown-prince-mbs-visits -turkey-as-countries-normalise-ties.

Abir, Mordechai. *Ethiopia and the Red Sea: The Rise and Decline of the Solomonic Dynasty and Muslim European Rivalry in the Region*. Abingdon: Frank Cass, 1980.

Adam, Hussein M. "Formation and Recognition of New States: Somaliland in Contrast to Eritrea." *Review of African Political Economy* 21, no. 59 (1994): 21–38.

Adam, Hussein M., and Richard Ford, eds. *Mending Rips in the Sky: Options for Somali Communities in the 21st Century*. Lawrenceville: Red Sea Press, 1997.

Adegbola, Oluseyi, Jacqueline Skarda-Mitchell, and Sherice Gearhart. "Everything's Negative about Nigeria: A Study of US Media Reporting on Nigeria." *Global Media and Communication* 14, no. 1 (2018): 47–63.

Adhanom, Tedros. *Ethiopia's Foreign Policy: Regional Integration and International Priorities*. Africa Program Meeting Transcript. London: Chatham House, 2015.

"Africa Rising." *The Economist*. December 3, 2011. https://www.economist.com/leaders /2011/12/03/africa-rising.

Agathangelou, Anna M., and L. H. M. Ling. *Transforming World Politics: From Empire to Multiple Worlds*. Abingdon: Routledge, 2009.

"Ahlu-Sunna Waljama'a: State Minister and Goobaale Are Leading Soldiers Fighting against Us." *Goobjoog*. February 13, 2015. https://goobjoog.com/english/ahlu-sunna -waljamaa-state-minister-and-goobaale-are-leading-soldiers-fighting-against-us/.

Ahmad, Aisha. "The Security Bazaar: Business Interests and Islamist Power in Civil War Somalia." *International Security* 39, no. 3 (2014/15): 89–117.

Ahmed, Guled. "As Farmaajo Digs In with Qatari Backing, Somalia's Election Crisis Grows Worse." Middle East Institute. February 9, 2021. https://www.mei.edu/publications/ farmaajo-digs-qatari-backing-somalias-election-crisis-grows-worse.

Ahmed, Guled. "Far from a Benefactor, the Turkish Government is Exploiting Somalia's Fragility." Middle East Institute. October 21, 2021. https://www.mei.edu/publications/ far-benefactor-turkish-government-exploiting-somalias-fragility.

Akwei, Ismail. "The Real Story of the Last Days of Emperor Haile Selassie of Ethiopia - Face2Face Africa." Face2Face Africa. Accessed January 8, 2023. https://face2faceafrica .com/article/the-real-story-of-the-last-days-of-emperor-haile-selassie-of-ethiopia.

al-Anani, Khalil. "Upended Path: The Rise and Fall of Egypt's Muslim Brotherhood." *The Middle East Journal* 69, no. 4 (2015): 527–43.

Albrecht, Peter, and Maria-Louise Clausen. *Fragile States*. Copenhagen: Danish Institute for International Studies, 2022.

Alghoul, Diana. "Somalia Rejects Secret $80m Bribe to Stand against Qatar in Ongoing Boycott." *The New Arab*. June 12, 2017. https://www.newarab.com/news/revealed -somalia-rejects-secret-80m-qatar-blockade-bribe.

Ali, Nimo-ilhan. *Going on Tahriib: The Causes and Consequences of Somali Youth Migration to Europe*. London: Rift Valley Institute, 2016.

Aliboni, Roberto. *The Red Sea Region: Local Actors and the Superpowers*. Abingdon: Routledge, 1985.

Allison, Graham T. "Conceptual Models and the Cuban Missile Crisis." *American Political Science Review* 63, no. 3 (September 1969): 689–718.

Allison, Graham T. *Essence of Decision: Explaining the Cuban Missile Crisis*. Boston: Little, Brown, and Co., 1971.

Almezaini, Khalid S., and Jean-Marc Rickli, eds. *The Small Gulf States: Foreign and Security Policies before and after the Arab Spring*. London: Routledge, 2017.

Alushula, Patrick. "US Sanction Waiver Saves Safaricom Ethiopia Deal." *Business Daily*. June 22, 2021. https://www.businessdailyafrica.com/bd/corporate/companies/us -sanction-waiver-saves-safaricom-ethiopia-deal-3445994.

Anant, Victor. "The Colony that Rejected Freedom." *Daily Herald*. June 29, 1960.

Anna, Cara. "Ethiopia Armed Group Says It Has Alliance with Tigray Forces." *AP News*. August 11, 2021. https://apnews.com/article/africa-only-on-ap-ethiopia-b280e6622d6 6b7e7f9b12cd1d0041ae8.

Ansah, Tony. "The Narrative of Africa Rising." October 23, 2018. https://www .sdgphilanthropy.org/The-Narrative-of-Africa-Rising.

"Arab States Issue 13 Demands to End Qatar-Gulf Crisis." *Aljazeera*. July 12, 2017. https:// www.aljazeera.com/news/2017/7/12/arab-states-issue-13-demands-to-end-qatar-gulf -crisis.

Armijo, Leslie Elliott, and Saori N. Katada, eds. *The Financial Statecraft of Emerging Powers Shield and Sword in Asia and Latin America*. Basingstoke: Palgrave MacMillan, 2014.

Ayieko, Odindo. "Russia Finalizes Plans to Set Up Naval Base in Somaliland." *EABW News*. January 31, 2020. https://www.busiweek.com/russia-finalizes-plans-to-set-up -naval-base-in-somaliland/.

Ayoob, Mohammed. "Inequality and Theorizing in International Relations: The Case for Subaltern Realism." *International Studies Review* 4, no. 3 (2002): 27–48.

Bahadur, Jay. *Following the Money: The Use of the Hawala Remittance System in the Yemen-Somalia Arms Trade*. Geneva: The Global Initiative against Transnational Organized Crime, 2020.

Bailey, Rob, and Laura Wellesley. *Chokepoints and Vulnerabilities in Global Food Trade*. London: Chatham House, 2017.

Baldwin, William A. *Economic Statecraft*. Princeton: Princeton University Press, 1985.

Baloyi, Tintswalo. "What on Earth is Djibouti Doing?" *CAJ News Africa*. March 19, 2019. https://allafrica.com/stories/201903200216.html.

Baracuhy, Braz. "Geo-economics as a Dimension of Grand Strategy: Notes on the Concept and its Evolution." In *Geo-economics and Power Politics in the 21st Century: The Revival of Economic Statecraft*, edited by Mikael Wigell, Sören Scholvin, and Mika Aaltola, 14–27. Abingdon: Routledge, 2019.

Baran, Paul A. *The Political Economy of Growth*. New York: Monthly Review Press, 1957.

Barnes, Cedric, and Harun Hassan. "The Rise and Fall of Mogadishu's Islamic Courts." *Journal of Eastern African Studies* 1, no. 2 (2017): 151–60.

Bassi, Marco. "The Relativistic Attitude in Development: Reflections on the Implementation of the Ethiopian Multinational Constitution." *Archivio Antropologico Mediterraneo* 22, no. 21 (2) (2019). http://journals.openedition.org/aam/2319.

Bayart, Jean-François. *The State in Africa: The Politics of the Belly*. London: Longman, 1993.

Bayart, Jean-François, and Stephen Ellis. "Africa in the World: A History of Extraversion." *African Affairs* 99, no. 395 (2000): 217–67.

Bell, J. Bowyer. *The Horn of Africa: Strategic Magnet in the Seventies*. New York: National Strategy Information Center, 1973.

Bergman, Ronen, and David D. Kirkpatrick. "With Guns, Cash and Terrorism, Gulf States Vie for Power in Somalia." *The New York Times*. July 22, 2019. https://www.nytimes.com/2019/07/22/world/africa/somalia-qatar-uae.html.

Berhane, Daniel. "Ethiopia: Al-Amoudi Pledges 1.5 Billion Br. for Renaissance Dam." *Horn Affairs*. September 12, 2011. https://hornaffairs.com/2011/09/12/ethiopia-al-amoudi-pledges-1-5-billion-br-for-renaissance-dam/.

Berhe, Aregawi. *A Political History of the Tigray People's Liberation Front (1975–1991): Revolt, Ideology and Mobilisation in Ethiopia*. Los Angeles: Tsehai, 2009.

Berhe, Aregawi. "The Origins of the Tigray People's Liberation Front." *African Affairs* 103, no. 413 (2004): 569–92.

Berridge, Geoff R., and Alan James. *A Dictionary of Diplomacy*. Basingstoke: Palgrave MacMillan, 2003.

Bezabeh, Samson A. "Citizenship and the Logic of Sovereignty in Djibouti." *African Affairs* 110, no. 441 (2011): 587–606.

Blackwill, Robert D., and Jennifer M. Harris. *War by Other Means: Geoeconomics and Statecraft*. Cambridge, MA: Harvard University Press, 2016.

Blanchard, Jean-Marc F., and Norrin M. Ripsman. "A Political Theory of Economic Statecraft." *Foreign Policy Analysis* 4, no. 4 (October 2008): 371–98.

Bøås, Morten, and Kathleen M. Jennings. "Insecurity and Development: The Rhetoric of the 'Failed State'." *European Journal of Development Research* 17, no. 3 (2006): 385–95.

Bogale, Samuel. "Ethiopia Recalls All Diplomats but Ambassadors, Finance Heads." *Fortune*. July 24, 2021. https://addisfortune.news/ethiopia-recalls-all-diplomats-but-ambassadors-finance-heads/.

British Embassy Mogadishu. "UK Ambassador Launches Construction of the Hargeisa Bypass." May 4, 2021. https://www.gov.uk/government/news/uk-ambassador-launches-construction-of-the-hargeisa-bypass.

Brown, William. "A Question of Agency: Africa in International Politics." *Third World Quarterly* 33, no. 10 (2012): 1889–908.

Brown, William, and Sophie Harman, eds. *African Agency in International Politics*. Abingdon: Routledge, 2013.

Browning, Christopher S. *Constructivism, Narrative and Foreign Policy Analysis: A Case Study of Finland*. Frankfurt am Main: Peter Lang, 2008.

Bull, Hedley. *The Anarchical Society: A Study of Order in World Politics*. London: Macmillan, 1977.

Bunce, Mel, Suzanne Franks, and Chris Paterson, eds. *Africa's Media Image in the 21st Century From the "Heart of Darkness" to "Africa Rising"*. Abingdon: Routledge, 2017.

Cafiero, Giorgio. "The UAE's Expansionist Agenda in Yemen Is Playing Out on Socotra." *DAWN MENA*. April 8, 2022. https://dawnmena.org/the-uaes-expansionist-agenda-in-yemen-is-playing-out-on-socotra/.

Cannon, Brendon J. "Foreign State Influence and Somalia's 2017 Presidential Election: An Analysis." *Bildhaan: An International Journal of Somali Studies* 18, no. 1 (2019): 20–49.

Cannon, Brendon J., and Federico Donelli. "Asymmetric Alliances and High Polarity: Evaluating Regional Security Complexes in the Middle East and Horn of Africa." *Third World Quarterly* 41, no. 3 (2019): 505–24.

Carmichael, Tim. "Bureaucratic Literacy, Oral Testimonies, and the Study of Twentieth-Century Ethiopian History." *Journal of African Cultural Studies* 18, no. 1 (2006): 23–42.

Carr, Edward H. *The Twenty Years' Crisis, 1919–1939: An Introduction to the Study of International Relations*. 2nd ed. London: Macmillan, 1946.

Caulk, Richard. *Between Jaws of Hyenas: A Diplomatic History of Ethiopia (1876-1896)*. Wiesbaden: Harrassowitz Verlag, 2002.

Center for International Security and Cooperation. "Al Ittihad Al Islamiya." Stanford University. Accessed January 13, 2023. https://cisac.fsi.stanford.edu/mappingmilitants/profiles/al-ittihad-al-islamiya.

Central Intelligence Agency. *The Aden Treaty: Implications for Warning*. Washington: Strategic Warning Staff, 1981. https://www.cia.gov/readingroom/docs/CIA-RDP83B01027R000300150004-8.pdf.

Chang, Ha-Joon, and Jostein Hauge. "The Concept of 'Developmental State' in Ethiopia." In *The Oxford Handbook of the Ethiopian Economy*, edited by Fantu Cheru, Christopher Cramer, and Arkebe Oqubay, 824–41. Oxford: Oxford University Press, 2019.

Cheru, Fantu, Christopher Cramer, and Arkebe Oqubay. "Introduction." In *The Oxford Handbook of the Ethiopian Economy*, edited by Fantu Cheru, Christopher Cramer, and Arkebe Oqubay, 3–16. Oxford: Oxford University Press, 2019.

"China's EximBank Withholds $339 Mln in Funds to Ethiopia, Cites Debt Repayment Pressures." *Reuters*. August 16, 2021. https://www.reuters.com/article/ethiopia-debt-idAFL8N2PN47O.

Chipaike, Ronald, and Matarutse H. Knowledge. "The Question of African Agency in International Relations." *Cogent Social Sciences* 4, no. 1 (2018). https://doi.org/10.1080/23311886.2018.1487257.

Chong, Alan, and Matthias Maass. "Introduction: The Foreign Policy Power of Small States." *Cambridge Review of International Affairs* 23, no. 3 (2010): 381–2.

Clapham, Christopher. *Africa and the International System: The Politics of State Survival*. Cambridge: Cambridge University Press, 1996.

Clapham, Christopher. "The Ethiopian Developmental State." *Third World Quarterly* 39, no. 6 (2018): 1151–65.

Clapham, Christopher. "The 'Longue Durée' of the African State." *African Affairs* 93, no. 372 (1994): 433–9.

Clarke, Jeremy. "Eritrea Rejects U.N. Report It Backs Somali Rebels." *Reuters*. March 16, 2010. https://www.reuters.com/article/idUSLDE62F297.

Clover, Charles, and Michael Peel. "China Tries Chequebook Diplomacy in Southeast Asia." *Financial Times*. November 7, 2016. https://www.ft.com/content/abb35db2-a4cc-11e6-8b69-02899e8bd9d1.

"Commentary: The Myth about China's 'Chequebook Diplomacy'." *Xinhua*. May 12, 2017. http://www.xinhuanet.com/english/2017-05/12/c_136277532.htm.

Compagnon, Daniel. "The Somali Opposition Fronts: Some Comments and Questions." *Horn of Africa* 13, no. 1–2 (1990): 29–54.

Connell, Dan. "Inside the EPLF: The Origins of the 'People's Party' & Its Role in the Liberation of Eritrea." *Review of African Political Economy* 28, no. 89 (2001): 345–64.

Connell, Dan, and Tom Killion. *Historical Dictionary of Eritrea*. 2nd ed. Plymouth: Scarecrow, 2011.

"Constitution of the Federal Democratic Republic of Ethiopia." December 8, 1994. Accessed January 11, 2023. https://www.refworld.org/docid/3ae6b5a84.html.

Coulibaly, Brahima Sangafowa. "In Defense of the 'Africa Rising' Narrative." *Africa in Focus*. June 27, 2017, https://www.brookings.edu/blog/africa-in-focus/2017/06/27/in-defense-of-the-africa-rising-narrative/.

Cowell, Alan. "Ethiopian Drive against Somalia Bogs Down." *The New York Times.* October 8, 1982. Section A, Page 1.

Dahir, Abdinor Hassan. *Foreign Engagements in the Horn of Africa: Diversifying Risks and Maximising Gains.* Istanbul: TRT World Research Centre, 2019.

Davis, Patricia A. *The Art of Economic Persuasion: Positive Incentives and German Economic Diplomacy.* Ann Arbor: University of Michigan Press, 1999.

de Mesquita, Bruce Bueno. "Foreign Policy Analysis and Rational Choice Models." *Oxford Research Encyclopedia of International Studies.* January 11, 2018. Accessed December 30, 2022. https://oxfordre.com/internationalstudies/view/10.1093/acrefore /9780190846626.001.0001/acrefore-9780190846626-e-395.

de Regt, Marina, and Medareshaw Tafesse. "Deported before Experiencing the Good Side of Migration: Ethiopians Returning from Saudi Arabia." *African and Black Diaspora: An International Journal 9*, no. 2 (2015): 228–42.

de Waal, Alex. *The Real Politics of the Horn of Africa: Money, War and the Business of Power.* Cambridge: Polity, 2015.

"Death Toll Hits 120 from 3-Day Fighting in Central Somalia." *Garowe Online.* October 26, 2021. https://www.garoweonline.com/en/news/somalia/death-toll-hits-120-from-3 -day-fighting-in-central-somalia.

"Declaration of National Commitment (Arta Declaration)." May 5, 2000. Accessed January 16, 2023. https://www.peaceagreements.org/viewmasterdocument/1682.

Deng, Francis Mading. *War of Visions: Conflict Identities in Sudan.* Washington: The Brookings Institution, 1995.

Desplat, Patrick, and Terje Østebø, eds. *Muslims in Ethiopia: The Christian Legacy, Identity Politics and Islamic Reformism.* New York: Palgrave Macmillan, 2013.

Devonshire-Ellis, Chris. "Eritrea Joins The Belt and Road Initiative." Silk Road Briefing. November 28, 2021. Accessed February 3, 2023. https://www.silkroadbriefing.com/ news/2021/11/28/eritrea-joins-the-belt-and-road-initiative/.

Dittmer, Jason, and Joanne Sharp, eds. *Geopolitics: An Introductory Reader.* London: Routledge, 2014.

Donelli, Federico. *Turkey in Africa: Turkey's Strategic Involvement in Sub-Saharan Africa.* London: IB Tauris, 2021.

Donelli, Federico, and Ariel Gonzalez-Levaggi. "Crossing Roads: The Middle East's Security Engagement in the Horn of Africa." *Global Change, Peace & Security 33*, no. 1 (2021): 45–60.

Donham, Donald L. "Old Abyssinia and the New Ethiopian Empire: Themes in Social History." In *The Southern Marches of Imperial Ethiopia: Essays in History and Social Anthropology*, edited by Donald L. Donham and Wendy James, 3–48. Cambridge: Cambridge University Press, 1986.

Doty, Roxanne Lynn. "Foreign Policy as Social Construction: A Postpositivist Analysis of U.S. Counterinsurgency Policy in the Philippines." *International Studies Quarterly 37*, no. 3 (September 1993): 297–320.

"DP World Inaugurates New Container Terminal at Berbera." *The Maritime Executive.* June 28, 2021. https://maritime-executive.com/article/dp-world-inaugurates-new -container-terminal-at-berbera.

"DP World and Somaliland Open New Container Terminal in Berbera Port." *Port Technology.* June 24, 2021. https://www.porttechnology.org/news/dp-world-and -somaliland-open-new-container-terminal-in-berbera-port/.

Drezner, Daniel W. *The Sanctions Paradox: Economic Statecraft and International Relations.* Cambridge: Cambridge University Press, 1999.

Dunn, Kevin C., and Timothy M. Shaw, eds. *Africa's Challenge to International Relations Theory*. London: Palgrave Macmillan, 2001.

Ehteshami, Anoushiravan, and Emma C. Murphy. *The International Politics of the Red Sea*. Abingdon: Routledge, 2011.

Elbagir, Nima, Barbara Arvanitidis, Tamara Qiblawi, Gianluca Mezzofiore, Mohammed Abo Al Gheit, and Darya Tarasova. "Russia is Plundering Gold in Sudan to Boost Putin's War Effort in Ukraine." *CNN*. July 29, 2022. https://edition.cnn.com/2022/07/29/africa/sudan-russia-gold-investigation-cmd-intl/index.html.

Embassy of Ethiopia. "WB, IMF Pledge Over $5b For Ethiopia's Economic Reform." December 11, 2019. https://ethiopianembassy.org/wb-imf-pledge-over-5b-for-ethiopias-economic-reform-december-11-2019/.

Embassy Nairobi. "Somalia - Political Perspectives from Dubai." Wikileaks Cable: 08NAIROBI2619_a. November 20, 2008. https://wikileaks.org/plusd/cables/08NAIROBI2619_a.html.

Encyclopaedia Britannica Online, s.v. "Bab el-Mandeb Strait." Accessed May 10, 2022. https://www.britannica.com/place/Bab-El-Mandeb-Strait.

Ennis, Crystal A. "Reading Entrepreneurial Power in Small Gulf States: Qatar and the UAE." *International Journal* 73, no. 4 (2018): 573–95.

"Erdogan Calls on UAE Businesses to Invest in Turkey." *France 24*. February 15, 2022. https://www.france24.com/en/live-news/20220215-erdogan-calls-on-uae-businesses-to-invest-in-turkey.

"Erdogan Says Saudi Crown Prince MBS to Visit Turkey Next Week." *Aljazeera*. June 17, 2022. https://www.aljazeera.com/news/2022/6/17/erdogan-says-saudi-crown-prince-mbs-to-visit-turkey-next-week.

"Erdogan Says Somalia Invited Turkey to Explore for Oil Offshore." *Aljazeera*. January 21, 2020. https://www.aljazeera.com/economy/2020/1/21/erdogan-says-somalia-invited-turkey-to-explore-for-oil-offshore.

"Eritrea: Another Venue for the Iran-Israel Rivalry." *Stratfor*. December 11, 2012. https://worldview.stratfor.com/article/eritrea-another-venue-iran-israel-rivalry.

"Eritrea: President Isaias Arrives in Tehran on Official Working Visit to Iran." May 18, 2008. Accessed January 25, 2023. https://allafrica.com/stories/200805191594.html.

"Eritrea Condemns New U.S. Sanctions." *Reuters*. November 13, 2021. https://www.reuters.com/article/uk-ethiopia-conflict-idUKKBN2HY09G.Eritrean Ministry of Information.

"Eritrea's Statement at the Meeting of High - Level Officials of Red Sea and Gulf of Aden." *Madote*. April 22, 2019. http://www.madote.com/2019/04/eritreas-statement-at-meeting-of-high.html.

Erlich, Haggai. *Ethiopia and the Middle East*. Boulder: Lynne Rienner, 1994.

Erlich, Haggai. *Ras Alula and the Scramble for Africa: A Political Biography: Ethiopia & Eritrea 1875–1897*. Lawrenceville: Red Sea Press, 1996.

Erlich, Haggai. *Saudi Arabia and Ethiopia: Islam, Christianity, and Politics Entwined*. Boulder: Lynne Rienner, 2007.

Erlich, Haggai. *The Struggle over Eritrea*. Stanford: Hoover Institution, 1983.

Eshete, Tibebe. "The Root Causes of Political Problems in the Ogaden, 1942–1960." *Northeast African Studies* 13, no. 1 (1991): 9–28.

"Ethiopia Claims Victory over Security Council's Support for African Mediation in Nile Dam Row." *The Arab Weekly*. July 10, 2021. https://thearabweekly.com/ethiopia-claims-victory-over-security-councils-support-african-mediation-nile-dam-row.

"Ethiopia to Get $140 Mln in Loans from Saudi Arabia." *Reuters*. December 19, 2019. https://www.reuters.com/article/ethiopia-economy-idUKL8N28T2EG.

"Ethiopia Recalls Dozens of Diplomats, Closes Consulates in Various Countries." *Addis Standard*. July 8, 2021. https://addisstandard.com/breaking-ethiopia-recalls-dozens-of -diplomats-closes-consulates-in-various-countries/.

"Ethiopian Constitution of 1931." July 16, 1931. Accessed January 4, 2023. https://www .abyssinialaw.com/laws/constitutions/the-1931-ethiopian-constitution-english-version /download.

"Ethiopian Khat Triggers Farmaajo's Dispute with PM Roble Ahead of Nairobi Trip." *Garowe Online*. August 8. 2021. https://www.garoweonline.com/en/news /somalia/ethiopian-khat-triggers-farmaajo-s-dispute-with-pm-roble-ahead-of -nairobi-trip.

"EXCLUSIVE: Top Officials behind Missing Soldiers in Eritrea Exposed." *Garowe Online*. June 13, 2021. https://www.garoweonline.com/en/editorial/exclusive-top-officials -behind-missing-soldiers-in-eritrea-exposed.

Federal Research Division. *Ethiopia: A Country Study*. 4th ed. Washington: Library of Congress, 1993.

Feltman, Jeffrey. "A Perspective on the Ethiopian-U.S. Relationship after a Year of Conflict." United States Special Envoy for the Horn of Africa. United States Department of State. November 1, 2021. https://www.state.gov/a-perspective-on-the -ethiopian-u-s-relationship-after-a-year-of-conflict/.

Fick, Maggie, and Alexander Cornwell. "In Peace between Ethiopia and Eritrea, UAE Lends a Helping Hand." *Reuters*. August 8, 2018. https://www.reuters.com/article/us -ethiopia-eritrea-emirates-insight-idUSKBN1KT1QX.

Fisher, Jonathan, and David M. Anderson. "Authoritarianism and the Securitization of Development in Africa." *International Affairs* 91, no. 1 (January 2015): 131–51.

Fox, Annette Baker. *The Power of Small States: Diplomacy in World War II*. Chicago: University of Chicago Press, 1959.

Frank, Andre Gunder. *The Development of Underdevelopment*. New York: Monthly Review Press, 1966.

Fraser-Rahim, Muhammad. "In Somalia, Iran Is Replicating Russia's Afghan Strategy." *Foreign Policy*. July 17, 2020. https://foreignpolicy.com/2020/07/17/iran-aiding-al -shabab-somalia-united-states/.

French, John R. P., and Bertram Raven. "The Bases of Social Power." In *Studies in Social Power*, edited by Dorwin Cartwright, 259–69. Ann Arbor: University of Michigan Press, 1959.

Gaas, Mohamed Husein. "Qatari Involvement in the Horn of Africa: A Kingmaker and a Successful Mediator?" In *Religion, Prestige and Windows of Opportunity?*, edited by Stig Jarle Hansen, 53–60. Aas: Norwegian University of Life Sciences, Noragric Working Paper no. 48, 2013.

Gaffey, Conor. "Eritrea Becomes Latest African Nation to Side with Saudi Arabia in Spat with Qatar." *Newsweek*. June 14, 2017. https://www.newsweek.com/qatar-crisis-eritrea -saudi-arabia-625356.

Gallagher, Kevin P. "Yuan Diplomacy." *Aljazeera*. February 29, 2012. https://www.aljazeera .com/opinions/2012/2/29/yuan-diplomacy/.

Gambrell, John. "Mysterious Air Base Being Built on Volcanic Island Off Yemen." *AP News*. May 25, 2021. https://apnews.com/article/mysterious-air-base-volcanic-island-yemen -c8cb2018c07bb5b63e1a43ff706b007b.

Gambrell, Jon. "UAE-Backed Yemen Leader Says His Troops at Island Air Base." *AP News*. June 15, 2021. https://apnews.com/article/yemen-middle-east-business-628ae4a2d20 e074e7e5f43fda2df46b6.

Gambrell, Jon. "UAE Dismantles Eritrea Base as it Pulls Back after Yemen War." *AP News.* February 18, 2021. https://apnews.com/article/eritrea-dubai-only-on-ap-united-arab -emirates-east-africa-088f41c7d54d6a397398b2a825f5e45a.

Gardarello, Angelo. "Russia Supplies Eritrea with New Drones-Kamikazes, and Could Open a Base on the Red Sea." *Meridiano 42.* May 8, 2022. https://www.meridiano42.it/ en/2022/05/08/russia-supplies-eritrea-with-new-drones-kamikazes-and-could-open-a -base-on-the-red-sea/.

Gause III, F. Gregory. *Beyond Sectarianism: New Middle East Cold War.* Doha: Brookings Doha Center, 2014.

Gebre, Samuel, and Alonso Soto. "Ethiopia in Talks to Restructure $1 Billion More of Debt." Bloomberg. July 7, 2021. https://www.bloomberg.com/news/articles/2021-07-07 /ethiopia-in-negotiations-to-restructure-1-billion-more-of-debt-kqte6iuj.

Gebreluel, Goitom. "The Tripartite Alliance Destabilising the Horn of Africa." *Aljazeera.* May 10, 2021. https://www.aljazeera.com/opinions/2021/5/10/the-tripatriate-alliance -that-is-destabilisng-the-horn-of-africa.

"General Tahalil: Most of Eritrean-Trained Soldiers Returned to Somalia." *Garowe Online.* January 1, 2023. https://www.garoweonline.com/en/news/somalia/general-tahalil -most-of-eritrean-trained-soldiers-returned-to-somalia.

Getachew, Addis. "Turkey Seeks Preferential Trade Deal with Ethiopia." *Anadolu Agency.* February 15, 2021. https://www.aa.com.tr/en/economy/turkey-seeks-preferential-trade -deal-with-ethiopia/2145955.

Giraudy, Agustina, Eduardo Moncada, and Richard Snyder. "Subnational Analysis: Theoretical and Methodological Contributions to Comparative Politics." *Revista de Ciencia Política* 41, no. 1 (2021): 1–34.

GlobalSecurity.org. "Bab al-Mandab Strait." Accessed May 11, 2022. https://www .globalsecurity.org/military/world/yemen/bab-al-mandab.htm.

Gogwilt, Christopher. *The Fiction of Geopolitics: Afterimages of Culture, from Wilkie Collins to Alfred Hitchcock.* Stanford: Stanford University Press, 2000.

Goldstein, Joshua S., and John R. Freeman. "U.S.-Soviet-Chinese Relations: Routine, Reciprocity, or Rational Expectations?" *The American Political Science Review* 85, no. 1 (March 1991): 17–35.

Goodwin, Stephanie A. "Impression Formation in Asymmetrical Power Relationships: Does Power Corrupt Absolutely?" Master's Thesis, University of Massachusetts Amherst, 1993. https://scholarworks.umass.edu/cgi/viewcontent.cgi?article=3371&context=theses.

Gordon, Murray. *Slavery in the Arab World.* New York: New Amsterdam, 1989.

Goth, Goth Mohamed. "Somaliland: President Silanyo Concludes 8 Days Working Visit to the U.A.E." *Somaliland Current.* June 14, 2015. https://www.somalilandcurrent.com/ somalilandpresident-silanyo-concludes-8-days-working-visit-to-the-u-a-e/.

GRAIN. *SEIZED! The 2008 Land Grab for Food and Financial Security.* Briefing. Rome: GRAIN, 2008. https://grain.org/article/entries/93-seized-the-2008-landgrab-for-food -and-financial-security.

Gray, Colin S. *The Geopolitics of Super Power.* Lexington: University Press of Kentucky, 1988.

Grimm, Sonja, Nicolas Lemay-Hébert, and Olivier Nay. "'Fragile States': Introducing a Political Concept." *Third World Quarterly* 35, no. 2 (2014): 197–209.

Grygiel, Jakub J. *Great Powers and Geopolitical Change.* Baltimore: Johns Hopkins University Press, 2006.

Guerrero, Laura, K. Peter A. Andersen, and Walid A. Afifi. *Close Encounters: Communication in Relationships.* 5th ed. Thousand Oaks: SAGE, 2018.

Hagmann, Tobias. *Stabilization, Extraversion and Political Settlements in Somalia*. London: Rift Valley Institute, 2016.

Hagmann, Tobias. "The Somali Region of Ethiopia Must Write Their Own Narrative." *The Africa Report*. March 11, 2021. https://www.theafricareport.com/71431/the-somali -region-of-ethiopia-must-write-their-own-narrative/.

Haile, Semere. "The Origins and Demise of the Ethiopia-Eritrea Federation." *Issue: A Journal of Opinion* 15 (1987): 9–17.

Handel, Michael I. *Weak States in the International System*. 2nd ed. London: Frank Cass, 1990.

Hanreider, Wolfram F. "Dissolving International Politics: Reflections on the Nation-State." *American Political Science Review* 72, no. 4 (December 1978): 1276–87.

Harb, Malak, and Elias Meseret. "Qatar Pulls All Its Troops from Djibouti-Eritrea Border." *AP News*. June 14, 2017. https://apnews.com/article/243ba2f8ef5841a5a2eeeb3 c9e6edccf.

Hasan, Mohamed-Rashid S., and Salada M. Robleh. "Islamic Revival and Education in Somalia." In *Educational Strategies among Muslims in the Context of Globalization: Some National Case Studies*, edited by Holger Daun and Geoffrey Walford, 141–63. Leiden: Brill, 2004.

Hasan, Yusuf Fadl. "Some Aspects of the Arab Slave Trade from the Sudan, 7th-19th Century." *Sudan Notes and Records* 58 (1977): 85–16.

Hassan, Mohamed Olad. "Islamic Leader Urges Greater Somalia." *AP News*. November 18, 2006. https://www.hiiraan.com/news2/2006/nov/islamic_leader_urges__greater _somalia__.aspx.

Hassan, Mohamed Olad. "Somalia Releases Nearly $10M Seized from UAE Plane Four Years Ago." *Voice of America*. May 19, 2022. https://www.voanews.com/a/somalia -releases-nearly-10m-seized-from-uae-plane-four-years-ago/6580817.html#:~:text =The%20Somali%20government%20has%20released,a%20low%20point%20ever %20since.

Hellyer, Hisham A., and Ziya Meral. "Will the Page Turn on Turkish-Egyptian Relations?" Commentary." Carnegie Endowment for International Peace. March 19, 2021. Accessed January 13, 2023. https://carnegieendowment.org/2021/03/19/will-page-turn -on-turkish-egyptian-relations-pub-84124.

Heng, Yee-Kuang, and Syed Mohammed Ad'ha Aljunied. "Can Small States be More than Price Takers in Global Governance?" *Global Governance* 21, no. 3 (2015): 435–54.

Henneberg, Ingo. "Horn of Africa Cooperation: Mixed Responses to New Regional Bloc." *The Africa Report*. September 9, 2020. https://www.theafricareport.com/40994/horn-of -africa-cooperation-mixed-responses-to-new-regional-bloc/.

Henze, Paul B. *Layers of Time: A History of Ethiopia*. New York: Palgrave, 2000.

Hermann, Charles F., Charles W. Kegley Jr., and James N. Rosenau, eds. *New Directions in the Study of Foreign Policy*. London: Allen & Unwin, 1987.

Hermann, Margaret G. "How Decision Units Shape Foreign Policy: A Theoretical Framework." *International Studies Review* 3, no. 2 (2001): 47–81.

Hermann, Margaret G., and Charles F. Hermann. "Who Makes Foreign Policy Decisions and How: An Empirical Inquiry." *International Studies Quarterly* 33, no. 4 (December 1989): 361–87.

Hilsman, Roger. *The Politics of Policy Making in Defense and Foreign Affairs*. New York: Harper & Row, 1971.

Hirt, Nicole, and Abdulkader Saleh Mohammad. "The Lack of Political Space of the Eritrean Diaspora in the Arab Gulf and Sudan: Torn between an Autocratic Home and

Authoritarian Hosts." *Mashriq & Mahjar: Journal of Middle East Migration Studies* 5, no. 1 (2018): 101–26.

Hoehne, Markus V., Dereje Feyissa, Mahdi Abdile, and Clara Schmitz-Pranghe. *Differentiating the Diaspora: Reflections on Diasporic Engagement 'for Peace' in the Horn of Africa*. Working Paper 124. Halle: Max Planck Institute for Social Anthropology, 2010.

Holleis, Jennifer, and Kersten Knipp. "Sudan Snubs UN, Opens Arms to Russia." *Deutsche Welle*. April 21, 2022. https://www.dw.com/en/sudan-cold-shoulder-for-un-warm -embrace-for-russia/a-61526111.

Holt, Peter M. *The Mahdist Sudan, 1881–1898: A Study of Its Origins, Development, and Overthrow*. Oxford: Clarendon, 1958.

"Hopeless Africa." *The Economist*. May 11, 2000. https://www.economist.com/node/333429.

Hopkins, Terence K., and Immanuel Wallerstein. *World-Systems Analysis: Theory and Methodology*. Beverly Hills: Sage, 1982.

Houghton, David Patrick. "Reinvigorating the Study of Foreign Policy Decision Making: Toward a Constructivist Approach." *Foreign Policy Analysis* 3, no. 1 (January 2007): 24–45.

Houreld, Katherine. "Iranian-Supplied Arms Smuggled from Yemen into Somalia, Study Says." *Reuters*. November 10, 2021. https://www.reuters.com/world/iranian-supplied -arms-smuggled-yemen-into-somalia-study-says-2021-11-10/.

Howell, John. "Horn of Africa: Lessons from the Sudan Conflict." *International Affairs* 54, no. 3 (July 1978): 421–36.

Hudson, Valerie M. "Foreign Policy Analysis Beyond North America." In *Foreign Policy Analysis Beyond North America*, edited by Klaus Blummer and Valerie M. Hudson, 1–13. Boulder: Lynne Rienner, 2015.

Huliaras, Asteris, and Sophia Kalantzakos. "The Gulf States and the Horn of Africa: A New Hinterland?" *Middle East Policy* 24, no. 4 (2017): 63–73.

Imtilak Real Estate. "Saudi Arabia Tops the List of Foreign Investments in Turkey." July 5, 2022. Accessed January 18, 2023. https://www.imtilak.net/en/articles/saudi-arabia-tops -list-foreign-investments-turkey.

"إنفوغرافيك.. أهمية باب المندب ومخاطر تهديدات الحوثي." *Sky News Arabia*. July 26, 2018. https:// www.skynewsarabia.com/middle-east/1167884.

InfoMigrants. "Thousands of Ethiopian Migrants Stuck in Yemen, IOM." September 8, 2021. Accessed January 11, 2023. https://www.infomigrants.net/en/post/34921/ thousands-of-ethiopian-migrants-stuck-in-yemen-iom.

Ingebritsen, Christine, Iver Neumann, Sieglinde Gstöhl, and Jessica Beyer, eds. *Small States in International Relations*. Seattle: University of Washington Press, 2012.

International Crisis Group. *Intra-Gulf Competition in Africa's Horn: Lessening the Impact*. Brussels: International Crisis Group, 2019.

International Crisis Group. *Somalia and the Gulf Crisis*. Brussels: International Crisis Group, 2019.

International Crisis Group. *The United Arab Emirates in the Horn of Africa*. Brussels: International Crisis Group, 2018.

International Organization for Migration. "Funding Needed to Assist over 100,000 Ethiopian Migrants Returning from the Kingdom of Saudi Arabia." March 30, 2022. Accessed January 11, 2023. https://www.iom.int/news/funding-needed-assist-over -100000-ethiopian-migrants-returning-kingdom-saudi-arabia.

"Israel Using Eritrean Bases to Spy on Iran." *Ynet News*. November 12, 2012. https://www .ynetnews.com/articles/0,7340,L-4318720,00.html.

Issa-Salwe, Abdisalam M. *The Collapse of the Somali State: The Impact of the Colonial Legacy.* London: Haan Associates, 1996.

Ivudria, Godfrey. "Legal Tussle over Dolareh Port Escalates as DP World Demands Djibouti to Respect Concession Agreement." *EABW News,* December 7, 2020. https://www.busiweek.com/legal-tussle-over-dolareh-port-escalates-as-dp-world-demands-djibouti-to-respect-concession-agreement/.

Jackson, Donna R. "The Ogaden War and the Demise of Détente." *The Annals of the American Academy of Political and Social Science* 632, no. 1 (2010): 26–40.

Jackson, Robert H. *Quasi-States: Sovereignty, International Relations and the Third World.* Cambridge: Cambridge University Press, 1993.

James, Frank L. *The Unknown Horn of Africa: An Exploration from Berbera to the Leopard River.* London: George Philip & Son, 1890.

Jaycox, Edward V. K. "Sub-Saharan Africa: Development Performance and Prospects." *Journal of International Affairs* 45, no. 1 (1992): 85–95.

Jesman, Czeslaw. "Egyptian Invasion of Ethiopia." *African Affairs* 58, no. 230 (1959): 75–81.

Johnson, Keith. "Trump Reaches for Checkbook Diplomacy to Counter China." *Foreign Policy.* October 8, 2018. https://foreignpolicy.com/2018/10/08/trump-reaches-for-checkbook-diplomacy-to-counter-china/.

Jok, Jok Madut. *War and Slavery in Sudan.* Philadelphia: Pennsylvania Press, 2001.

Jones, Christopher M. "Bureaucratic Politics and Organizational Process Models." *Oxford Research Encyclopedia of International Studies.* November 20, 2017. Accessed December 30, 2022. https://oxfordre.com/internationalstudies/view/10.1093/acrefore/9780190846626.001.0001/acrefore-9780190846626-e-2.

Kabbani, Nader. "The Blockade on Qatar Helped Strengthen Its Economy, Paving the Way to Stronger Regional Integration." The Brookings Institution. January 19, 2021. https://www.brookings.edu/blog/order-from-chaos/2021/01/19/the-blockade-on-qatar-helped-strengthen-its-economy-paving-the-way-to-stronger-regional-integration/.

Käihkö, Ilmari. "Big Men Bargaining in African Conflicts." In *African Conflicts and Informal Power: Big Men and Networks,* edited by Mats Utas, 181–204. London: Zed Books, 2012.

Kaplan, Morton A. "An Introduction to the Strategy of Statecraft." *World Politics* 4, no. 4 (July 1952): 548–76.

Kaplan, Robert D. "Ethiopia's Problems Aren't Postcolonial." *Foreign Policy.* July 9, 2021. https://foreignpolicy.com/2021/07/09/ethiopias-problems-arent-postcolonial/.

Katzenstein, Peter. *Small States in World Markets: Industrial Policy in Europe.* Ithaca: Cornell University Press, 1985.

Keller, Edmond J. "The Politics of State Survival: Continuity and Change in Ethiopian Foreign Policy." *The Annals of the American Academy of Political and Social Science* 489, no. 1 (1987): 76–87.

Keohane, Robert. *After Hegemony: Cooperation and Discord in the World Political Economy.* Princeton: Princeton University Press, 1984.

Keohane, Robert, and Joseph S. Nye. *Power and Interdependence: World Politics in Transition.* New York: Little, Brown, and Co., 1977.

Kepel, Gilles. *Jihad, on the Trail of Political Islam.* Boston: Harvard University Press, 2002.

Khatib, Lina. "Qatar's Foreign Policy: The Limits of Pragmatism." *International Affairs* 89, no. 2 (2013): 417–31.

Kibreab, Gaim. *African Refugees: Reflections on the African Refugee Problem.* Trenton: Africa World Press 1985.

Killion, Tom. *Historical Dictionary of Eritrea*. London: Scarecrow, 1998.

Knorr, Klaus. *The Power of Nations: The Political Economy of International Relations*. New York: Basic Books, 1975.

Korany, Baghat, and Ali E. Hillal Dessouki. *The Foreign Policies of Arab States: The Challenge of Change*. 2nd ed. Boulder: Westview Press, 1991.

Kubálková, Vendulka, ed. *Foreign Policy in a Constructed World*. Armonk: M.E. Sharpe, 2001.

Kuschminder, Katie, Lisa Andersson, and Melissa Seigel. "Migration and Multidimensional Well-Being in Ethiopia: Investigating the Role of Migrants Destinations." *Migration and Development* 7, no. 3 (2018): 321–40.

Lauren, Paul Gordon. "Ultimata and Coercive Diplomacy." *International Studies Quarterly* 16, no. 2 (June 1972): 131–65.

Le Corre, Philippe. "What China's Checkbook Diplomacy Means for Europe." *Politico*. May 12, 2016. https://www.politico.eu/article/what-chinas-checkbook-diplomacy-means-for-europe/.

Le Sage, Andre. "Somalia: Sovereign Disguise for a Mogadishu Mafia." *Review of African Political Economy* 29, no. 91 (2002): 132–8.

Lecadet, Clara, and Medareshaw Tafesse Melkamu. "The Expulsion of Ethiopian Workers from Saudi Arabia (2013–2014): The Management of a Humanitarian and Political Crisis." *Annales d'Ethiopie* 31 (2016): 225–43.

Lefebvre, Jeffrey. "Red Sea Security and the Geopolitical-Economy of the Hanish Islands Dispute." *Middle East Journal* 52, no. 3 (1998): 367–385.

Lefebvre, Jeffrey A. *Arms for the Horn: U.S. Security Policy in the Horn of Africa, 1953–91*. Pittsburgh: University of Pittsburgh Press, 1991.

Lefebvre, Jeffrey A. "Middle East Conflicts and Middle Level Power Intervention in the Horn of Africa." *Middle East Journal* 50, no. 3 (1996): 387–404.

Legum, Colin, and Bill Lee. *Conflict in the Horn of Africa*. New York: Africana Publishing, 1977.

Leitner, Matthias E. "Conflict Resolution in Northern Ethiopia and Geopolitics." International Institute for Middle East and Balkan Studies. December 27, 2020. Accessed January 13, 2023. https://www.ifimes.org/en/researches/conflict-resolution-in-northern-ethiopia-and-geopolitics/4713#_ftnref3.

Lenin, Vladimir Ilyich. *Imperialism, the Highest Stage of Capitalism*. Petrograd: Life and Knowledge Publishers, 1917.

Levy, Jack S. "Deterrence and Coercive Diplomacy: The Contributions of Alexander George." *Political Psychology* 29, no. 4 (August 2008): 537–52.

Lewis, Aidan. "Egypt's Sisi Opens Naval Base Close to Border with Libya." *Reuters*. July 4, 2021. https://www.reuters.com/world/middle-east/egypts-sisi-opens-naval-base-close-border-with-libya-2021-07-03/.

Lewis, Ioan M. "The Somali Conquest of the Horn of Africa." *The Journal of African History* 1, no. 2 (1960): 213–30.

Li, Yi. "Saudi Arabia's Economic Diplomacy through Foreign Aid: Dynamics, Objectives and Mode." *Asian Journal of Middle Eastern and Islamic Studies* 13, no. 1 (2019): 110–22.

Ligle, Dr. "Bossaso: A Somali Success Story ...PICS." Somalia Online. September 4, 2009. https://www.somaliaonline.com/community/topic/34066-bossaso-a-somali-success-story-pics/?do=findComment&comment=511436.

Lipson, Charles. "International Cooperation in Economic and Security Affairs." *World Politics* 37, no. 1 (October 1984): 1–23.

Luttwak, Edward N. "From Geopolitics to Geo-Economics: Logic of Conflict, Grammar of Commerce." *The National Interest*, no. 20 (1990): 17–23.

Lynch, Colum. "U.N. Report Cites Outside Military Aid to Somalia's Islamic Forces." *The Washington Post*. November 15, 2006, A13.

Maasho, Aaron. "UAE to Give Ethiopia $3 Billion in Aid and Investments." *Reuters*. June 16, 2018. https://www.reuters.com/article/ozabs-uk-ethiopia-emirates -idAFKBN1JC07G-OZABS.

Machiavelli, Niccolo. *The Prince*. New York: Oxford University Press, 1984.

Madain Project. "as-Sahaba Mosque." Accessed January 21, 2023. https://madainproject .com/as_sahaba_mosque_(massawa).

Marchal, Roland, and Zakaria M. Sheikh. "Salafism in Somalia: Coping with Coercion, Civil War and Its Own Contradictions." *Islamic Africa* 6, no. 1–2 (2015): 135–63.

Marcus, Harold G. "The Foreign Policy of the Emperor Menelik 1896–1898: A Rejoinder." *The Journal of African History* 7, no. 1 (1966): 117–22.

Marqaati. *2016 State of Accountability in Somalia: Unrestrained Corruption*. Mogadishu: Marqaati, 2017.

Marqaati. *Five Years of Stasis: Accountability in Somalia*. Mogadishu: Marqaati, 2022.

Marqaati. *State of Accountability in Somalia in 2020: Towards Authoritarianism*. Mogadishu: Marqaati, 2020.

Marsai, Viktor, and Máté Szalai. "The 'Borderlandization' of the Horn of Africa in Relation to the Gulf Region, and the Effects on Somalia." *Journal of Borderlands Studies*, 2021. https://doi.org/10.1080/08365655.2021.1884118.

Martinez, Michael. "Top Somali Militant Killed in U.S. Operation, Pentagon Says." *CNN*. September 5, 2014. https://edition.cnn.com/2014/09/05/world/africa/somali-militant -killed/index.html.

Maru, Mehari Taddele. *A Regional Power in the Making: Ethiopian Diplomacy in the Horn of Africa*. Occasional Paper 261. Johannesburg: South African Institute of International Affairs, 2017.

Mason, Robert. "Small-State Aspirations to Middlepowerhood: The Cases of Qatar and the UAE." In *Unfulfilled Aspirations: Middle Power Politics in the Middle East*, edited by Adham Saouli, 157–82. Oxford: Oxford University Press, 2020.

Mason, Robert, and Simon Mabon, eds. *The Gulf States and the Horn of Africa: Interests, Influences and Instability*. Manchester: Manchester University Press, 2022.

Mastanduno, Michael. "Economic Statecraft, Interdependence, and National Security: Agendas for Research." *Security Studies* 9, no. 1–2 (1999): 288–316.

Mastanduno, Michael, David A. Lake, and G. John Ikenberry. "Toward a Realist Theory of State Action." *International Studies Quarterly* 33, no. 4 (December 1989): 457–74.

Mathisen, Trygve. *The Functions of Small States in the Strategies of the Great Powers*. Oslo: Universitetsforlaget, 1971.

Matthies, Volker. *The Siege of Magdala: The British Empire against the Emperor of Ethiopia*. Princeton: Markus Weiner, 2010.

Mattlin, Mikael, and Mikael Wigell. "Geoeconomics in the Context of Restive Regional Powers." *Asia Europe Journal* 14, no. 2 (2016): 125–34.

Maxwell, Daniel, and Merry Fitzpatrick. "The 2011 Somalia Famine: Context, Causes, and Complications." *Global Food Security* 1, no. 1 (2012): 5–12.

Mazrui, Ali A. "Black Africa and the Arabs." *Foreign Affairs* 53, no. 4 (1975): 725–42.

Mazrui, Ali A. "The Black Arabs in Comparative Perspective: The Political Sociology of Race Mixture." In *The Southern Sudan: The Problem of National Integration*, edited by Dunstan M. Wai, 47–81. London: Frank Cass, 1973.

McGowan, Patrick, Scarlet Cornelissen, and Philip Nel, eds. *Power, Wealth and Global Equity: An International Relations Textbook for Africa*. Cape Town: University of Cape Town Press, 2006.

Meester, Jos, Willem van den Berg, and Harry Verhoeven. *Riyal Politik: The Political Economy of Gulf Investments in the Horn of Africa*. CRU Report. Den Haag: Clingendael, Netherlands Institute of International Relations, 2018.

Mello, Alex, and Michael Knights. "West of Suez for The United Arab Emirates." *War on the Rocks*. September 2, 2016. https://warontherocks.com/2016/09/west-of-suez-for -the-united-arab-emirates/.

Menkhaus, Ken. "Governance without Government in Somalia: Spoilers, State Building, and the Politics of Coping." *International Security* 31, no. 3 (2007): 74–106.

Mesfin, Berouk. "Ethiopia's Role and Foreign Policy in the Horn of Africa." *International Journal of Ethiopian Studies* 6, no. 1/2 (2012): 87–113.

Mesfin, Berouk. *The Eritrea-Djibouti Border Dispute*. Situation Report. Addis Ababa: Institute for Security Studies, 2008.

Metaferia, Getachew. *Ethiopia and the United States: History, Diplomacy, and Analysis*. New York: Algora, 2009.

Michaud, Nelson. "Bureaucratic Politics and the Shaping of Policies: Can We Measure Pulling and Hauling Games?" *Canadian Journal of Political Science* 35, no. 2 (2002): 269–300.

"Midroc Investment Group to Beef up Ethiopia's Edible Oil Processing Capacity with US$1 Billion Planned Investment." *Food Business Africa*. November 2, 2021. https:// www.foodbusinessafrica.com/midroc-investment-group-beefs-up-ethiopias-edible-oil -processing-capacity-invests-us1-billion-in-new-facility/.

Migdal, Joel S. *Strong Societies and Weak States: State-Society Relations and State Capabilities in the Third World*. Princeton: Princeton University Press, 1988.

Miller, Rory, and Harry Verhoeven. "Overcoming Smallness: Qatar, the United Arab Emirates and Strategic Realignment in the Gulf." *International Politics* 57, no. 1 (2020): 1–20.

Mintz, Alex, and Karl DeRouen. *Understanding Foreign Policy Decision Making*. Cambridge: Cambridge University Press, 2010.

Miran, Jonathan. "Mapping Space and Mobility in the Red Sea Region, c.1500-1950." *History Compass* 12, no. 2 (2014): 197–216.

Mitzer, Stijn, and Joost Oliemans. "Secretive UAE Air Force Aircraft Deployed To War-Torn Ethiopia." *Oryx*. December 30, 2021. https://www.oryxspioenkop.com/2021/12/ secretive-uae-air-force-aircraft.html.

Mitzer, Stijn, and Joost Oliemans. "UAE Air Bridge Supports Ethiopian Military in Tigray War." *Oryx*. October 8, 2021. https://www.oryxspioenkop.com/2021/10/uae-air-bridge -supports-ethiopian.html.

Mohamed, Hassan Adan, and Amina Abdulkadir M. Nur. *The Puntland Experience: A Bottom-up Approach to Peace and State Building*. Garowe: Puntland Development Research Center, 2008. https://www.interpeace.org/wp-content/uploads/2008/07/2008 _SomP_PDRC_Interpeace_A_Bottom_Up_Approach_To_Peace_And_Statebuilding _EN.pdf.

"Mohamed Said Guedi: Businessman with a Midas Touch." *Arabian Post*. November 8, 2019. https://thearabianpost.com/mohamed-said-guedi-businessman-with-a-midas -touch/.

Moisio, Sami. "Towards Geopolitical Analysis of Geoeconomic Processes." *Geopolitics* 23, no. 1 (2018): 22–9.

Morgenthau, Hans J. *Politics among Nations: The Struggle for Power and Peace*. New York: Alfred A. Knopf, 1948.

Morse, Edward L. "The Transformation of Foreign Policies: Modernization, Interdependence and Externalization." *World Politics* 22, no. 3 (1970): 371–92.

Mukhashaf, Mohammed. "Yemen Separatists Seize Remote Socotra Island from Saudi-Backed Government." *Reuters*. June 21, 2020. https://www.reuters.com/article/us -yemen-security-separatists-idUSKBN23S0DU.

Müller, Tanja. "Assertive Foreign Policy in a 'Bad Neighbourhood': Eritrean Foreign Policy Making." In *2016 International Conference on Eritrean Studies*, edited by Zemenfes Tsighe, Saleh Mahmud Idris, Yonas Mesfun Asfaha, Senai Woldeab Andemariam, Rediet Kifle Taddesse, and Ghebrebrhan Ogubazghi, 631–51. Asmara: National Higher Education and Research Institute, 2016.

Müller, Tanja. "Representing Eritrea Geopolitics and Narratives of Oppression." *Review of African Political Economy* 43, no. 150 (2016): 658–67.

Mumbere, Daniel. "Eritrea President Discusses Regional Developments, Investment with UAE Crown Prince." *AfricaNews*. July 4, 2018. https://www.africanews.com /2018/07/04/eritrea-president-discusses-regional-developments-investment-with -uae-crown//.

Musa, Ahmed M., Oliver Vivian Wasonga, and Nadhem Mtimet. "Factors Influencing Livestock Export in Somaliland's Terminal Markets." *Pastoralism* 10, no. 1 (2020). https://doi.org/10.1186/s13570-019-0155-7.

Mutambo, Aggrey. "China's Version of Mediation for the Horn of Africa." *The East African*. March 21, 2022. https://www.theeastafrican.co.ke/tea/news/east-africa/china-s-version -of-mediation-for-the-horn-of-africa-3754916.

Mutambo, Aggrey. "Disputed Oil Blocks at Stake as Law Gives Somalia Power to Sell." *The East African*. February 18, 2020. https://www.theeastafrican.co.ke/tea/news/east-africa /disputed-oil-blocks-at-stake-as-law-gives-somalia-power-to-sell-1436974.

Myatt, Frederick. *The March to Magdala: The Abyssinian War of 1868*. London: Leo Cooper, 1970.

Naidoo, Tamara. "The Grand Game: Gulf Interests in the Horn of Africa." *The Horn Bulletin* 3, no. 2 (2020): 1–9.

Nair, Deepthi. "Dubai's DP World and Ethiopia Strike $1bn Deal to Develop Trade and Logistics Corridor." *The National*. May 6, 2021. https://www.thenationalnews.com/ business/markets/dubai-s-dp-world-and-ethiopia-strike-1bn-deal-to-develop-trade -and-logistics-corridor-1.1218039.

Neack, Laura, Jeanne A. K. Hey, and Patrick J. Haney, eds. *Foreign Policy Analysis: Continuity and Change in Its Second Generation*. Englewood Cliffs: Prentice Hall, 1995.

Negash, Tekeste. *Eritrea and Ethiopia: The Federal Experience*. Uppsala: Nordic Africa Institute, 1997.

"New Era Heralded as Turkey-UAE Ink Dozens of Investment Deals." *Daily Sabah*. November 24, 2021. https://www.dailysabah.com/business/economy/new-era -heralded-as-turkey-uae-ink-dozens-of-investment-deals.

"New Somali Alliance Threatens War." *BBC*. September 12, 2007. http://news.bbc.co.uk/2/ hi/africa/6990928.stm.

Newbery, Katharina M. B. "State Identity Narratives and Threat Construction in the Horn of Africa: Revisiting Ethiopia's 2006 Intervention in Somalia." *Journal of Eastern African Studies* 15, no. 2 (2021): 255–73.

"News: After the Launch of La Gare Downtown Luxury Complex Addis Abeba City Poised to Build at Least Four Similar Joint Projects." *Addis Standard*. November 20,

2018. https://addisstandard.com/news-after-the-launch-of-la-gare-downtown-luxury -complex-addis-abeba-city-poised-to-build-at-least-four-similar-joint-projects/.

Nichols, Michelle. "Iran Is New Transit Point for Somali Charcoal in Illicit Trade Taxed by Militants: U.N. Report." *Reuters*. October 9, 2018. https://www.reuters.com/article/us -somalia-sanctions-un-idUSKCN1MJ158.

Nkiwane, Tandeka C. "Africa and International Relations: Regional Lessons for a Global Discourse." *International Political Science Review* 22, no. 3 (2001): 279–90.

Nye, Joseph S. *Bound to Lead: The Changing Nature of American Power*. New York: Basic Books, 1990.

Nye, Joseph S. *Soft Power: The Means to Success in World Politics*. New York: Public Affairs, 2004.

Nye, Joseph S. *The Future of Power*. New York: Public Affairs, 2011.

Ojulu, Ojot Miru. "Large-Scale Land Acquisitions and Minority/Indigenous Communities' Rights under Ethnic Federalism in Ethiopia: A Case Study of Gambella Regional State." Unpublished PhD Diss., Bradford University, 2013. http://hdl.handle.net/10454/6291.

Olson, James S. *The Peoples of Africa: An Ethnohistorical Dictionary*. London: Greenwood, 1996.

"Omani-Somaliland Joint Venture to Establish Cement Factory in Berbera." *Somaliland*. July 19, 2019. https://www.somaliland.com/business/omani-somaliland-joint-venture -to-establish-cement-factory-in-berbera/.

Organization of African Unity. *Border Disputes among African States*. AHG/Res. 16(I), July 17–21, 1964.

Orlando, Ludovic. "Back to the Roots and Routes of Dromedary Domestication." *Proceedings of the National Academy of Sciences of the United States of America* 113, no. 24 (2016): 6588–90.

Ottaway, Marina, and David Ottaway. *Ethiopia: Empire in Revolution*. New York: Africana, 1978.

Özbaran, Salih. *The Ottoman Response to European Expansion: Studies on Ottoman-Portuguese Relations in the Indian Ocean and Ottoman Administration in the Arab Lands during the Sixteenth Century*. Istanbul: The Isis Press, 1994.

Pandey, Ashutosh. "Is Africa a Victim of Bias by International Investors?" *Deutsche Welle*. August 14, 2020. https://www.dw.com/en/africa-imf-bias-discrimination-debt -international-investors/a-54564359.

Pankhurst, Richard. *An Introduction to the Economic History of Ethiopia, from Early Times to 1800*. Woodford Green: Lalibela House, 1961.

Pankhurst, Richard. *The Ethiopian Borderlands: Essays in Regional History from Ancient Times to the End of the 18th Century*. Lawrenceville: The Red Sea Press, 1997.

Pankhurst, Richard. "The Trade of Southern and Western Ethiopia and the Indian Ocean Ports in the Nineteenth and Early Twentieth Centuries." *Journal of Ethiopian Studies* 3, no. 2 (1965): 37–74.

Pateman, Roy. *Eritrea: Even the Stones Are Burning*. Lawrenceville: Red Sea Press, 1998.

Pateman, Roy. "Eritrea, Ethiopia, and the Middle Eastern Powers: Image and Reality." *Northeast African Studies* 8, no. 2/3 (1986): 23–39.

Patman, Robert G. "Soviet–Ethiopian Relations: The Horn of Dilemma." In *Troubled Friendships: Moscow's Third World Ventures*, edited by Margot Light, 110–39. London: British Academic Press, 1993.

Patterson, Soren, and John Custer. "Six Deep Dives into China's Checkbook Diplomacy." *AIDDATA*, January 23, 2018. https://www.aiddata.org/blog/six-deep-dives-into-chinas -checkbook-diplomacy.

Paul, Andrew. *A History of the Beja Tribes of the Sudan*. Cambridge: Cambridge University Press, 2012.

Peel, Michael, Camilla Hall, and Heba Saleh. "Saudi Arabia and UAE Prop up Egypt Regime with Offer of $8bn." *Financial Times*. July 10, 2013. https://www.ft.com/content /7e066bdc-e8a2-11e2-8e9e-00144feabdc0.

Pelton, Robert Young. "Puntland Marine Police Force Enter Eyl." *Somalia Report*. March 2, 2012. https://piracyreport.com/index.php/post/2978/Puntland_Marine_Police_Force _Enter_Eyl_#:~:text=At%20the%20request%20of%20the,piracy%20program%20to %20the%20townspeople.

Peltz, Jennifer. "UN Report: Banned Somali Charcoal Exports Pass through Iran." *AP News*. October 13, 2018. https://apnews.com/article/united-nations-ivory-coast-us -news-global-trade-al-qaida-9b2bcd2c5b354e83b2882cd147e17385.

"People's Democratic Programme of the Tigray People's Liberation Front (TPLF)." May 1983. Accessed January 23, 2023. https://www.marxists.org/history/erol/ethiopia/ tigray-program.pdf.

Phillipson, David W. *Foundations of an African Civilisation: Aksum & the Northern Horn 1000 BC - AD 1300*. London: James Currey, 2012.

Plaut, Martin. *Understanding Eritrea: Inside Africa's Most Repressive State*. Oxford: Oxford University Press, 2016.

Poole, James, and Laura Millan Lombrana. "Nevsun Finds a White Knight in Zijin With $1.41 Billion Deal." *Bloomberg*. September 5, 2018. https://www.bloomberg.com/news /articles/2018-09-05/zijin-mining-to-buy-nevsun-resources-for-1-41-billion-in-cash.

Porter, Bruce D. *The USSR in Third World Conflicts: Soviet Arms and Diplomacy in Local Wars 1945–1980*. Cambridge: Cambridge University Press, 1984.

Powell, Robert. "The Problem of Absolute and Relative Gains in International Relations Theory." In *Cooperative Models in International Relations Research*, edited by Michael D. Intriligator and Urs Luterbacher, 127–150. Boston: Springer, 1994.

Prichard, James C. *Researches into the Physical History of Mankind: Ethnography of the African Races*. Sherwood: Gilbert & Piper, 1837.

Quackenbush, Stephen. "The Rationality of Rational Choice Theory." *International Interactions* 30, no. 2 (2004): 87–107.

Rabasa, Angel, Peter Chalk, Kim Cragin, Sara A. Daly, Heather S. Gregg, Theodore W. Karasik, Kevin A. O'Brien, and William Rosenau. *Beyond Al-Qaeda: Part 2, The Outer Rings of the Terrorist Universe*. Arlington: RAND Corporation, 2006.

Ram, Krishnamurthy V. *Anglo-Ethiopian Relations, 1869 to 1906: A Study of British Policy in Ethiopia*. New Delhi: Concept Publishing, 2009.

Rawlence, Ben. *Black and White: Kenya's Criminal Racket in Somalia*. Nairobi: Journalists for Justice, 2015.

"Remittance from Ethiopians Living Abroad Reaches $3.8 Billion." *Ethiopian Monitor*. April 21, 2022. https://ethiopianmonitor.com/2022/04/21/remittance-from-ethiopians -living-abroad-reaches-3-8-billion/.

Renders, Marleen. *Consider Somaliland: State-Building with Traditional Leaders and Institutions*. Leiden: Brill, 2012.

Research Directorate of the Immigration and Refugee Board of Canada. "Somalia: The 22 December 1997 Peace Accord in Mogadishu and Subsequent Developments." SOM29118.E. April 1, 1998 https://www.refworld.org/docid/3ae6ab53c.html.

Reva, Denys. *Ten Years on, Is Somali Piracy Still a Threat?*. ISS Today. Pretoria: Institute for Security Studies, 2018. https://issafrica.org/iss-today/ten-years-on-is-somali-piracy -still-a-threat.

Rodney, Walter. *How Europe Underdeveloped Africa*. Dar es Salaam: Tanzania Publishing House, 1972.

Rosen, Armin. "What Is an Expensive, Idyllic Resort Doing in Eritrea?" *The Atlantic*. March 23, 2013. https://www.theatlantic.com/international/archive/2013/03/what-is -an-expensive-idyllic-resort-doing-in-eritrea/274424/.

Rosencrance, Richard, and Arthur A. Stein, eds. *The Domestic Bases of Grand Strategy*. Ithaca: Cornell University Press, 1993.

Rugh, William A. "The Foreign Policy of the United Arab Emirates," *Middle East Journal* 50, no. 1 (1996): 57–70.

"Russia, Ethiopia Ink Military Cooperation Agreement." *Anadolu Agency*. July 12, 2021. https://www.aa.com.tr/en/africa/russia-ethiopia-ink-military-cooperation-agreement /2302337.

Samatar, Abdi Ismail. *The State and Rural Transformation in Northern Somalia, 1884– 1986*. Madison: University of Wisconsin Press, 1989.

Sanderson, George N. "The Foreign Policy of the Negus Menelik, 1896–1898." *The Journal of African History* 5, no. 1 (1964): 87–97.

"Saudi Crown Prince to Visit Turkey in Move to Boost Ties, Erdogan Says." *Reuters*. June 17, 2022. https://www.reuters.com/world/middle-east/saudi-crown-prince-visit-turkey -june-22-erdogan-2022-06-17/.

"Saudi Withdraws Its Troops from Yemen's Socotra." *Middle East Monitor*. May 7, 2020. https://www.middleeastmonitor.com/20200507-saudi-withdraws-its-troops-from -yemens-socotra/.

Sauldie, Madan M. *Super Powers in the Horn of Africa*. New York: APT Books, 1987.

Schelling, Thomas. *Arms and Influence*. New Haven: Yale University Press, 1966.

Scholvin, Sören, and Mikael Wigell. "Geo-economic Power Politics: An Introduction." In *Geo-economics and Power Politics in the 21st Century: The Revival of Economic Statecraft*, edited by Mikael Wigell, Sören Scholvin, and Mika Aaltola, 1–13. Abingdon: Routledge, 2019.

Scholvin, Sören, and Mikael Wigell. "Power Politics by Economic Means: Geoeconomics as an Analytical Approach and Foreign Policy Practice." *Comparative Strategy* 37, no. 1 (2018): 73–84.

Schraeder, Peter J. *United States Foreign Policy toward Africa: Incrementalism, Crisis and Change*. Cambridge: Cambridge University Press, 1994.

Schwab, Peter. "Cold War on the Horn of Africa." *African Affairs* 77, no. 306 (1978): 6–20.

Schwab, Peter. "Rebellion in Gojam Province, Ethiopia." *Canadian Journal of African Studies / Revue Canadienne des Études Africaines* 4, no. 2 (1970): 249–56.

Seddiq, Yasser. "Iranian Support to Houthis via Eritrea: Reality or Myth?" *Ahram Online*. June 15, 2015. https://english.ahram.org.eg/NewsContent/2/8/132655/World/Region/ Iranian-support-to-Houthis-via-Eritrea-Allegations.aspx.

Selassie, Bereket Habte. *Eritrea and the United Nations and Other Essays*. Trenton: Red Sea Press, 1989.

Semret, Nemo. "Pay Any Prize, Bear Any Burden." EthioReference. June 5, 2021. Accessed January 13, 2023. https://ethioreference.com/archives/28349.

Shahwan, Najla M. "UAE-Israel Intelligence Base on Yemeni Island of Socotra." *Daily Sabah*. September 5, 2020. https://www.dailysabah.com/opinion/op-ed/uae-israel -intelligence-base-on-yemeni-islandof-socotra/amp.

Sheik-Abdi, Abdi. "Somali Nationalism: Its Origins and Future." *The Journal of Modern African Studies* 15, no. 4 (1977): 657–65.

Sheikh, Abdi. "Al Shabaab Leader Urges Somalis to Battle Old Enemy Ethiopia." *Reuters*. March 11, 2014. https://www.reuters.com/article/us-somalia-alshabaab-leader-idU SBREA291OL20140310.

Sherman, Richard. *Eritrea: The Unfinished Revolution*. New York: Praeger, 1980.

Silberman, Leo. "Ethiopia: Power of Moderation." *Middle East Journal* 14, no. 2 (1960): 141–52.

Sishagne, Shumet. *Unionists and Separatists: The Vagaries of the Ethio-Eritrean Relation, 1941–1991*. Hollywood: Tsehai Publishers, 2007.

Smith, Denis Mack. *Mussolini*. New York: Alfred A. Knopf, 1982.

Snyder, Jack. *Myths of Empire: Domestic Politics and International Ambition*. Ithaca: Cornell University Press, 1991.

Solomon, Salem. "Observers See Several Motives for Eritrean Involvement in Yemen." *Voice of America*, January 9, 2015. https://www.voanews.com/a/observers-see-several -motives-eritrean-involvement-yemen/3138689.html

Solomon, Salem. "Russia-Eritrea Relations Grow with Planned Logistics Center." *Voice of America*. September 2, 2018. https://www.voanews.com/a/russia-eritrea-relations -grow-with-planned-logistics-center/4554680.html.

"Somali President Makes His First Foreign Trip to UAE." *Hiraan Online*. June 19, 2022. https://www.hiiraan.com/news4/2022/Jun/186693/somali_president_makes_his_first _foreign_trip_to_uae.aspx.

"Somalia: Farmaajo Seeks Saudi Arabia Intervention in Controversial Berbera UAE Military Base." *Radio Dalsan*. February 24, 2017. http://allafrica.com/stories/201702240588.html.

"Somalia: Former PMPF Director Lauds UAE's Support for Puntland." *Garowe Online*. April 28, 2018. https://www.garoweonline.com/en/news/puntland/somalia-former -pmpf-director-lauds-uaes-support-for-puntland.

"Somalia: Prime Minister of Somalia Meets with UAE's Deputy PM, Discuss Increased Support to Somalia." *Radio Dalsan*. March 4, 2014. https://allafrica.com/stories /201403041646.html.

"Somalia: Puntland Signs Deal to Develop Bosaso Port with Dubai's P&O Ports." *Garowe Online*. April 6, 2017. https://www.garoweonline.com/en/news/puntland/somalia -puntland-signs-deal-to-develop-bosaso-port-with-dp-world.

"Somalia: UAE Confirms to Continue Supporting Puntland Troops." *Garowe Online*. April 14, 2018. https://www.garoweonline.com/en/news/puntland/somalia-uae-confirms-to -continue-supporting-puntland-troops.

"Somalia: UAE Pledges Continued Support for Puntland Marine Forces." *Horseed Media*. March 28, 2014. https://horseedmedia.net/somalia-uae-pledges-continued-support -puntland-marine-forces-145629.

"Somalia Chides Its Regions for Cutting Ties with Qatar." *Aljazeera*. September 22, 2017. https://www.aljazeera.com/news/2017/9/22/somalia-chides-its-regions-for-cutting-ties -with-qatar.

"Somalia Received Saudi Aid the Day It Cut Ties with Iran: Document." *Reuters*. January 17, 2016. https://www.reuters.com/article/us-somalia-saudi-iran-idUSKCN0UV0BH.

"Somalia Seizes $9.6m from UAE Plane in Mogadishu." *Aljazeera*. April 9, 2018. https:// www.aljazeera.com/news/2018/4/9/somalia-seizes-9-6m-from-uae-plane-in -mogadishu.

"Somaliland Agrees to UAE Military Base in Berbera." *BBC*. February 13, 2017. https:// www.bbc.com/news/world-africa-38956093.

"Somaliland UAE Military Base to Be Turned into Civilian Airport." *Reuters*. September 15, 2019. https://www.reuters.com/article/us-somalia-emirates-idUSKBN1W00FI.

Sparke, Matthew. "Geoeconomics, Globalisation and the Limits of Economic Strategy in Statecraft: A Response to Vihma." *Geopolitics* 23, no. 1 (2018): 30–7.

Spence, Jack. "Africa: What Does the Future Hold?" *Strategic Review for South Africa* 19, no. 2 (2000): 1–14.

Steil, Benn, and Robert E. Litan. *Financial Statecraft: The Role of Financial Markets in American Foreign Policy*. New Haven: Yale University Press, 2006.

Stern, Eric, and Bertjan Verbeek, eds. "Whither the Study of Governmental Politics in Foreign Policymaking? A Symposium." *Mershon International Studies Review* 42, no. 2 (1998): 205–55.

Strange, Susan. "What Is Economic Power, and Who Has It?" *International Journal* 30, no. 2 (1975): 207–24.

Stuart, Douglas T. "Foreign-Policy Decision-Making." In *The Oxford Handbook of International Relations*, edited by Christian Reus-Smit and Duncan Snidal, 576–93. Oxford: Oxford University Press, 2010.

"Sunridge Gold Sold Its 60% Share in Eritrea Mine to China." *TesfaNews*. November 6, 2015. https://tesfanews.net/sunridge-gold-sold-its-eritrea-mine-to-china/.

Suuley, Yaxy Bisle. "Op-Ed: The Dawn of Democracy in Puntland: A Promising Start and a Hopeful Future." *Garowe Online*. October 25, 2021. https://www.garoweonline.com/en/opinions/op-ed-the-dawn-of-democracy-in-puntland-a-promising-start-and-a-hopeful-future.

Tadesse, Medhane. *Turning Conflict to Cooperation: Towards an Energy-Led Integration in the Horn of Africa*. Addis Ababa: Friedrich-Ebert Stiftung, 2003.

Tadesse, Medhane, and John Young. "TPLF: Reform or Decline?" *Review of African Political Economy* 30, no. 97 (2003): 389–403.

Tan, Qingshan. "Explaining U.S.-China Policy in the 1990s: Who Is in Control?" *Asian Affairs: An American Review* 20, no. 3 (1993): 143–160.

Tareke, Gebru. *Ethiopia: Power and Protest*. Lawrenceville: Red Sea Press, 1996.

Tedla, Michael Weldeghiorghis. "The Eritrean Liberation Front: Social and Political Factors Shaping Its Emergence, Development and Demise, 1960–1981." Master's Thesis, Leiden University, 2014. https://hdl.handle.net/1887/32998.

Tekle, Amare. "The Determinants of the Foreign Policy of Revolutionary Ethiopia." *The Journal of Modern African Studies* 27, no. 3 (1989): 479–502.

Tekle, Tesfa-Alem. "Ethiopia Loses Its 19pc Stake in Berbera Port: Somaliland Minister." *The East African*. June 11, 2022. https://www.theeastafrican.co.ke/tea/rest-of-africa/ethiopia-stake-in-port-of-berbera-3845366.

Tessema, Seleshi. "Mutual Growth Drives Turkish Investment in Ethiopia." *Anadolu Agency*. January 17, 2020. https://www.aa.com.tr/en/africa/mutual-growth-drives-turkish-investment-in-ethiopia/1705411.

The Government of Ethiopia. "The Federal Democratic Republic of Ethiopia Foreign Affairs and National Security Policy and Strategy." Ministry of Information. November 2002. https://chilot.me/wp-content/uploads/2011/08/national-security-policy-and-strategy.pdf.

"The Transitional Federal Charter of the Somali Republic." February 2004. Accessed January 13, 2023. https://www.ilo.org/dyn/travail/docs/2177/Transitional%20Federal%20charter-feb%202004-English.pdf.

The White House. "Executive Order on Imposing Sanctions on Certain Persons With Respect to the Humanitarian and Human Rights Crisis in Ethiopia." September 17, 2021. https://www.whitehouse.gov/briefing-room/presidential-actions/2021/09/17/executive-order-on-imposing-sanctions-on-certain-persons-with-respect-to-the-humanitarian-and-human-rights-crisis-in-ethiopia/.

The White House. "Statement by NSC Spokesperson Emily Horne on National Security Advisor Jake Sullivan's Call with His Highness Sheikh Mohammed bin Zayed Al Nahyan, The Crown Prince of Abu Dhabi." June 30, 2021. https://www.whitehouse.gov /briefing-room/statements-releases/2021/06/30/statement-by-nsc-spokesperson-emily -horne-on-national-security-advisor-jake-sullivans-call-with-his-highness-sheikh -mohammed-bin-zayed-al-nahyan-the-crown-prince-of-abu-dhabi/.

Tiruneh, Andargatchew. "Eritrea, Ethiopia, and Federation (1941–1952)." *Northeast African Studies* 2/3, no. 3/1 (1980-81/1981): 99–119.

Touval, Saadia. "The Organization of African Unity and African Borders." *International Organization* 21, no. 1 (1967): 102–27.

"TPLF MANIFESTO." ገብሬል የድረጅት ጋዜጣ. September 25, 2016. Accessed January 23, 2023. https://www.goolgule.com/tplf-manifesto/.

"TPLF-Manifesto –1968 E.C." February 1976. Accessed January 23, 2023. https://tassew .wordpress.com/tplf-manifesto-1968-e-c/.

"Treaty of Wuchale." May 2, 1889. Accessed January 4, 2023. https://africanlegends.files .wordpress.com/2016/10/ethiopie_traite-de-wuchale.pdf.

Trimingham, J. Spencer. *Islam in Ethiopia.* Oxford: Oxford University Press, 1952.

Tun, Zaw Thiha. "How Petrodollars Affect the U.S. Dollar." Investopedia. Accessed December 30, 2022. https://www.investopedia.com/articles/forex/072915/how -petrodollars-affect-us-dollar.asp.

Turhan, Yunus. "Turkey's Foreign Aid to Africa: An Analysis of the Post-July 15 Era." *Journal of Balkan and Near Eastern Studies* 23, no. 5 (2021): 795–812.

"Turkey Accuses UAE of Financing Terrorists in Somalia." *Garowe Online.* May 1, 2020. https://www.garoweonline.com/en/news/somalia/turkey-accuses-uae-of-financing -terrorists-in-somalia.

"Turkey, Somalia Sign MoU to Boost Cooperation on Investments." *Horn Diplomat.* June 22, 2021. https://www.horndiplomat.com/2021/06/22/turkey-somalia-sign-mou-to -boost-cooperation-on-investments/.

"UAE: Withdrawal from Assab, Build-Up on Perim." *Gulf States Newsletter.* Issue 1122. March 18, 2021. https://www.gsn-online.com/article/uae-withdrawal-assab-build-perim.

"UAE Air Bridge Provides Military Support to Ethiopia Gov't." *Aljazeera.* November 25, 2021. https://www.aljazeera.com/news/2021/11/25/uae-air-bridge-provides-military -support-to-ethiopia-govt.

"UAE Denounces Seizure of Cash and Plane in Somalia." *Reuters.* April 10, 2018. https:// www.reuters.com/article/us-somalia-politics-emirates-idUSKBN1HH21V.

"UAE Forces 'Occupy' Sea and Airports on Yemen's Socotra." *Aljazeera.* May 4, 2018. https://www.aljazeera.com/news/2018/5/4/uae-forces-occupy-sea-and-airports-on -yemens-socotra.

Uhlig, Siegbert, Alessandro Bausi, and Baye Yimam, eds. *Encyclopaedia Aethiopica*, vol. 4. Wiesbaden: Harrassowitz Verlag, 2010.

Ulrichsen, Kristian Coates. "The Geopolitics of Insecurity in the Horn of Africa and the Arabian Peninsula." *Middle East Policy* 18, no. 2 (2011): 120–35.

UN Tribune. "UN Report: UAE, SAUDI Using Eritrean Land, Sea, Airspace and, Possibly, Eritrean Troops in Yemen Battle." November 2, 2015. http://untribune.com/un-report -uae-saudi-leasing-eritean-port-using-eritrean-land-sea-airspace-and-possibly-troops -in-yemen-battle/.

United Nations. "Africa Rising in Business, Trade, Innovation, Deputy Secretary-General Says at Harvard Event, Urging Lifting of Barriers to Create Equal Opportunity." January 21, 2020. https://press.un.org/en/2020/dsgsm1384.doc.htm.

United Nations General Assembly. "Eritrea: Report of the United Nations Commissioner in Eritrea." A/RES/617(VII), December 17, 1952. https://undocs.org/en/A/RES/617(VII).

United Nations General Assembly. "Eritrea: Report of the United Nations Commission for Eritrea; Report of the Interim Committee of the General Assembly on the Report of the United Nations Commission for Eritrea." A/RES/390(V)A-B, December 2, 1950. https://undocs.org/en/A/RES/390(V).

United Nations Office for the Coordination of Humanitarian Affairs. "2021 Somalia Humanitarian Needs Overview." March 9, 2021. https://reliefweb.int/attachments/3faf9fa4-3879-3a53-ab25-a093731a7bae/20200903_HNO_Somalia.pdf.

United Nations Security Council. "Report of the Monitoring Group on Somalia and Eritrea Pursuant to Security Council Resolution 1916." S/2011/433. July 18, 2011. https://www.undocs.org/S/2011/433.

United Nations Security Council. "Report of the Monitoring Group on Somalia and Eritrea Pursuant to Security Council Resolution 2002." S/2012/544. July 13, 2012. https://www.undocs.org/S/2012/544.

United Nations Security Council. "Report of the Panel of Experts on Somalia Submitted in Accordance with Resolution 2444." S/2019/858. November 1, 2019. http://undocs.org/S/2019/858.

United Nations Security Council. "Resolution 1846." S/RES/1846. December 2, 2008. Accessed January 16, 2023. https://digitallibrary.un.org/record/642811/files/S_RES_1846%282008%29-EN.pdf?ln=en.

United Nations Security Council. "Resolution 1907." S/RES/1907. December 23, 2009. Accessed January 23, 2023. https://digitallibrary.un.org/record/673859/files/S_RES_1907%282009%29-EN.pdf?ln=en.

United Nations Security Council. "Resolution 1916." S/RES/1916. March 19, 2010. Accessed January 23, 2023. https://daccess-ods.un.org/tmp/3024535.17913818.html.

United Nations Security Council. "Resolution 2444." S/RES/2444. November 14, 2018. Accessed January 23, 2023. https://digitallibrary.un.org/record/1652454/files/S_RES_2444%282018%29-EN.pdf.

United States Department of State. "290. Circular Airgram From the Department of State to Certain African Posts." CA-9629. March 21, 1964. Accessed January 8, 2023. https://history.state.gov/historicaldocuments/frus1964-68v24/d290.

United States Department of Treasury. "Treasury Designates al-Shabaab Financial Facilitators." October 17, 2022. Accessed January 17, 2023. https://home.treasury.gov/news/press-releases/jy1028.

United States Energy Information Administration. "Maritime Chokepoints Critical to Petroleum Markets." March 2, 2021. https://www.eia.gov/todayinenergy/detail.php?id=330.

United States Energy Information Administration. "The Bab el-Mandeb Strait Is a Strategic Route for Oil and Natural Gas Shipments." August 27, 2019. https://www.eia.gov/todayinenergy/detail.php?id=41073.

Utas, Mats, ed. *African Conflicts and Informal Power: Big Men and Networks*. London: Zed Books.

van de Walle, Nicolas. *African Economies and the Politics of Permanent Crisis, 1979–1999*. Cambridge: Cambridge University Press, 2001.

Venkataraman, Manickam, and Solomon Mebrie. "Eritrean-Yemeni Relations." In *Regional Security in the Post-cold War Horn of Africa*, edited by Roba Sharamo and Berouk Mesfin, 281–307. Addis Ababa: Institute for Security Studies, 2011.

Verhoeven, Harry. "Africa's Next Hegemon." *Foreign Affairs*. April 12, 2015. https://www
.foreignaffairs.com/articles/ethiopia/2015-04-12/africas-next-hegemon.

Verhoeven, Harry. *Black Gold for Blue Gold? Sudan's Oil, Ethiopia's Water and Regional
Integration*. Chatham House Briefing Paper. London: Chatham House, 2011.

Verhoeven, Harry. "The Gulf and the Horn: Changing Geographies of Security
Interdependence and Competing Visions of Regional Order." *Civil Wars* 20, no. 3
(2018): 333–57.

Vertin, Zach. *Red Sea Rivalries: The Gulf, the Horn and New Geopolitics of the Red Sea*.
Doha: Brookings Doha Centre, 2019.

Vertin, Zach. *Turkey and the New Scramble for Africa: Ottoman Designs or Unfounded
Fears?* Doha: Brookings Doha Center, 2014.

Vertzberger, Yaacov Y. "Bureaucratic-Organizational Politics and Information
Processing in a Developing State." *International Studies Quarterly* 28, no. 1 (1984):
69–95.

Wai, Dunstan M. "African-Arab Relations: Interdependence or Misplaced Optimism?" *The
Journal of Modern African Studies* 21, no. 2 (1983): 187–213.

Wai, Dunstan M. "African-Arab Relations from Slavery to Petro-Jihad." *A Journal of
Opinion* 13 (1984): 9–13.

Wallerstein, Immanuel. *The Politics of the World-Economy: The States, the Movements and
the Civilizations*. Cambridge: Cambridge University Press, 1984.

Walsh, Declan. "Foreign Drones Tip the Balance in Ethiopia's Civil War." *The New York
Times*. December 20, 2021. https://www.nytimes.com/2021/12/20/world/africa/drones
-ethiopia-war-turkey-emirates.html.

Waltz, Kenneth. *Man, the State and War*. New York: Columbia University Press, 1959.

Waltz, Kenneth. "The Emerging Structures of International Politics." *International Security*
18, no. 2 (Fall 1993): 44–79.

Waltz, Kenneth. *Theory of International Politics*. New York: McGraw-Hill, 1979.

Wang, Qingxin Ken. "Recent Japanese Economic Diplomacy in China: Political Alignment
in a Changing World Order." *Asian Survey* 33, no. 6 (1993): 625–41.

Warburg, Gabriel. *Islam, Sectarianism and Politics in Sudan since the Mahdiyya*. London:
Hurst & Co., 2003.

Warton, C. Dale. *Geopolitics and the Great Powers in the Twenty-First Century*. Abingdon:
Routledge, 2007.

Wayne, Tony. "What Is Economic Diplomacy and How Does It Work?" *Foreign Service
Journal*. January/February 2019. https://www.afsa.org/what-economic-diplomacy-and
-how-does-it-work.

Wendt, Alexander. *Social Theory of International Politics*. Cambridge: Cambridge
University Press, 1999.

Wigell, Mikael. "Conceptualizing Regional Powers' Geoeconomic Strategies: Neo-
Imperialism, Neo-Mercantilism, Hegemony, and Liberal Institutionalism." *Asia Europe
Journal* 14, no. 2 (2016): 135–51.

Wight, Martin. *Systems of States*. Leicester: Leicester University Press, 1977.

Wight, Martin. "Why is There No International Theory?" In *Diplomatic Investigations:
Essays in the Theory of International Politics*, edited by Herbert Butterfield and Martin
Wight, 12–33. London: Allen & Unwin, 1966.

Wohlfarth, William Curtis. *The Elusive Balance: Power and Perceptions during the Cold
War*. Ithaca: Cornell University Press, 1993.

Womack, Brantly. *Asymmetry and International Relationships*. Cambridge: Cambridge
University Press, 2016.

Woodward, Peter. *The Horn of Africa: State, Politics and International Relations*. 2nd ed. London: I.B. Tauris, 2002.

Wu, Friedrich, and Koh De Wei. "From Financial Assets to Financial Statecraft: The Case of China and Emerging Economies of Africa and Latin America." *Journal of Contemporary China* 23, no. 89 (2014): 781–803.

Yasin, Yasin Mohammed. "Political History of the Afar in Ethiopia and Eritrea." *Africa Spectrum* 43, no. 1 (2008): 39–65.

"Yemen: Mysterious Airbase Gets Built on Mayun Island." *Aljazeera*. May 25, 2021. https://www.aljazeera.com/news/2021/5/25/yemen-mysterious-airbase-gets-built-on-mayun-island.

Yihdego, Zeray W. "Ethiopia's Military Action against the Union of Islamic Courts and Others in Somalia: Some Legal Implications." *The International and Comparative Law Quarterly* 56, no. 3 (2007): 666–76.

Yihun, Belete Belachew. "Ethiopian Foreign Policy and the Ogaden War: The Shift from "Containment" to "Destabilization," 1977–1991." *Journal of Eastern African Studies* 8, no. 4 (2014): 677–91.

Yilmaz, Şuhnaz. "Middle Powers and Regional Powers." *Oxford Bibliographies*. Accessed September 27, 2017. https://www.oxfordbibliographies.com/view/document/obo-9780199743292/obo-9780199743292-0222.xml.

Ylönen, Aleksi. "A Critical Appraisal of Realist International Relations Concepts in the Horn of Africa – Persian Gulf Relations: The State, Power, and Agency." *Cadernos de Estudos Africanos* 43 (2023). https://journals.openedition.org/cea/.

Ylönen, Aleksi. "Eritrea: A Sub-Regional Menace?" In *The Horn of Africa since the 1960s: Local and International Politics Intertwined*, edited by Aleksi Ylönen and Jan Záhořík, 88–105. Abingdon: Routledge, 2017.

Ylönen, Aleksi. "External Power Competition in the Horn of Africa: Somaliland's Quest for International Recognition and Development." *RUSI Journal* 166, no. 6–7 (2022): 74–82.

Ylönen, Aleksi. *On State, Marginalization, and Origins of Rebellion: The Formation of Insurgencies in Southern Sudan*. Trenton: Africa World Press, 2017.

Ylönen, Aleksi. "Positivism or Understanding? The Complexity of Analyzing the Objectives of Armed Opposition Groups." *Critical Review* 33, no. 1 (2021): 128–44.

Ylönen, Aleksi. "Talking Nile: Historical Aspects, Current Concerns, and the Stalemate in Grand Ethiopian Renaissance Dam Negotiations." *The Horn Bulletin* 3, no. 4 (2020): 1–10.

Ylönen, Aleksi. "The Dragon and the Horn: Reflections on China–Africa Strategic Relations." *Insight on Africa* 12, no. 2 (2020): 145–59.

Ylönen, Aleksi, and Alexander Meckelburg. "Ethiopia: Between Domestic Pressures and Regional Hegemony." In *Africa's Thorny Horn: Searching for a New Balance in the Age of Pandemic*, edited by Giovanni Carbone, 122–48. Milan: Ledizioni, 2021.

Yodfat, Aryeh Y. "The Soviet Union and the Horn of Africa." *Northeast African Studies* 1, no. 3 (1979–1980): 1–17.

Young, John. "Regionalism and Democracy in Ethiopia." *Third World Quarterly* 19, no. 2 (1998): 191–204.

Young, Karen E. "A New Politics of GCC Economic Statecraft: The Case of UAE Aid and Financial Intervention in Egypt." *Journal of Arabian Studies* 7, no. 1 (2017): 113–36.

Youngs, Richard. "Geo-economic Futures." In *Challenges for European Foreign Policy in 2012: What Kind of Geo-Economic Europe?*, edited by Ana Martiningui and Richard Youngs, 13–17. Madrid: FRIDE, 2011.

Yüksel, Engin, and Haşim Tekineş. *Turkey's Love-In with Qatar: A Marriage of Convenience.* CRU Report. Den Haag: Clingendael, Netherlands Institute of International Relations, 2021.

Zagare, Frank C. "Reconciling Rationality with Deterrence." *Journal of Theoretical Politics* 16, no. 2 (2004): 107–41.

Zakaria, Fareed. *From Wealth to Power: The Unusual Origins of America's World Role.* Princeton: Princeton University Press, 1998.

Zakaria, Fareed. "Realism and Domestic Politics: A Review Essay." *International Security* 17, no. 1 (Summer 1992): 177–98.

Zelalem, Zecharias, and Will Brown. "First Migrants Released from Saudi Detention Centres Arrive Home after Telegraph Investigation." *The Telegraph.* January 27, 2021. https://www.telegraph.co.uk/global-health/climate-and-people/first-migrants-released -saudi-detention-centres-arrive-home/.

Zewde, Bahru. *A History of Modern Ethiopia.* Oxford: James Currey, 2001.

Zimmerman, Robert F. *Dollars, Diplomacy, and Dependency: Dilemmas of US Economic Aid.* Boulder: Lynne Rienner, 1993.

INDEX

www.ingramcontent.com/pod-product-compliance
Lightning Source LLC
Chambersburg PA
CBHW071849270326
41929CB00013B/2160